Preventing Stress, Improving Productivity

D1328641

In one study made of European workers, twenty-eight per cent of employees reported that stress affects their health and their performance at work. This is a serious problem for the performance of individual organisations and as a consequence, for national economies. *Preventing Stress, Improving Productivity* investigates the ways in which companies can combat stress by changing the workplace to reduce stress rather than by treating an already stressed individual.

Costs and benefits of stress prevention in general are discussed, with an emphasis on approaches that involve both the individual and the place of work. This is followed by eleven chapters each concentrating on examples of best practice from a different European country with one case study analysed in detail.

Preventing Stress, Improving Productivity identifies five factors that are critical for a stress reduction programme to work, both in terms of employee well-being and from a financial point of view. The most successful strategies combine participation from workers and support from top management. Useful as a reference for psychologists and consultants, this book will also be an invaluable aid to managers in the day-to-day running of organisations.

Michiel Kompier is Professor of Work and Organisational Psychology at the University of Nijmegen in the Netherlands. **Cary Cooper** is BUPA Professor of Organisational Psychology and Health at the University of Manchester Institute of Science and Technology (UMIST).

Preventing Stress, Improving Productivity

European case studies in the workplace

Edited by
Michiel Kompier
and Cary Cooper

London and New York

First published 1999
by Routledge
11 New Fetter Lane, London EX4P 4EE

Simultaneously published in the USA and Canada
by Routledge
29 West 35th Street, New York, NY 10001

Typeset in Bembo by
The Florence Group Ltd, Stoodleigh, Devon
Printed and bound in Great Britain by
TJ International Ltd, Padstow, Cornwall

British Library Cataloguing in Publication Data
A catalogue record for this book is available from the British
Library

Library of Congress Cataloging in Publication Data
Kompier, Michiel
    Preventing stress, improving productivity: European case
studies in the workplace/Michiel Kompier and Cary Cooper.
        p.   cm.
    Includes bibliographical references and index.
    1. Job stress – Europe – Prevention – Case studies.
2. Labor productivity – Europe – Case studies. 3. Industrial
hygiene – Europe – Case studies. I. Kompier, Michiel.
    II. Title.
HF5548.85.C656 1999
658.3'82–dc21   98–35612
                                                    CIP

ISBN 0–415–16556–3(hbk)
ISNB 0–415–16557–1(pbk)

Contents

Figures

Tables

Contributors

Sebastiano Bagnara, Multimedia Communication Laboratory, University of Siena, Italy.

Alberto Baldasseroni, Service of Occupational Health, Health Company of Florence, Italy.

Beate Beermann, Bundesanstalt für Arbeitsschutz, Dortmund, Germany.

Marc Buelens, Department of Organisational Behaviour, Vlerick School of Management, University of Gent, Belgium.

Susan Cartwright, Manchester School of Management, University of Manchester, United Kingdom.

Theo Compernolle, Ponos Research Centre for Stress-Productivity and Health, Vlerick School of Management, University of Gent, Belgium/Free University, Amsterdam, the Netherlands.

Cary Cooper, Manchester School of Management, University of Manchester, United Kingdom.

Hubert De Neve, Janssen Pharmaceutica, Belgium.

Sabine Geurts, Department of Work and Organisational Psychology, University of Nijmegen, the Netherlands.

Luís Graça, National School of Public Health, Lisbon, Portugal.

Robert Gründemann, TNO Work and Employment, Hoofddorp, the Netherlands.

Irene Houtman, TNO Work and Employment, Hoofddorp, the Netherlands.

Raija Kalimo, Department of Psychology, Finnish Institute of Occupational Health, Helsinki, Finland.

Michiel Kompier, Department of Work and Organisational Psychology, University of Nijmegen, the Netherlands.

Karl Kuhn, Bundesanstalt für Arbeitsschutz, Dortmund, Germany.

Paula Liukkonen, Department of Economics, University of Stockholm, Sweden.

Ellis Lourijsen, TNO Work and Employment, Hoofddorp, the Netherlands.

Bo Netterstrøm, Clinic of Occupational Medicine, Hillerød Hospital, Hillerød, Denmark.

Oronzo Parlangeli, Multimedia Communication Laboratory, University of Siena, Italy.

Elisabeth Petsetaki, National School of Public Health, Athens, Greece.

Steven Poelmans, Instituto Superior de Estudios Empresariales, University of Navarra, Spain.

Rose Rafferty, Aer Rianta, Dublin, Ireland.

Jef Rombouts, Janssen Pharmaceutica, Belgium.

Stefano Taddei, Multimedia Communication Laboratory, University of Siena, Italy.

Riccardo Tartaglia, Service of Occupational Health, Health Company of Florence, Italy.

Töres Theorell, Divisions of Psychosocial Factors and Health, and of Occupational Health, Department of Public Health, Karolinska Institute/ National Institute for Psychosocial Factors and Health, Stockholm, Sweden.

Salla Toppinen, Department of Psychology, Finnish Institute of Occupational Health, Helsinki, Finland.

Kurt Wahlstedt, Department of Occupational and Environmental Medicine, University Hospital, Uppsala/Swedish Foundation for Occupational Health and Safety among State Employees, Sweden.

Lynne Whatmore, Manchester School of Management, University of Manchester, United Kingdom.

Richard Wynne, Work Research Centre Ltd., Dublin, Ireland.

Foreword

Stress at work was complained of by one in four employees according to a recent survey of working conditions across the Member States of the European Union: one in five complained of burn-out. Stress can have major consequences for both individuals and their households, for company productivity and morale and for society. In 1993, a European Conference 'Stress at Work: a call for action' discussed strategies to confront what appeared to be a growing phenomenon. Policymakers, employers' representatives, trade unionists and researchers from the different Member States of the European Union exchanged views on how best to tackle stress at work. At the end of the Conference the Belgian Minister of Labour, at that time the President of the Council of Ministers, invited the European Commission to take action.

Analysis of the action necessary at European Union level to prevent stress at work was identified by the Commission to be a priority in its 1996–2000 Programme concerning safety, hygiene and health at work. To assist in this work, the Commission asked its tripartite Advisory Committee for Safety, Hygiene and Health Protection at Work to investigate the issue. The Committee set up a working group that included among its recommendations the production of intervention and cost-benefit studies and the exchange of information on best practices as well as their evaluation.

This book is indeed a contribution to the need for more and better examples of good practice at European level. The cases, all written by well known experts in the field, bring to the fore that stress prevention is not only possible, but is worthwhile for employees and companies alike. I hope managers, trade unionists and researchers will find plenty of food for thought in it and will answer the call for action first launched at that Conference in 1993.

I particularly commend the editors, Professor Kompier and Professor Cooper, for their courage and dedication in producing a volume that so clearly demonstrates how, in spite of the variety of conditions in different European countries, we can learn from each other and achieve both a healthier and more productive workplace.

Clive Purkiss
Director, European Foundation for the Improvement of Living and Working Conditions

Chapter 1

Introduction: Improving work, health and productivity through stress prevention

Michiel Kompier and Cary Cooper

As the nature of work in the developed world undergoes more and more change, as organisations downsize, de-layer and out source, so the stresses and strains on employees increase. In the United States, it is estimated that 54 per cent of sickness absence is in some way stress related (Elkin and Rosch, 1990). In Europe as well, the costs are high. From a recent study by the European Foundation for the Improvement of Living and Working Conditions (Paoli, 1997) it appears that 28 per cent of over 15,000 European workers report that stress is a work–related health problem. In many developed countries the total cost of workplace pressure has been estimated at roughly 10 per cent of gross national product (Cartwright and Cooper, 1997; Cooper *et al.*, 1996; Karasek and Theorell, 1990), stemming from sickness absence, labour turnover, premature retirement due to ill health, escalating health insurance and expenditure on treatment of the consequences of stress.

While a great deal of research (for example, Cooper, 1995) has been devoted to identifying the sources of workplace stress and its links to adverse health and organisational outcomes, little has been done to focus on interventions to improve working environments. In reviewing the practice overall of stress prevention and intervention at the workplace, three conclusions may be drawn. First, although there is a considerable amount of activity in the field of stress management, it is disproportionally concentrated on reducing the effects of stress, rather than reducing the presence of stressors at work (Cooper and Payne, 1988; Cox, 1993; ILO, 1992; Kahn and Byosiere, 1992; Murphy, 1984, 1986, 1996; Quick and Quick, 1984). To put it differently, stress management activities focus on secondary and tertiary prevention, rather than primary prevention (Kompier and Marcelissen, 1990; Kompier *et al.*, 1998; Murphy, 1984, 1986; Quick and Quick, 1984). Whereas the latter involves interventions aimed at eliminating, reducing or altering stressors in the working situation, the former two are aimed at the effects of stress, with secondary prevention concerning the helping of employees (who are already showing signs of stress) from getting sick (for example, by increasing their coping capacity); and tertiary prevention concerning treatment activities for employees with serious stress-related health problems (for example, stress counselling/employee assistance programmes, the rehabilitation after long-term absenteeism). Second, most activities are primarily aimed at the individual rather than at the workplace or the organisation, in other words, a worker-oriented approach, for instance, by improving employees' skills to manage, resist or reduce stress (Ivancevich and Matteson, 1987; McLeroy et al., 1988; Murphy, 1996), as opposed to a job or organisation-oriented approach, for instance, by job redesign or in some way changing the corporate culture or management style (Kelly, 1992; Kopelman, 1985). Moreover, as Kahn and Byosiere (1992) conclude in their literature review: 'Even the programs that aim at stress inhibition tend to address subjective rather than objective aspects of the stress sequence; almost none consider the organisational antecedents (policy and structure) that intensify or reduce the presence of objective stressors' (p. 633).

A third peculiarity in the practice of stress prevention concerns the lack of a systematic risk assessment ('stress audit', identifying risk factors and risk groups) as well as of serious research into the effects of all these activities (Kahn and Byosiere, 1992). In the words of Kahn and Byosiere (1992): 'The programs in stress management that are sold to companies show a suspicious pattern of variance; they differ more by practitioner than by company. When practitioners in any field offer sovereign remedies regardless of the presenting symptoms, patients should be wary' (p. 623).

Against the background of (1) clear evidence of the relationship between psychosocial work characteristics and health (Cartwright and Cooper, 1997; Cooper and Marshall, 1976; Cox, 1988; Johnson, 1986; Karasek and Theorell, 1990; Siegrist et al., 1990; Uehata, 1991; Vaernes et al., 1991), (2) national and international legislation that put the emphasis on risk assessment and combating risks by changing the stressful situation (Cooper et al., 1996; Cox, 1993; Kompier et al., 1994), and (3) the basic idea of prevention, that is, eliminating the stress producing situation (prevention at the source), the current practice of stress prevention and intervention seems disappointing.

Given the current status of stress prevention, a question that deserves attention is why it is that companies express a preference for 'post hoc' individual-directed interventions, as opposed to primary or job/organisational interventions. At least four factors seem to contribute to this rather one-sided 'individual'-oriented approach (see Kompier et al., 1998):

1   Senior managers are often inclined to blame personality and lifestyle factors of employees who are absent from work or report health complaints, rather than the job or organisational factors, for which they are responsible. Senior management also often point to the potential role of stressful life events (family problems such as a divorce or the loss of a beloved), or responsibilities and obligations in the family life (raising children for example). Of course, on the micro-level (i.e. on the level of the individual employee) stressors at work are often accompanied by

stressors in one's family situation (Evans and Bartolomé, 1984; Frone *et al.*, 1992; Watkins and Subich, 1995), but because of the mutual influence and spill-over between both domains, the causes and consequences can hardly be disentangled. Furthermore, holding individual characteristics responsible for differences in experienced stress, one cannot explain why some occupations show significantly more stress complaints and higher sickness absence rates than others (for example, Cooper and Payne, 1988). A risk attached to this view is that the employee is regarded as being 'guilty' of his or her own health problems, that is 'blaming the victim' (McLeroy *et al.*, 1988), with the potential threat in the workplace being overlooked. Logically, this approach also leads to one-sided recommendations to reduce stress, that is, concentrating more on the individual employee than on changing the stressful working conditions.

2   The second reason may be found in the nature of psychology itself, with its emphasis on subjective and individual phenomena. Many psychology-oriented stress researchers are primarily interested in stress as a subjective and individual phenomenon. To some extent, this may be a legacy of the strong tradition in psychology to focus on individual differences (i.e. differential psychology), and on individual counselling and therapy (i.e. clinical psychology). In this context, a warning seems appropriate against 'psychologism', that is, the explanation of (a sequence of) societal events from an individual-psychic point of view. Because of this orientation, the potential impact of more 'objective' or 'collective' risk factors in the work situation (e.g. poor management, work-overload and bullying), may go unnoticed and untreated (see Frese and Zapf, 1988).

3   The third reason is of a methodological nature. In stress research, there is a gap between what 'theory' preaches (that is, properly designed longitudinal studies, involving a randomised control group, collecting both subjective and objective measures that are analysed properly with statistical techniques), and what is possible in practice (Kahn and Byosiere, 1992; Murphy, 1996). One of the main reasons for this gap is the difficulty of conducting methodological 'sound' interventions and evaluation studies in an ever-changing organisational environment. In the 1990s, not only the context of work is rapidly changing, but also 'work' itself. Work organisations are in a constant state of change, due, in part, to new production concepts (for example, team based work, lean production methods, telework), 'the flexible workforce' concept, the 24-hour economy, the increased utilisation of information technology, and the changing structure of the work force (for example, more women working). These changes clearly affect the work behaviour of employees, work group processes, as well as the organisational structure and culture. As a consequence, it is practically impossible to find two companies with comparable stress problems at the beginning of any intervention programme, of which the control company agrees not to undertake any action for a

period of three or four years (the period a researcher might like to choose for an intervention project). A related problem is that it is often not in a company's interest to facilitate 'sound scientific research' in the context of an ongoing business, involving interlopers from outside (i.e. researchers) and detailed data collection on the scene of sometimes confidential information. Senior managers can regard research of this kind as a nuisance to the primary organisational processes and objectives.

4   A fourth factor may be found in the discipline segregation within stress research, with a tendency of researching to neglect the collection of more objective data on the impact of stress and its prevention. Work and organisational psychologists concentrate primarily on 'soft' outcome variables (e.g. motivation, satisfaction, effect and health complaints), and are well-known for their questionnaire-oriented approach. Traditionally, it has been rather unusual for stress researchers to co-operate with economists, for example, in order to study the potential 'hard' outcome measures (e.g. productivity, sickness absence rates and accident rates), as well as the financial effects of interventions. To put it differently, a history of gaining empirical insight in costs and benefits is merely lacking in stress research.

Research in the field should in the future include some of the following: first, stress researchers should not only address 'soft' outcome variables (for example, motivation and satisfaction), but extend their focus to also include 'hard' outcome variables (for example, productivity and sickness absenteeism). Whereas work and organisational psychologists have often stated that an adequate stress prevention programme may positively affect productivity and sickness absenteeism, until now they have not laid down a sufficiently strong empirical foundation for this position (see also Kopelman, 1985). For too long, stress prevention advocates have based their arguments on a moral or humanistic appeal to the good employer (that is, on 'industrial charity'), or on legal regulations (for example, working conditions legislation). It is beyond doubt that these are important and strong arguments. Still, it may well be that they are not enough, since these arguments are not those that primarily affect senior management, who are more 'bottom line' driven.

Second, in order to increase the impact of stress prevention in the workplace, more emphasis should be placed on such factors as the quality of product and services, organisational flexibility, continuity, absenteeism, productivity, labour market facets and improved competitivity; and for there to be a multi-disciplinary approach rather than the traditional mono-disciplinary one (for example, co-operation with economists and ergonomists).

And finally, the demonstration of examples of good preventive practice is considered as a *sine qua non* for developing effective stress prevention procedures and for the involvement of both social partners in this field (i.e. employers and employees) (Kompier *et al.*, 1994). These examples may be crucial when attempting to answer the question: 'How well – and why – do stress prevention programmes work?'

Thus, one of the major purposes of this book is to analyse and compare projects that may provide an alternative to the *post hoc* individual-oriented approach described earlier. Our aim is to carefully and systematically analyse and compare examples of good practice in stress prevention, taking one example from eleven European Union member states. In doing so, we hope to show and explore the possibilities and benefits of stress prevention, both for the worker and the organisation.

Since one of the shortcomings of stress research is its disciplinary segregation, we also wanted to relate psychosocial work characteristics, such as high demands, low control and low support – and health and safety in general – to other policy areas, that is, productivity, labour market facets, company image, human resources management, total quality management, and so forth. We hope to answer such questions as:

- which are the corporate motives for these projects?
- which instruments were used in order to identify risk factors and risk groups?
- which measures were selected and why?
- how were these measures implemented?
- to what extent were these projects successful?
- what were the encouraging and obstructing factors?

The core of this volume consists of eleven case studies from eleven European Union member states: Finland, the Netherlands, Belgium (Belgium and Luxembourg are combined), United Kingdom, Denmark, Sweden, Germany, Ireland, Portugal, Greece and Italy. We were not successful in identifying cases in Spain, France or Austria.

All the contributors have tried to present their country and their project in a comparable framework. First, the country is introduced. The contributors were asked to address such questions as: Is stress an important policy issue? Is there a legal framework for stress prevention? Are there any factors considered as main stressors? Are there any occupational and other groups considered to be at special risk? Is there a national monitoring system? Are there examples of good preventive practice available? Are stress interventions mainly oriented on the (work) organisation or on the individual employee, or both? Are there, on a national level, reliable statistics on the costs of stress at work, its impact on the health and performance of employees and companies, and on the benefits of stress prevention? Given the differences between the various countries, some of the authors were able to present detailed answers to these questions, whereas others were not.

Second, each case-chapter introduces the company under study, with information on the motives for the project, the first signals of stress and the (project) organisation of the current project. Next, the authors explore how risk factors and risk groups were identified, which (and why) measures were chosen, how they were implemented, and finally, how the project was evaluated: the effects, the costs and the benefits, whether there were any lessons to be learned, and so forth. Table 1.1 presents the range of industrial sectors that is covered by the case studies.

The eleven case-chapters are preceded by two chapters that more generally address occupational stress and stress prevention in Europe. The second chapter, from Sabine Geurts and Robert Gründemann, presents a general overview of the state of affairs with respect to work stress and stress prevention in Europe.

In Chapter 3, Paula Liukkonen, Susan Cartwright and Cary Cooper investigate an important theme in the area of occupational health and safety, and of working conditions policy, looking at the costs and benefits of stress prevention in organisations. Raija Kalimo and Salla Toppinen, in Chapter 4, describe and analyse an impressive longitudinal Finnish project of research and organisational development in a forest industry corporation. In Chapter 5, Ellis Lourijsen, Irene Houtman, Michiel Kompier and Robert Gründemann present a case from a Dutch hospital, 'Healthy working for health'. This project constitutes one of the 'examples of good practice' which at the beginning of the 1990s was initiated by the Dutch Ministry of Social Affairs and Employment. Chapter 6, by Steven Poelmans, Theo Compernolle, Hubert De Neve, Marc Buelens and Jef Rombouts, examines a large Belgian pharmaceutical company. The case from the United Kingdom, Chapter 7 (Lynne Whatmore, Susan Cartwright and Cary Cooper), is situated in the public sector. In Chapter 8, Bo Netterstrøm presents a Danish case on self-regulation among bus drivers, 'a classic high strain occupation'. Chapter 9, by Töres Theorell and Kurt Wahlstedt, concentrates on mail processing in

Table 1.1 Overview of industry sectors and case studies

Case	Chapter	Country	Industry sector
1	4	Finland	Forestry
2	5	The Netherlands	Hospital
3	6	Belgium	Pharmaceutical company
4	7	United Kingdom	Public sector
5	8	Denmark	Bus company
6	9	Sweden	Postal service
7	10	Germany	Hospital
8	11	Ireland	Airport management company
9	12	Portugal	Bank
10	13	Greece	Hospital
11	14	Italy	School of nursing

Sweden. Two related sub-cases are analysed: a postal sorting terminal and mail delivery. In Chapter 10, Beate Beermann, Karl Kuhn and Michiel Kompier present a German project, a health circle, which is a popular organisational concept in Germany, again in a hospital. Chapter 11, by Richard Wynne and Rose Rafferty focus on an Irish airport management company. In Chapter 12 Luis Graça and Michiel Kompier discuss an ongoing project in a large bank organisation in Portugal. Chapter 13, by Elisabeth Petsetaki, concentrates on so-called support groups in the health-care sector. Situated also in the health-care sector is the case from Italy (Chapter 14, Sebastiano Bagnara, Alberto Baldasseroni, Oronzo Parlangeli, Stefano Taddei, and Riccardo Tartaglia), which looks at a school of nursing.

The eleven case studies are followed by a final chapter by Michiel Kompier and Cary Cooper, which considers the current status with respect to occupational stress and its prevention in the various countries that are discussed in this book. A more detailed comparison and evaluation is made of the eleven cases, with some final conclusions being drawn as a result.

Bibliography

Cartwright, S. and Cooper, C.L. (1997) *Managing Workplace Stress*, London and Thousand Oaks, California: Sage Publications.

Cooper, C.L. (1995) *Handbook of Stress, Medicine and Health*, Florida: CRC Press.

Cooper, C.L., Liukkonen, P. and Cartwright, S. (1996) *Stress Prevention in the Workplace: Assessing the Costs and Benefits to Organisations*, Dublin: European Foundation for the Improvement of Living and Working Conditions.

Cooper, C.L. and Marshall, J. (1976) 'Occupational sources of stress: A review of the literature relating to coronary heart disease and mental ill health', *Journal of Occupational Psychology*, 49: 11–28.

Cooper, C.L. and Payne, R. (eds) (1988) *Causes, Coping and Consequences of Stress at Work*, Chichester: John Wiley and Sons.

Cox, T. (1988) 'Psychobiological factors in stress and health', in Fisher, S. and Reason, J. (eds) *Handbook of Life Stress, Cognition and Health*, Chichester: Wiley and Sons, pp. 603–28.

Cox, T. (1993) *Stress Research and Stress Management: Putting Theory to Work*, HSE contract research report, no. 61/1993.

Elkin, A.J. and Rosch, P.J. (1990) 'The person-environment fit approach to stress: Recurring problems and some suggested solutions', *Journal of Organizational Behavior*, 11: 293–307.

Evans, P. and Bartolomé, F. (1984) 'The changing pictures of the relationship between career and family', *Journal of Occupational Behavior*, 5: 9–21.

Frese, M. and Zapf, D. (1988) 'Methodological issues in the study of work stress: objective versus subjective measurement of work stress and the question of longitudinal studies', in Cooper, C. and Payne, R. (eds) *Causes, Coping and Consequences of Stress at Work*, New York: John Wiley and Sons Ltd.

Frone, M.R., Russell, M. and Cooper, M.L. (1992) 'Antecedents and outcomes of work–family conflict: Testing a model of the work–family interface', *Journal of Applied Psychology*, 77: 65–78.

International Labour Office (ILO) (Di Martino, V.) (1992) *Conditions of Work Digest. Preventing Stress at Work*, 11, (2), Geneva: ILO.

Ivancevich, J.M. and Matteson, M.T. (1987) 'Organisational level stress management interventions: A review and recommendations', in Ivancevich J.M. and Ganster D.C. (eds) *Job Stress: From Theory to Suggestion*, New York: Haworth Press, pp. 229–48.

Johnson, J.V. (1986) *The Impact of Workplace Social Support and Work Control Upon Cardiovascular Disease in Sweden*, Stockholm: Division of Environmental and Organisational Psychology.

Kahn, R.L. and Byosiere, P. (1992) 'Stress in organisations', in Dunnette, M.D. and Hough, L.M. (eds) *Handbook of Industrial and Organizational Psychology*, Palo Alto, California: Consulting Psychologists Press, (2nd edn), 3, pp. 571–650.

Karasek, R.A. and Theorell, T. (1990) *Healthy Work. Stress, Productivity, and the Reconstruction of Working Life*, New York: Basic Books.

Kelly, J. (1992) 'Does job-redesign theory explain job-redesign outcomes?' *Human Relations*, 45, (8) 753–74.

Kompier, M.A.J., De Gier, E., Smulders, P. and Draaisma, D. (1994) 'Regulations, policies and practices concerning work stress in five European countries', *Work and Stress*, 8, (4): 296–318.

Kompier, M.A.J., Geurts, S.A.E., Gründemann, R.W.M., Vink, P. and Smulders, P.G.W. (1998) 'Cases in stress prevention: The success of a participative and step-wise approach', *Stress Medicine*, 14, 155–68.

Kompier, M.A.J. and Marcelissen, F.H.G. (1990) *Handboek Werkstress* Amsterdam: Nederlands Instituut voor Arbeidsomstandigheden.

Kopelman, R. (1985) 'Job redesign and productivity: A review of the evidence', *National Productivity Review*, pp. 237–55.

McLeroy, K.R., Bibeau, D., Steckler, A. and Glanz, K. (1988) 'An ecological perspective on health promotion programs', *Health Education Quarterly*, 15, 351–77.

Murphy, L.R. (1984) 'Occupational stress management: a review and appraisal', *Journal of Occupational Psychology*, 57: 1–15.

Murphy, L.R. (1986) 'A review of organisational stress management research', *Journal of Organisational Behaviour Management*, 8: 215–27.

Murphy, L.R. (1996) 'Stress management in work settings: A critical review of the health effects', *American Journal of Health Promotion*, 11, (2): 112–35.

Paoli, P. (1997) *Second European Survey on Working Conditions 1996*, Dublin: European Foundation for the Improvement of Living and Working Conditions.

Quick, J.C. and Quick, J.D. (1984) *Occupational Stress and Preventive Management*, New York: McGrawHill.

Siegrist, J., Peter, R., Junge, A., Cremer, P. and Seidel, D. (1990) 'Low status control, high effort at work and ischaemic heart disease: prospective evidence from blue-collar men, *Social Science Medicine*, 31: 1127–34.

Uehata, T. (1991) 'Karoshi due to occupational stress-related cardiovascular injuries among middle-aged workers in Japan', *Japanese Science of Labour*, 67, (1): 20–28.

Vaernes, R.J., Myhre, G., Aas, H.; Hommes, T., Hansen, I. and Tonder, O. (1991) 'Relationships between stress, psychological factors, health and immune levels among military aviators', *Work and Stress*, 5, 5–16.

Watkins, C.E. and Subich, L.M. (1995) 'Annual Review, 1992–1994: Career development, reciprocal work/non-work interaction, and women's workforce participation', *Journal of Vocational Behavior*, 47: 109–63.

Chapter 2

Workplace stress and stress prevention in Europe

Sabine Geurts and Robert Gründemann

2.1 Introduction

The purpose of this chapter is to present an overview of the various initiatives that have been taken by European companies to prevent or reduce workplace stress. For this purpose, we will use a broad definition of 'stress'. This definition includes not only psychosocial stressors (e.g. poor job content, poor work organisation, poor social relationships and social conditions at work), but also physical stressors in the workplace (e.g. lack of safety, ergonomic shortcomings, stressful ambient factors), as well as work-related psychological health problems ('strains'). Consequently, in overviewing the practice of 'stress prevention' in Europe, we will take into account all initiatives and activities that are directed at (1) the reduction (or elimination) of psychosocial and/or physical stressors in the workplace, (2) the reduction (or elimination) of work-related ill health, absenteeism and permanent work incapacity, and (3) the improvement or promotion of health at the workplace.

In the first part of this chapter (2.2) the context of workplace stress in Europe will be discussed. In three sections, background information is provided on the scope of workplace stress (2.2.1), developments in the area of workplace stress (2.2.2), and the socio-political and legislative context of workplace stress (2.2.3). In the second part of this chapter (2.3), the practice of stress prevention in Europe is discussed. First, a conceptual framework of stress prevention is presented (2.3.1). Subsequently, we discuss the method (2.3.2) and the results (2.3.3) of a research survey conducted by the European Foundation for the Improvement of Living and Working Conditions among 1,451 European companies (Wynne and Clarkin, 1992). This study was used to answer the following four questions about the practice of stress prevention in European companies:

1 What is the nature of stress prevention activities?
2 What are the motives for stress prevention activities?
3 Who are the participants in stress prevention activities?
4 What are the characteristics of the active companies in stress prevention?

The chapter ends with some summarising and concluding remarks, as well as with some future prospects (2.4).

2.2   Context of workplace stress in Europe

2.2.1   The scope of workplace stress

The number of European workers who suffer from excessive pressures in the workplace is impressive. Out of 137 million workers in the European Community, approximately 10 million annually fall victim to accidents or sickness as a result of their work (Bloemhoff *et al.*, 1993). For 8,000 of these workers the consequences are fatal. The total amount paid out yearly in benefits to the sufferers of occupational diseases and accidents is estimated at 20 billion ECU (*ibid.*) Available absence and disability figures show large differences between the various European countries (Gründemann *et al.*, 1994). For example, in Portugal and the Netherlands nearly 8 per cent of all working days are lost annually due to sickness, in contrast to less than 4 per cent in Denmark. The number of workers who are long-term or permanently unfit for work is highest in the Netherlands (12 per cent of its total work population), and lowest in Ireland (3 per cent of its total work population). The absence and disability figures of the different European countries are, however, difficult to compare due to differences in the definition of sickness absence and disability, the measurement of absence and disability figures, the population that is used to calculate the figures and the regulations governing absenteeism and disability. A detailed description and comparison of absence and disability data and arrangements between the European member states is presented by Gründemann and Van Vuuren (1997).

There is a range of expensive direct and indirect costs due to absenteeism and disability. For example:

- in the UK 177 million working days were lost in 1994 as a result of absence due to sickness; this equates to over 13.2 billion ECU in lost productivity at a cost of 630 ECU per employee (Balcombe and Tate, 1995).
- German employers in 1993 paid up to 30.5 billion ECU for the social security insurance of their workers (Doukmak and Huber, 1995).
- Belgium, with an absenteeism rate of approximately 7 per cent, paid 2.4 billion ECU on sickness benefits in 1995 and 0.6 billion ECU for benefits to do with work accidents and occupational diseases, a total of about 1,000 ECU per employee (Van Damme, 1995).
- In the Netherlands in 1993 the costs of benefits for absenteeism and disability arrangements totalled approximately 16.6 billion ECU; 4.1 billion ECU for sickness benefits and 12.5 billion ECU for disability benefits (Gründemann, 1995).

These figures relate to the benefits paid through the social security schemes for each country. Figures concerned with other costs of ill health of workers are more difficult to obtain. There is, however, some information available about the cost of work-related diseases and accidents directly related to the work environment. For example, in Denmark (Jensen, 1996) it has been estimated that the work environment accounts for 15 per cent of the total sickness behaviour among 15–66 year olds and 20 per cent of sickness absence: the socio-economic costs of these work–related diseases and accidents in 1992 were estimated at between 3 billion and 3.7 billion ECU (based on a working population of approximately 3 million). The cost to the British economy of work accidents and work-related ill health in 1990 has been calculated at between 2 per cent and 3 per cent of the total Gross Domestic Product, or a typical year's economic growth (Davies and Teasdale, 1994). Although the methods used to calculate the costs of absenteeism and ill health diverge, it is evident that the scale of the issue is immense and that a lot of money could be saved by even a moderate reduction in absenteeism caused by ill health.

In terms of job and organisational problems, it has been estimated that about half of all absences is related to stress in the workplace (Schabracq et al., 1996). In a Dutch study among 15,000 recently disabled workers, 55 per cent of the interviewees reported a direct (causal) relationship between aspects of their work (the physical and mental workload and the general working conditions) and the health problems which caused their disability (Gründemann et al., 1991). An extensive survey on working conditions conducted by the European Foundation (Paoli, 1997) among a representative sample of 15,800 workers from fifteen European Union member states, underlines these figures. The results reveal that 57 per cent of the European workers felt that their health is negatively affected by their work, and approximately one-third (28 per cent) felt that their health and safety is at risk because of their work. Backache, general stress complaints and overall fatigue in particular were mentioned as being related to poor working conditions (by, respectively, 30 per cent, 28 per cent and 20 per cent). Moreover, a quarter (23 per cent) of the workers reported to have missed one or more working days during the past twelve months because of work-related health problems (on average, four days per worker were lost). Backache and stress complaints were particularly prevalent in southern European countries (Greece, Italy, Spain and Portugal), as well as in Luxemburg, Finland and Sweden. Ireland showed the lowest level of health complaints. The lowest self-reported absence incidence was found in Sweden, Denmark and the United Kingdom, in contrast with Germany and Austria, of which both showed the highest self-reported absence incidence.

2.2.2 Developments in the area of workplace stress

It is plausible to assume that in the next century workplace stress might increase due to substantial changes in the nature of work itself, the context of work and the constitution of the working population (cf. Cartwright and Cooper, 1997). Because of the changing nature of work undertaken by the European working population, mental and emotional risk factors in particular seem on the increase. A comparison between the results of the Second European Survey on Working Conditions 1996 (Paoli, 1997) and the First European Survey on the Work Environment, carried out five years earlier (Paoli, 1992), reveals that time constraints have increased sharply. Figure 2.1 shows the percentage of European workers that, at least half of the time, experienced a high pace of work.

From Figure 2.1 we can conclude that a growing number of European workers are spending most of their working time performing high-speed work (35 per cent in 1991 and 43 per cent in 1996) and working tight deadlines (38 per cent in 1991 and 45 per cent in 1996). With the exception of Germany and Greece, the increasing work pace is perceived in all European Union member states. The highest number of workers to experience high-speed work is in the Netherlands (59 per cent of workers work 'at least half of the time' and 38 per cent work 'all the time' at very high speed). The United Kingdom has the highest percentage of workers whose job involves working to tight deadlines (63 per cent of workers work 'at least half of the time' and 45 per cent work 'all the time' to tight deadlines). With regard to physical risk factors, the results reveal that these have stabilised during the past five years, although they are still prevalent (Paoli, 1997): stressful ambient factors (for example, noise, polluted air, too high or too low temperatures, vibration) are experienced by approximately a quarter of the workers, a third reported having to carry heavy loads, meanwhile, half the respondents experienced having to work in painful or tiring positions.

The second European survey (Paoli, 1997) further shows that for the majority of the workers (67 per cent) the work pace is dictated more by the customers and the clients (especially in trade and catering sectors) than by machines (reported by only 22 per cent). This directly relates to the growing number of workers who are employed in the service sector (59 per cent in 1991 compared with 63 per cent in 1996), at a cost to the falling numbers working in the agriculture sector (8 per cent in 1991 and 6 per cent in 1996) and manufacturing sector (34 per cent in 1991 and 31 per cent in 1996) (Paoli, 1997). Although in all European Union member states, the service sector is the most important economically, this is particularly true for north and west Europe. For example, in the Netherlands three out of four workers are employed in the service sector (CBS, 1998). The growth of this sector implies an expanding scope of specific risk factors that are attached to meeting customers' demands, such as working hours that fall beyond the regular nine-to-five schedule (i.e. the twenty-four-hour economy). Results of the second European survey (Paoli, 1997) show that a substantial number of workers (33 per cent) have irregular working hours or work shifts (mostly in catering, transport and energy production). Moreover, half of the workers (55 per cent)

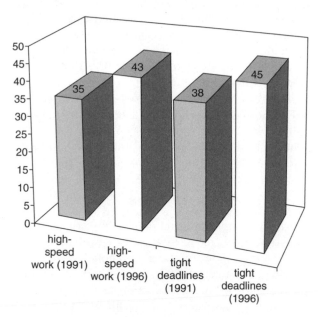

Figure 2.1 Increase in work pace 1991–1996. Percentage of workers exposed to high-speed work and tight deadlines

Source: Paoli, 1997

work at least one Saturday per month, 29 per cent at least one Sunday per month, and 21 per cent work at night at least once per month.

These developments (the rise of the service sector and the twenty-four hour economy) are illustrative of the rapidly changing context of work. Work organisations keep transforming due to, among other things, new production concepts and the flexibilisation of work practices (for example, team-based work), and the increased utilisation of information technology. The changing context of work is illustrated in the second European survey (Paoli, 1997). A substantial number of the European workers appears to be involved in team-based work: 55 per cent has the possibility to rotate tasks with colleagues, and 46 per cent jointly decides on organisational issues, such as the division of tasks, timetables and production objectives. Particularly high incidences of team-based work are found in the Netherlands, the United Kingdom, Sweden and Denmark. Results of the second European survey also reveal that for a third (38 per cent) of the European workers, working with computers is an occasional feature and for 18 per cent it is a permanent feature.

Finally, the constitution of the work population itself is changing. Not only is the process of ageing of concern (31 per cent of the European working population has reached the age of 45 or older, whereas only 13 per cent is younger than 25), but the number of women entering the work force is also steadily growing. Whereas in 1991 39 per cent of the European working population was female, this has increased to 42 per cent in 1996. This development implies a growing number of dual career families. In addition to the changes in the organisation of work practices triggered by this development (for instance, the introduction of flexitime and part-time work), there are specific risks attached, such as the 'spill-over' from work to family life and vice versa (Evans and Bartolomé, 1984; Watkins and Subich, 1995), and an increase in commuting time (a quarter of the European workers spend over one hour a day commuting, with the Netherlands and the United Kingdom experiencing the longest commuting times).

2.2.3 Sociopolitical and legislative background

In Europe in the 1990s, there is an increasing interest at government level in reducing workplace absenteeism and the premature exit of the employee from the workplace as a result of bad working conditions and workplace stress (Gründemann and Van Vuuren, 1997). This increased attention is a relatively recent phenomenon. The introduction of the European Framework Directive (the Directive on Safety and Health of Employees at Work of 12 June 1989) was a stimulus in this, but also other aspects have played a role.

First, there is the increasing cost of social security due to increased unemployment, making the issue of unemployment the most prominent problem within the European Union at this time. Second, there is growing international competition inside and outside the European Union. The third point relates to the globalisation of the production process, whereby international companies transfer their business to cheaper developing countries. All three aspects point in the same direction: the costs of labour have to be reduced so as to keep (industrial) employment in Europe. The costs of social security have a great effect on labour costs and on the price of products. Thus countries with a relatively high expenditure in the field of social security are concerned to maintain competiveness in the international market.

Another aspect is the financing problem (budgetary deficits) of national governments. The costs of social security form a substantial part of this problem. Governments have used the introduction of the European Monetary Union (EMU) as an argument to make an extra effort to put their government finances in order. However, the financing of the social security system in the near future is in question due to the rising average age of the working population, with the move towards a society made up of fewer young people and more elderly people. This issue mainly relates to the financing of insurance benefits due to prolonged work incapacity or invalidity and the old-age pension, with support for these benefit schemes under pressure as a result of these population trends.

In addition to the financial and economic arguments, social and ethical arguments also feature to a limited extent. Observers point, for example, to the undesirable situation whereby large groups of the population are outside the labour process and hence outside normal social intercourse. This means that insufficient use is being made of capacities present in society and the situation also has an adverse effect on the health and welfare of this group and their families.

Employer organisations are also worried about the competitive position of national industry. In general, they support an active government policy regarding workplace absenteeism, but are against too much financial responsibility resting with the companies. The trade unions are opposed to increasing financial responsibilities for employees. This social partner stresses the relation between ill health and aspects of work and argues that employers are responsible for the working environment. Still, unions often respond to policies and initiatives from governments and employer organisations and essentially do not take a different position on the issue of absenteeism and ill health.

The current pressures on social protection budgets, including those for sickness and disability benefits, offer good opportunities for preventive activities at the workplace. All the major players have an interest in the prevention of health problems of workers: governments welcome a decline in the general level of absenteeism; employers are pleased to decrease the financial responsibility of the company; and employees enjoy the benefits of better health and well-being.

In some European countries there are joint (national) programmes between employers and employees – and, generally, also with national governments – to combat workplace absenteeism and to reduce work-related ill health in companies. For example in 1989, the Finnish government, the employer organisations and the unions discussed the possibilities of a programme to extend the working capacity of older workers. These discussions led to the implementation of a comprehensive 'maintenance of workability programme'. In Denmark the government started a campaign in 1994 under the title 'social engagement of companies'. The aim of this campaign is to promote and support workplace initiatives and activities directed at improving the situation of long-term absentees and avoiding exclusion from the work force due to reduced work capacities. In Norway the government and the social partners agreed in 1991 on a national programme to reduce absenteeism. In Portugal the government and the organisations of employers and employees signed a historical agreement in 1991 on health and safety at work. This agreement included activities directed at the prevention of occupational diseases and the rehabilitation and reintegration of disabled workers.

Not only on a national level is legislation in the field of working conditions developed or sharpened, but the European Commission as well has devoted particular attention to the harmonisation of legislation in this area. Among other things, various European directives on health and safety at work have become active, with consequences for policies on working conditions on a national level. The Framework Directive on Health and Safety embodies the concept of risk assessment, that is, the assessment of health and safety risks to the employees. In terms of employer obligations, the major topics covered are (1) the provision of protective, preventive and emergency services, (2) comprehensive information in the area of health and safety, and (3) full consultation and participation rights to employees on matters affecting workplace health and safety. In addition to these framework directives, special directives are aimed at, for instance, the use of work equipment, the use of personal protective equipment, the manual handling of loads, and work with display screen equipment.

2.3   Practice of stress prevention in Europe

The increased familiarity with European legislation on working conditions, and the increased awareness of and concern about health and safety risks in the workplace by various national parties, have created a supportive background for the development of stress prevention activities in the workplace. Although a great deal of activity is going on in this field, the state of development in Europe had previously never been properly addressed (cf. Kahn and Byosiere, 1992; Kompier et al., 1994 and 1998). Little was known about the prevalence and the nature of stress prevention activities at a European level (or, for that matter, at a national level), or about the motives and the major players in the field. This is in contrast to the stress prevention practice found in the United States. The major reasons for US companies becoming involved in stress prevention activity were clearly understood, since the structure of health care costs in the US implied a genuine economic incentive. Moreover, the US approach to stress prevention was typically focused on risk factors for single stress-related health problems (such as heart disease), and interventions were consequently aimed at changing health-related behaviour of the worker. Furthermore, stress prevention programmes in the United States placed little emphasis on the issue of worker participation and provided little evidence of any interventions at the level of the work environment. In the US context participation means taking part in the programmes, and does not include involvement in the decision-making process.

In response to the lack of knowledge about the practice of stress prevention and intervention in Europe, the European Foundation initiated a research programme to obtain a general overview of the type of 'health activities' that took place in workplaces in Europe, the motives to initiate these activities, the role of worker participation in these initiatives, and the characteristics of the companies that were active in this area. Their report, titled 'Under Construction' (Wynne and Clarkin, 1992), presents the results of an extensive research survey conducted among 1,451 companies from seven European Union member states. It should be noted, that the focus of the researchers in this study was not specifically 'stress prevention' activities, but on workplace 'health activities'. However, the activities they were interested in fall within our definition of 'stress prevention' activities, as described in the introduction to this chapter as 'all initiatives and activities that are directed at the reduction (or elimination) of psychosocial and/or physical job stressors, work-related ill health, absenteeism and permanent work incapacity, or that are directed at the improvement or promotion of health at the workplace'. More detailed information on the method (i.e. sample and questionnaire content) and the specific results of this particular study will be discussed later in this section (2.3.2 and 2.3.3 respectively). First, we will present a theoretical framework that will guide our perspective on the nature of stress prevention activities.

2.3.1   A conceptual framework for stress prevention

Two facets in particular will be considered in looking at the prevention of stress, (1) worker- versus work-oriented interventions and (2) primary versus secondary/tertiary interventions.

- Worker-oriented interventions focus on the individual (or group) in such a way that employees learn to deal more effectively with experienced stress or to modify their appraisal of a stressful situation so that the perceived threats are reduced.
- Work-oriented interventions focus on the work environment (or organisation) in such a way that the fit between an individual worker and the workplace is improved.
- Primary prevention is concerned with taking action to modify or eliminate the sources of stress.
- Secondary/tertiary prevention is essentially aimed at the reduction or elimination of the effects of stress. Secondary prevention concerns preventing employees, who are already showing signs of stress, from getting sick (for example, by increasing their coping capacity), and tertiary prevention concerns treatment activities for employees with serious stress-related health problems (for example, the rehabilitation after long-term absenteeism).

By combining worker versus work-oriented interventions and primary versus secondary/tertiary interventions, a conceptual framework arises, as is presented in Figure 2.2, indicating four types of stress prevention activities (Kompier and Marcelissen, 1990; Kompier et al., 1998).

Examples of interventions that are categorised in the first quadrant include job enrichment, increasing workers' autonomy and participation in decision-making, and changing work time schedules. Interventions in the second quadrant are similar to those in the first quadrant, but directed at employees who already show signs of stress (for example, special work schedules for older workers or for those recovering from serious health problems, such as a heart

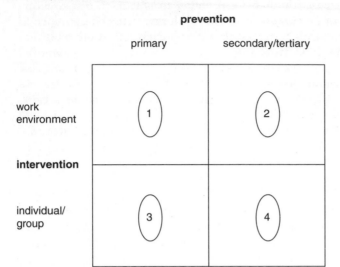

Figure 2.2 A framework for stress prevention and intervention

Source: Kompier and Marcelissen, 1990

attack). Examples of interventions in the third quadrant, often affecting groups rather than specific individuals, are found in the domains of personnel policy (for example, training and development, providing career opportunities, selection, and pre-employment medical examination) and health promotion (for example, corporate fitness programmes and relaxation training programmes). Measures categorised in the fourth quadrant are often directed at specific individuals with serious stress-related problems (for example, rehabilitation after sick leave, post-traumatic stress assistance programmes, and response or symptom directed techniques such as relaxation and psychotherapy).

In reference to Chapter 1 of this book, in its overview of the literature concerned with what kind of stress prevention activities are prevalent, not only in Europe but also in the United States (for example see, Cooper and Payne, 1988; Cox, 1993; Kahn and Byosiere, 1992; Murphy, 1984, 1986 and 1996), three conclusions may be drawn. First, activities in the field of stress management are disproportionally concentrated on reducing the effects of stress, rather than its sources (Cooper and Payne, 1988; Cox, 1993; International Labour Office, 1992; Kahn and Byosiere, 1992; Murphy, 1984, 1986 and 1996). To place it within the terms of the conceptual framework presented in Figure 2.2, stress preventive activities seem to focus primarily on secondary and tertiary prevention, rather than on primary prevention (Murphy, 1984 and 1986). Second, and as a consequence of the relatively high prevalence of secondary and tertiary interventions, most activities seem to be primarily directed at the individual, rather than at the work environment or the organisation. In other words, a worker-oriented approach is followed more often than a work-oriented approach (cf. Ivancevich and Matteson, 1987; Kelly, 1992; Kopelman, 1985; McLeroy et al., 1988; Murphy 1996). Third, a systematic risk assessment (i.e. identifying risk factors and risk groups), as well as serious research into the effects of all the activities, are often lacking in the practice of stress prevention (Kahn and Byosiere, 1992; Kompier et al., 1998).

A general conclusion which may be drawn from the available literature reviews is that stress prevention activities focusing on the sources of stress in the work environment (quadrant 1) are less prevalent than activities in the other three quadrants.

Let us now take a closer look at what kind of stress prevention activities have been undertaken in recent years by the companies that participated in the European research survey (Wynne and Clarkin, 1992). First, we will provide information about some important methodological aspects of this particular study, that is, how the companies were selected for participation in the study, what characterised the responding companies, and which issues were addressed in the questionnaire (2.3.2). The next section (2.3.3) presents the results of the survey, addressing respectively the four central questions that were presented in the introduction to this chapter.

2.3.2   European research survey: Method

Sample

A research questionnaire was sent to 6,157 companies from seven European Union member states: to 1,419 German, 535 Greek, 804 Irish, 725 Italian, 803 Dutch, 1,215 Spanish, and 656 British companies (each company received one questionnaire). In drawing up the national samples, no attempt was made to achieve a sense of representativeness. In practice, many different sampling strategies were used (business directories and in-house databases were the predominant sources from which the samples were drawn). The only stipulations in drawing the samples were that at least two regions within each country should be involved, and that at least 200 companies should receive a questionnaire. In most cases, the selected companies were located in areas of heavy concentration of industry, and within more rural areas.

In all, 1,451 companies responded to the questionnaire (the response rate was 23.6 per cent). More specifically, 161 German (response: 11 per cent), 200 Greek (response: 37 per cent), 138 Irish (response: 17 per cent), 202 Italian (response: 28 per cent), 207 Dutch (response: 26 per cent), 312 Spanish (response: 26 per cent), and 231 British (response: 35 per cent) companies participated. The participating companies did not form a representative sample in terms of company size, sector of industry and trade union membership.

The average company size tended to be large in comparison to the average size of enterprises in most countries: only 15 per cent of the responding companies could be considered small (i.e. less than 100 workers); over 30 per cent of the companies, offered employment to more than 500 workers; in the remainder of the companies sampled, 100 to 500 workers were employed. Of all responding companies, 27.2 per cent was a multinational.

With regard to the different sectors of industry, the sample was biased towards the manufacturing sector, whereas the service sectors and the agriculture sector were under-represented. In the break down of figures; 18.4 per cent of the responding companies operated in the public sector, 75.5 per cent operated in the private sector, and 6.1 per cent classified themselves as 'other'. The majority of the sample (64 per cent) was involved in manufacturing (22 per cent from metal manufacturing, mechanical, electrical and instrument engineering; 17 per cent from extraction and processing industries; and 25 per cent from 'other' manufacturing industries). The remainder of the sample came largely from the services sectors – transport and communications (approximately 7 per cent), banking and finance distributive trades (approximately 6 per cent) and 'other' services (11 per cent). Only 2 per cent of the sample was active in the agriculture sector.

According to the researchers, the sample was further biased towards the older industries where trade union membership levels tend to be higher. More specifically, in half of the responding companies, 50 to 100 per cent of the workers were members of trade unions; 18 per cent of the sample had a trade union membership between 25 and 50 per cent; and 33 per cent had a trade union membership up to 25 per cent.

Questionnaire

When drawing up the research questionnaire different sections were developed. For the purpose of this chapter, that is, answering the four central questions raised in the introduction section, the following three sections were particularly useful:

*   Section A ('company details') sought demographic details, such as company size, sector of industry and trade union membership.
*   Section B ('actions for health') sought information about the nature of actions which have taken place in recent years. The companies were given 30 activities that were categorised by the researchers in the following five areas:

    1   health screening activities (for example, periodic health screening for all personnel and periodic health screening for 'at risk' staff);
    2   healthy behaviour activities (for example, alcohol and non-smoking policies and exercise facilities);

3   organisational interventions (for example, job design programmes, flexibility of work time and training in human resource management skills) which were primarily aimed at the reduction of psychosocial job stressors;

4   safety and physical environment activities (for example, toxic substance control, protective clothing/equipment and changing various aspects of the physical environment) which were primarily aimed at the reduction of physical job stressors;

5   social and welfare activities (for example, counselling support, community and social programmes, and 'stress control' programmes).

Unfortunately, no questions were asked about policies and procedures on sickness absence and permanent work incapacity.

•   Section C ('establishing action for health') concerned the process of how actions became established in the company (i.e. the motives, responsibilities, and the participants).

2.3.3   European research survey: Results

Question 1:   What is the nature of stress prevention activities?

Figure 2.3 (p. 22) presents an overview of the thirty activities that have been categorised into the conceptual framework for stress prevention and intervention, presented earlier (see Figure 2.2). Figure 2.3 also reports, for each of the thirty activities, the percentage of responding organisations that claimed that the activity had taken place recently within their company. One specific activity, presented as 'stress control', is excluded from this figure, because in the questionnaire it was not clarified what specifically was meant by 'stress control'. Therefore, it is impossible to categorise this activity into one of the four quadrants (this specific activity will be addressed in 'Question 2').

Contrary to our expectations that were based on literature reviews, the most prevalent class of activities concerned preventive measures directed at the work environment (quadrant one). Within this quadrant, we have distinguished between activities that are directed at the reduction of psycho-social versus physical stressors (the former are shown in bold). As can be seen, actions directed at the reduction of physical stressors had taken place to a large extent. About three-quarters of the responding companies claimed to have introduced protective clothing and equipment (80 per cent), machinery guards (76 per cent), improvements in lighting (76 per cent), ventilation (76 per cent), heating (73 per cent) and noise reduction (68 per cent). Primary preventive work-directed measures aimed at the reduction of psychosocial stressors were reported less frequently: half of the responding

	prevention	
	primary	**secondary/tertiary**
work environment	protective clothing/equipment (80%) machinery guards (76%) changes to lighting (76%) changes to ventilation (76%) changes to heating/air-conditioning (73%) noise reduction (68%) toxic substance control (56%) **flexibility of working time (56%)** **training in human resource management skills (55%)** changes to interior design (56%) changes to individual workspaces (54%) **work organisation programmes (47%)** automating hazardous processes (47%) **redesign of shift schedules (24%)** 1	individual job (re)design programmes (39%) changes to individual workspaces (54%) redesign of shift schedules (24%) 2
individual/group	3 health screening for all personnel (51%) rest/social/shower facilities (47%) health screening for at risk staff (46%) health education (40%) no smoking policy (37%) healthy diet policy (37%) alcohol policy (28%) community/social programmes (25%) exercise facilities (23%) exercise/lifestyle classes (10%)	4 welfare support programme (31%) counselling support (30%) support programmes alcoholics/gamblers (16%) policy on alcohol/substance abuse (28%)

The leftmost label **intervention** applies to the rows (work environment, individual/group).

Figure 2.3 Interventions and preventive actions in 1,451 organisations in seven EU countries

Sources: Kompier and Marcelissen, 1990; Wynne and Clarkin, 1992

Note: The activities in quadrant 1 in bold differ from the other activities in this quadrant in that they are directed at the reduction of psychosocial rather than physical stressors in the workplace

companies claimed to have introduced more flexible working hours (56 per cent), training in human resource management skills (55 per cent) and work organisation programmes, that is, designing how jobs fit together (47 per cent). Furthermore, 24 per cent of the responding companies reported having redesigned their shift schedules, although it is unclear whether this reorganisation took place at a group level or on an individual basis (see also quadrant two).

The next dominant class of activities was also primary preventive, but directed at the individual or group rather than at the work itself (quadrant three). About half of the companies reported periodic health screening for all personnel (51 per cent) or for 'at risk' staff (for example, staff using dangerous chemicals, 46 per cent), and the introduction of rest-, social- and shower-facilities. A minority reported that special policies on alcohol (28 per cent), smoking (37 per cent) and healthy diet (37 per cent), as well as exercise facilities (23 per cent), were developed within their company.

The least prevalent activities concerned secondary and tertiary preventive measures, directed at the individual (quadrant four). Counselling support (30 per cent) and welfare programmes (31 per cent) were provided by about only one-third of the responding companies. The prevalence of secondary and tertiary work-oriented interventions (quadrant two) took a moderate position. Out of all the companies, 54 per cent claimed to have changed individual workspaces (see also quadrant one), 39 per cent claimed to have (re)designed individual jobs, and 24 per cent reported having redesigned shift schedules (see also quadrant one).

To summarise, activities directed at the individual, rather than at the work environment, and activities directed at reducing the effects of work stress (i.e. secondary/tertiary prevention), rather than its sources (i.e. primary prevention), were not disproportionally present, as had been expected from the literature reviews (Cooper and Payne, 1988; Cox, 1993; Kahn and Byosiere, 1992; Kompier et al., 1998; Murphy, 1984, 1986 and 1996). There may be at least three explanations for the perhaps overly rosy picture of the state of European stress prevention practice that this chapter paints. First, we have used a broad definition of the term 'stress prevention', also including actions aimed at the reduction of physical rather than psychosocial stressors. When taking a closer look at the type of primary preventive work-directed measures most prevalent in the participating companies (quadrant one), we noticed that measures directed at the reduction of psychosocial stressors were less frequent than measures directed at the reduction of physical stressors. Second, one may assume that the responding companies (23 per cent of those who were asked to participate) were probably the ones which were the most active in the area of 'stress prevention'. Consequently, these probably do not represent what actually happens on a larger scale. In fact, as mentioned earlier, the responding companies were larger than average, with a strong bias towards the manufacturing sector (more than 60 per cent were involved in manufacturing, whereas recent figures reveal that only 30 per cent of European workers are employed in this economic sector; see Paoli, 1997). This also explains the high incidence of activities in the area of safety and physical work environment. A final explanation, is legislation. Most of the activities directed at safety and ambient factors were the subject of legislation. This brings us to the various motives behind the instigation of certain activities.

Question 2: What are the motives for stress prevention activities?

The participating companies in the survey were asked a question in regard to what extent each of ten possible factors had prompted one or more of the thirty activities within their company. Among the external motives, legislative provisions on both a European and on a national level appeared to be the most important factors, and were mentioned by 80 per cent of the companies. Among the most important internal motives were health problems (77 per cent), problems of employee morale (73 per cent), personnel and welfare problems (76 per cent) and productivity and performance problems (72 per cent). More than half of the responding companies mentioned absenteeism (63 per cent), company public image (61 per cent) and accident rates (56 per cent) as internal pressures. Industrial relations (41 per cent) and employee turnover (29 per cent) were mentioned the least as important motives.

A separate question involved the benefits that had been observed within the company as a result of one or more of the thirty activities. The benefits that were mentioned most often were the improvement of employee morale (78 per cent), improvement of health in the work force (76 per cent), the reduction of personnel and welfare problems (62 per cent) and of absenteeism (63 per cent), and the improvement of productivity and performance (62 per cent) and of industrial relations (62 per cent).

An interesting finding is that the motives for undertaking one or more of the thirty activities did not always correspond with the benefits that were observed. The most extreme difference was found for 'industrial relations'. The improvement of industrial relations was only mentioned as a motive by 41 per cent of the companies, whereas 62 per cent reported this as an important benefit from the activities that had been undertaken within their company.

Another interesting point is when the companies were asked whether or not 'stress control' activities had recently taken place, only 11 per cent of the 1,451 companies reported 'yes'. Although, as noted earlier, it was not further clarified what exactly was meant by 'stress control', this finding indicates that most activities that we consider as 'stress prevention' activities are not considered or recognised as such by the responding companies (see also, Kompier et al., 1994).

Question 3: Who are the participants in stress prevention activities?

The companies were also asked what specific groups were involved in various stages of one or more of the thirty activities. Six potentially involved parties were distinguished: (a) management, (b) employee representatives (for example, works council), (c) trade union representatives, (d) health and safety representatives, (e) occupational health staff and (f) external consultants. In order to facilitate answering the question, an idealised process of stress prevention was described, involving four steps: (1) the initial idea, (2) the planning, (3) the implementation and (4) the evaluation. These four steps bear a similarity to the five steps outlined in most of the subsequent chapters in this book: ((1) preparation, (2) problem analysis, (3) choice of measures, (4) implementation and (5) evaluation). The 'planning' phase in the European study can be seen as a combination of the 'problem analysis' and 'choice of measures' phases in the following chapters. In addition, four levels of involvement in the process were envisaged: information provision (the lowest level of involvement), consultation, participation and responsibility (the highest level of involvement). The main findings revealed that management was most involved in the process of stress prevention in all four steps, and with the highest degree of participation (80 per cent of the managers reported high involvement in Step 1 and Step 4, and about 60 per cent reported high involvement in Steps 2 and 3). The next most involved groups were employee representatives and health and safety representatives, showing the same pattern of involvement in the various steps as managers, that is, relatively high involvement in the beginning and at the end of the project, and lower involvement in the middle steps. Although in the implementation phase (Step 4) over half of the managers, employee representatives and health and safety representatives reported participating in decision making, the majority of the managers (over 70 per cent) reported carrying financial responsibility for the measures taken, in contrast to a minority (less than 40 per cent) of the other two groups. The remaining parties (trade union representatives, external consultants and occupational health staff) played less prominent roles, both in terms of when they were involved and the extent of their participation. In contrast to the parties just discussed, the external consultants showed a relatively high level of involvement during Step 2 and Step 3. In general, the results showed that in all four steps management carried responsibility, whereas the level of involvement of the other five parties rarely exceeded the level of participation.

Question 4: What are the characteristics of the active companies in stress prevention?

A series of multi-variate regression analyses was performed in order to find out what characterised the companies that were most active in stress prevention.

As independent variables ('predictors') four types of factors were included: (1) company demographics (for example, size and trade union membership), (2) company health characteristics (for example, the existence of an occupational health department, health policies and a health budget), (3) the prompting factors (or motives) that we have discussed in answering question two, and (4) the participation level of the six parties that we have discussed in answering question three. The dependent variables in the analyses were the five categories of activities that were presented earlier (2.3.2): (1) health screening activities, (2) healthy behaviour activities, (3) organisational interventions, (4) safety and physical environment activities and (5) social and welfare activities. Table 2.1 presents an overview of the specific 'predictors', as well as information on whether they significantly predicted each of the five 'stress prevention' activities.

Overall, the highest levels of prediction were found for health screening activities and healthy behaviour activities (respectively 38 per cent and 36 per cent of the variance was explained). The lowest levels of prediction were found for the organisational interventions, and the safety/physical environment activities (respectively 20 per cent and 23 per cent of the variance was explained). Of the variance in social/welfare activities a moderate amount of variance (28 per cent) was explained.

With respect to company demographic variables, company size in particular was strongly and consistently associated with the various stress prevention activities, indicating that larger companies were more active in this area. The level of trade union membership was positively associated only with healthy behaviour activities and social/welfare activities, and not with organisational or safety/physical environment activities. This is surprising, as trade unions are often in favour of work-oriented activities, and can be suspicious of activities directed primarily at the individual ('blaming the victim'). However, it is possible that the trade unions did not succeed in their attempt to initiate and introduce work-oriented measures.

With regard to the company health characteristics that explained specific stress prevention activities, a high overall level of activity was typical of companies that had resources as well as policies to reduce work-related stressors and ill health or to promote health at the workplace. In fact, companies with health budgets and health policies that were assisted by an occupational health department and/or specific health and safety committees were most active in the field.

The various prompting factors were not predictive of health screening activities, but were significantly associated with the other four types of activities. They played the greatest role in predicting healthy behaviour activities, as well as safety/physical environment activities. The most active companies were the ones whose activities were primarily triggered by internal motives, particularly by staff morale. This finding indicates that when work force morale is given as a reason to initiate workplace health activities, then such

Table 2.1 Significant predictors (+) of various 'stress prevention' activities

predictors	health screening activities	healthy behaviour activities	organisational interventions	safety and physical environment activities	social and welfare activities
company demographics					
size	+	+	+		+
sector					
ownership					
trade union membership		+			+
premises					
company health					
occupational health	+	+		+	+
health and safety committee	+	+	+	+	
health policy	+	+	+		+
health budget	+		+	+	+
health priority			+		
prompting factors					
legislation		+		+	
personnel problems					
health problems					
staff morale		+	+	+	+
absenteeism				+	
productivity/ performance				+	
staff turnover					
industrial relations					
public image		+			
accident rates		+	+		+
participation level					
management		+			
staff					
trade union					
health and safety representatives	+			+	
occupational health staff				+	
external consultants		+			
% variance explained	38%	36%	20%	23%	28%

Source: Wynne and Clarkin, 1992

activities are far more likely to take place. Interestingly, the presence of health problems was not at all predictive of any of the five types of activities.

Finally, the level of participation of the various parties revealed that involvement of health and safety representatives was most predictive of health screening activities and safety/physical environment activities. High involvement of management and external consultants was only strongly associated with healthy behaviour activities. These findings suggest that management relies primarily on individually-oriented interventions. This is not necessarily true for external consultants, as they may have unsuccessfully attempted to introduce other types of measures (in fact, management has the final decision in regard to what measures are actually taken).

Surprisingly, the participation level of trade unions was not associated with any of the five types of activities, suggesting that trade unions may play only a marginal role in the establishment of 'stress prevention' activities in the workplace.

2.4   Concluding remarks and future prospects

The purpose of this current chapter is to present an overview of the various initiatives and activities that have been taken by European companies to prevent or reduce 'workplace stress'. We have argued that for a growing number of European workers workplace stress is a common phenomenon, due to the changing nature and context of work. We have also tried to make clear that concern about workplace stress and stress prevention is growing among national governments and social partners in the European Union. Based on a European research survey conducted among 1,451 companies, drawn from seven European Union member states (Wynne and Clarkin, 1992), we have tried to answer the following questions about the practice of stress prevention in European companies: (1) what is the nature of stress prevention activities? (2) what are the motives for stress prevention activities? (3) who are the participants in stress prevention activities? and (4) what are the characteristics of active companies in stress prevention?

With respect to the first question, the results showed that a wide variety of activity has been going on in the area of 'stress prevention' (although these activities may not always be considered as 'stress prevention' activities by the companies). The results of the survey did not show, as was expected from literature reviews, that individually-oriented and secondary/tertiary preventive activities were undertaken more often than the work-oriented and primary preventive activities. However, this picture is probably too favourable, representing particularly the large-sized and most active companies in the area of stress prevention, with a strong bias towards the manufacturing sector ('selection bias'). Moreover, the primary preventive and work-oriented activities that were most prevalent within the responding companies were directed at the reduction of physical rather than psychosocial stressors.

In looking at the second question, both external motives (i.e. legislation) and internal motives (i.e. reducing health problems and personnel/welfare problems and improving staff morale and productivity/performance) were reported by the companies as playing a role in prompting 'stress prevention' activities. Surprisingly, although 'health problems' and 'personnel/welfare problems' were often reported as a motive, neither motive was predictive of what activities were actually undertaken by the participating companies. Factors that were reported as important motives and were predictive of at least two out of five types of activity were 'staff morale' and 'legislation'.

Turning to the third question, the results showed that in all four steps of stress prevention programmes (i.e. initial idea, planning, implementation and evaluation) management was the most involved and carried the highest responsibility.

With respect to question four, the results showed that a high overall level of stress prevention activity was typical of large-sized companies who had resources (such as the existence of occupational health staff and health budgets) and policies in the area of stress prevention, and who considered the improvement of staff morale as an important reason to start these activities. The results further suggest that trade unions only play a marginal role in (or have a minor influence on) the establishment of stress prevention activities, particularly when it concerns work-oriented, rather than worker-oriented, interventions. There seems to be considerable room for improvement in this regard in the future.

We conclude here with some key challenges that will need to be faced in the future. First, the awareness of and concern about stress prevention should be considered not only in north and west European countries, but be particularly taken into account in south European countries where the quality of the work environment is still below the average (Smulders et al., 1996). Furthermore, the knowledge of workplace stress and stress prevention should move beyond the circle of 'professionals' in the field, and into all workplaces to those who actually use it for implementation purposes. Both employers' organisations and employees (or trade unions) should realise that stress prevention is mutually beneficial. For employers there are bottom-line benefits to be gained, while for employees and trade unions there is the potential to use stress prevention as a means to improve working conditions.

A second challenge is to provide examples of good practice in the area of stress prevention. Recently, Kompier and his colleagues (1998) presented successful examples of preventive practice in ten Dutch companies. They derived five key factors which they consider to be at the heart of a successful approach. These involve: (1) a stepwise and systematic approach, (2) an adequate problem analysis, (2) a combination of measures directed at both the work environment and the individual, (4) worker participation and (5) top management support. In our opinion, particular attention should be devoted to methods and tools to assess workplace stress that can also be used by non-professionals in the workplace (cf. Kompier and Levi, 1993),

Third, a major challenge is the adequate analysis of the costs and benefits of stress prevention activities, in terms of, for instance, finances, productivity and absence reduction. In order to carry out an adequate and complete costs-benefit analysis, professionals from various academic communities (for example, psychologists, economists and ergonomists) should join forces. Although there is some evidence from the United States of the costs and benefits that operate there, particularly concerning 'single issue' (for example, lifestyle) programmes (Mossink and Licher, 1998), translation to the European context is impossible, mainly due to differences in health care cost structures. Research on this issue needs, therefore to be stimulated and conducted within a European context (cf. Cooper et al., 1996).

Bibliography

Balcombe, J. and Tate, G. (1995) *Ill-health and Workplace Absenteeism in the United Kingdom: Initiatives for Prevention*, Dublin: European Foundation for the Improvement of Living and Working Conditions (Working Paper).

Bloemhoff, A., Lourijsen, E., Smulders, P. and De Gier, E. (1993) *European Legislation on Health and Safety at Work: How Much Do Small and Large Businesses in the Netherlands Know About It?* Report no. 93.011, Leiden: NIPG-TNO.

Cartwright, S. and Cooper, G.L. (1997) 'The growing epidemic of stress', in S. Cartwright and C.L. Cooper (eds), *Managing Workplace Stress*, pp. 1–24. London: Sage Publications Ltd.

CBS (Central Bureau for Statistics) *Statistisch Jaarboek 1998* (Yearbook on Statistics 1998), Voorburg/Heerlen CBS.

Cooper, C.L., Liukkonen, P. and Cartwright, S. (1996) *Stress Prevention in the Workplace: Assessing the Costs and Benefits to Organisations*, Dublin: European Foundation for the Improvement of Living and Working Conditions.

Cooper, C.L. and Payne, R. (eds) (1988) *Causes, Coping and Consequences of Stress at Work*, Chichester: John Wiley and Sons.

Cox, T. (1993) *Stress Research and Stress Management: Putting Theory to Work*. HSE contract research report, no. 61/1993, Nottingham: University of Nottingham.

Davies, N.V. and Teasdale, P. (1994) *The Costs to the British Economy of Work Accidents and Work-related Ill Health*, London: Health and Safety Executive.

Doukmak, B. and Huber, B. (1995) *Ill-health and Workplace Absenteeism in the Federal Republic of Germany: Initiatives for Prevention*, Dublin: European Foundation for the Improvement of Living and Working Conditions (Working Paper).

Evans, P. and Bartolomé, F. (1984) 'The changing pictures of the relationship between career and family', *Journal of Occupational Behaviour, 5*, (21).

Gründemann, R.W.M. (1995) *Ill-health and Workplace Absenteeism in the Netherlands: Initiatives for Prevention*, Dublin: European Foundation for the Improvement of Living and Working Conditions (Working Paper).

Gründemann, R.W.M., Nijboer, I.D. and Schellart, A.J.M. (1991) *Arbeidsgebondenheid van WAO-intrede; onderzoeksresultaat: Fase 1* (Work-relatedness of disability; Research result: phase 1), Den Haag: Ministerie van Sociale Zaken en Werkgelegenheid.

Gründemann, R.W.M., De Winter, C.R. and Smulders, P.G.W. (1994) *Absenteeism in the European Union*, Dublin: European Foundation for the Improvement of Living and Working Conditions.

Gründemann, R.W.M. and Van Vuuren C.V. (1997) *Preventing Absenteeism at the Workplace*, European Research Report, Dublin: European Foundation for the Improvement of Living and Working Conditions.

International Labour Office (Di Martino, V.) (1992) *Conditions of Work Digest. Preventing stress at work*, 11, (2): Geneva.

Ivancevich, J.M. and Matteson, M.T. (1987) 'Organisational level stress management interventions: a review and recommendations', in J.M. Ivancevich and D.C. Ganster (eds), *Job Stress: from Theory to Suggestion*, pp. 229–48, New York: Haworth Press.

Jensen, P.L. (1996) *The Costs of Work-related Diseases and Work Accidents in Denmark*, Copenhagen: Arbejdstilsynet.

Kahn, R.L. and Byosiere, Ph. (1992) 'Stress in organisations', in M.D. Dunnette and L.M. Hough (eds) *Handbook of Industrial and Organisational Psychology*, (2nd edition), 3, pp. 571–650, Palo Alto, California: Consulting Psychologists Press.

Kelly, J. (1992) 'Does job-redesign theory explain job redesign outcomes?' *Human Relations*, 45, (8) 753–74.

Kompier, M.A.J. and Marcelissen, F.H.G. (1990) *Handboek Werkstress*, Amsterdam: Nederlands Instituut voor Arbeidsomstandigheden.

Kompier, M.A.J. and Levi, L. (1993) *Stress at Work: Causes, Effects and Prevention*, Dublin: European Foundation for the Improvement of Living and Working Conditions.

Kompier, M.A.J., De Gier, E., Smulders, P. and Draaisma, D. (1994) 'Regulations, policies and practices concerning work stress in five European countries', *Work and Stress*, 8, (4): 296–318.

Kompier, M.A.J., Geurts, S.A.E., Gründemann, R.W.M., Vink, P. and Smulders, P.G.W. (1998), 'Cases in stress prevention: the success of a participative and stepwise approach', *Stress Medicine*, 14, 155–68.

Kopelman, R. (1985) 'Job redesign and productivity: a review of the evidence', *National Productivity Review*, pp. 237–55.

McLeroy, K.R., Bibeau, D., Steckler, A. and Glanz, K. (1988) 'An ecological perspective on health promotion programs', *Health Education Quarterly*, 15, 351–77.

Mossink, J. and Licher, F. (1998) *Costs and Benefits of Occupational Safety and Health 1997*, Amsterdam: NIA-TNO.

Murphy, L.R. (1984) 'Occupational stress management: a review and appraisal', *Journal of Occupational Psychology*, 57: 1–15.

—(1986) 'A review of organizational stress management research', *Journal of Organizational Behavior Management*, 8: 215–27.

—(1996) 'Stress management in work settings: A critical review of the health effects', *American Journal of Health Promotion*, 11, (2): 112–35.

Paoli, P. (1992) *First European survey on the work environment 1991–1992*, Dublin: European Foundation for the Improvement of Living and Working Conditions.

—(1997) *Second European Survey on Working Conditions 1996*, Dublin: European Foundation for the Improvement of Living and Working Conditions.

Schabracq, M.J., Winnubst, J.A.M. and Cooper, G.L. (eds) (1996) *Handbook of Work and Health Psychology*, Chichester: John Wiley and Sons.

Smulders, P.G.W., Kompier, M.A.J. and Paoli, P. (1996) 'The work environment in the twelve EU-countries: Differences and similarities', *Human Relations*, 49, (10): 1291–1313.

Van Damme, J. (1995) *Ill-health and Workplace Absenteeism in Belgium: Initiatives for Prevention*, Dublin: European Foundation for the Improvement of Living and Working Conditions (Working Paper).

Watkins, C.E., and Subich, L.M. (1995) 'Annual Review, 1992–1994: Career participation', *Journal of Vocational Behavior*, 47: 109–63.

Wynne, R. and Clarkin, N. (1992) *Under Construction: Building for Health in the EC Workplace*, Dublin: European Foundation for the Improvement of Living and Working Conditions.

Chapter 3

Costs and benefits of stress prevention in organisations

Review and new methodology

Paula Liukkonen, Susan Cartwright and Cary Cooper

3.1 Introduction

The financial costs of stress can be considered and measured at a national, organisational and individual level. Similarly, the cost benefit analysis of stress prevention and stress reduction activities can be assessed from these three different perspectives. Depending on which perspective is selected, the results and economic consequences can vary. For example, what is measured as a cost at the level of public administration need not mean costs at the level of private enterprise. In the United Kingdom, hospital treatment costs for workers who develop stress-related illness are typically borne by the National Health Service and are not a direct cost to the employer. At an organisational level, the direct costs of stress-related absence are reflected in productivity losses, lost opportunities, increased recruitment and retraining costs and the like. In the same way, employees loss of welfare, i.e. inability to continue to work in the same job, does not necessarily imply costs for the organisation.

In many EU countries, knowledge regarding the costs of industrial injuries, sickness, health and safety exists at a national level. This is often the result of work carried out by economists and health economists. Sophisticated models and methodologies have recently been developed to help countries assess the socio-economic costs of stress at a national level (Levi and Lunde-Jensen, 1996). However, differing employment provisions and pay structures, employment classification systems and statistics across EU member states often serve to complicate meaningful comparisons between countries.

The degree of recognition and the priority placed on the problem of stress varies among European countries both at a national and employer level. Some indication of the costs of stress can be gained from several European and national studies. According to one report (Commission of the European Communities, 1992) on occupational accidents and diseases within the EU, approximately 8,000 people die each year as a result of occupational accidents and disease, a further 10 million suffer some form of work related accident or disease, and the annual compensation paid for these injuries and illnesses is estimated at European Currency Unit (ECU) 20,000 million.

A report by the Nordic Council of Ministers (Lunde-Jensen, 1994) calculated that the economic costs of work-related sickness and accidents in four Nordic countries ranged from 2.5 per cent of gross national product in Denmark to over 10 per cent in Norway. (See also Chapter 2.)

Evidence also indicates that absence from work due to psychological disorders is rising, whereas the rate of absenteeism emanating from more traditional sources (for example, back problems) has remained relatively stable. Between 1981 and 1991, the percentage of workplace absence attributed to psychological disorders in Denmark rose from 12 per cent to 26 per cent (Danish Working Environment Service, 1996). It has been suggested (Balemans, 1994) that work stress is responsible for a considerable proportion of these absences. More recent figures released for the UK by the Health and Safety Executive (HSE, 1997) estimate that 30 million days are lost each year as a result of work-related injuries and ill health. Furthermore, employers' liability insurance costs have increased by 250 per cent over a ten year period to £738 million in 1995.

In contrast, methods for calculating sickness and deficiencies in health and safety at an organisational level are less well developed. Although action to reduce workplace stress can be initiated at a national level, as exemplified by the Dutch government's policy programme 'Stress at Work' (Vromans, 1994), such initiatives are primarily aimed at increasing awareness and encouraging companies to make stress prevention an integral part of their normal company practice rather than compelling them to do so. The Swedish government has also played a particularly active initiating role in stress prevention. Through the Swedish Working Life Fund (Arbetslivsfonden), it has made significant funds available to organisations for health promotion and health improvement projects. However, organisations are required to contribute at least half of the investment costs themselves (Lunde-Jensen, 1996; Nilsson, 1994; see also this volume Chapter 9). Because the onus of responsibility for implementing stress prevention activities lies with the employers, the financial wisdom of investing in this type of activity has to be demonstrated. Although growing litigation fears, certainly in the UK, may have contributed to motivate organisations to seriously consider ways to address the problem of workplace stress, most organisations have yet to be fully convinced of the positive financial benefits to be gained from maintaining a healthy workforce.

In seeking to present a means of developing a 'business case' to justify organisational expenditure in this area, this chapter will:

1   briefly review the current research evidence on the costs and benefits of different types of stress interventions (section 3.2);
2   consider the extent to which the collection and analysis of organisational data can be used to detect early signs of positive or negative development in employee health and well being (sections 3.3. and 3.4);
3   present a model ('Oskar') for conducting a cost benefit analysis of any

stress intervention measures which an organisation may decide to introduce (section 3.5).

3.2 Stress interventions and their effectiveness

Typically, as discussed in Chapters 1 and 2, stress intervention strategies fall into three broad categories: primary, secondary and tertiary (Murphy, 1988). Primary level interventions are concerned with modifying or eliminating the sources of stress (stressors) inherent in the workplace in order to adapt the environment to better fit the individual. Secondary level interventions focus on the individual and are concerned with increasing awareness and extending the physical and psychological resources of employees to enable them to minimise the damaging effects of stress and manage stress more effectively. Tertiary interventions are also targeted at the individual but unlike secondary level interventions, their role is recuperative rather than preventative. That's to say, tertiary interventions are concerned with providing treatment, rehabilitation and recovery services to individuals who are already suffering from quite severe ill health problems as a result of stress.

There are examples of all three types of intervention operating within European organisations, although stress prevention activities tend to be confined to large organisations employing more than 500 employees (Cartwright and Cooper, 1996; Wynne and Clarkin, 1992; see also this volume Chapter 2). In the UK, stress interventions tend to involve stress management activities, i.e. training and health promotion programmes and the provision of employee counselling services. Whereas in the Scandanavian countries, particularly in Sweden, emphasis is placed more on primary prevention through changing or redesigning work organisation and culture.

Tertiary prevention

There is well documented evidence (Berridge et al., 1997; Cooper and Sadri, 1991) to suggest that counselling is effective in improving the psychological well-being of employees and has considerable cost benefits in terms of reduced sickness absence. However, such evaluations have not incorporated productivity measures nor considered the effects on attrition rates. Significant improvements in mental health and self-esteem as a result of counselling may improve the abilities and confidence of individuals to pursue and secure alternative job opportunities in potentially less stressful work environments, which may have costs to the organisation.

Secondary prevention

In common with other forms of training, the effectiveness and potential cost benefits of secondary level interventions has been even less rigorously evaluated. Based on self-report measures, stress management activities would seem to have a modest effect in temporarily reducing experienced stress (Cooper *et al.*, 1996; Murphy, 1988; Sallis *et al.*, 1987). However, in isolation, not only do these beneficial effects appear to decay over time, but evidence would seem to indicate that success varies according to the form such activities take and the individual receptiveness to the techniques employed (see Chapter 4). Research which has examined the impact of lifestyle and health promotion activities has reached roughly similar conclusions (Ivancevich and Matteson, 1988). In terms of cost benefit analysis, most research which has evaluated the impact of secondary interventions has tended to utilise behavioural and affective employee self-report measures rather than productivity or other financial indices to gauge success and failed to incorporate administrative and programme costs or establish suitable control groups.

Primary prevention

This also holds true for most evaluated studies of primary level interventions, with certain exceptions. Brulin and Nilsson (1994) evaluated 1,500 randomly selected projects funded by the Swedish Working Life Fund. Apart from significant improvements in employee satisfaction and motivation levels, such projects were shown to minimally improve productivity output by 10 per cent and reduce production errors and delivery times. Terra (1995) has demonstrated that job redesign and the implementation of self-regulating teams as a means of stressor reduction resulted in a 50 per cent decrease in sickness absence in the metal can industry. A recent review of stress intervention practice (Cooper *et al.*, 1996) provides two examples of more thorough cost benefit analysis studies of primary (Kvarnstrom, 1996) and integrated stress intervention programmes (Nijhuis *et al.*, 1996) which incorporated pre- and post-performance and absence data and showed significant cost benefits over and above the implementation costs.

One of the major difficulties in evaluating the costs and benefits of stress intervention in organisations is that critical success factors, key processes and performance indicators have to be clearly defined from the outset. With post-intervention, it is almost impossible to reconstruct the procedure. Stress has financial consequences for organisations both in the short and long term. Some of the consequences can be measured using quantitative methods, for example personnel costs, while others require qualitative measurement, for example, the organisation's capacity or health (Cooper *et al.*, 1996). These dimensions will be discussed in the following section.

3.3   Organisational performance and results

Organisational results have traditionally been regarded purely as financial (monetary) results and their other dimensions have not been considered

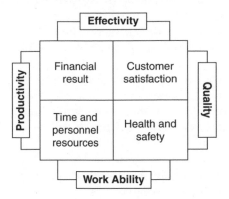

Figure 3.1 Four performance dimensions, plus measures of operational rationality, productivity, effectivity, quality and work capacity

(Liukkonen, 1996). As companies have begun to pay more attention to factors other than economic goals, methods of measuring results have needed to become more versatile. Consequently, the need for versatile performance analysis has followed the use of multidisciplinary result measurement. In order to make clear the importance of the working environment and the issue of employee health for the future of the company, it is necessary to re-examine the results concept and to understand its different dimensions.

Companies' financial performance measures, such as liquidity, solvency, renumerativeness and profitability, measure historical data. It would be fair to say that these measurements give a historical view of what has already happened. In order to look forward it is necessary to consider other dimensions. Performance analysis should therefore include an element of predictive information as regards present and future employee health. As the measurement of results plays such a central role in overall performance analysis, it is important to analyse the content of this new multidisciplinary result concept and then consider how it can be used.

Four dimensions of company results

Company results are made up of both quantitative and qualitative measures. The quantitative measures consist of information taken from the company's profit and loss account and balance sheet. Hours worked, personnel statistics and personnel reports show the levels of staffing and competency that have been used to achieve the financial result. The customers' level of appreciation for products and services is demonstrated by qualitative measures. Measurements of customer satisfaction show how effective a company has been in satisfying customer's requirements and providing value for the customer. All these findings including any data relevant to the work environment and employee health can be presented in a report, showing the organisation's collective health and capacity. Such a report might contain opinion surveys, environmental appraisals, as well as different types of employee health appraisals.

The operational measures of productivity, effectivity and quality are subordinate to the results concept. Many working environment studies, intended to show the benefit of measures implemented, report on side issues alone, that is, productivity, effectivity and quality, omitting how profits have been improved through measures taken.

Combined reporting of the result's different dimensions gives a picture of how cause, result and effect are related. Often, it is precisely these relationships that remain uninvestigated, resulting in the company not recognising the need to introduce improvements to the working environment or employee health. Cost/benefit analysis can be used to provide the answer to the question of whether or not the investment under consideration would be profitable to carry out. While such calculations are necessary, it is also important to establish how the company results, and those factors that influence their development, are affected by the proposed measures in the long term. Measurement should be focused on the main issue (the company's performance development) rather than on sub-issues.

3.4   Towards a new organisational performance analysis

3.4.1   Introduction: Everything is measured – apart from the whole

Relatively well-developed methods exist for calculating and analysing the state of the working environment and employee health (Liukkonen, 1997). The main problem is one of communication within the company and particularly communication between the different organisational functions. Accountants measure financial development, production managers measure the cost of production, in the personnel and salary departments staffing costs are calculated, while working environment and employee health organisations try to justify their measures by drawing attention to reduced sick leave, work place injury costs, or early retirement costs. There seems to be little communication between these numerate experts, with the result that everyone has partial knowledge of the results, while no-one actually gets to see the whole picture. Thus it is important to find a common 'company language' and methods of combined reporting, where the results from different areas can be presented together. Combined reporting provides the company with a complete picture of its results and the factors that can influence them in the short and long term.

Consequently, being able to see the whole picture, and creating concurrency that facilitates long-term development, is a fundamental concept in the following report which outlines a new organisational performance analysis method. This multidisciplinary analytical method requires increased communication between the different functions of an organisation.

3.4.2   Figures as a basis for decisions

The operation activity of a company is controlled on the basis of financial information. Company operational control should also include information regarding customer satisfaction, employee health and the levels of staff and competence with which the company results have been achieved. When considering the question of why important information that could be used as a basis for decisions is not used, senior managers typically reply that operational decisions are made on the basis of numerical information. So long as personnel managers, company doctors and working environment specialists are unable to communicate their knowledge in a numerical format, these facts about the working environment and employee health will continue to be ignored when it comes to making decisions. Meaningful information for senior managers is almost exclusively information that is purely numerical. Other information, that could provide a more rounded picture of a company's competitiveness and the factors affecting it, is consequently not always used, despite the fact that the information exists within the company.

This is often the major problem and not the actual method of calculation. How is it possible to get the different parts of an organisation, as well as different experts, to communicate with each other so that complex issues such as stress and its economic and humanistic consequences can be surveyed? The survey should be both a learning and development process, so that those participating develop knowledge as to how cause and effect are related. When the organisation's different 'expert functions' have such comprehensive knowledge of their own areas of work, they can then reduce their knowledge to such a level that a subject expert from a completely different field can understand and participate in the refinement of the information. Sometimes this is needed for a joint development project, but at other times a single diagram showing the organisation's different dimensions may be sufficient. This joint production of knowledge is at the core of preventative work environment and health and safety work, i.e. understanding what it is that one should avoid. The method of calculation is simply a tool for the procurement of knowledge and not the ultimate goal.

Are companies aware of which factors affect the long- and short-term development of results? Business economics, and the key figures used, give a picture of what has already happened. Therefore, the key financial figures provide a historical view of the company. In order to look forward, and maintain and increase organisational performance, a different type of

Figure 3.2 Weak financial situation, but strong organisation

information is needed. Companies need meaningful information about the quantitative and qualitative values that affect profit development – information about customer satisfaction, employee health, work capacity, staff, competence and time utilisation.

3.4.3 Illustration: Four company profiles

Weak financial situation, but strong organisation

Figure 3.2 shows a company with a weak financial situation, that is, an organisation with extensive financial difficulties. The company management are lacking up-to-date information about customer satisfaction and furthermore are unaware of the company's capacity. A company with strong organisa-

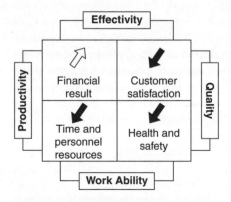

Figure 3.3 Sound finances, but weak organisation

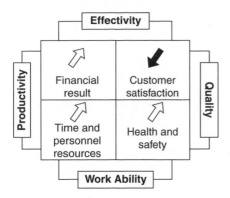

Figure 3.4 Sound finances, but customer problems

tional capacity is on the road to failure because of badly run finances. Many of the companies that were stripped during the 1980s either look like this or have already gone bankrupt. Such companies had unique competence but could not afford to make the necessary investments in production.

Sound finances, but weak organisation

Figure 3.3 shows the opposite development of Figure 3.2. If only the key financial figures are taken into account, the company appears to be performing well and because the company has sound finances there is no real interest in measuring other values. The company management are oblivious to early signs that customers are turning to competitors, key personnel are leaving the company and those that are left are suffering from poor motivation and lack of job satisfaction. Organisational capacity and competitiveness are collapsing.

Sound finances, but customer problems

Figure 3.4 shows a company with customer problems. A powerful and dynamic organisation handles customer problems in a manner that will not affect financial development. A weak organisation lacks this dynamism and in the long run, customer problems can lead to financial problems. The manner in which customer problems are dealt with is, therefore, decisive for whether financial development is positive or negative.

Weak financial situation and low customer satisfaction, but strong organisation

Figure 3.5 shows a company where financial result and customer satisfaction reveal a negative development, while the internal result measures, such as

Figure 3.5 Weak financial situation and low customer satisfaction, but strong organisation

staffing and work capacity, show the opposite. The company has financial problems that may lead to the need for extensive reorganisation. Many companies that were set up to provide employment and were started with the aid of grants, look like this. Although customers are satisfied as long as they receive free or substantially subsidised service, the organisation lacks viable business ideas. Employees are committed and motivated for success, but the organisation has no financial stability.

3.5   'Oskar' – a method for more effective performance measurement

3.5.1   What is Oskar?

This section gives an account of a multidisciplinary method for effective and more all-round performance analysis. The analysis takes into account working environment and employee health variables, as well as traditional measures. This method of analysis has been developed in Finland, Sweden and Norway during the last five years. Almost 300 organisational analyses have been carried out in different areas from industry to health care. The method is known as 'Oskar'. Oskar is a trade-marked company analysis model. The model can also be used for performance analysis with emphasis on quantitative and qualitative values. The name Oskar comes from the measurement of the organisations collective capacity and result development ('Organisationens Samlade Kapacitet och Resulttutveckling').

In order that causes as well as effects can be extracted from the Oskar model, productivity, effectivity and quality are also taken into consideration.

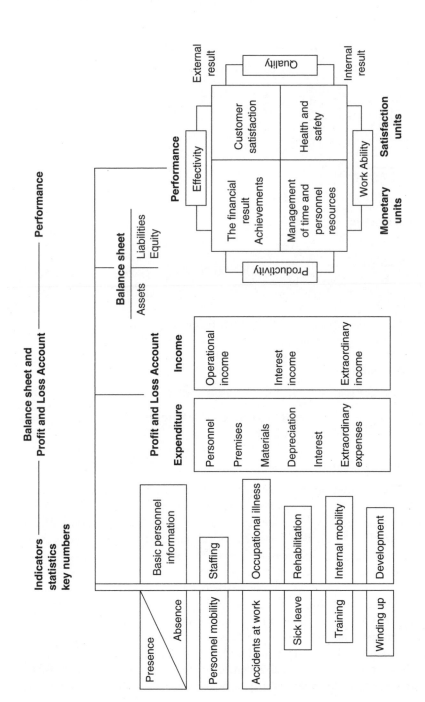

Figure 3.6 Oskar

The Oskar analysis contains the following reports with respect to performance analysis:

- *Financial administration:*

    Profit and loss account and balance sheet
    Financial measures
    Operational measures
    Different dimensions of results

- *Customer satisfaction:*

    Technical quality
    Functional quality
    Company profile

- *Time utilisation:*

    Workforce and staffing
    Production and through times
    Non-value added time

- *Competence:*

    Current and desired competence profile
    Competence utilisation

- *Personnel reporting:*

    Personnel statistics
    Workforce costs
    Employee turnover
    Development and winding-up costs

- *Employee health and working environment:*

    Physical working environment
    Psychological working environment
    Stress
    Health
    Work capacity
    Risk analysis

As well as the measuring scheme, a graphic is used to highlight the multidisciplinary report's combined results. This results diagram can be used to assess a company's capacity and drive. It gives a combined picture of a company's operations and can also be used for performance analysis. The Oskar analysis shows the areas in which corrective measures are needed to improve a company's profitability and employee health.

Management accounting and analysis are not purely numerical exercises. In many companies, sections of the financial reporting have been delegated to profit centres, teams and project groups. Financial reporting has moved closer to the production process and its users. This means that the need for clarity, comprehensibility and user-friendliness has become even greater. Those who work with financial reporting and performance analysis require an overview of all operations within the company. Formulating a system for improved performance analysis is often a learning process that involves the whole of a working group. Interest in product calculations is increasing, management accounting is becoming 'finances for all'. The Oskar analysis helps those responsible for results and profit centres to analyse the whole of the organisation.

All the information needed for an Oskar analysis already exists within a company. However, the information is spread over a variety of different departments/functions. A systematic and combined account of all the company's quantitative and qualitative values is required. Such a report should be multidisciplinarial and should contain meaningful information about the reasons for positive/negative development of results. Information about the conditions that affect an organisation's long-term capacity utilisation and competitiveness should be made discernible and known to those responsible for results.

This method can also be used for carrying out business analyses. When analysing a company's activities, the starting point is a summary of results combining the organisation's four areas of performance: finances, customer satisfaction, personnel and their utilisation of time, and finally employee health. A combined report covering these four areas, provides us with the company's organisational capacity and future prospects.

3.5.2 Oskar: An example of company analysis

We now turn to a Swedish example from the banking world and a company analysis carried out using the Oskar method. Unfortunately, one suspects that it is possible to find many such organisations in similar circumstances.

If we look at the bank's profit and loss account, we see that the bank has an excellent financial performance; the key financial figures show a positive development. However, approximately 80 per cent of its income is derived from interest. In reality, all that is required to achieve this is that interest rates for lending are higher than those for the bank's own borrowing. Consequently, the bank is living on easily earned interest money. Income from the provision of services is very modest. It is precisely this overview of financial results that the company management usually show to illustrate the organisation's financial performance. If we change the perspective and instead ask the customers how they perceive the bank's performance, a survey of customer satisfaction shows that the customers are highly dissatisfied in a number of areas. They are dissatisfied with the level of service offered by the bank, the accessibility of their personnel and the information provided.

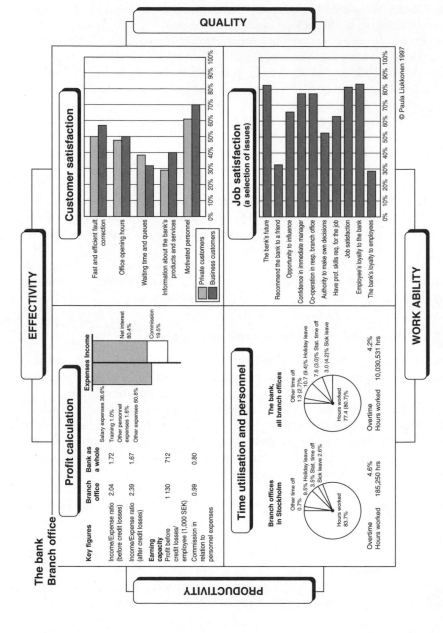

Figure 3.7 Oskar: a Swedish example from the banking world

In terms of customer satisfaction, on studying this diagram an industrial manager would regard the company as being on the brink of bankruptcy. His or her organisation could not sustain such low figures. Customer satisfaction is seldom 100 per cent in any organisation, the bank, however, should be closer to 70 or 80 per cent.

But how is the work organised? If we look at the bank's time utilisation, we find that it has alarmingly low figures. Absenteeism is high and overtime is extensive. A large proportion of employees have more than fifteen years service. Rationalisation is carried out in the form of structural changes and mergers, and many of the older employees feel they are insufficiently competent to deal with these changes.

Under the heading of job satisfaction and psychosocial health (Job satisfaction in Figure 3.7), the figures are quite dramatic. The staff do not feel good, they do not perceive the bank as being loyal towards them, they lack competence development/training and have limited opportunities to influence their own work. These things can all have a negative effect on employee health and can cause stress.

The bank's financial status is good, while customer satisfaction is very low. The personnel summary and time utilisation figures show the first warning signs and part of this is evident in the box on job satisfaction and psychosocial health (Job satisfaction in Figure 3.7). How long will the bank stay at the top with its excellent financial performance?

This is an example of a multidisciplinarial business performance analysis using the Oskar method. Oskar illustrates the bank's performance from different perspectives and also provides a first warning indication as to where to take corrective action.

Cost and benefit analyses are necessary, but so too is a serious investment in multidisciplinarial performance analysis, with an emphasis on finances, personnel and employee health. During capitalism's golden years, it was sufficient to measure and follow cash flows. Now, knowledge regarding people, health and safety, and the organisation's capacity, is also required.

Figure 3.7 shows a company with sound finances but with problems in three related areas; personnel (staffing and competence), customer satisfaction (complaints about the lack of service capacity and poor accessibility) and employee health (risk of ill-health through stress, limited opportunity to influence their own work and deficient competence). The scenario is, nevertheless, typical for companies with strong finances. The early signs of negative results development are not detected when things are going well for a company. Problems are given the opportunity to amass, thus steering things towards a more serious crisis. After a number of Oskar analyses had been conducted, it was found that it was important for industrial, as well as service companies, to present a combined picture of those factors affecting development of results.

Therefore, working environment and health and safety appraisals are not isolated activities, carried out independently from the rest of a company's activities; rather, they are measures that are an essential part of a combined results report. If a company wants satisfied customers, the first step is to ensure the health and working environment of its employees. It is necessary to initiate and maintain a simultaneous and positive development in all four of the results dimensions (finances, time utilisation, customer satisfaction and employee health).

3.5.3   Oskar: Experiences and further perspective

Research and the Oskar analyses (Liukkonen, 1996) have shown that the key financial figures, in particular the operational measures of effectivity, productivity and quality, are inadequate for detecting early indications of conditions that may jeopardise a company's capacity in different areas. Instead it is customer satisfaction, working environment and health appraisals that clearly show when an organisation's capacity is insufficient. Furthermore, the causes, such as excessive or inadequate staffing levels, excessive work rates, omitted or misguided investments in competence and so forth, can be acquired from the Oskar analysis. Cause, result and effect are made apparent and performance analysis becomes more than a numerical exercise. A learning process has been started.

During recent years, almost 300 Oskar analyses have been carried out at different workplaces throughout Scandanavia. The analysis method has evolved and been formulated according to company requirements. At times it has been a question of how a company should cope with extensive rationalisation, or how to simultaneously develop and wind-up different operations, how to make an organisation more customer-orientated, or why leadership and co-operation factors are not working. These companies have invested in their competitiveness and employee health.

The analyses have been carried out by economists especially trained for the purpose, company analysts, consultants or by the company's own personnel in a multidisciplinarial group, made up of accountants, personnel/product managers, production personnel and personnel from working environment and company health units.

Occasionally, companies have needed assistance from external analysts in order to appreciate their own situation, but usually the Oskar analysis is carried out by the company's own personnel. The analytical work is formulated in such a way that theoretical lessons are mixed with practical numerical and analytical exercises, based on the workplace's own material. Such group exercises increase understanding and also respect for each other's competence. The joint development work strengthens the co-operation between the different departments of the organisation providing everyone with the opportunity to succeed in their work.

Oskar is a review technique that makes it possible to carry out a multifaceted analysis of a company and a survey of conditions affecting the development of financial performance. Experience suggests that it is extremely important to reduce financial data to a level such that other subject experts can understand the content. In the same way it is important that health and medical experts adapt their facts, regarding working environment and health, so that accountants can understand their message. A report should provide the opportunity to connect causes, results and effects. It is only then, after finding the connections, can it be claimed that working environment and health organisations have supplied meaningful information. Oskar is an example of a conceptual model that makes it possible to communicate this important information over subject boundaries.

3.6 Conclusions

Many of the difficulties in establishing the cost effectiveness of stress intervention activities occur because there is a lack of integrated measurement. In other words, the multiple and diverse impact which stress can have on a business is insufficiently recognised and so, at best, measurement of effectiveness is partial. In the main, decisions to implement stress intervention strategies tend to be driven by those in the Human Resources or Occupational Health functions. The kinds of indices selected for evaluation often reflect their measurement perspective and are based on the data which is most readily available and accessible to that function, i.e. health and personnel costs. As this chapter has argued a wider and more holistic perspective is necessary so as to fully establish both the costs of stress and the benefits which can be gained from adopting proactive stress prevention policies. The key to this process lies in collating and combining the different kinds of data, both objective and subjective measures, which often already exist in the company, so as to appreciate the 'full picture'. By establishing systems to monitor this data on a continuing basis, organisations can not only assess the efficacy of their efforts to reduce stress but also identify the early warning signs of a potential problem.

Bibliography

Balemans, A. (1994) 'Further perspectives on stress at work', in European Conference on Stress at Work: A Call for Action, pp. 157–161, Dublin: European Foundation for the Improvement of Living and Working Conditions.

Berridge, J., Cooper, C.L. and Highley-Marchington, C. (1997) Employee Assistance Programmes and Workplace Counselling, Chichester: Wiley.

Brulin, G. and Nilsson, T. (1994) Arbetsutveckling och förbättract producktvitet (Development of work and improved producivity), Stockholm: Arbetslivfonden.

Cartwright, S. and Cooper, C.L. (1996) Managing Mergers, Acquisitions and Strategic Alliances: Integrating People and Cultures, Oxford: Butterworth-Heinemann.

Commission of the European Communities (1992) European Year of Safety, Hygiene and Health Protection at Work, Leiden: NIPG-TNO.

Cooper, C.L. and Sadri, G. (1991) 'The impact of stress counselling at work', in P.L. Perrewe (ed.) Handbook of Job Stress (Special Issue), *Journal of Social Behaviour and Personality*, 6 (7): 411–23.

Cooper, C.L., Liukkonen, P. and Cartwright, S. (1996) *Stress Prevention in the Workplace: Assessing the Costs and Benefits to Organisations*, Dublin: European Foundation for the Improvement of Living and Working Conditions.

Danish Working Environment Service (1996) *The Costs of Work-related Diseases and Work Accidents in Denmark*, (Rep. 9/1996), Copenhagen: Arbejdstilsynet.

Health and Safety Executive (1997) *Successful Health and Safety Management*, London HMSO: UK Health and Safety Executive.

Ivancevich, J.M. and Matteson, M.T. (1988) 'Promoting the individual's health and well being', in C.L. Cooper, and R. Payne (eds) *Causes, Coping and Consequences of Stress at Work*, 267–301, Chichester and New York: John Wiley.

Kvarnstrom, S. (1996) 'From Taylorism to 1000 objective oriented groups: Experiences of a cultural revolution in an industrial concern', in C.L. Cooper, P. Liukkonen and S. Cartwright (eds) *Stress Prevention in the Workplace: Assessing the Costs and Benefits to Organisations,* pp. 12–25, Dublin: European Foundation for the Improvement of Living and Working Conditions.

Levi, L. and Lunde-Jensen, P. (1996) *Economic Benefits from Stress Prevention in the European Community*, Dublin: European Foundation for the Improvement of Living and Working Conditions.

Liukkonen, P. (1996) *Measuring an Organisation's Capacity – How Great is the Development Potential?*, Bjärred: Acadmia Adacta.

Liukkonen, P. (1997) *The Company Barometer – the Successful Company's Key Figures*, Helsinki: Edita.

Lunde-Jensen, P. (1994) 'The costs of occupational accidents and work related sickness in Nordic countries', *Janus*, 18 (4): 25–26.

Murphy, L.R. (1988) 'Workplace interventions for stress reduction and prevention', in C.L. Cooper, and R. Payne (eds) *Causes, Coping and Consequences of Stress at Work*, pp. 301–31, Chichester and New York: Wiley.

Nijhuis, F., Lendfers, M.L., De Jong, A., Janssen, P. and Ament, A. (1996) 'Stress related interventions on construction work', in C.L. Cooper, P. Liukkonen and S. Cartwright (eds) *Stress Prevention in the Workplace: Assessing the Costs and Benefits to Organisations*, 26–47, Dublin: European Foundation for the Improvement of Living and Working Conditions.

Nilsson, C. (1994) 'New strategies for the prevention of stress at work', in *European Conference on Stress at Work: A Call for Action*, 84, Dublin: European Foundation for the Improvement of Living and Working Conditions.

Sallis, J.F., Trevorrow, T.R., Johnson, C.C., Howell, M.F., and Kaplan, R.M. (1987) 'Worksite stress management: a comparison of programs', *Psychology and Health 1987*, 1, 237–53..

Terra, N. (1995) 'The prevention of job stress by redesigning jobs and implementing self-regulating teams', in L.R., Murphy, J.J. Hurrell, S.L. Sauter and G.P. Keita, (eds) *Job Stress Interventions*, pp. 264–83, Washington DC: American Psychological Association.

Vromans, I. (1994) 'Stress prevention at work', in *European Conference on Stress at Work: A Call for Action*, pp. 86–8, Dublin: European Foundation for the Improvement of Living and Working Conditions.

Wynne, R. and Clarkin, N. (1992) *Under Construction: Building for Health in the EC Workplace*, Dublin: European Foundation for the Improvement of Living and Working.

Chapter 4

Finland: Organisational well-being

Ten years of research and development in a forest industry corporation

Raija Kalimo and Salla Toppinen

4.1 Introduction: Psychosocial factors in work life in Finland

In the latter half of the 1990s, Finland is rapidly recovering from the deepest economic recession in its history. The recession, which started in 1992, was preceded by a period of high productivity and economic growth during most of the 1980s. From the viewpoint of research and development on psychosocial factors and stress prevention, the 1980s was a period of many opportunities. The knowledge basis and attitudinal readiness had already started to grow during the late 1970s through research, information and training. In order to cope with the downturn in the economy in the early 1990s, business reacted mostly with restrictive policies, including company mergers and the reduction in personnel. As a result, unemployment at its peak rocketed to over 19 per cent, and has come down only slowly during 1997. This situation increased the need and demand for psychosocial knowledge and services, so that reorganisations could be made as smoothly as possible. Another need was to monitor, and intervene against, the anticipated negative consequences, such as increased stress and burn-out.

Stress prevention is seen as the duty of the employer and as a part of the overall occupational health care and safety at the work place. Legal obligations for ensuring occupational health and safety are based primarily on two laws, the Occupational Health Care Act of 1978, and the Occupational Safety Act, which was revised in 1987. Both of these and their lower level specifications give orders concerning psychosocial factors. Finland also follows the recommendations of ILO and WHO.

4.1.1 Occupational Health Care Act (1978)

All employers are obligated to organise occupational health services for his/her employees; services must also be available for the self-employed; the emphasis is on prevention; and sufficient personnel have to be available for the service system.

The principal activities of occupational health services (OHS) are to identify health hazards at work, to assess their consequences to the workers' health, to propose and initiate preventive and control measures, to provide health-based criteria for a healthy and safe work environment, and to provide appropriate diagnostic and therapeutic services for persons with occupational diseases. Among other components of working life, the law covers psycho-social factors.

According to the Act and the lower level statutes, working conditions, in-cluding work organisation and psychosocial factors, have to be monitored systematically. To implement this regulation, specific methods have been developed, for instance to assess psychic stresses at work (Elo, 1986; Elo et al., 1992). The statutes stipulate that occupational health professionals must participate in professional training at least once in five years. The training includes topics related to stress and psychosocial factors.

One important step towards a comprehensive approach in the promotion of occupational health was the agreement of the labour market organisations on the maintenance of work ability in 1990. This function was later included in the Decision of the Ministry of Social Affairs and Health on occupational health care (1348/94). It means 'all activities by which the employer, the employees and the co-operation bodies at the work place jointly promote and support the work ability and functional capacity of every worker at every phase of his/her career'.

In 1989 the Finnish government approved the National Programme for Development of OHS. It pointed out eighteen target areas, several of which are related to psychosocial factors, for the development of OHS.

After the achievement of these targets was evaluated the Occupational Health Care Act was amended (Decree of the Council of State, 1994). The targets of occupational health care thus cover, in addition to the prevention of risks, a healthy and safe environment, a well-functioning work organisa-tion, the prevention of work-related diseases, and the maintenance and improvement of the ability to work. Among the factors that must be taken into account are: physical and psychological strain caused by work; specific risk of illness due to the work environment and due to the individual's char-acteristics; the health status of the employee and his/her capacity to work and function. The Decree also obligates the assessment of the work demands and functional capacity of the worker in order to estimate (among other things) the measures needed to improve the work environment, work organis-ation and working capacity. The Decree further emphasises the importance of co-operation between the employer and the employees in taking these measures. The employer must resort to health-care specialists and the neces-sary experts in order to comply with the law. The experts include specialists in occupational psychology.

The Decree uses the term 'good occupational health practice', which means preventive, comprehensive and multidisciplinary action with continuous evaluation. The prerequisites of psychological well-being are integrated as an essential component into the total approach. A guidebook on the matter for work places and OHS personnel was published in 1997 by the Ministry of Social Affairs and Health together with the Finnish Institute of Occupational Health (Good Occupational Health Practice, 1997).

The coverage of occupational health care in Finland is 92 per cent of salaried employees. The scope of activities covers prevention, promotion of health and work ability as well as curative care. The OHS systems of Sweden and the Netherlands are similar in scope, but such systems are rare elsewhere. The Finnish system has proved to be flexible and capable of being innovated when needed.

4.1.2 Occupational Safety Act (1987)

The Occupational Safety Act of 1987 has several clauses which refer to psychosocial factors. The employer's general obligation is to make sure that the work is not harmful to the health of the worker. Health is considered to include both physical and mental health. Another clause obligates the employer to consider the mental well-being of the worker when planning the work and working conditions. Furthermore, the law stipulates that the worker's psychological resources have to be taken into account in the adjustment of the work and work methods to suit the worker. Training and guidance must be given in risk prevention. Prevention means here the adoption of appropriate techniques for performing the work and for preventing accidents.

The Occupational Safety Act in itself is a skeleton law. Soon after enforcement of the law, the National Board of Safety prepared instructions on the application of the law to field inspections (Psychosocial Factors in Labour Inspection, 1989). These instructions interpreted the stipulations of the Act very broadly from the psychosocial point of view. For instance, problems in the social climate of the work place are considered as a possible harm to one's health, and therefore attention has to be paid to these problems. According to the Act, planning in which psychosocial factors have to be taken into account is interpreted as a continuous process taking place on many levels in the work organisation. These instructions supported the idea of preventing stressors already at an early stage and of promoting psychological well-being. However, they are not in the letter of the law, and therefore are not mandatory. A proposal to amend the law itself towards the spirit of the interpretations has been made to the Ministry of Social Affairs and Health by a senior labour inspection official in psychology in the Ministry. This proposal contains, among other things, a clause on the prevention of bullying and harassment in the workplace.

4.1.3   Monitoring of job stress at national level

Several systems for assessing working conditions have been developed. Nationwide quality of work life surveys based on personal interviews on working conditions, including job stressors, have been conducted by Statistics Finland in 1977, 1984, 1990 and 1997. Between 1977 and 1990 both positive and negative trends could be seen. The work had become more challenging and autonomous, but time pressure had increased and social interaction had become more negative (Report of working conditions, 1991).

The Ministry of Labour has a barometer on working conditions with the emphasis on employment conditions and psychosocial factors. It has been applied three times, in 1994, 1995 and 1996 (Ylöstalo et al., 1997). One of the main trends noted was that psychological stress, especially time pressure is increasing. The Finnish Institute of Occupational Health (FIOH) has collected the first set of data in 1997 with a new comprehensive surveillance system of working conditions and occupational health (Kauppinen et al., 1997). This effort will be updated every three years. The Institute is conducting also another survey the emphasis of which is on OH services (Räsänen et al., 1994).

Work-related stress is a common problem among the Finns. Speed and time pressures are cited as the most common stressors. According to the working life barometer, 65 per cent of women and 52 per cent of men perceived that time pressure had increased in 1996 (Ylöstalo et al., 1995 and 1997). Another area where a steady increase has been noted since 1994 is in conflicts between the workers and the management (a 17 per cent increase in 1996). On the whole, work is seen as becoming increasingly more stressful, with approximately every second employee in 1996 reporting that their mental work load had increased.

According to one population study, serious burn-out was prevalent in 7.3 per cent of the working population in 1997 (Kalimo and Toppinen, 1998a). Burn-out was found to have a direct relation to feelings of insecurity and instability due to reorganisations for economic reasons. The risk of burn-out was doubled in organisations which had laid off employees (odds ratio 2.02; 95 per cent confidence interval 1.6–2.6) and which had not hired replacements (odds ratio 2.0; 95 per cent confidence interval 1.6–2.5). The risk of burn-out was even higher in organisations where a threat of dismissal was perceived.

Differences in the prevalence of burn-out between occupational and economic sectors reflected feelings of insecurity and increased workloads due to a reduction of the labour force, changes in the structure of the organisations and the quality of contracts. In the banking and insurance sectors, which have gone through a period of mergers and a dramatic reduction of personnel, 65 per cent showed at least some symptoms of burn-out. This figure was about the same in the agriculture and forestry sectors where fundamental changes encompassing whole lifestyles are taking place, and where the future is for many unknown. Restaurant and hotel businesses have adopted increasingly a policy of short, unstable contracts leading to an unstable work force. Two-thirds of the employees experienced symptoms of burn-out to varying degrees. Serious burn-out was more common than average in some sectors of human services, for example, in teaching (11 per cent), and also in sectors where the risk factors are combined with a largely unqualified labour force, for example, repair and maintenance (9 per cent). Cynicism, one symptom of 'burn-out syndrome,' was alarmingly high in public administration (serious in 20 per cent of the cases). Public administrators in the 1990s have had to make cuts in social security and public services spending, a move which is seen as a violation against the values of a welfare society.

4.1.4 Steps towards psychosocial improvements at work

On the whole, it seems that the recognition of stress as a workplace hazard and pressures in its prevention have increased during the economically difficult times of the 1990s. When the basic legislation was passed, the laws acted as a stimulus to increase awareness and knowledge and thereby also to encourage employers to exceed the minimum defined by the laws. When the amendment to the Occupational Safety Act was enforced in 1987, large-

Table 4.1 Three levels of maintenance of work ability activities

	Level 1	Level 2	Level 3
Target group	all employees	subjects with threatening decrease of work ability	subjects with decreased work ability
Identification	assessment of health promotion needs	symptoms, morbidity, own or other initiative, OHS records	morbidity, diminished ability to perform work tasks, OHS health examinations
Actions	preventive activities, health promotion, promotion of individual lifestyle, development of work and work environment, development of work organisations	definition of actual problem, adaptation of work to individual properties, replacement, personal health advancement, early rehabilitation	treatment of diseases, rehabilitation, re-education, replacement

Source: Matikainen, 1998

scale training of industrial designers and other planners began to take place. The Finnish Institute of Occupational Health, the main expert organisation in the field, has offered training on stress and its prevention and has published guidebooks and training material since the early 1980s.

The development of stress prevention was progressing steadily up until the early 1990s. Since then economic problems in Finland and decisions often made on the basis of short-sighted economic interests, have created new problems. But although job stress is of concern, happily, one can conclude that Finnish workers are well-informed about these problems and their prevention. The gap between being informed and having attitudinal readiness for change is, unfortunately, wide however. This is so even in cases where the problems are well-defined and the needs for improvement are specified. The demand for organisational surveys on stress assessment and consultations for the implementation of development actions has greatly increased during the past few years at the Finnish Institute of Occupational Health. If there is action, the emphasis is on work organisation rather than individual stress management, which has never really been adopted as a strategy for dealing with work stress in Finland.

4.1.5 Stress prevention as a part of maintenance of work ability

The trend in Finland is for stress prevention to be seen as an integral part of the overall strategy of maintenance of work ability (MWA), the basis of which was laid down in the agreement made by the Labour market organisations in 1990. This strategy defines actions on three levels (Table 4.1) (Matikainen, 1997; 1998).

Level 1 involves primarily developmental actions targeted at work, work organisations and the employees. They are based on the needs and initiatives of the work place and are preferably carried out as a part of its 'normal' functions. Level 2 involves preventive actions mobilised by some signs of alarm. Actions on level 3 are mostly those that belong in traditional occupational health care. On all levels co-operation between the management of the company and the occupational health care is important. Actions on level 3 also demand contact with rehabilitation and social insurance organisations.

In order to facilitate action along the above lines the Finnish Institute of Occupational Health established in 1994 a Work Ability Center, which has, as first step, given training, counselling and guidance to organisations, labour unions and OH services around the country. This activity is supported by the Social Security organisations which are under pressure due to the early retirement age (the average in 1997 was 59 years). Currently, only 10 per cent of the population remain at work until they are entitled to the old age pension.

4.1.6 Conclusion

Finland has a long tradition in the consideration of work stress as a possible health and safety hazard. Stress-related productivity concerns are increasing. Legislation developed since the 1970s, gives broad obligations to employers for the control of psychosocial hazards. The knowledge basis for this is grounded in research projects carried out in companies and risk groups, as well as in several regular nationwide monitoring systems. Stress and burn-out are regular training themes in many professional groups and constant topics of interest in the media. As a whole, this infrastructure gives a multi-faceted basis for workplace reforms on stress reduction, which gradually started to increase in number at the end of the 1980s. In spite of this interest, the indicators of work-life stress have risen during the 1990s. The macro-economics recession, related unemployment and diminished labour force have triggered many stressors, especially time pressure, excessive total work load, insecurity and deterioration of co-operation at workplaces. As a result, indi-cators of stress and burn-out are on the increase. In this situation we are fortunate to have a knowledge basis and infrastructure for countermeasures. It is, however, difficult to solve such problems with ad hoc organisational actions. Organisations which have already developed stress control strategies on a long-term basis are better equipped for coping with the consequences of acute problem situations.

4.2 The study company: Introduction

Our study company is one of the biggest forest industry enterprises in Europe. The core products of the company are fine papers, publication papers, pack-

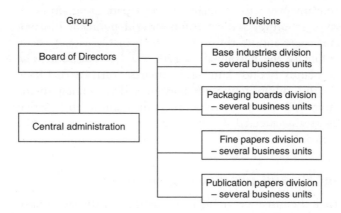

Figure 4.1 Organigram of the company

aging boards and sawn timber. The company employs about 19,000 people in production, research and development tasks, as well as in sales and marketing. Most of the company's operations are located in Finland, but more than 80 per cent of its consolidated sales derive from exports and overseas operations. The organisational structure of the company is complex. In addition to line organisation, organisation is divided into several regions, as well as four divisions (Figure 4.1).

The company has gone through major changes during the past decades both in its operations and in its organisational composition. The work has become psychologically more abstract and demanding, while the physical demands have decreased. Buying and selling companies and operations has become increasingly common; this also means a sense of insecurity for some of the personnel. In the past few years the effects of the EU and other international criteria of quality and of environmental issues have also demanded new adjustment to the markets. It has been necessary to make profits not only by increasing production, but by higher quality standards, as well as by making the most out of the 'human capital'. This means investing in the well-being and health of the personnel and thereby lowering the costs incurred by sickness absenteeism and turnover. It also means increasing the motivation, commitment and innovativeness of the personnel. Changes in working practices and the principles of personnel training are taking place, and more emphasis is placed on management issues, such as promotion of quality, management by results and co-operation.

During 1996 a merger with another major forest company took place and the main task of the personnel administration was to implement the personnel changes and to bring into line the two organisational cultures. An agreement was made with employee representatives to develop co-operation between domestic companies and to start similar co-operation between companies abroad. Several development programmes were initiated, the most important of which were a company-wide total quality management programme, a training and education programme for the personnel working outside Finland, and training for the management.

The total turnover rate of the personnel in 1996 was 3.7 per cent. The turnover rate varies constantly because large-scale organisational restructuring and investments change the composition of the personnel. The sickness absenteeism rate is higher among the hourly-paid workers than among the salaried staff. This situation is greatly affected by the agreement on wages and the conditions of employment.

4.3   Motives, signals and project organisation

The study company took the initiative in 1984 to collaborate with the Finnish Institute of Occupational Health in order to carry out an investigation on the working conditions and to launch a health promotion and stress prevention

programme in the company. The initiative came from the central occupational health care unit, which co-operated closely with the general management, staff and the safety specialists. A pilot study was first done by the Finnish
Institute of Occupational Health (FIOH) to investigate the need and feasibility
of an action-oriented project. Negotiations between the management, staff
groups and the labour unions in the company led to an agreement on a complex action-research programme between the company and the FIOH (Kalimo
et al., 1993).

Two committees were formed to take care of the undertaking: the Programme Advisory Committee (PA Committee) and the Programme
Management Committee (PM Committee). The responsibility of the PA
Committee was to see that the interests of various bodies in the company
were taken into account at the planning stage. Its duty was also to follow-
up the implementation of the programme according to plan. Representatives
of the staff groups, the occupational health care unit and the safety committee
were members of the PA Committee. The hourly-paid workers, who form
the largest staff category, had two representatives. Two senior representatives
of the research community, one from the FIOH, and one from the Social
Insurance Institution were also invited to sit on the PA Committee. A
member of the board of directors of the company acted as the chairperson.
Altogether there were eleven members on the PA Committee.

The PM Committee had six members, including the chief OH physician
as the chairperson, the safety manager, the personnel manager, an information
specialist and two researchers from the FIOH, one of whom was also a member on the PA Committee.

The duty of the PM Committee was to make a proposal for the plan and
to oversee its implementation in practice. The duty of the researchers was
to carry out the investigation. The company representatives were responsible
for all the arrangements within the company for initial information activities, data collection and feedback. The researchers informed about the main
issues in the investigation, both before data collection and at the time of
giving feedback on the results.

A draft plan for the programme was prepared by the PM Committee, and
was revised according to the comments of the PA Committee. The Scientific
Committee of the FIOH reviewed and approved the plan. After these preparations the programme plan was discussed in the company's staff meetings.
The researchers and the OHS staff participated in several of these meetings
and gave further information.

A similar project organisation was set up for the ten-year follow-up phase
in 1996. The participants represented the same groups from the company.
Because of the international coverage of the follow-up, the personnel manager
of the international sector was also involved. The responsible FIOH researcher
was again involved in both the PA and PM Committees, and the other FIOH
researcher in the PM Committee. This time, the social security organisation

Table 4.2 Financing of the project (in US dollars)

	1986–1993	1990–1993	1996–1999
Finnish Work Environment Fund	Salary of a researcher, 3 years, $65,000	Salary of a researcher, 3 years. Some laboratory expenses, $75,000	Salary of a researcher, 3.5 years, $75,000
Social Insurance Institution	Financial support. All data analysis, $120,000	–	–
Finnish Institute of Occupational Health	Salary of the responsible researcher and assistants part-time, $40,000	Salary of the responsible researcher and assistants part-time, $30,000	Salary of the responsible researcher and assistants part-time, $95,000
Company	Costs due to lost working time and travel of the staff, $155,000	Costs due to lost working time and travel of the staff. Some laboratory expenses, $75,000	Costs due to lost working time and travel of the staff. Material expenses, $250,000
Total	$380,000	$180,000	$420,000

was not involved in the project. The present occupational health manager of the company, who was the chairperson of the PM Committee, was actively involved in research and training outside this project as well. The PA Committee was chaired by the vice-president of the corporation.

In both phases FIOH was responsible for the scientific basis of the undertaking, while the company itself dealt with the administration and information. Policy issues and action strategies in the company were discussed and planned together but the company had the final responsibility. In between the two main phases of the project, an additional more focused study on the stress of project managers was made based on the initiative of the company.

Financing for the entire project was gained from various sources. The main contributors and their share of the budget can be seen in Table 4.2.

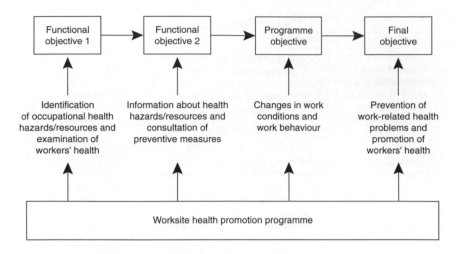

Figure 4.2 Simplified model of functional and outcome objectives in a worksite health promotion programme

4.4   Analysis: Risk factors and risk groups

4.4.1   Introduction

The functional objectives of the research and development project were to investigate working conditions, health and well-being, and their inter-relationships (see Figure 4.2). The programme objective was to design development projects and to implement and evaluate changes in work conditions and work behaviour. The final objective of the project was the prevention of work-related health problems, the prevention of stress and the promotion of workers' health.

The whole process started in 1984 with a pilot study and was still continuing at time of publication (see Figure 4.3).

4.4.2   Pilot survey, 1984

A pilot study was made in 1984 to investigate the need and feasibility of an action-oriented programme and to recognise possible problems in the working conditions, as well as stress-related health problems of the personnel. A total of 500 people from various personnel groups (about 5 per cent of the total personnel) were randomly selected to participate in the survey. Out of this group 130 people did not respond, and were replaced. The final number of accepted questionnaires was 468.

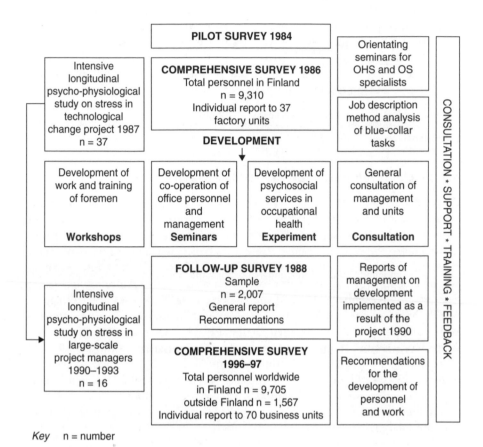

Key   n = number

Figure 4.3 Phases of the programme

The questionnaire consisted of 182 items on work-related factors, as well as subjective health indicators, namely demographic data, work characteristics, work environment, management and co-operation, job satisfaction, needs for work development, occupational safety and occupational health issues, symptoms of strain and functional capacity. Some of the items on work characteristics and symptoms of strain and functional capacity were based on earlier studies (Elo *et al.*, 1992; Goldberg, 1978), and some of the items were based on earlier experiences from studies on similar matters. The questionnaire was distributed to the workplaces and the respondents filled out the questionnaires during working hours.

The descriptive results from the study revealed the following problems in the working conditions: lack of challenge and a low level of skill utilisation in many jobs, some weaknesses in the management practices, and lack of opportunities for participation in planning and decision-making. On the basis of the results, action was deemed necessary, and a more comprehensive investigation concerning the total personnel and the working conditions was planned. Key roles were given to the occupational health and safety personnel in promoting the undertaking among the entire personnel. In order to increase their readiness to participate in this task, two-day seminars on the background philosophy and issues of the project were organised. The seminar material was published in the staff paper, where also several articles on psychological and social factors at work and their health effects were published.

4.4.3   Comprehensive survey, 1986: Baseline

A questionnaire survey, which was based on the experiences from the pilot study, was carried out in 1986. The questionnaire included 209 items on work-related factors, such as task content, work organisation, co-operation, management, as well as health-related variables, such as symptoms of strain (General Health Questionnaire, GHQ: Goldberg, 1978), and personal resources and risk factors (Sense of Coherence, SOC: Antonovsky, 1987; Self-esteem: Rosenberg, 1962; Type A behaviour: Järvikoski and Härkäpää, 1987). Most of the work-related variables were based on measures, which were developed and widely used in the FIOH (Elo et al., 1992), and the other work-related items were formulated for this study. Demographic data were also included. Altogether thirteen sum scales were formed of selected individual items. The reliability of the sum scales were tested and were found to be satisfactory (between 0.6 and 0.9, except for isolation, which was 0.58).

The questionnaire was distributed to every employee at his/her workplace. For the analysis the employees were divided into five occupational groups according to company practices (700 managers, 850 office personnel, 1,000 foremen, 300 technical staff and 6,500 hourly paid workers). Altogether 74 per cent of the personnel (9,350) responded, the lowest response rate being among the hourly-paid workers (68 per cent). The results were reported for each business unit (37 units) and some more reports were prepared on request. Information on the results was also given in the staff paper and in various meetings.

During this period, the researchers also consulted the management of the company and the different units about the possibilities to utilise the results. Information about the results was given in several articles in the staff paper, and the management of the company obligated the units to use the results for the development of the work and the personnel.

4.4.4   Job analysis of blue-collar tasks

Job stressors were assessed also with a job description technique (Elo, 1986). This method has been developed by the FIOH for the purpose of assessing psychic stressors in association with the monitoring of the work environment. The method has proved useful for screening purposes. It includes general information on stressors at work, instructions for the use of the method, suggestions for the assessment of the need for corrective measures, and a checklist containing the most important stressors at work and overall assessment of psychic stress.

The job description method was applied by a committee which included, for example, an OHS representative and the foreman whose job it was to monitor the tasks of the hourly-paid workers. The data collected by this method were compared where possible with the results obtained by the questionnaire. The employees themselves in their answers gave higher scores on risk factors in the work situation than the group who had drawn up the job description.

4.4.5   Development projects and actions for office personnel and foremen, 1986–1988

The results of the questionnaire showed that some problems were 'general problems' which concerned the personnel as a whole, and some were specific to some personnel groups (see Table 4.3).

The groups whose situation was the most problematic were later selected as target groups for development actions (see sections 4.5 and 4.6). Data from these groups are in bold typeface in Table 4.3. The office personnel, most of whom are women, felt that their position at work had weakened over the years. Their other problems included: poor possibilities for advancement, job insecurity, unsatisfactory remuneration systems, insufficient communication with superiors, lack of possibilities for participation, and lack of feedback. The office personnel also reported mental strain and frequent psychosomatic symptoms.

The work role of the foremen had changed the most along with new technological developments and ways of organising work. New leadership styles and practices needed to be developed. The foremen had a direct link to production and maintenance, and their role therefore was crucial in the development of work and working conditions. Satisfaction with the management was found to be very important for the well-being of the employees. The foremen found their work to be demanding and independent, but they also reported a need for training in management skills, for improving the flow of information and increased possibilities for advancement.

4.4.6   Development of psychosocial services in occupational health

Because the activities of the occupational health services (OHS) had, in general, been meagre with regard to psychological issues, the prerequisites for these activities were deemed necessary. The co-operation within OHS, and between OHS and production were studied and promoted in a separate development project. The connections between the company's OHS and local mental health services were improved (see sections 4.5 and 4.6).

4.4.7 Intensive psychophysiological study, 1987

One group of personnel in particular was facing a fundamental techno-logical change in their sector of paper production. A psychophysiological stress study assessing how the personnel succeeded in coping with the change process was carried out in 1987. The stressfulness of the management of a large-scale investment project was assessed with psychological and bio-chemical measurements. The stress hormone level of the subjects was compared to the stress level of a control group, in which the employees were not involved in a technological change project. The members of the test group showed signs of being under more strain and they reported stronger levels of exhaustion than did the control group. The conclusion was that in future supportive activities should be organised to prevent the negative effects of such stressful project periods. An attempt in this direction was made within the context of two later investment projects (see section 4.6.4, and Kalimo et al., 1992).

4.5   Choice of development measures

4.5.1   Criteria and priorities

On the basis of the baseline assessment, two basic approaches were considered: (1) reorganisation of work and training of management through the mobili-sation of actions as a long-term process in the organisation, and (2) implemen-tation of specific development projects (see Figure 4.3). For the first purpose, problem areas were defined on the basis of the risk analysis and recommend-ations for improvements were given to the company. This purpose was deemed to be best served with actions planned and initiated among the personnel within the company with some support from the research team if needed. For the second purpose, four specific development projects were planned and launched by the project team.

   The criteria for the choice of the above measures were:

- presence of a serious problem in the work and/or well-being in the personnel;
- an expressed need in the survey for improvements at work or in health services and;
- estimated readiness of a work unit or a personnel group to participate.

Table 4.3 Results from baseline survey: problems in work and well-being, and need for work development in different occupational groups

Problems in work, %	Managers	Office personnel	Foremen	Technical staff	Hourly paid workers	Whole personnel
Own position at work has weakened	16	17	14	11	11	12
Very little possibilities for advancement	23	55	38	35	51	47
Job insecurity	5	10	7	3	9	8
Present system of remuneration does not motivate	11	20	10	17	16	16
Lack of support from superiors	9	15	8	7	14	13
Dissatisfaction with the management	8	8	5	9	6	6
Lack of possibilities for participation	10	29	18	21	28	23
Lack of feedback	25	48	25	33	39	37
Time pressure (often)	41	22	29	29	18	21
Need for work development (useful, mean %)						
Improving the flow of information	34	53	53	48	49	49
More discussions between superiors and staff	48	57	48	52	45	47
More possibilities for advancement	47	39	43	47	24	30
Strain symptoms (often, %)						
Mental strain	3	3	2	5	3	3
Psychosomatic symptoms	2	3	2	2	3	3
Absent from work due to overstrain or tiredness	5	5	4	5	8	7

The selection of the measures was also affected by the capacity of the project group, as regards time and personnel resources to consult workplaces.

Priority in the choice of targets of action was given on the one hand to those groups who were in key roles in the organisation, and could therefore have a radiating effect. This included foremen, managers of technological change projects, and occupational health services. On the other hand, office personnel was chosen as a focus of action from those groups with assessed risks.

4.6   Implementation of development actions

4.6.1   Co-operation of office personnel and management

Three company-level meetings were arranged for the office personnel and their supervisors from different units during 1986–87 (see Figure 4.4). Seminars in which office employees and supervisors from the same units participated at the same time were planned. The seminars were led by a personnel training specialist in eight units during 1987–88. Some seminars were put into practice later. The aim of the seminars was to develop team work and to search for better practices for co-operation. One of the aims was also to improve the work atmosphere by increased participation and more efficient communication. About 530 office employees and supervisors participated in the development seminars and programmes. Follow-up methods were planned during the seminars.

4.6.2   Work and training of foremen

A paper mill was selected as the target for the development of the work of the foremen on the basis of the results from the questionnaire survey indicating needs for work redesign, as well as promoting well-being of the personnel. Foremen in this mill were interviewed by a psychologist in 1987 (see Figure 4.5). The interview aimed to clarify the present duties and the role of the foremen, as well as to highlight current problems. After the interviews, a two-day seminar was organised for all 115 of the foremen by the psychologist and the safety manager. The background, current status and future role of the foremen were analysed. Numerous needs for changes were recognised, and actions were planned. Critical incidents in sixteen foremen's work were studied as a part of the development project by OHS. Individual interviews gave information on the coping strategies of the foremen in stressful situations. On the basis of this information, another seminar was held on the development and co-ordination of production and maintenance tasks. Some foremen (18 in total) from two paper mills participated in the seminar, and the co-operation was planned to be continued and followed up. At the same time a systematic training programme for all new foremen was initiated at company level.

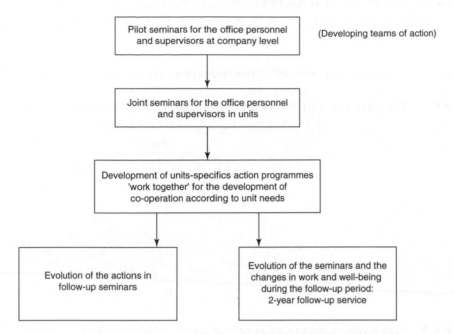

Figure 4.4 Development process of the co-operation between the office personnel and supervisors

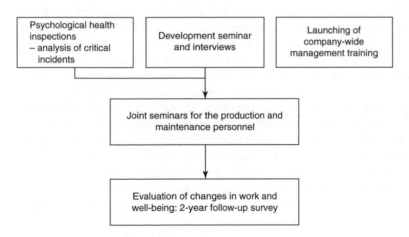

Figure 4.5 Development process of the work of the foremen

4.6.3   Psychosocial services in occupational health

The development of occupational health services was made according to the principles of participative action research, which meant that a consulting psychologist from outside the FIOH worked in the company's central OHS for three and a half months. The psychologist evaluated the need for help with work-related psychological problems, and made plans for integrating the psychologist's role as a health promoter into the company's OHS practice. The psychologist planned psychological health inspections and carried these out together with the OH specialists. The foremen were selected as one target group: the other target group comprised the total personnel of the mill, which operated in the same city as the company's central OHS. The psychologist consulted the OH specialists and gave training in psychological matters concerning work and health psychology, such as stressors at work and their relation to well-being, strain symptoms and the interaction between the individual and work. The psychologist prepared a report on the communication between the OHS and the units, as well as between the OHS and the public health services in matters concerning mental health problems and their treatment.

4.6.4   Intensive psychophysiological study 1990–1993

An intensive four-year stress monitoring an intervention project (between 1990–1993) was initiated among the top management of two major construction undertakings in the company, on the basis of the positive experiences from the earlier psychophysiological stress study of a change process (see section 4.4.7). The aims were to recognise job stressors and resources in the management of large-scale industrial construction projects, and to study the role of group cohesiveness in co-operation and commitment, and in the accumulation of psychological and psychophysiological symptoms of strain. A further aim was to study the need of psychological support during such a project. Two groups of managers, each comprising eight men, responsible for a similar construction project, were followed-up with monthly hormone assessments and frequent interviews. The manager of the first group was nominated by the company board. He in turn selected the other members on the basis of his previous acquaintance with them. Some of them had previous successful project experience with each other; this was the 'cohesive' group. The strategy for the compilation of the other group was different: the company board nominated all the members primarily on the basis of their technical expertise without using co-operation experience as a criterion. This second group was the 'disjointed' group. The results showed that the composition of the group, i.e. whether it was cohesive or disjointed, was an important predictor of the functions of the team. Towards the end of the project the quality of co-operation was poorer and commitment to work lower in the disjointed group than in the cohesive group ($p < 0.01$ and $p < 0.06$). The cohesive group was significantly better off in terms of stress level and stress management (Kalimo et al., 1992).

The levels of cortisol decreased towards the end of the project ($p < 0.01$) in the cohesive group but not in the disjointed group. Also, the levels of noradrenaline decreased in the cohesive group ($p < 0.001$) but increased in the disjointed group ($p < 0.05$). The cohesive group displayed a greater readiness for using the available consultations than the other group. Both groups assessed the possibility for support as useful, especially with regard to their personal role as managers (Kalimo and Toppinen, 1998b).

4.6.5   Reorganisation of work and training of management: development action based on recommendations

Apart from problems in the target groups outlined in section 4.6.4, the baseline assessment pointed out a number of other more general needs for improvement. Therefore recommendations with alternative proposals for their implementation were given on the following topics: developing the content of monotonous tasks; developing leadership; personnel development; planning a support system for the change processes; integrating maintenance and support functions with production; improving co-operation between office staff and their superiors; encouraging shop floor participation; increasing psychological resources for the prevention of stress; and increasing the OHS personnel's knowledge of psychology.

Recommendations were reported to the management of the company and they were included in the unit reports. These recommendations and their implementation are given in depth in section 4.7.2. A member of the research team attended the meetings where representatives of the personnel and the management, as well as OHS and safety personnel, discussed the reports and possible actions to be taken.

4.7   Evaluation

In this evaluation we will first discuss whether the programme objectives were achieved (4.7.1 to 4.7.5). Next we will discuss the costs and benefits of this project, and the collaboration in this project (4.7.6 and 4.7.7).

4.7.1   Sample survey, 1988: Two-year follow-up

The first follow-up survey was carried out in 1998 two years after the baseline survey. The aim was primarily to evaluate the results of the development processes implemented as a result of the baseline survey among the office personnel and their supervisors, and among the foremen. A 20 per cent sample of the personnel, including those who were involved in the

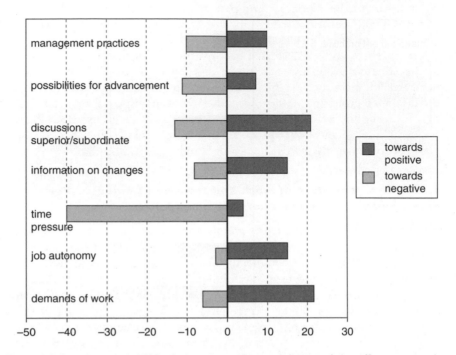

Figure 4.6 Sample survey 1988: changes in working conditions of the office personnel during the two-year follow-up period (1986–1988)

Note: Direction of change: no change was reported by 60–80 per cent of the respondents

development projects, was chosen. The response rate was 82 per cent and the number of respondents was about 2,000. As previously, data were collected on work conditions, stress and health indicators. Furthermore, the respondents were asked to assess whether they found the interventions positive or negative.

The evaluation of the interventions, as well as the overall development of work, was for the most part positive. As expected, there were no differences in the health indicators. The office personnel regarded the development of their work during the first follow-up period favourably (see Figure 4.6). On the one hand, increased automation had made their work more challenging, demanding and independent. On the other hand, time pressure was greater than before. About half of the respondents felt that the joint seminars for both the superiors and the office personnel had improved communication, and about three-fourths had found the seminars to have a positive impact on the work atmosphere. Most of the office personnel hoped that such seminars would continue to be organised in the future.

The work of the foremen had become more challenging and demanding

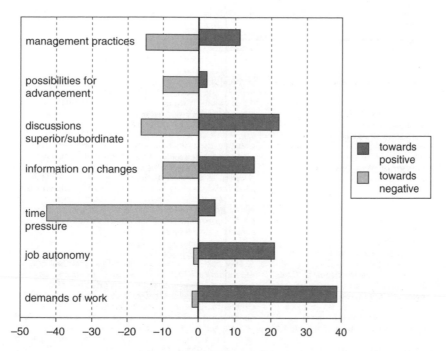

Figure 4.7 Sample survey 1988: changes in working conditions of the foremen during the two-year follow-up period (1986–1988)

Note: Direction of change; no change was reported by 60–90% of the respondents

(see Figure 4.7). They had discussions with their superiors more frequently, but they reported also some negative features of development in their superiors' work. Possibilities for advancement were seen to be more limited than before. The foremen were also concerned with training needs in communication and technical skills.

4.7.2   The management's report, 1990: Four-year follow-up

In order to evaluate comprehensively the development processes initiated on the basis of the baseline survey, the company management was asked to give a report. It was prepared by a member of the board of directors together with the chief occupational health manager. The report was requested from the management instead of the units in order to maximise its reliability. As the top management is not responsible to any other body in the company, it does not need to demonstrate activity simply to gain merit from the others. Their role would thus allow them to say that the project did not help them to

Table 4.4 Overview of actions and results in relation to nine central issues based on the baseline survey

Recommendation	Implementation
1. Reorganisation of monotonous tasks This means increased task variety and a broadening of the task structure. Training must be given for broader jobs. This will also facilitate replacement of employees and improves the mastery of work in situations of change. The factory unit in which monotony is a major problem should organise trials of this kind.	Gradual automation of all monotonous mechanised tasks in the package industry, where monotony was a big problem, had been planned. The plan had been put into action by automating the repetitive tasks at the end of the production process in the factory where the problems had been most severe. Discussions on changing the tasks had been started between different personnel groups and the management in several factory units. The management had suggested job rotation as a means of eliminating monotony. This proposal, however, was not approved by the workers nor by the labour unions. The monotony was alleviated through the integration and combination of production tasks and maintenance tasks in some sectors (see recommendation no. 5).

2. Development of leadership
Training in leadership skills should be made an essential part of the development of the management. This can be achieved by a refocusing of the strategies and practices of management training. Emphasis should be given to the development of skills, regular communication and supervisor support.
 	
3. Personnel development
A personnel training and development system should be developed. This must include both a long-term personnel development plan and a plan for a flexible system of training to react quickly to changing needs of production and organisation. Small-scale training events should be organised at the shop-floor level.
	A new post had been established for the chief of personnel development. The training system was completely revised based on the principle of continuous development, and a personnel training centre 'management school' was set up. The programme had three levels, for both newly recruited and experienced managers. Some of the courses lasted for several weeks. Leadership skills belonged to the main topics in the programme.
	    A system of regular discussions for planning and evaluation between the supervisor and each staff member had been initiated, and the decision was made to carry out such discussions in the whole company. The project team had prepared guidelines for this purpose. These discussions had been carried out between the foremen and their superiors in all the factories, and between the foremen and their staff members in some of them.
	    Individual development plans for the staff members were made. An extensive language training programme and various other training programmes were started in collaboration with local training organisations. It became possible to sit exams at university level. A support system for training was established among the personnel.
	    The company was nominated the Educator of the Year in Finland in 1989.

4. Support system for change processes
A system of support and personal development of the staff should be planned and integrated in the major investment programmes and other large-scale change processes. The system should offer support to the personnel during a change process.
	The management of change processes was included as a part of the training of managers.
	    A three-year research-intervention project was started in order to follow-up and to support the management groups of two large-scale programmes of investment and change.
	    New types of meetings of managers in the regional units of the company had been organised with the help of a consultant. The discussions included cases of change projects and other important management issues.

Table 4.4 cont.

Recommendation	Implementation
5. Integration of maintenance and support functions with production The problems occurring in maintenance and planning functions can be prevented by integrating these functions more closely with production. A better understanding of the production process is necessary for the maintenance and the design personnel. Partial reorganisation of tasks and co-ordination of the functions would also be important. 　The motivation potential of office work should be increased through better understanding of the production and through long-term planning of the work.	Co-operation between the production and the maintenance personnel had increased in all sectors. The skills of the production personnel had been extended through training and guidance to cover also maintenance tasks. In a new factory, these two functions had been combined already from the start. 　The responsibility of the personnel management had increasingly been shifted to the production managers, according to the view that every supervisor is the personnel manager of his/her staff. 　The purchasing activity had been delegated to the factory units from a previously centralised unit.
6. Improvement of co-operation of the office staff and the managers The workshops for improving co-operation between office staff and managers, started during the research project, should be continued in all units. Follow-up workshops should be arranged at agreed time intervals. The proposals of the workshops should be put into action, and their results should be controlled. The model of the development of co-operation applied in the workshops should be applied in the units and adopted as a daily routine.	Workshops for the personnel groups in question had been organised and continued in all the factories. The problems and ways of improving co-operation were dealt with in the supervisor/staff discussions.
7. Encouragement of shop floor participation Participation can be increased, for example, through departmental staff groups. One of the targets of participation should be an increase in the flow of information and better awareness of the staff concerning the overall goals of work and the needs of the clients. This would increase the meaningfulness and the mastery of work.	A representative of the staff was given the opportunity to participate in the meetings of the board of directors. The departments had started to organise regular meetings for the whole staff. The departments and the paper machine units selected representative staff groups to act as 'unofficial management groups'. 　Strengthening of staff participation was accepted as one of the goals to be facilitated in the supervisor/staff discussions.
8. Increasing psychological resources and preventing stress Well-being of personnel should be an issue to be integrated into all normal functions of the company in the same way as production and technology. A necessary precondition for this is increased awareness based on information and training, especially in the personnel management and occupational health services. A consultative support system for the OHS personnel should be developed. Discussion of issues related to workload and stress should be regular topics at the meetings of the OHS.	Information and guidelines for action were included in the training of the management and of the occupational health personnel. 　The system of regular health examinations conducted by the OHS was revised. The work stress questionnaire was adopted as a method in these examinations in order to screen for problems as early as possible. 　The activities of the occupational health personnel in the recognition of musculoskeletal disorders and early rehabilitation were increased.
9. Increasing the OHS personnel's knowledge of psychology A need for increased awareness and recognition of psychological factors both in decisions concerning individuals and the organisation was noted. Also the company would profit from consultations with a psychologist. The availability of such consultations should be the aim of the company. This service could be available either within the OHS, personnel development, or the personnel management.	Psychological well-being was taken as one of the main topics in the training of occupational health personnel. Co-operation between the factories and local mental health services was increased. Research and training collaboration with the Finnish Institute of Occupational Health was increased.

improve the company if this was indeed the case. The units, in turn, might be biased to report actions on a less evident basis simply to gain merit, since they had been encouraged by the management to apply the study results for their development. On the other hand the units may have independently implemented some improvements which were not known to the top management. Therefore, the report given by the directors may be a somewhat limited picture rather than a fully comprehensive one of the situation at the evaluation phase.

The company had made improvements in all nine issues which had been recommended after the baseline survey. Some of them were company-wide strategic actions, some concerned specific staff groups, and others were local improvements in the factories. Table 4.4 presents an overview of actions and results on nine issues that were based on the baseline survey

According to the report, the research results themselves served as the central motive for all the changes. The recommendations were the impulse for initiating the actions, but in many cases development continued as a result of the experiences gained. All in all, at this step the project matched well the goals of organisational change formulated in the beginning.

4.7.3   Comprehensive survey, 1996–1997: Ten-year follow-up

In 1996–1997 another survey concerning the company's entire work force and units in Finland as well as abroad was carried out. It was initiated by the OHS and the management of the company. In order to maintain the comparability between this survey and the first comprehensive survey (in 1986), the questionnaire was very similar to the first one with regard to items on work and working conditions. In addition, several validated measures on work ability, competence, innovativeness and burn-out were added. Demographic data on the subjects was collected so that it was possible to link anonymously but individually the two databases with different identification codes. This gave an opportunity to further investigate the relationships between work and health from a longitudinal perspective. The aim of the study was to evaluate the work environment, work organisation, job demands and health of the personnel in order to obtain an overall picture of the company's strengths and weaknesses in these areas. This information was intended for use both for the assessment of previous development as well as of possible needs for further improvements throughout the entire company.

The questionnaire was translated into seven languages and distributed to 19,000 people working in all the units of the enterprise across the world, of whom about 11,000 responded. The overall response rate was 61 per cent. Individual reports for sixty-five business units containing the results of the unit and the comparison between the unit and the other units of the company were given in information meetings in 1997. In these meetings the vice-

Table 4.5 Wishes for development and what happened during the ten-year follow-up period (1986–1996)

	1986 This measure would be useful in developing my work, %	1988 Evaluation of development	1996 Evaluation of development
More information about changes	49	+	
More discussions between superiors and subordinates	47	+	+
New machines and equipment	43	+	
Development of co-operation among the personnel	38	+	+
Changing accepted procedures	33	+	+
Training for superiors/ activities of superiors	32	+	+
More initial instruction and guidance about work tasks	32	+	+
Better possibilities for career advancement	30	–	
A slower work pace	29	–	–
Improving safety at work	25	+	+
Giving more independence to work groups	24	+	+
Reorganising work	22	+	+
Clarification of operational values/goals	21	+	
Swapping tasks with someone else for a while	21	+	+
Automation of work	20	+	
More work phases – broader tasks	14	+	+

Key: + = The development of work has been more often positive than negative.
– = The development of work has been more often negative than positive.
blank = This item was not included in the study.

president of Occupational Health and Safety and either one of the researchers from the FIOH reported the results and gave information about the problematic areas in the work of different personnel groups, and made suggestions for improving the work. The scientific work and statistical analysis of the results still continues.

4.7.4   Wishes for development of work and their fulfilment, 1985–1996

A list of several possible measures of developing work were included in the questionnaire, and the respondents evaluated whether each of these measures would be useful in developing their own work. These evaluations were made in 1986 and in 1996. In the two-year follow-up in 1988 and in the ten-year follow-up in 1996 the respondents evaluated the changes that had taken place in their work during the past two years. The trend of these evaluations, as well as the proportions of those respondents who thought that the measures would be useful, are given in Table 4.5.

It is clear from Table 4.5 that on almost all issues the trends have been favourable. There are two exceptions to this 'rule': possibilities for career advancements have decreased and work pace, as we have seen before, has increased.

4.7.5   The company in view of external comparison: Stressors and strains in the ten-year follow-up phase

The preliminary results of the ten-year follow-up showed that time pressure was the greatest problem at work. Time pressure had increased during the past two years according to more than half of the employees. In the total labour force 47 per cent reported the same trend in 1994 (Statistics Finland, 1994). The increase in work pace was a negative sign of development in these ten years. In general, the work was considered challenging and independent, and the work role remained clear. The personnel were also quite satisfied with the management and the support of their superiors. Thirty per cent of them reported an increase in employee/management discussions and 18 per cent saw improvement in the management practices in general, while in the total population 14 per cent saw improvement in the management support. The employees of the company nevertheless hoped for more interaction between the superiors and the staff. The organisational climate was evaluated by most as relaxed and cosy, but quite often also as conservative and prejudiced. Co-operation of the personnel was assessed good by 80 per cent and 25 per cent felt that it had improved (9 per cent said it had worsened) during the past two years. An opposite trend has been noted in the total population: 7 per cent reported a deterioration and 5 per cent an improvement in personnel relations. Job security was perceived as slightly better in the company than in the total population. Work in the company seems to be polarised regarding overall stressfulness: 36 per cent considered it stressful and 20 per cent not stressful at all. The corresponding figures in the total population were 11 per cent and 38 per cent. The overall level of stress remained quite low, and work ability, competence and health were evaluated as being good among the personnel. In the company, 81–88 per cent of staff members assessed their own psychological working capacity as good, and severe burn-out was prevalent only in 3 per cent, while the corresponding figure was 66 per cent for work ability and 7.3 per cent for burn-out in the total population (Kalimo and Toppinen, 1998a).

Further recommendations for future development

Although the psychosocial work conditions in the company were relatively good and the indicators of stress rather low, many possibilities for further improvements were noted. After the results of the 1996 survey had been reported and discussed in several meetings for the representatives of the management and/or personnel, the PA Committee made recommendations for further improvements. The company board approved their distribution throughout the company with a letter of obligation for their implementation. Many of the plants and other units included these activities in their budget for 1998. The following actions were proposed:

MANAGEMENT PROCEDURES

To the entire personnel:

- The opinions of the personnel are to be surveyed by means of an annual questionnaire in all business units.
- The operational values of the corporation are defined and discussed so that they will be internalised and applied to practical procedures.
- The flow of information will be improved, for example by increasing the use of internet and express news bulletins.
- The organisation and work procedures are improved in order to enrich work and diminish speed and time pressures and stress related to them, with a special emphasis on sufficient human resources and avoidance of overlapping tasks.

PERSONNEL DEVELOPMENT

- Every employee's personal resources, qualifications and needs for further development will be assessed in order to formulate an individual development programme to be included in the personnel data system.
- Personnel development will be the main focus of the human resource services, and sufficient resources in terms of manpower and time will be allocated for this purpose.
- The general concept designed for the personnel development activities will be carried out, taking care of its main aspects (management training, internationalisation, promoting multiple skills, team work, the profile of the company's Industrial Institute).
- The age structure of the personnel, with its consequences, will be taken into consideration when recruiting new personnel.

PERFORMANCE OF THE PERSONNEL

- Testing the physical fitness of the personnel will be included in the health examination programme so that every employee is made aware of his/her own health and physical condition, and will get guidance for improving them (personal revisable fitness programme).
- Rehabilitation activities will be intensified among all age groups, but especially among those over 50 years of age, so that everyone gets an opportunity for rehabilitation when necessary; remaining at work until the normal retirement age is the goal.
- Occupational health services will pay special attention to persons at risk of burn-out.
- Improvements at the workplace, based on individual needs, will be strengthened in order to be effectively rehabilitative.
- Job changes will be facilitated and encouraged.
- Facilities for fitness exercises will be arranged for the personnel either on the company premises or as purchased services.

ARRANGEMENTS AT WORK AND AT WORKPLACES

- The group division of the salaried staff will be abandoned.
- The system of orientating new workers will be improved, utilising more the know-how of older workers.
- Customer awareness will be improved so that every employee will know the expectations of internal and external customers concerning his/her own work.
- Safety risk assessment and management activities will be further improved.
- The implementation of new technology will be made more effective by developing ergonomics and the work environment.
- Possibilities for more flexible work arrangements will be created, and the development of multiple skills will be supported by increasing team work.

4.7.6   Costs and benefits: Evaluation of goals and effects

The benefit in relation to the cost is a crucial issue, and one which is difficult to measure in a large and complex project. This analysis will be continued in the present undertaking. One implicit indication of the benefit to the company may be the fact that each step has prompted continuation of the collaboration. The scientific results do not yet match the costs, but the remaining one and a half years of the project are reserved for scientific work based on the gathered data and experience. The value of the material, including the follow-up information ten years later which evaluates thousands of people and their working conditions, is immensely useful from a scientific standpoint, and can be used for the study of the determinants of health and the functions of an organisation.

In addition to the follow-up data collected in the questionnaire survey, data on sickness absences and their causes during the ten-year follow-up were also collected. It was realised that this data can be used only for epidemiological purposes, for example, to see which factors assessed in the first phase could possibly predict absence and its health-related causes over time. However, it is not feasible to use these data for the evaluation of the present project on a comprehensive basis. There are several reasons for this. First, the systems for recording absenteeism vary in different units and groups. Second, the company has reduced the number of personnel in the units located in Finland. Moreover, selection may have affected the factors related to sickness absenteeism. The same problems come up also in the use of other organisational wellness indicators, such as the quantity and the quality of the production.

Many other uncontrollable factors may affect the same outcome that interventions are meant to affect. In spite of a project, the company continues living its own life, including changes in production, markets, organisation and personnel. For this reason it was not possible to maintain the originally intended case-control design in the action projects implemented in some parts of the organisation.

For reasons of lack of control over the above mentioned factors, the evaluation of the impact of the actions involved in the project was based primarily on data closely related to the activities implemented. This means primarily process evaluation instead of outcome evaluation, i.e. assessing whether changes that are expected to lead to improvement of individual and organisational wellness actually took place.

The programme was successful in achieving its functional objectives and to a certain degree also in its participatory approach. The expectations of the research group were exceeded with regard to the extent of the field participation as a whole. The programme objectives were also achieved: action was taken in all recommended areas by the management and the interventions implemented as a part of the programme were perceived positively. Another method that was found to be feasible was the use of direct assessments of the personnel and the management regarding the changes and their effects. The specific direct evaluation of the development actions by the staff who participated in them was generally positive. A positive trend was obvious also in issues where development needs had been expressed in the first baseline survey.

4.7.7   Collaboration: Resource allocation and different interests

One of the aims in running the project was to follow a participatory approach. Although the company as a whole was actively involved, worker participation remained limited. In view of the large total number of workers, their immediate participation was marginal. The mechanism for workers participation in a large, geographically dispersed company can only be through representatives. The workers had a few representatives in the present programme which was built on a company-wide strategy. It became obvious that participatory democracy did not work satisfactorily. Even workers who were involved in the interventions could not always make the connection between the actions and the programme.

The impacts of the programme on the interest of the organisation in collaboration and exchange with the research team were greater than expected. The programme demonstrated that a successful field impact may lead to a gradually increasing demand for consultative support. The more the company learned about itself the more it wanted to have consultations for the application of the knowledge. This showed that flexible resource allocation is one important factor in programmes of this kind.

Collaboration between a company and a research and development organisation may involve some differences in interests, as in this case. The company was primarily interested in getting reliable information and in using it for its own development. The FIOH researchers were interested also in critical case analyses, controlled evaluations and scientific reports. This conflict of interest caused some tension throughout the programme. For instance, the researchers wanted personal identification on the questionnaires to facilitate follow-up studies. The employees were first against this, but approved the proposal after extensive negotiations.

Another controversial issue revolved around, who should participate in the surveys. The company members did not accept sampling, whereas the researchers regarded total participation of the personnel as unnecessary and time-consuming. The company members thought it necessary that, for the success of eventual interventions, everybody should have an opportunity for baseline reporting. Their point of view was followed, and the chosen strategy probably increased overall staff commitment.

The interim report on the baseline survey was jointly planned to include only preliminary company-wide results. This plan was made for the research group to be able to have an experimental group/control group design in the intervention phase. This shows that two important aspects regarding participatory research and development had not been taken into account: first, the collaborators in the field do not like to wait for years for feedback and second, the experimental/control group design is hardly feasible.

On the company's request, an interim report on the baseline survey results was made for each main factory unit on their own data and using some company-wide data for comparison. This was followed by a request by the factories for consultation with the researchers. The conflict between scientific goals and practical goals was obvious: while the results were utilised everywhere at the work place, the possibilities for controlled actions were weakened from the research point of view, and the time reserved for scientific work was in part spent in the field.

The same tendency for excessive demand from the company is evident also at the time of the ten-year follow-up report. Only an explicit agreement made during the planning phase on the duration of the periods of company feedback and scientific reporting can safeguard time for the latter. As a whole, a great deal of flexibility is demanded from both parties in order for the collaboration to succeed.

4.8   Conclusions

This multifaceted company-wide research and development cycle began in 1986 and has continued through the 1990s. During the first years of the project several development actions were launched in order to improve factors which were found unsatisfactory in the working conditions. The noted differences in health and well-being of the personnel were explained to a considerable degree by the differences in the working conditions. The idea of taking the best out of the 'human capital' also in terms of promoting the well-being of the personnel has finally made a breakthrough. The project has shown that the best results can be achieved by combining the development of work and the development of the personnel. The knowledge on psychological well-being and on factors which affect psychological well-being at work has definitely increased in the company and thereby also its own readiness to continue development. It can be concluded that the project has had a snowball effect in the company.

Parts of the strategy of this programme were adopted also in a programme to be carried out in an oil refinery company (Talvi et al., 1994). Many other organisations are carrying out smaller-scale surveys and short-cycle development with stress prevention as the focus. The positive development in the participation of the company itself for the development of work and personnel was also seen during the ten-year follow-up period of this project.

The scope of this programme in both extent of content and length of time is greater than the average. The research and development cycle has moved forward one step again. A tentative plan has been made in the company that in ten years time there may possibly be a new evaluation.

Bibliography

Antonovsky, A. (1987) *Unraveling the mystery of health*, San-Francisco: Jossey-Bass.

Elo, A-L. (1986) *Assessment of Psychic Stress Factors at Work*, Helsinki: Institute of Occupational Health.

Elo, A.-L., Leppänen A., Lindström K. and Ropponen, T. (1992) 'Occupational Stress Questionnaire: User's Instructions', *Reviews 19*, Helsinki: Institute of Occupational Health.

Finnish Institute of Occupational Health (1994) *Occupational Safety Act. Instructions and Guidance on the Application of the Occupational Safety Act, 299/58–509/93*, 35th revised edition, Helsinki: Finnish Institute of Occupational Health.

Goldberg, D.P. (1978) *Manual of the General Health Questionnaire*, Slough: National Foundation for Educational Research.

Järvikoski, A. and Härkäpää, K. (1987) 'A brief type A scale and the occurrence of cardiovascular symptoms', Scandinavian Journal *Rehab* Medicine, 3: 115–20.

Kalimo, R., Harju A., Leskinen J. and Nykyri, E. (1992) 'Work load, psychophysiological strain and coping of innovation project management in industry', *Scandinavian Journal of Work, Environment and Health*, 18(2): 130–2.

Kalimo, R., Olkkonen, M. and Toppinen, S. (eds) (1993) 'People in Progressing Production: I Research and development project in industry', *People and Work*, 7(4) (in Finnish with Abstract in English).

Kalimo, R. and Toppinen, S. (1998a) *Työuupumus Suomen työikäisellä väestöllä*, ('Burnout in Finnish working population'), Helsinki: Institute of Occupational Health.

Kalimo, R. and Toppinen, S. (1998b) *Large-scale Project Management: Group Cohesiveness, Commitment and Strain*, Helsinki: Institute of Occupational Health.

Kauppinen, T., Aaltonen, M., Lehtinen, S., Lindström, K., Näyhä, S., Riihimäki, H., Toikkanen, J. and Tossavainen, A. (1997) *Työ ja terveys Suomessa v. 1997* ('Work and Health in Finland 1997'), Helsinki: Institute of Occupational Health.

Matikainen, E. (1998) *Workplace Health Promotion*, European Network Workplace Health Promotion.

Matikainen, E. (1997) Työkykyä ylläpitävä toiminta ('Maintenance of work ability'), in *Hyvä työkyky* ('Good work ability'), Helsinki: Institute of Occupational Health, Insurance Company Ilmarinen.

Ministry of Social Affairs and Health (1978) *Occupational Health Care Act*, Unofficial translation, 1996, no. 743, Helsinki: Ministry of Social Affairs and Health.

Ministry of Social Affairs and Health (1996) *Decree of the Council of State on occupational health care prescribed as the responsibility of the employer and on the occupational health care of entrepreneurs and other self-employed persons*, Unofficial translation, 950/94, Helsinki, 1994: Ministry of Social Affairs and Health.

Ministry of Social Affairs and Health (1997) *Hyvä työterveyshuoltokäytäntö. Opas toiminnan suunnitteluun ja seurantaan*, ('Good occupational health in practice. Guidebook for planning and evaluation'), Helsinki: Institute of Occupational Health.

Ministry of Social Affairs and Health (1998) *Työterveyshuollon valtakunnalliset kehittämislinjat* ('National programme for the development of occupational health services'), Helsinki: Ministry of Social Affairs and Health.

National Board of Safety (1998) Henkinen työsuojelu valvontatoiminnassa ('Psychosocial factors in labour inspection'), *Circular 2/89*, 1086/68/89. Helsinki: National Board of Safety.

Räsänen, K., Peurala, M., Kankaanpää, E., Piirainen, H., Notkola, V. and Husman, K. (1994) *Occupational Health Care in Finland 1992*, Helsinki: Institute of Occupational Health (In Finnish).

Rosenberg, M. (1962) 'The association between self-esteem and anxiety', *Journal of Psychiatric Research*, 1: 135–52.

Talvi, A., Järvisalo, J., Knuts, L-R., Kaitaniemi, P. and Kalimo, R. (1994) *Työikäisen terveyden edistäminen* ('Health promotion for working-age people. Health promotion needs as recognized by the occupational health service of Neste Oy in

1988–1991'), Turku: Publication of the Social Insurance Institution, ML: 131 (in Finnish with Abstract in English).

Työolokomitean mietintö (1991) ('Report of working conditions'), 37, Report of a Commission, Helsinki: Finland.

Ylöstalo, P., Kauppinen, T. and Heikkilä, A. (1995) *Statistics Finland 1994*.

—(1996) *Työolobarometri marraskuu 1995* ('Work conditions barometer November 1995'), Helsinki: Ministry of Labour.

—(1997) *Työolobarometri lokakuu 1996* ('Work conditions barometer October 1996'), Helsinki: Ministry of Labour.

Chapter 5

The Netherlands: A hospital, 'Healthy Working for Health'

Ellis Lourijsen, Irene Houtman,
Michiel Kompier and Robert Gründemann

5.1   Introduction: Work stress in the Netherlands

In the Netherlands, work stress and work stress prevention and intervention in particular are considered to be main topics in occupational medicine, in occupational psychology, and in the view of many practitioners responsible for work and health issues in organisations, ranging from the works council to the human resource manager (see, for example, Van der Beek *et al.*, 1996). This relates to the fact that work stress has been found to be a major risk factor for the whole work force; it is considered to be responsible for a large amount of absenteeism and drop out from work, and is, therefore, to blame for high costs, to the individual, the company, and society.

Surveys representative of the Dutch work force show a steady increase in work stress risks: the percentage of employees indicating they have to work at a high work pace has increased from 3 per cent in 1977 to 56 per cent in 1993 (CBS, 1987 to 1994). The most recent data indicate a further increase (CBS, 1995, 1996). The data from the European Foundation for the Improvement of Living and Working Conditions ('EF') indicate that an overall rise in 'time pressure' has taken place over the whole of Europe. The Dutch employees, however, who ranked the highest in Europe on this topic in the EF's first survey of 1991–1992, showed an increase which was even more than average in 1995. Whereas 'working at a high pace for at least 50 per cent of the time' increased from 35 per cent to 42 per cent for the European mean over the period 1991/1992 to 1995, in the Netherlands it increased from 47 per cent to 58 per cent (Paoli, 1992; 1997).

Psychological dysfunctioning account for about one-third of the employees who are diagnosed unfit for work each year in the Netherlands (CTSV Central Surveillance of the Social Insurances, 1996). These psychological problems are not so much due to psychiatric disorders but are mainly the result of (over)strain, burn-out, chronic exhaustion and depression. There are indications that the proportion who are diagnosed unfit for work due to psychological dysfunctioning is increasing (Houtman, 1997).

Approximately 58 per cent of the employees who dropped out from work in 1990 for about one year due to psychological disorders, claim that this was due to a considerable extent to work. This percentage was somewhat higher than average (Gründemann et al., 1991). A more recent survey reports comparable figures on the work-relatedness of drop out from work due to psychological dysfunctioning (Van Engers, 1995). In the study by Gründemann et al. (1991) there was also an 'expert opinion' on the 'work-relatedness' of the drop-out, the expert being a medical doctor who had studied the files relating to the cases. Weighing up the different opinions, the researchers estimated the 'real' work-relatedness of the drop-out to be between 34 per cent and 50 per cent (Gründemann and Schellart, 1993).

These high percentages of people who are absent from work, or who are diagnosed unfit for work after one year of absence, indicate that high costs are involved. The costs involved with sickness absenteeism due to psychological problems are estimated at around 1.7 billion guilders per year, which is 40 per cent of the total estimated costs for absenteeism. The costs for disability pensions due to psychological disorders are estimated to be about 2.7 billion guilders per year (42 per cent of the total estimated costs for disability pensions), and the medical costs associated with psychological disorders are estimated at 290 million guilders per year (about 26 per cent of the total estimated costs) (Koningsveld and Mossink, 1997). Absence and drop out from work due to psychological problems are therefore one of the most expensive health problems that the Netherlands has to deal with.

In the Netherlands, work stress has been an important policy issue. It was in 1990, with the enforcement of Article 3 of the Working Conditions Act, that 'work stress' became a high priority. This Article also promoted risk-management at the source. At the beginning of the 1990s, several 'examples of good practice' were initiated in different branches of industry by the Ministry of Social Affairs and Employment. These studies were longitudinal in nature and were performed in a hospital, in a construction company, in regional institutes for mental welfare, and in a metal-products company. In this chapter we describe, one of these projects, the 'hospital example', in more detail. Other prevention and intervention projects in the Netherlands, financed by the Ministry or otherwise, are described in Kompier et al. (1996).

Since 1994 the legislation on Working Conditions has been adjusted to fit the European framework directive on health and safety at work (89/391/EEC) which was enforced on 1 January 1993 (Kompier et al., 1994). The adjustment of the Working Conditions Act was implemented together with a first adjustment in the regulations on sickness absenteeism. This resulted in more responsibility for employers and employees with respect to risk management and social security aspects.

Preventive action at company and sector levels seems to have been increasing significantly since the most recent adaptations in legislation on Working Conditions and in the regulations on absenteeism (Houtman, 1997).

Both with respect to sickness absenteeism and the numbers who drop out of work, and in particular in the case of psychological dysfunctioning, the effects on various sectors has been highly significant. Table 5.1 shows trends in absence percentages for different sectors in the Netherlands. The drop in absenteeism seen in 1994 is generally considered due to changes in the legislation on social security. The figures indicate that not only in the past, but at present as well, absence is high in the health care sector. Relative to other sectors, the percentage of employees diagnosed disabled for work after one year of sickness absence is large in this sector as well (see, for example, Gründemann *et al.*, 1991). These facts are major reasons for the selection of the study performed in the health care sector which is presented in this chapter.

Preventive action is considered to be effective by many practitioners as well as employers, but there are hardly any studies in which a sound methodological approach is used and the effects of the intervention procedure is tested against a control. In recent programming studies, the need is expressed to seriously expand on studies evaluating interventions in a more 'scientific' way (for example, Van der Beek *et al.*, 1996). In general, prevention and interventions can be directed either at the individual or at the (working) environment. Ideally, risk management is considered most effective when its focus is directed at the source, i.e. the working environment. Research indicates, however, that preventive measures directed at the individual level, training courses for example, are still highly popular measures, particularly in the case of prevention or intervention of work stress (Houtman, 1997).

Against this background, this chapter presents 'an example of good practice' in work stress management situated in a hospital. It is known that not only disablement due to psychological problems but risks for work stress are highly prevalent in this sector (Houtman *et al.*, 1994). The risks are, however, found to be quite different between occupational groups working in hospitals (Smulders, 1990). The heterogeneous nature of such organisations is one of the reasons that a tailor-made and step-by-step strategy in prevention and intervention of work stress and psychological problems is often requested, as the example presented will show.

5.2   Introduction to the Waterland hospital

The prevention project described here was carried out in the Waterland hospital in Purmerend, during 1991–1995. Waterland is a general hospital that resulted from a merger of two hospitals in Purmerend. In 1995, it employed approximately 850 people, working in five sectors: the care sector (432 employees), care support sector (116 employees), facilities sector (159 employees), information sector (41 employees) and general affairs sector (31 employees, including management and staff services). The majority of employees were female (82 per cent) and the average employee age was 35 years. Their level

Table 5.1 Trends in absence percentages for the different sectors in the Netherlands

Sector	1991	1992	1993	1994	1995
Agriculture	7.2	6.3	6.9	3.4	3.3
Construction industry	9.9	9.4	8.6	3.5	3.1
Industry	8.1	7.8	7.7	4.4	4.1
Commercial (profit) services (catering, retail and wholesale trade)	6.7	6.6	6.6	4.2	3.9
Commercial (profit)services (transportation)	7.2	6.9	7.0	3.8	3.5
Non-profit services (e.g. hospitals, education etc.)	10.2	9.5	9.8	6.2	6.2

Source: Houtman, 1997
Note: In 1994 the absenteeism compensation at company level radically changed, and is considered to be highly responsible for changes in the absence figures.

of education was fairly high, ranging from secondary education/vocational training (over 40 per cent of the employees) to higher professional education or university (more than one-third of the employees). The average term of employment was 6.5 years.

In 1991 at the start of the project, the absenteeism rate was 8.9 per cent (excluding maternity leave), which was considerably higher than the national average for hospitals in that year (6.5 per cent). The occupational health and safety committee was then responsible for the preparation and evaluation of policy on working conditions. In this matter, the committee worked closely with the Works Council's Committee for safety, health and well-being. The sectors were responsible for measures to improve working conditions. Just before the project began, the hospital issued a paper on absenteeism which indicated why absenteeism merited attention and how it intended to deal with it. The high absenteeism rate was considered symptomatic of problems in employees' health and their personal and/or work situation. Absenteeism leads to higher work pressure and adversely influences the quality of the service provided. The costs of absenteeism were also high. The hospital assumed that absenteeism could be influenced, and that supervisory staff could play an important role in this; they should be more intensively involved in the supervision of sick employees. In addition, a start was made with the formulation of a year plan for occupational health and safety, which the Working Conditions Act had recently required companies and organisations to do. The hospital was affiliated with the BVG (health care branch organisation) for its sickness insurance. The hospital itself was to cover the risk for a limited number of civil servants still employed after the merger.

5.3   Motives, signals and project organisation

5.3.1   Motives and signals

In 1991, the Waterland hospital had been pursuing an active policy for the improvement of working conditions and reduction of absenteeism, to which the personnel affairs and training department had also made a contribution. At that time, the absenteeism percentage was above average for the hospital sector, whereas its goal was to be an 'above average quality' hospital, both for patients and personnel. Consequently, in 1991 the hospital decided to set up a project to deal with absenteeism in a more structured way.

At the same time, TNO, the employer of the authors of this chapter, was looking for an enthusiastic hospital that was willing to serve as a model for a prevention project aimed at the reduction of absenteeism and drop out from work. This led to a joint project titled 'Healthy Working for Health' at the Waterland hospital.

The model project at the Waterland hospital was one of four carried out in 1991–1995 for the Ministries of Social Affairs and Employment, Health, Welfare and Sports, and the Aaf/Aof-national invalidity insurance funds. All four projects aimed to promote the health, safety and well-being of employees and therefore reduce absenteeism and drop out from work. They were also meant to serve as examples and result in a single strategy for use by other companies and organisations. The organisations' own responsibilities and employee participation played central roles in the projects.

To properly assess the influence of this approach, a control hospital was selected besides the Waterland hospital. This was the Diaconessen hospital in Leiden, which is similar to the Waterland hospital in terms of size, structure of the work force, training facilities and turnover. However, at the start of the project the absenteeism percentage at the Diaconessen hospital (7.1 per cent) was lower than at the Waterland hospital (8.9 per cent) (see Table 5.7). The Diaconessen hospital also pursued an active policy to improve working conditions and reduce absenteeism. However, this did not take place in the form of a special project as was the case at the Waterland hospital project, and the scope of its activities was also smaller.

The decision to carry out one of the model projects in the health care sector was related to the serious problems that intramural health care was facing in terms of work-related health. One study (Oversloot *et al.*, 1987) revealed that there were problems with the physical nature of the work (posture while lifting loads), psychological and emotional stress (work pace and dealing with patients), rosters (shift work) and employee participation in decision making. These factors increased the likelihood of work pressure, absenteeism, disablement and turnover in the sector. As the prevention project was intended to be used as an example case, TNO asked various branch organisations (NZf, CFO, FHZ, Abva/Kabo, Nieuwe Unie '91 and BVG) to approve the project method and actively support the project. Most of the organisations responded positively. During the project, TNO periodically provided them with progress reports and results.

5.3.2   Organisation of the project

Initially, the hospital and TNO made agreements on the co-ordination between the model project and the ongoing occupational health and safety activities at the hospital. The agreements were specified in a covenant between the hospital's board and TNO. As the organisation's independence played a central role in the project, the covenant also stipulated that the final responsibility for the project lay with the management of the hospital and that it was 'a hospital project'. TNO was only to play a supportive, guiding and advisory role, aimed at the implementation of working conditions policy in a broad sense and, within that context, at the project. To be able to do this, TNO employed experts in the fields of ergonomics, absenteeism and disability, stress, physical load, lifestyle programmes and occupational health and safety.

An internal project group

Based on the idea that an action research project can only succeed if it is supported by the entire organisation, a steering committee with a broad-based composition was selected to carry out the project. The 'Healthy Working for Health' steering committee comprised: the head of the care sector (also chairperson), the head of personnel affairs (also member of the occupational health and safety committee), two supervisory staff members (one from the care support sector and one from the facilities sector), the organisational expert, a Works Council member, a nurse and an operational member of the radiology department. The head of the care sector, the head of personnel affairs and the organisational expert were also members of the hospital's management team. The two TNO consultants were also members of the steering committee. The steering committee met once every three weeks for three hours.

Occupational health and safety care structure during the project

From the start, the model project was integrated into the hospital's normal working conditions policy. The hospital's management team was responsible for the occupational health and safety policy. The steering committee was responsible for the implementation and progress of the project, and played a central co-ordinating role in the implementation of working conditions policy during the project. The occupational health and safety committee, which had previously been established by the management, was to function under the steering committee's supervision for the rest of the project's duration.

The hospital uses one insurance doctor and one reporter (layman) for the employees on sick leave.

Introduction of the project into the hospital

To create support for the project and to give it a positive start, an initial meeting was organized for the complete work force in the local theatre in Spring 1992. The director and the chairmen of the steering committee and the Works Council explained the goals and organisation of the model project. The employees were then provided with further information during departmental meetings where attention was directed at the project and any questions from employees. The meetings were chaired by a member of the steering committee.

5.4   Analysis: Risk factors and risk groups

5.4.1   Methods

To gain a general impression of the problems in work and at the hospital, a limited number of supervisory and other staff, known as 'key respondents', were interviewed using existing check lists on job content and organisation of work, on working conditions, on social relations at work and on terms of employment (Kompier and Marcelissen, 1990). In addition, a study was made of the available data related to the diagnosis of those disabled for work, absenteeism and turnover.

The interviews revealed that there were organisation-related problems in the areas of job content, working conditions, terms of employment and to a lesser extent in the area of social relations at work. An analysis of absenteeism and turnover data revealed that the absenteeism and turnover percentages were the highest in the facilities sector. In addition, the people employed in this sector tended to be older and less highly educated than in the other sectors. 'Disability from work' as a cause of turnover was also seen more frequently in this sector. Absenteeism was relatively low in the care support and information sectors.

A closer study of the procedures of socio-medical guidance revealed they merited improvement, particularly where the role of supervisory staff was concerned. At the time of the interviews, measures were already being prepared for this.

On the basis of the problems identified, it proved fairly difficult to designate specific risk groups. It was still unclear which factors in particular led to problems and which departments or positions were affected the most. It was therefore decided to analyse the stress and health problems in more detail by conducting a survey among all employees and volunteers working at the hospital. The survey was conducted in mid-1992. The questionnaire used was largely based on validated instruments which pay attention, in a broad sense, to aspects of work and employee health (Gründemann et al., 1992). Questions were added to assess the need for activities in the area of lifestyle, such as a 'how to stop smoking' course and physical exercise. The absenteeism data for 1991 and 1992 were also analysed in more detail. On the basis of the survey, a number of positions were selected for further analysis using the WEBA method (WEBA is the Dutch abbreviation for 'well-being at work'; Vaas et al., 1995). This method can be used to determine job-related stress risks and learning and development opportunities. The WEBA method complies with the provisions of Section 3 of the Dutch Working Environment Act. An important characteristic of this method is that it also allows rules for improvement to be inferred.

The control hospital – the Diaconessen hospital – also participated in the survey, but only a random sample of 50 per cent of the employees were sent a questionnaire.

5.4.2   Risk factors and risk groups

Survey

There was a high response to the survey (72 per cent), which was well distributed among the sectors and departments. Table 5.2 compares the results of the Waterland hospital with those of a large external reference group (approximately 3,500 employees in hospitals; Oversloot et al., 1987) and the Diaconessen hospital in 1992.

The results for the Waterland hospital were quite favourable compared with those of the reference population. The Waterland workforce expressed significantly fewer complaints related to such matters as physical and psychological effort, organisation of work, physical working conditions/safety, supervision, colleagues and appreciation of their working environment. Which is five of the six aspects of work that could be compared. The general opinion of Waterland hospital employees was also significantly more favourable in 1992 than that of the reference population (94 per cent of the Waterland hospital employees said that they felt quite or reasonably comfortable with their work, whereas this was 'only' true for 82 per cent of the control group). There was no reference data on speed of work, emotional stress, (problems with) physical load, autonomy and emotional exhaustion. The hospital was comparable to the reference group with relation to job content, health complaints and sickness behaviour.

Compared with the Diaconessen hospital (also with an employee response of 72 per cent), employees of the Waterland hospital complained significantly more in relation to appreciation of their working environment. The hospitals were generally similar with respect to all other aspects.

Table 5.3 contains a brief summary of the organisation-related problems, which are problems that apply to all sectors or at least three of the four

Table 5.2 The results of the Waterland hospital compared with those of the reference
population and the Diaconessen hospital in 1992 (pre-assessment);
expressed as the average percentage of complaints per aspect.

Aspects considered	Reference population (n = 3522) %	Waterland pre-assessment 1992 (n = 687) %	Diaconessen pre-assessment 1992 (n = 455) %
Job content	11	10	12
Autonomy	–	33	31
Organisation of work	* 35	27	29
Work pace	–	36	38
Physical and psychological effort	* 44	35	35
Emotional stress	–	11	10
Physical load	–	39	38
Physical working conditions	* 28	26	28
Supervision and co-workers	* 27	18	19
Appreciation, reward and prospects	* 45	<u>38</u>	<u>30</u>
Health complaints	19	18	20
Emotional exhaustion	–	10	10
Sickness behaviour	31	30	29

Note: An asterisk before the reference population score denotes a significant difference to the
Waterland hospital score. An underlined score signifies a significant difference between the
Waterland hospital and the Diaconessen hospital (which means the probability that the
differences found are based on coincidence is less than 1 in 20: $p < 0.05$)

sectors. The fifth sector – the general sector – has been left out of consideration here due to its highly heterogeneous composition. Something is considered a problem if 20 per cent or more of the employees in at least three of the four sectors complained about the work.

Table 5.4 provides an overview of the main health complaints. Complaints were only listed if they had been vented by at least 20 per cent of the employees.

Need for lifestyle activities

Employees of the hospital proved to have a clear need for activities in the area of lifestyle, the most favourite being physical exercise (49 per cent) and activities in the area of 'healthy eating' (31 per cent). Of the smokers (27 per cent of the employees), 54 per cent said they would join a 'smoking cessation' course if it was offered by their employer. Ninety-four per cent of the employees was interested in a course in social skills.

Table 5.3 Organisation-related problems at the Waterland hospital (1992)

Job content and organisation of work	Explanation
Job content	In three of the four sectors, 21 per cent to 32 per cent of the employees found the work too simple (care sector excepted).
Effort/work pace	Forty-four to 56 per cent of the employees found the work either physically or psychologically very demanding. 55 per cent regularly worked under the pressure of time. 23 to 49 per cent said they had to work too fast/hard/much and did not have enough time to finish work.
Organisation of work	Twenty-four to 39 per cent of the employees said they were impeded in their work by others' shortcomings, unforeseen situations or the absence of others. Forty-four per cent indicated that normal work was often interrupted.
Autonomy	Thirty-three to 43 per cent complained about the lack of opportunity to organize certain aspects of work (e.g., work pace, work sequence and the time at which a task is carried out). The complaints did not apply to the information sector.
Working conditions: Interior climate	Sixty-four per cent of the employees were considerably troubled by heat, half of them by dry air or lack of fresh air, 26 per cent by fluctuations in temperature and 22 per cent by draught and wind.
Other working conditions	Of all the employees dealing with dangerous goods, radiation or infections (52 per cent), 51 per cent were afraid of adverse consequences from infections and 32 per cent from chemical agents. Of the employees wearing compulsory workwear (71 per cent), 41 per cent were not satisfied with it.
Physical load	Twenty-eight to 60 per cent complained about physical load. Common complaints were: frequently having to bend over or having to turn upper part of the body (60 per cent), walk (59 per cent) or stand (47 per cent) for a long, uninterrupted period, push/pull heavy loads (45 per cent) and lift heavy loads (44 per cent). Twenty-eight per cent of the employees had to make repetitive movements.
Information	A quarter of the employees thought they were not kept well enough informed of what was going on in the hospital. Thirty-three to 44 per cent said they received insufficient information on the dangerous aspects of their work.
Social relations at work: Supervision and co-workers	Twenty-one per cent were not satisfied with the day-to-day management. Twenty-two per cent felt insufficiently supported by their direct superiors. Twenty-three per cent said the day-to-day management took insufficient account of employees' remarks. Twenty-one per cent said that the day-to-day management did not have a correct impression of the employees.
Terms of employment: Lack of personnel, replacement and leave days Appreciation and training and career opportunities	Thirty-eight per cent hold the view that there was a lack of personnel in the department, 30 per cent frequently had to replace co-workers and 35 per cent could not take days off when they wanted to. Twenty-nine per cent of the employees felt insufficiently valued, 49 per cent thought they were underpaid for what they did and 35 per cent were not satisfied with their prospects. Forty-six to 52 per cent said that training and career opportunities were insufficient.

Table 5.4 Mental and physical health problems for the hospital and per sector (1992)

Problems for the entire hospital	Additional health problems per sector
VOEG (Questionnaire on psychosomatic symptoms) 36% often felt tired 36% frequently had back pain 31% often had a headache	Care: 27% had an empty feeling at the end of a work day 26% were sooner tired than normally 22% generally got up tired in the morning 27% frequently experienced pain in bones/muscles 21% had irritation of the skin due to work
Posture Movement Health Pain-related complaints during the past 12 months: in the lumbar region (43%) in the neck (26%) in the shoulder (20%)	Care support: none
Emotional exhaustion 21% overexerted themselves at work	Facilities: 20% generally got up tired in the morning 32% often complained about pain in bones/muscles 20% had problems with the knees during the past 12 months 20% were treated by a doctor
Sickness behaviour In the six months preceding the study: 53% had visited a doctor; 40% had occasionally stayed at home from work due to illness or accident	
24% suffered from work-related health complaints	Information: empty feeling at end of work day (21%) problems with wrist/hand (21%)

Absenteeism data

An analysis of absenteeism percentages for the hospital both at sectoral and departmental level revealed that the absenteeism percentage for the Waterland hospital as a whole was significantly higher in 1991 than the national hospital average (8.9 per cent versus 6.5 per cent, excluding maternity leave). At the sector level, only the absenteeism percentage in the facilities sector (higher) differed significantly from that in the other sectors in 1991. The differences in absenteeism percentage within each of the sectors were not significant, except in the domestic services section of the facilities sector. In other words, chance may be part of the reason for the differences found between the departments.

In 1992, there was a significant decrease in absenteeism for the entire hospital and in the facilities sector. In addition, there was no increase or decrease in absenteeism at either the sector or department levels.

Table 5.5 provides an overview of the 1991 and 1992 absenteeism percentages (excluding maternity leave) for the entire hospital and for each sector.

Table 5.5 Absenteeism percentage (excluding maternity leave) in 1991 and 1992 at the sector level and for the hospital as a whole

Sectors	Absenteeism percentage 1991	Absenteeism percentage 1992
Care	7.8	6.5
Care support	6.4	4.8
Facilities	16.9	9.6
Information	6.1	4.8
General affairs	3.7	2.9
Total	**8.9**	**6.5**

Furthermore, the absenteeism percentage (the only measure of absenteeism available at that time) did not indicate a clear relationship between absenteeism on the one hand and perception of work or health on the other. This was true at both the sector and department levels. It should be noted that, for reasons of privacy, the absenteeism data could not be linked to data from the questionnaires. That also made it more difficult to demonstrate any correlations between data from questionnaires and absenteeism data.

WEBA analyses

The positions of nurse, medical analyst, cook, archive assistant and operating theatre assistant were analysed using the WEBA method. These were jobs in departments with a relatively high number of complaints related to job content, physical and psychological effort, organisation of work, work pressure, appreciation of working environment and autonomy.

A general impression gained from the WEBA analyses was that there were major stress risks in virtually all departments. These risks were mainly associated with the lack or ambiguity of procedures, rules or agreements between departments.

The physical and stress risks at the medical archives were marked as alarming. Prevention was no longer a feasible option there and 'prevention of deterioration' merited the highest priority. This department was not only faced with a spatial problem (people have to work in a very small area), but also with technical, organisation and managerial problems. Technical because the archive system used constantly resulted in a lack of space. The organisational and managerial problems were related to the fact that agreements concerning work made with the departments served by the archives were either unclear or the departments failed to comply with them.

5.5   Choice of measures

5.5.1   *Object: Integrated health promotion*

The survey on the employees' work situation at the hospital showed a relatively positive score for the hospital compared with the reference hospitals. Nevertheless, there were a number of organisation-related problems, which seem to lead to some organisation-related and sector-specific health complaints. It was difficult to demonstrate a direct statistical relationship between problems/complaints and absenteeism at the hospital. However, according to the literature on absenteeism, the aspects studied here were likely to influence absenteeism to a greater or lesser extent.

Consequently, the choice of measures was based on a 'multi-track' policy, aimed at both the improvement of working conditions and employees' physical and mental health, and the intensification of inspection and supervision of absentees. An approach that combines three types of measures and positively influences employees' health and well-being in a more structured manner is an instance of integrated health promotion. Such an approach intends to go further than 'solely' removing health hazards from the workplace.

5.5.2   *Plan of action*

The steering committee held the view that all problems identified needed to be tackled. In order to arrive at a co-ordinated set of measures, they first examined the question of whether the problems identified could be solved. To do so, each problem was assessed to determine:

- whether the cause of the problem was sufficiently clear or required further investigation;
- what source-specific and non-source-specific measures the hospital could take;
- the cost of such measures;
- the expected (additional) yield.

This showed that the causes of some problems were insufficiently clear. In other cases, the problem and their possible solutions were clear, but the measures needed further elaboration. This prompted the steering committee to write a memo to the management team, providing the basis for a plan of action. The memo contained a list of all problems, classified according to job content and organisation of work, working conditions, social relations at work and terms of employment. Lifestyle activities constituted a separate category. The basis principle was to tackle the problems within the existing line organisation wherever possible. Problems specific to a certain sector were to be solved in that sector. A sub-project was to be started for any problems that could not be solved within the line organisation. The management team agreed with this plan of action.

5.5.3 Further elaboration of plan of action on the basis of sub-projects

The steering committee subsequently decided to start sub-projects for work pressure, interior climate, physical load, provision of information, working hours and rosters, training and career opportunities, managerial style and life-style. The purpose of the sub-projects was to (further) elaborate and implement measures and solutions. No further priorities were assigned. The sequence of the sub-projects was mainly determined by the clarity of the solutions and time and manpower available to carry out the projects. Table 5.6 provides a brief overview of the content and duration of the sub-projects.

Socio-medical guidance

In 1994 and 1995 the head of personnel affairs also elaborated procedures for absenteeism and socio-medical guidance. These included measures for the improvement of absenteeism registration, increasing direct supervisors' involvement in absenteeism and the periodic provision of absenteeism data to supervisors.

5.6 Preparation and implementation of sub-projects

5.6.1 Preparation and implementation

The steering committee assigned a steering committee member as co-ordinator for each category of problem (job content and organisation of work, working conditions, terms of employment, social relations at work, lifestyle). One of the co-ordinators' duties was to ensure that a well-substantiated proposal was committed to paper for the sub-projects formulated. Such a proposal directs attention to the problems that are to be addressed, the duration of the project, the manner in which problems are dealt with, the employees concerned, the expected cost and the manner in which employees are informed on the project. Each proposal was discussed by the steering committee and then sub-mitted one at a time to the management team for approval.

Responsibility for the implementation of each sub-project was given to a single project group (sometimes one employee). The progress and co-ordination of the various sub-projects were monitored by the steering committee. The five co-ordinators provided feedback on the state of affairs of the various sub-projects at every steering committee meeting. In this way, it was checked whether sub-projects were progressing according to plan or

Table 5.6 Content and duration of sub-projects

Sub-projects	Content
Job content and organisation of work Work pressure (1993–1994)	Inventory and implementation of measures in the areas of work planning, organisation of work and work processes and autonomy. Since measures in these areas have a great impact in terms of organisation, a small-scale project was initially set up in the internal nursing department.
Working conditions Interior climate (1993–1996)	A feasibility study was conducted into the possibilities of cooling the entire hospital with the existing systems and cooling options. A plan of action was subsequently developed, which was carried out in 1995–1996.
Physical load (1994–1995)	Closer inventory of causes and solutions, and implementation of measures. This, too, was a small-scale project started in the orthopaedics ward, pharmacy and operating theatres.
Information (1994–1995)	Determine what problems occur in the provision of information related to working conditions and dangerous aspects of work, and make an inventory of measures.
Terms of employment Working hours and rosters (1995)	Developing a plan of action to arrive at a better roster for the wards, taking account of the problems concerning replacement days and taking days off.
Training and career opportunities (1996)	Further elaboration of training and career policy.
Social relations at work Managerial style (1994–1995)	Developing measures to assist supervisory staff in such areas as work consultations and performance reviews.
Lifestyle Lifestyle and social skills (1994–1995)	Categorising possible activities in the areas of physical exercise, smoking, eating habits and social skills in consultation with providers of lifestyle programmes. Elaborating and offering specific programmes after approval from the management team.

whether interim adjustment of the schedule or implementation of the sub-projects was required.

During the sub-projects, the Works Council was informed and consulted on project proposals and the implementation of the projects by the Works Council's representative on the steering committee. If the Works Council's consent or advice was required for the implementation of measures, the hospital director would specify this at the regular consultative meetings of the Works Council.

Each sub-project was concluded with a final report which, after the approval from the steering committee, was given final approval by the management team, which actually commissioned each sub-project. In order to keep the employees informed during the project, of proposed or implemented measures, the steering committee organised a 'theme day' for personnel at the end of 1994. During this day, everyone was comprehensively informed of all the activities carried out by the steering committee and the occupational health and safety committee. Employees also informed each other of any projects in their own departments.

5.6.2 Measures

At the end of 1995 some of the measures described had already been implemented, others were carefully elaborated proposals that still required formal approval

Not all of the problems identified had been dealt with. Choices were made – mostly for practical reasons – and it is envisaged that solutions for some problems will be conceived and implemented in the near future.

Two new positions

In 1994, the management team created two new positions: the occupational health and safety/environmental officer and the physical load adviser. The occupational health and safety/environmental officer co-ordinates the formulation and implementation of policy on working conditions and the physical load adviser advises supervisory staff on how physical load can be limited and prevented.

Job content and organisation of work

As part of the 'work pressure' project in the internal nursing department, a number of specific improvements were introduced related to the organisation of work and employee participation, such as:

• better co-ordination between the supply and demand of care by charting the number of admissions per specialist and introducing a computer program that shows the number of beds occupied in the department;

- improvement of internal communication and accessibility of the department by:

  1   appointing a department secretary to take telephone calls;
  2   installing a computer at the desk to provide employees with better access to relevant information;
  3   introducing telephone consultation time for family, as well as designating permanent liaisons to convey information to the family;

- training employees in 'assertive communication', to make them better able to deal with comments from co-workers, management or specialists and to tell others when they function below par.

There were also developments underway at the hospital which, in the long term, may contribute to further improvement of job content and organisation of work in the nursing sector, such as the 'job differentiation and care methods' project. This project, which was carried out relatively autonomously from the 'Healthy Working for Health' project, took place in the nursing sector and initially explored opportunities for differentiating between different types of nursing position. It also looked at any consequences for the manner in which care was provided and the organisation of work (care methods). If properly put into practice, job differentiation may help make positions more attractive (in WEBA terms) and improve the quality of the care provided.

Working conditions

In the 'physical load project', management, employees of the orthopaedics, pharmacy and operating theatre departments, and a consultant and ergonomist from TNO worked closely together to develop a package of measures for each individual department. Initially, the problems relating to physical load were examined for each department, followed by categorisation of potential solutions. Then the people involved evaluated the various solutions on the basis of the following criteria:

1   Does the solution contribute to a reduction of physical load?
2   Is the solution desirable, available and financially feasible?
3   Would implementation of the solution have organisational consequences?

This approach has already resulted in a coherent package of measures for the orthopaedic and pharmacy departments.

The following measures have been proposed for the orthopaedic department:

- a special bed lift/fork-lift truck and periodic maintenance of the beds, to facilitate bed transport;
- an (alternative) lift to facilitate changing the sheets and patient care;

- a special toilet seat that helps the patient stand up and supports for the patient beside the toilet.

Measures for the pharmacy include:

- a movable table, adjustable in height, for unwrapping infusion bags and distilled water, combined, if required, with a pallet truck so the infusion bags can be easily transported to the wards;
- automatic doors at the pharmacy to allow transport using heavy trolleys;
- a trial set-up to determine what – in terms of physical load – is the best workplace for dispensing medicines and working with computer screens.

The increasing number of health complaints from people working at the central medical archives prompted a closer assessment of physical load by a human movement scientist from TNO. The following measures were taken almost immediately:

- Trolleys were made to facilitate transporting boxes of files;
- The file boxes were fitted with handles and made more suitable for stacking, reducing the need for bending, lifting and carrying;
- The archives room was modified, reducing the need for bending or reaching when storing files;
- File holders were made to improve medical registration work (especially finding the right codes for diagnoses and treatments);
- Computer workplaces were modified (such as height-adjustable chairs);
- The roster was improved, allowing personnel to rotate the various activities, leaving more room for personal initiative and responsibility, and monthly team meetings were organised to discuss problems at work.

In recent years, various equipment has been purchased for the entire hospital, including a CTG unit, lifts, pumps and infusion stands.

Social relations at work

In 1994, supervisory staff was trained to conduct performance reviews. The 'managerial style' project also gave further support to supervisory staff in the performance of their duties by:

- providing courses in dealing with rewards, in accordance with the new reward system;
- providing a course in supervising absenteeism, providing supervisory staff with instruments for supervising their ill employees;
- providing separate management courses for heads of department and team leaders;

- establishing a network for support between colleagues, in which supervisory staff meet in groups to exchange experiences;
- establishing an individual training schedule, thereby enabling supervisory staff to supplement their knowledge and skills.

The measures proposed to improve work consultations, such as the formulation of objectives and preconditions by the management team and offering training and support to supervisory staff, were postponed by the management team for the time being, to prevent too many activities from taking place at the same time.

Social skills and lifestyle

The primary purpose of activities in the area of social skills and lifestyle is to promote the physical and mental health of employees, resulting in healthy employees who will be less susceptible to illness and drop out from work. The following measures were implemented:

- a stress management course for all supervisory staff; from 1995 on, all employees were given the opportunity to take this course;
- a course on 'how to deal with aggression and violence' for employees of the psychiatric ward and emergency room;
- the oncology department – where staff is frequently confronted with suffering and death – has had a guidance group for several years where people can talk about each other's experiences; the structural introduction of such groups at other wards is being considered;
- a 'communication techniques' course (talking to patients);
- a 'dealing with the public' course for employees of the outpatient department, radiology department, first aid and reception;
- programmes for employees interested in stopping smoking and a healthy diet.

Socio-medical guidance

In recent years the following measures were taken in this area:

- Supervisory staff have been given clearly defined tasks in the area of socio-medical guidance. These tasks are set down in the socio-medical guidance manual.
- Following adjustments to the registration of sick leave, absenteeism data is now regularly reported directly back to supervisors, enabling them to take further action.
- To prevent absenteeism, sick leave is reported to the immediate superior.

- Half of the employees are visited at home by a reporter on the first day of sick leave. The other half is visited before the sixth day of sick leave.
- With a view to a quick recovery and work rehabilitation of employees on (long-term) sick leave and to prevent them from ceasing work altogether, recoveries are also reported to the direct supervisor who regularly contacts (i.e. once every three to four weeks) a sick employee.
- The immediate superior draws up a return-to-work plan before the eleventh week.
- The Socio-medical Team (SMT) discusses the opportunities for resuming work for employees on long-term sick leave and considers temporary or long-term modifications to the work.
- The aim is to involve supervisory staff more intensively in reducing sick leave in the coming years.

The measures are briefly summarised in Table 5.7.

5.7 Evaluation

The project was evaluated in the period from April to October 1995 and involved a repetition of the survey, an analysis of the absenteeism data and a cost-benefit analysis.

5.7.1 Effects

Improvements at the Waterland hospital

The post-assessment produced a high response (72 per cent), which was evenly distributed between the sectors and departments. The post-assessment showed that several important improvements had been made in employees' work situations. Figure 5.1 provides the results of the pre-assessment and post-assessment at the Waterland hospital, expressed as an average percentage of complaints for each aspect examined.

In 1995, the Waterland personnel expressed significantly fewer complaints related to aspects of job content, emotional stress and appreciation for working environment than in 1992. Improvements in the aspects of job content and emotional stress are of little practical value because the initial situation in those respects was already fairly positive (low percentage of complaints during pre-assessment). Moreover, the respondents now complained significantly more about the work pace, which seems to be a national phenomenon. Data from the Central Bureau of Statistics (CBS) showed that, of the developments in risk factors for work stress, the one relating to work pace is the least favourable (see section 5.1). In the Netherlands, this is more or less equally true for men and women, for all age brackets and for practically all sectors and occupations. For all other aspects, the situation at the hospital is similar to that of 1992.

Table 5.7 Measures already implemented and still to be implemented

Topics	Measures implemented in mid-1995	Measures to be implemented in 1995–1996
General	Two new positions: Occupational Health and Safety officer and physical load adviser	
Job content and organisation of work	*Internal nursing department (work pressure)* •coordination of care supply and demand •improvement of internal communication and accessibility •assertive communication training	*Care sector* •project for position differentiation and care methods
Working conditions	*Central medical archives (physical load)* improvement of: •transport/processing of files •workplaces with computer screens •rosters, team consultations, autonomy *Entire hospital* •purchase of aids	*Orthopaedics department (physical load)* Improvement of: •bed transport •cleaning beds and looking after patients •helping patients go to the toilet *Pharmacy (physical load)* Improvement of: •unpacking and transport of infusion bags and distilled water •transport of heavy trolleys •dispensing drugs/workplace with computer screen *Entire hospital* •improvement of interior climate •improvement of provision of information on occupational safety and health
Working conditions		*Care sector* •new rosters *Entire hospital* •training and career policy
Social relations at work	*Supervisory staff (managerial style)* •training in conducting performance reviews •absenteeism supervision course •management course	*Supervisory staff (managerial style)* •networks for support from co-workers •individual training plan •course in conducting performance and absenteeism interviews (team leaders) •improve work consultations
Lifestyle/social skills	*Supervisory staff* •stress management course *Employees of psychiatric ward/emergency room* •course in how to deal with aggression	*Employees* Course/programme: •stress management •communication techniques •dealing with the public •how to quit smoking, healthy food
Absenteeism/socio-medical guidance	*Supervisory staff* •periodic feedback on absenteeism figures to supervisory staff •sickness and recovery reports to direct superiors •regular contact with sick employees •visit by inspector between 1–6 days •return-to-work plan for week 11 *SMT* •studies opportunities for work rehabilitation or modification of work	*Supervisory staff* •greater involvement in reducing absenteeism

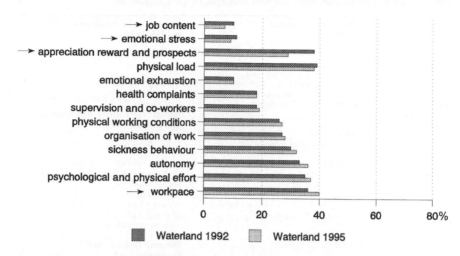

Figure 5.1 The results of the Waterland hospital in the pre-assessment (1992: n = 687) and the post-assessment (1995: n = 612), expressed as the average percentage of complaints per aspect.

Note: An arrow before a score signifies a significant difference in relation to the pre-assessment in 1992 (which means the probability that the differences found are based on coincidence is less than 1 in 20: p < 0.05)

The survey also showed a number of improvements in the work situation which are (possibly) associated with the measures already implemented. However, it is impossible to make 'definitive' statements about the relationship between measures on the one hand and effects on the other, because a mixture of measures were implemented which cannot be viewed in isolation from each other. In 1995 employees of the hospital appeared to complain less about the available aids, possibly as a result of the acquisition of aids. Supervisory staff training may also have contributed to the reduction in complaints related to the functioning of work consultations and being kept up-to-date of what is going on in the hospital. The activities in the area of socio-medical guidance have also borne fruits: most of the employees think their immediate superiors pay sufficient attention to sick employees and half of them think the treatment of sick employees has improved.

Of the measures at departmental level, those relating to physical load in the medical administration department seem to have particularly reduced work-related complaints.

The 'work pressure' project in the internal nursing department does not seem to have led to a significant reduction in the number of complaints about work pace, autonomy and organisation of work. According to the employees concerned, the work pressure has not diminished. They were, however, positive about the fact that a process of change has been initiated in the ward and have high expectations for the future; at the end of 1995 a number of the planned measures still had to be implemented. The project seemed to have 'stirred up' the department. The employees involved spoke of positive and more open communication related to bringing about improvement and change.

The 'physical load' project in the orthopaedics department and pharmacy was completed at the end of 1995. However, when it was being evaluated at the end of 1995, it was still too early to ascertain a reduction in complaints related to physical load and the locomotor system. Most of the measures still had to be implemented. A number of employees of the orthopaedics department did say that the project has contributed to an increased use of aids, which has changed working methods and made work more pleasant.

The Waterland hospital compared with the control hospital

Figure 5.2 compares the results of the post-assessment with those of the Diaconessen hospital, expressed in the average percentage of complaints per aspect examined.

In 1995, the Waterland personnel proved to be more positive about job content than the personnel at the Diaconessen hospital. However, they complained significantly more about autonomy, organisation of work, work pace, physical load and mental stress than their counterparts in the control hospital.

Improvements in the control hospital

An explanation for the differences between both hospitals in 1995 could be found in the developments that took place in the Diaconessen hospital in the period 1992–1995. Post-assessment in the Diaconessen hospital also produced a high response (68 per cent), which was evenly distributed between the sectors and departments. Figure 5.3 shows the results of the pre- and post-assessment for the Diaconessen hospital. This hospital also showed some significant improvements in comparison with 1992.

Employees of the Diaconessen hospital complained significantly less about the organisation of work and work pace. These improvements are possibly related to measures implemented in recent years to improve the organisation of work and managerial style.

On the basis of the quantitative comparison, it can be concluded that compared with 1992 there were significant improvements in the work situation at the Waterland hospital. Possibly as a result of the improvements in job content, the Waterland hospital now scores higher in this respect than the Diaconessen hospital. In 1992, appreciation for the working environment was still significantly less positive in the Waterland hospital than in the Diaconessen hospital. The major improvements in this region may have made

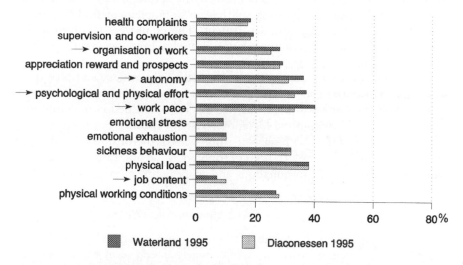

Figure 5.2 The results of the post-assessment in the Waterland hospital compared with those of the Diaconessen hospital (1995), expressed as the average percentage of complaints per aspect.

Note: An arrow before a score signifies a significant difference between the two hospitals (which means the probability that the differences found are based on coincidence is less than 1 in 20: p < 0.05)

the situation similar to that at the Diaconessen hospital. On the other hand, the Diaconessen hospital now scores significantly better on the aspects of physical and psychological effort, work organisation, work pace and autonomy.

It should be noted, however, that the Diaconessen hospital has also pursued an active occupational safety and absenteeism policy in recent years. Accordingly, the Diaconessen hospital is not a 'typical' control hospital. It is impossible to expect a hospital to not take measures in this area for a period of four years, the duration of this model project.

Another point is that the Waterland hospital has thus far taken measures of a more general nature, such as the development of the working conditions policy, formulation and implementation of procedures in the area of socio-medical guidance, and training programmes for supervisory personnel. Most of the more specific measures that may influence the aspects of work studied still need to be implemented, or have thus far only been implemented on a small scale, for example as part of the 'work pressure' and 'physical load' projects. Effects on these aspects of work can, in fact, only be expected in the long term.

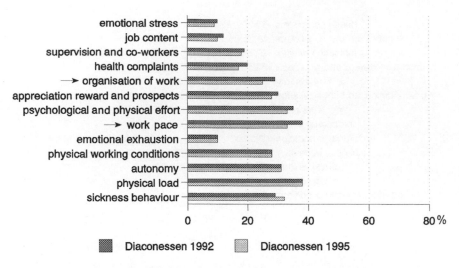

Figure 5.3 The results of the Diaconessen hospital in the pre-assessment (1992: n = 455) and the post-assessment (1995: n = 382), expressed as the average percentage of complaints per aspect.

Note: An arrow before a certain score signifies a significant difference in relation to the pre-assessment in 1992 (which means the probability that the differences found are based on coincidence is less than 1 in 20: p < 0.05)

More attention to sick employees and working conditions

Figure 5.4 provides employees' answers to the question of what improvements have resulted from activities concerning 'Healthy Working for Health' (no questions were asked related to deterioration).

The main results were improvement in dealing with sick employees (50 per cent) and working conditions in the hospital (45 per cent). In addition, 40 per cent of the employees thought that people were more involved in improving the work situation, and 37 per cent held the view that the atmosphere at work had improved. More than one-third saw an improvement in dealing with healthy employees and an improvement in the quality of care provided.

Furthermore, one-third of the employees replied that the activities made a positive contribution to health, well-being and job motivation. Activities as part of the project have only had a limited influence on employees' way of life. This is not surprising, as measures in this area have not yet been implemented.

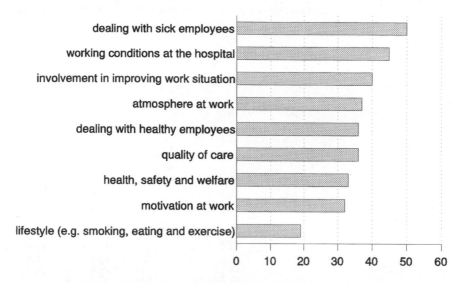

Figure 5.4 Employee opinions (in percentages) on the benefits of the 'Healthy Working for Health' project (post-assessment, Waterland, n = 612). All aspects indicate an 'improvement in/by'.

Working conditions and absenteeism as part of personnel policy

The project has provided a solid basis for more structured activities in the field of working conditions and absenteeism. As a result of the project, attention to working conditions and absenteeism is now an integral part of personnel policy. Sick employees resume work sooner because direct superiors are now personally responsible for the supervision of sick employees. Since the establishment of a Socio-medical Team (SMT), it is easier to talk about possibilities for modifying the work place.

Reduction in absenteeism

Table 5.8 provides an overview of the absenteeism data (excluding maternity leave) for the Waterland hospital, other control hospital and other Dutch hospitals (excluding university hospitals) for the period 1991–1995.

At the start of the project, the absenteeism percentage at the Waterland hospital was higher compared to the control hospital and to the sector in general. Both differences are significant. In 1991, the absenteeism percentage at the Waterland hospital started to fall rapidly, particularly between 1991 and 1992. There was a slight rise in 1993, probably due to two influenza epidemics in that year, which also explains the higher figure in the sector. In 1994, the sick leave percentage was close to the figure for the sector.

Table 5.8 Sickness absenteeism percentages in Waterland hospital, control group and Dutch hospitals (1991–1995) (excluding pregnancy and maternity leave)

Sickness Absenteeism	1991	1992	1993	1994	1995
Lost days per year (as percentage of calendar days)					
Waterland hospital	8.9	6.5	6.7	5.8	4.0
Control hospital	7.1	6.5	6.3	4.9	5.4
Dutch hospitals	6.5	5.5	5.8	5.3	6.6
Frequency per year (rate of sick reports)					
Waterland hospital	2.4	1.7	1.8	1.5	1.3
Control hospital	2.2	2.2	2.2	1.7	1.9
Dutch hospitals	1.9	1.7	1.9	1.5	1.5
Average duration per year (days)					
Waterland hospital	—	13.5	14.2	13.7	13.0
Control hospital	11.6	10.6	9.1	10.6	9.8
Dutch hospitals	11.4	12.1	11.4	12.8	15.1

Key: — = no data available

Source: Dutch Hospitals: BVG (1996)

In addition, the frequency of employees calling in sick decreased, while the average duration of absenteeism stabilised. These last two factors indicate that absenteeism in general – short, medium and long term – decreased. It should, however, be noted that the figures for the sector were possibly somewhat low in 1994 due to under-reporting of sick leave as a result of an amendment to the Sickness Benefit Act of 1 January 1994. In other words, the actual difference between absenteeism at the Waterland hospital and the sector could well be smaller in 1994.

The figures for 1995 show a further decrease of absenteeism for the Waterland hospital, even falling below the level of the control hospital and the sector. The 1995 difference between the Waterland hospital and the sector is significant. The development with respect to the absenteeism percentage at the Waterland hospital, the Diaconessen hospital, and the Dutch hospitals is depicted in Figure 5.5.

Cultural swing

As a result of the project and the many measures taken, many employees are under the impression that a great deal is possible at the Waterland hospital. Employees are more critical of their work situation and have less of a wait-and-see attitude when it comes to bringing about improvements, especially in departments where specific measures have already been taken. In general,

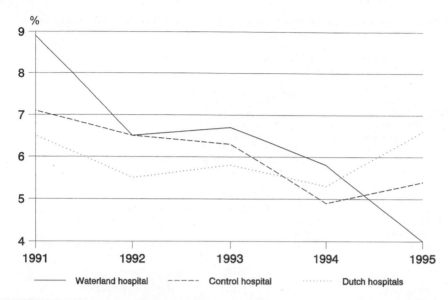

Figure 5.5 Absenteeism percentage at the Waterland hospital, the control hospital
and Dutch hospitals (excluding teaching hospitals), 1991–1995

Source: BVG

the project has made employees more aware of what is going on in the
various departments of the hospital, which has led to a better understanding
of each other and a more pleasant atmosphere.

Costs and benefits

Table 5.9 provides a general overview of the costs and benefits of the 'Healthy
Working for Health' project. The costs have been divided into three categories,
namely technical measures, courses/training programmes and organisational
measures. Most of the technical measures concern fairly small investments
debited to the year in which they are made. Investments exceeding
NLG 5,000, which include the pharmacy doors, the CTG unit and the lift, are
written down over ten years. Three-tenths of the investments (1992–1994) are
listed in the table. No account is taken of the time value of money, which
means that the interest rate is not considered when calculating these amounts.

The 'courses/training programmes' cost item comprises 50 per cent of the
total costs. This includes programmes dealing with aggression, sick leave interviews and stress management. In addition to the costs of hiring external
training institutes, the cost of time spent by all the employees taking part in
such courses/programmes (time multiplied by average salary) is included.
Although this cost item was debited to the years 1992–1994, the 'benefits'

Table 5.9 Overview of costs and benefits of the 'Healthy Working for Health'
project (1992–1994)

Costs of measures in 1992–1994 (in Dutch guilders) (total write-down period is parenthesised)		Benefits in 1992–1994 (in Dutch guilders)	
Technical measures.		Proceeds from reduction of	
Patient toilet modifications	2,000	absenteeism: gross estimate (not adjusted for decrease in the sector):	
Automatic doors in pharmacy		Absenteeism in 1991 = 8.9% (costs: 3,026,000)	
(10 years)	3,000	Reduction in absenteeism in 1992:	
Trolley for file transport	2,000	$8.9\% - 6.5\% = 2.4 \times 340{,}000$	816,000
File boxes with handles	300	Reduction in absenteeism in 1993: $8.9\% - 6.7\% = 2.2 \times 340{,}000$	748,000
CTG unit (10 years)	30,000	Reduction in absenteeism in 1994:	
Lift (10 years)	1,800	$8.9\% - 5.8\% = 3.1 \times 340{,}000$	1,054,000
Electronic stop devices	5,000		
		Gross total	**2,618,000**
Modification of work places with computer screens	2,700	Net estimate (adjusted for decrease in the sector) Reduction in absenteeism in 1992: 2.4 – 1.0 (decrease in sector) = $1.4 \times 340{,}000$	476,000
Courses and training programmes		Reduction in absenteeism in 1993: 2.2 – 0.7 (decrease in	
How to deal with criticism		sector) = $1.5 \times 340{,}000$	510,000
Performance reviews		Reduction in absenteeism in 1994: 3.1	
Absenteeism policy		– 1.2 (decrease in	
Management		sector) = $1.9 \times 340{,}000$	646,000
Stress management			
How to deal with aggression and violence			
Total:	579,330		
Organisational measures Once-only:			
•Specifying tasks			
•Establishing consultative structures			
Total of once-only costs:	79,155		
Annually recurring (× 3 years):			
•Environmental/ occupational safety and health tasks			
•Participation in consultations			
•Sick leave inspection			
Total annually recurring costs:	466,440		
Total	**1,171,725**	**Net total**	**1,632,000**

of those courses and programmes are expected to be still perceptible in the years to come. The current benefits cannot be more specifically quantified and have therefore not been included in the table.

The 'organisational measures' costs item accounts for 46 per cent of the total costs. As in the case of courses/training programmes, the costs are mainly caused by the time spent by the employees involved. They are split into once-only and recurrent costs. Once-only costs involve costs such as setting up consultative structures and specifying tasks. The recurrent costs include the salary of the occupational health and safety officer and participation in consultations. The recurrent costs are entered on the balance sheet for three years (annual amount multiplied by three).

The benefits side of the table only includes the cost savings achieved due to reduction of absenteeism. The absenteeism and concomitant costs for 1991 are taken as the baseline situation. In 1991, the absenteeism percentage was 8.9 per cent. Each per cent of absenteeism reduction over the years 1992–1994 resulted in a saving of NLG 340,000 (assuming that the costs of 1 per cent sick leave equal 1 per cent of the total gross salary, which totalled NLG 34 million in 1991). No account is taken of benefits such as improved working atmosphere or increased productivity.

Two approaches were then chosen. The first was to calculate the difference between the costs and benefits for 1992–1994, which results in a positive result of NLG 1.4 million. The second approach takes account of the decreasing absenteeism percentage in the sector (Dutch hospitals; source BVG). If an adjustment is made for that, the benefits total NLG 1,632,000. In other words, the difference between the costs and benefits is still positive at NLG 460,275 (it should be noted that the costs side has not been adjusted for the investments usually made in the sector). In both cases, there is a positive result. Furthermore, the measures are expected to bear more fruit in the coming years, possibly resulting in an even more positive result.

5.7.2 Lessons

Negative factors

Although all parties in the hospital were supposed to participate in the project, this proved difficult to realise. Interviews with some of the steering committee members demonstrated that middle management felt insufficiently involved in the project and the activities aimed at cutting absenteeism. The presence of the steering committee was even used as an excuse by them for not being actively involved with absenteeism.

It was also difficult to actively involve operational personnel in the steering committee's activities. In retrospect, the appointment of operational personnel to the steering committee proved problematic. There was a major difference in knowledge and skills between the various steering committee members.

Operational personnel were often insufficiently equipped to actively participate in steering committee discussions, which frequently gave them the
impression of 'being unable to keep up'. The management team representatives, on the other hand, often had extensive background information on the
topics to be discussed, which is why they often felt that steering committee
meetings were progressing slowly.

Another problem was the steering committee's mandate. Although the
management team was represented in the steering committee by three people,
the steering committee was not in a position to make autonomous decisions.
Such decisions were made by the management team on the basis of memos
from the steering committee. Especially at the start of the project, these documents were often sent back to the steering committee for additions or revision,
which slowed down the project's progress. This method was changed during
the project, and the management team switched to testing only the main
outlines of proposed decisions after which they were worked out in further
detail by the steering committee.

Finally, the long period between problem analysis (pre-assessment) and
actual implementation of measures (more than a year) proved a major impedi-
ment for maintaining support for the project. Once data from the pre-
assessment were known, it proved difficult to determine when something
was a problem and when it was not. The steering committee set a relatively
arbitrary limit of 20 per cent, which means that an item from the questionnaire is considered a problem if complaints are received from at least 20 per
cent of the respondents. The committee subsequently discussed criteria for
setting priorities in great detail. Ultimately, it decided to address all the problems. The order in which this was done was primarily determined by the
degree to which the problems and possible solutions are clear and whether
there was sufficient manpower to carry out the activities. The result of this
method was that it took a long time before employees had any feedback on
the project after the survey had been taken. This caused them to be rather
sceptical about the project's progress.

Positive factors

TNO's request to the hospital to take part in the model project came at the
right time, as there was sufficient consensus to act on absenteeism and the
hospital had just begun to organise a structure within which a project such
as this one could be carried out. This enabled the hospital to meet the
requirements set by TNO's clients (ministries, disablement funds), while at
the same time optimum use could be made of the support which was provided
as part of the study.

The systematic approach was very important in directing structured attention at the reduction of absenteeism. The hospital used the 'kick-off' meeting
to inform its personnel that it was going to take serious action to reduce

absenteeism. The meetings with key figures at the beginning of the project soon provided an impression of the problems at the hospital. The survey further quantified this picture, both in terms of risk factors and risk groups. The survey also had a legitimising effect with respect to the problems to be dealt with, since it provided every employee with the opportunity to give his/her opinion on the work situation. The survey also provided information on more delicate subjects, such as managerial style, support from co-workers and matters such as discrimination and sexual harassment.

The socio-medical guidance course enhanced the supervisory personnel's involvement in the reduction of absenteeism. It is expected that, in the future when supervisory staff become responsible for absenteeism in their department, their level of involvement will increase.

Involving employees in sub-projects has proved to be very important for acquiring support for improvements and actually implementing measures. Employees who are directly involved are indispensable for conceiving solutions, as they face the problems identified on a daily basis and, eventually, have to work in the improved situation. From the start of the 'physical load' project, for example, employees were closely involved in carefully defining problems and the choice and implementation of solutions. This style of approach was greatly appreciated by those involved.

The kick-off meeting, subsequent departmental meetings and the theme day have also proved to be excellent means to involve employees (more intensively) in the project. The kick-off meeting and departmental meetings produced support for the project. During the theme day, a few months before the evaluation, the hospital was informed in detail of all activities of the steering committee and occupational health and safety committee. Many employees were keen to tell what had taken place in their department and what they had achieved.

The project's spin-off effect was also considerable. During the project, uniforms were replaced and nurses were given the opportunity to wear trousers, a new reward system will be introduced (propagating a tit-for-tat policy in a positive and negative sense), and a liaison was appointed for sexual harassment. These matters might also have been introduced without the project, but not as quickly.

Table 5.10 provides a brief overview of the main positive and negative factors in the project.

If the hospital were to repeat the project

If the hospital were to start reducing absenteeism again, it would approach several matters differently. It would again choose a systematic approach, but not necessarily in the form of a project (although that does provide the best preconditions for such an approach). A smaller steering committee would be established, which would only assist in determining the activities and assigning

Table 5.10 Negative and positive factors in the 'Healthy Working for Health' project

Negative factors	Positive factors
Little involvement of middle management in the project and activities to reduce absenteeism.	Sufficient commitment in the hospital to counteract absenteeism.
Many different levels of expertise in the steering committee, making it too big and not decisive enough.	Setting up a project to structurally reduce absenteeism.
	Quantification of risk factors and groups by means of a survey.
Lack of clarity on the mandate of the steering committee members who are also members of the management team.	Absenteeism supervision course for supervisory staff.
	Involving employees in the implementation of sub-projects.
Too much time between problem analysis and implementation of measures.	Organising theme day for all employees on occupational safety and health.
Lack of clarity on when something is a problem and how to further prioritise measures.	The project accelerated the introduction of certain measures (spin-off effect).
Insufficient level of employee involvement in the project.	

responsibilities for the various parts. From the beginning, supervisors would be made responsible for reducing absenteeism in their departments and be judged on the results of their actions. This would increase their level of involvement in the problem. The personnel affairs and training department would fulfil a supportive and co-ordinative role in this, enabling the various departments to benefit from each other's experiences. This department could also provide supervisors with the necessary absenteeism information. Employees would be kept better informed, for example by linking the results of the survey to absenteeism data and discussing them during work consultations. External expertise would again be used for certain matters, because the organisation itself does not have all the necessary specific knowledge and expertise.

5.8   Follow-up

All in all, the project can be called a success. It has made an important contribution to a systematic reduction in absenteeism. Furthermore, since a number of measures have yet to be implemented, a further decrease in absenteeism can be expected in the near future. This forecast is confirmed by the 1995 absenteeism figures.

The project was officially completed in 1995. The hospital will, however, continue along its chosen path and pay more attention to employees' health and the reduction of absenteeism in the coming years. Assisted by the occupational health and safety committee (which will take over the steering committee's task) and committee for safety, health and well-being, the management team will retain a co-ordinating task in improving working conditions and reducing absenteeism. Supervisors will play an increasingly important role in the actual improvement of working conditions and controlling absenteeism. They do not stand alone in this, but can count on active assistance from various parties inside and outside the hospital, such as the occupational health and safety committee, occupational health and safety officer, physical load adviser, personnel affairs department, company doctor, Occupational Health Service with which the hospital recently became affiliated, and possibly other experts.

Bibliography

BVG-Jaarverslag (1991–95) (BVG Annual Report 1991–95), Zeist: BVG.
——(1996) (BVG Annual Report 1996), Zeist: BVG.
CBS (Central Bureau for Statistics) (1978, 1981, 1984, 1987) *LeefSituatie Onderzoek* ('Life Conditions Survey') 1977, 1980, 1983, 1986: *Kerncijfers* ('Core Figures'), *1977, 1980, 1983, 1986*, Heerlen: CBS.
——(1990–97) *Doorlopend Leefsituatie Onderzoek (1989–1995): Kerncijfers*, ('Continuing Life Conditions Survey 1989–95: Core figures'), Heerlen: CBS.
CTSV (Central Surveillance of the Social Insurances) (1996) *Stand van ziekteverzuim en arbeidsongeschiktheid* ('Absence and disability for work'), vierde kwartaal, Zoetermeer: CTSV.
Gründemann, R.W.M., Nijboer, I.D. and Schellart, A.J.M. (1991) *Arbeidsgebondenheid van WAO-intrede. Deelrapport I: resultaten van de enquête onder WAO-ers* ('Work-relatedness of disability: Report I: Results from the survey on disabled employees'), Den Haag: SDU.
Gründemann, R.W.M. and Schellart, A.J.M. (1993) *Arbeidsgebondenheid van WAO-intrede. Deelrapport 3: Enquête en dossier vergeleken* ('Work-relatedness of disability: Report III: Survey and file compared'), Den Haag: SDU.
Gründemann, R.W.M., Lourijsen, E.C.M.P. and Kompier, M.A.J. (1992) *Voorbeeldproject Gezond Werken aan Gezondheid. Vragenlijst ten behoeve van stap 2* ('Demonstration project Healthy Working for Health'), Leiden: TNO-PG.
Houtman, I.L.D. (ed.) (1997) *Trends in arbeid en gezondheid 1996* ('Trends in work and health 1996'), Amsterdam: NIA TNO.
Houtman, I.L.D., Smulders, P.G.W., Bloemhoff, A. and Kompier, M.A.J. (1994) Bedrijfs- en beroepsgebonden werkstress-risico's en ontwikkelingen hiervan in de tijd ('Risks for work stress by branch and occupation, and developments in time'), *Tijdschrift voor Sociale Gezondheidzorg*, 72 (3): 128–38.
Kompier, M.A.J. and Marcelissen, F.H.G. (1990) *Handboek Werkstress* ('Handbook of Work Stress'), Amsterdam: NIA.
Kompier, M., De Gier, E., Smulders, P. and Draaisma, D. (1994) Regulations, policies

and practices concerning work stress in five European countries, *Work and Stress*, 8 (4): 296–318.

Kompier, M.A.J., Gründemann, R.W.M., Vink, P. and Smulders P.G.W. (1996) *Aan de slag! Tien praktijkvoorbeelden van succesvol verzuimmanagement* ('Now to work! Ten examples of the successful reduction of sickness absenteeism'), Alphen a/d Rijn: Samson.

Koningsveld, E.A.P. and Mossink, J. (1997) *Kerncijfers maatschappelijke kosten van arbeidsomstandigheden* ('Core figures on societal costs of working conditions'), Den Haag: VUGA.

Oversloot. J.S., De Winter, C.R. and Schlatmann, M.J.T. (1987) *Werknemers in de intramurale gezondheidszorg over hun arbeid en gezondheid* ('Employees in inpatient health care about their work and health'), Den Haag: Ministerie van Sociale Zaken en Werkgelegenheid.

Paoli, P. (1992) *First European Survey on the Work Environment 1991–1992*, Dublin: European Foundation for the Improvement of Living and Working Conditions.

——(1997) *Second European Survey on the Work Environment 1995*, Dublin: European Foundation for the Improvement of Living and Working Conditions.

Smulders, P.G.W. (1990) De arbeidssituatie van twaalf beroepsgroepen in de intramurale gezondheidszorg ('The work situation of twelve occupational groups in the inpatient health care'), *Tijdschrift voor Sociale Gezondheidszorg*, 68, 247–55.

Vaas, S., Dhondt, S. and Peeters, M.H.H. (1995) *De WEBA-methode. Deel 1 WEBA-analyse handleiding* ('Manual Well-being at work'), Alphen aan den Rijn/Zaventem: Samsom BedrijfsInformatie.

Van der Beek A.J., Frings-Dresen, M., Van Dijk, F.J.H., Houtman, I.L.D. and Fortuin, R.J. (1996) *Arbo-risicobeheersing en sociaal-medische begeleiding* ('Work risk control and socio-medical counselling'), Den Haag: RGO.

Van Engers, R.W. (1995) *Overspannen in de Ziektewet; een onderzoek naar de oorzaken en het verloop van ziekteverzuim wegens overspanning,* ('Overstrain and absenteeism: Determinants and course of absence'), Amsterdam: Gemeenschappelijk Administratiekantoor (GAK).

Chapter 6

Belgium: A pharmaceutical company

Steven Poelmans, Theo Compernolle,
Hubert De Neve, Marc Buelens and
Jef Rombouts

6.1 Introduction: Work stress in Belgium

6.1.1 Stress as a policy issue

At the time of the case study (1993–1994) presented in this chapter, Belgium had no legal enforcement focusing on the psycho-social health risks at the workplace. However, since the Belgian Minister for Labour and Employment took office in 1991, it was clear that stress in the workplace was to be one of her policy priorities. Several studies were carried out by the Belgian government in order to collect data on this matter.

A study on the causes of long-term absence from work (i.e. longer than one month), based on an analysis of the files of the National Health Service (Swinnen *et al.*, 1994), showed that psycho-social stress is the fourth cause of absenteeism (10 per cent), after musculoskeletal problems (28 per cent), accidents (17 per cent) and infectious diseases (12 per cent). Taking stress-related disorders, such as ulcers, asthma, migraine or back problems into account as well, adds an extra 25 per cent to the 10 per cent. The authors concluded that stress is at least partially responsible for long-term absenteeism in one-third of the cases. Only taking into account the 10 per cent, this entails a yearly disability insurance cost of 10 billion Belgian Francs (i.e. US$366 million) for the Belgian state, treatment costs and organisational costs not included.

During the Belgian chairmanship of the European Social Council (1993), the Minister for Labour and Employment, Miet Smet, organised an international conference on stress at work, in collaboration with the European Foundation for the Improvement of Living and Working Conditions. This was the situation at the time of this case study.

In October 1995 the Minister for Labour and Employment organised another national conference on stress at work, in which the results of further studies were presented. One study was an inventory of initiatives and experiences in stress management in Belgium (Compernolle and Poelmans, 1996). The purpose of the study was to find out to what extent Belgian employers prevented or managed stress, and what their motivations were. The authors collected in-depth data from ten companies and surveyed a sample of 644 personnel managers of the biggest Belgian companies (those with more than fifty employees). This represented a response percentage of 13 per cent. The ten case studies, one of them the case study in this chapter, provide useful information on the process of stress management. The most important results were that 66 per cent of the sample experience stress as a moderate to very important problem in their organisation, whereas 25 per cent took stress-related initiatives, most frequently elicited by individual problems or department crises. For 47 per cent of the personnel managers the reduction of absenteeism is the most important motivation to manage stress in the future. The respondents indicated several positions should be involved in corporate stress management: the personnel manager (66 per cent), the depart-ment manager or supervisor (52 per cent), the Central Executive Officer (CEO) (52 per cent), the medical officer (50 per cent), and members of the committee for safety and health (42 per cent). This indicates the importance of a multidisciplinary approach of stress management. A large number of the respondents were interested in more information (68 per cent) and learning from experiences of other organisations (59 per cent). At the same conference the Minister announced the start of the Ponos Stress Research Centre at De Vlerick School voor Management at the University of Ghent and introduced the Belgian version of the European directive.

At the time of writing the first normative data for Belgium will soon be available from the BELSTRESS survey, a European longitudinal prospective research project, which studies the relationship between perceived job stress measured using the Karasek model: psychological demands, decision latitude and social support (Karasek and Theorell, 1990), and coronary heart disease and absenteeism (Coetsier *et al.*, 1996).

6.1.2 Legal framework in Belgium

On the 4 August 1996 the law concerning the 'Well-being of Employees during the Execution of their Work' came into effect (Belgisch Staatsblad/Moniteur Belge 18/09/1996). This law is based on the European directive that offers a framework for health and safety in the workplace (89/391/EEC). Article 5 of the Belgian law is very similar to article 6 of the European directive. It states:

> The employer takes the necessary measures to promote the well-being of the employees in the execution of their work. The employer applies the general principles of prevention:
> (a) preventing risks, (b) evaluating the risks which cannot be avoided, (c) combating the risks at source, (d) replacing what is dangerous by what is not dangerous or less dangerous, (e) giving priority to measures aimed at

collective protection rather than individual protection, (f) adapting work to the individual, especially with regard to the design of the workplaces, the choice of work equipment and the choice of working and production methods, with a view, in particular, to making monotonous work and work at a predetermined work rate more tolerable and to reducing their effect on health, (g) limiting risks as much as possible, taking into account technical developments, (h) limiting risks of serious injuries by taking priority material measures, (i) planning prevention and implementation of an employee well-being policy, with a view to a system approach in which the following elements are integrated: technique, organisation of work, working conditions, social relations and environmental factors, (j) informing the employee about the nature of his job, the job-related risks and the measures that aim to prevent or reduce the risks.

An important difference with the European framework directive is the obligation for every employer to promote well-being in the workplace. Another difference with other European legislation is that the Belgian legislator defined well-being at work in a broad sense: it includes safety and health at work, psycho-social stress, ergonomics, hygiene, work environment and the influence of the work environment on working conditions. This means that employers are now not only held responsible for health and safety, but also for psycho-social stress caused by work.

Hence, Belgium joins the European countries that have translated the European directive into a national law. However, Sweden and the Netherlands are the only two countries to have added specific stress prevention directives to their law on working conditions (Kompier et al., 1994; Kwantes and Hoogendijk, 1994). This legal framework is important. Kompier et al. (1994) demonstrated that only in the European countries which have such a statutory framework are corporate initiatives taken to prevent stress. According to information from the Belgian Ministry of Labour (Van Hamme, 1997), in Belgium too, a Royal Decree will soon be implemented, specifying all aspects of risk inventory of psycho-social stress. This Royal Decree was adapted, taking into account different remarks of the social partners. The most important adaptations were:

- The goal of the Royal Decree is explicitly described as 'dealing with the negative consequences of stress by approaching the different aspects the employer controls'.
- An integrative approach was emphasised by considering stress as one of the possible risk factors in the workplace that can threaten the health of the employee and that have to be dealt with in the course of the risk analysis the employer is obliged to undertake.
- A list of attention points attached to the text was rewritten to match the Karasek-model.

6.2   Introduction to Janssen Pharmaceutica

Janssen Pharmaceutica (J.P.) was founded in 1953, when Dr Paul Janssen began drugs research at the family business run by his parents in Flanders. Since then the company has become a leading international pharmaceutical enterprise. J.P. has affiliated companies in forty-three countries employing more than 16,000 people worldwide. Janssen's medical and scientific research activities are centralised in the Janssen Research Foundation. In Europe, and in many parts of the world, Janssen research products are distributed by Janssen-Cilag. In 1961 Janssen became a wholly owned subsidiary of Johnson and Johnson, the largest pharmaceutical company in the world. In Belgium more than 1,100 of the 3,240 Janssen employees are involved in the research and development of new drugs for people, animals, crops and plants. J.P. is active in various branches of medicine, including psychiatry, anaesthesia, gastroenterology, mycology, parasitology, immunology, allergy, oncology, virology and cardiovascular disease. Drugs developed by Janssen include among others Fentanyl ®, Risperdal ®, Prepulsid ®, Motilium ®, Imodium ®, Sporanox ® and Nizoral ®. About 14 per cent of Janssen's annual turnover is placed back into research and development. This substantial investment is essential, as the average cost of developing a new drug has increased dramatically in recent years. The cost for the development of a new drug is estimated at 500 million US dollars. In addition to its research activities, Janssen conducts the chemical and pharmaceutical production and international marketing of its own drugs. Locally, the pharmaceutical production is concentrated in Beerse, while chemical production is carried out at nearby Geel, where 352 employees prepare the basic ingredients of Janssen products in three chemical plants. This paper focuses on the Belgian plants and offices in Beerse, Geel and Olen where – at the time of the study – about 3,261 people worked. Figure 6.1 presents the organigram of Janssen Pharmaceutica.

Recently a pharmaceutical plant was built in Beerse for the production of liquid formulations. To satisfy needs for extra capacity in the chemical production sector, a new chemical plant was built at Geel that also started production in 1996.

6.3   Motives, signals and project organisation

At the time of the case study, in 1993, J.P. was going through an important period of change. For the first time in its history, the company was forced to freeze its budgets and recruiting efforts because of an unprecedented stabilisation in the growth of the pharmaceutical sector. At the same time, the employees were experiencing fundamental changes. The high standards imposed by the Food and Drug Administration and Boards for Animal Protection, created continuing pressure. Several re-engineering projects in the process control activities had created feelings of uncertainty. The appointment

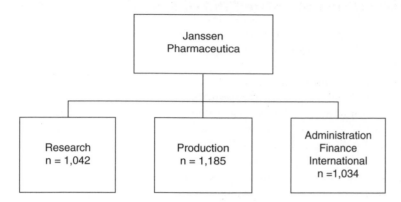

Figure 6.1 Organisation chart of Janssen Pharmaceutica (Plants at Beerse, Geel and Olen)

of several top executives, recruited from competing companies for the pharmaceutical, quality and chemical production departments, changed leadership and management styles. The company evolved from a hierarchic to a matrix organisation. The changes were drastic and because the employees had no influence on most changes they caused insecurity and feelings of loss of control.

At that time J.P. had already been running an employee assistance programme for many years, highlighting such topics as smoking, Aids, hepatitis and other risks. Several years before J.P. carried out a non-smoking programme. In a survey following this programme 70 per cent of the employees asked for measures to be taken against stress, and the unions and the works council considered stress an important enough topic to recommend doing something about it. This was the first signal for the company to manage stress in a more explicit way. The professional organisation of the company managers organised lectures on the subject which were given by one of the co-authors, of this chapter, Theo Compernolle. The company planned a stress management programme to provide a general support network, but ultimately the subject was considered too 'personal' and had to give way to more important business priorities.

In this period of change, the medical officer and his team observed several signals indicating that the level of organisational stress was reaching alarming levels. Several individuals dropped out with severe mental health problems. When the medical officer reported his findings to the human resources manager, he was met with a low-key reception because 'social elections' were coming up. In Belgium, companies with one hundred employees or more have a works council, consisting of employee and employer representatives. Companies with fifty or more employees have a committee for health and safety, consisting of employee representatives. Every four years, when the 'social elections' take place, these employee representatives are elected from a list compiled by the trade unions. In the elections the role of the trade unions is paramount. Giving special attention to organisational stress problems seemed like opening Pandora's box. Eventually, convinced of the seriousness of the situation, the medical officer reported his concern to the CEO, who acknowledged the problem, but requested more data to support a decision. The main questions were:

1   What are the stress levels of our company?
2   Is this level higher compared to others?
3   Where exactly can the problem be located?
4   What can be done about this problem?

No such data existed. The only information available was on individual cases of stress. Therefore a company-wide survey was organised.

6.4   Analysis: Risk factors and risk groups

The definition of stress throughout the survey was: 'The perception of dysfunctioning in the work situation, which is experienced as a threat', for instance the threat of losing one's position in the company. Different expressions of this perception of threat are: state anxiety, psychosomatic complaints and a negative perception of work, such as adverse working conditions, lack of job satisfaction, poor social relationships and adverse terms of employment.

6.4.1   Method

A stratified sample of 324 employees was selected, controlling for six selection criteria: gender, age, department (operations/research/general), hierarchical level and seniority (see Table 6.1).

They were invited by the medical officer who guaranteed anonymity and discretion. The respondents could choose one of three possible dates to fill in a questionnaire collectively in a company auditorium. Respondents who could not attend any of the sessions, were replaced by a randomly chosen respondent meeting the same requirements. The nine-page survey consisted of five parts and seventy-two items. The five parts related to personal data, experience of stress, psychosomatic complaints, work, and a previously organised non-smoking programme. Within every scale inter-item correlations were calculated as well as item-test correlations. All items with $r_{it} < 0.30$ (item-total correlation) were removed.

Table 6.1 Distribution of the sample over the different strata

	Total population	Sample
Seniority:		
< 5 years	963	81
5–15 years	1,334	143
> 15 years	964	99
Department:		
Administration/Finance/International	1,034	96
Production	1,185	117
Research	1,042	108
Hierarchical level:		
Blue collar	445	47
White collar	1,963	195
Management and professionals	739	66
Senior management	104	15
Gender:		
Male	2,125	210
Female	1,136	113
Age:		
≤ 30 years	1,010	94
31–45 years	1,648	168
≥ 46 years	609	61
Total	3,261	324

Questionnaire

The questionnaire consisted of five parts.

I PERSONAL DATA

- Seniority: < 5 years/5–15 years/> 15 years. In this context we will use the term 'seniority' to indicate the number of years of employment in the company. By senior employees we mean the employees who have been employed for a longer time in the company.
- Department: production/research/general, financial and international services
- Hierarchical level: blue collar/white collar/management and professionals/senior management
- Gender: male/female
- Age: ≤ 30 years/31–45/≥ 46

2 EXPERIENCE OF STRESS

Stress levels were assessed using the 'Zelfbeoordelingsvragenlijst' method, a Dutch adaptation of the State Trait Anxiety Inventory (STAI), which has the population of the Dutch town of Leiden as reference group (Spielberger,

1983; Van der Ploeg, 1979). The STAI measures the state of anxiety and uncertainty or the 'tendency of people to react to psychological stress with different levels of intensity'. The survey consists of twenty statements (for example, 'I feel nervous'), which are evaluated on a scale of one to four, (1 = 'not at all', to 4 = 'a lot'). This results in a minimum score of 20 and a maximum score of 80, with a high score indicating that the subject experiences more stress. Cronbach's alpha for this scale was 0.94.

3   PSYCHOSOMATIC COMPLAINTS

This section, drawn up by Janssen's health department, identified fifteen psychosomatic complaints, such as hand tremors, stomach-ache, headache, sleeping disturbances, and so forth. These statements were scored on the same four-point scale. An item was considered a complaint if the score was three (quite a lot) or four (a lot). The score is the number of complaints. This results in a minimum score of zero and a maximum score of fifteen, with a high score indicating more psychosomatic complaints. Cronbach's alpha for this scale was 0.82.

4   WORK

The training manager of J.P. selected these questions from several questionnaires. The respondents had to answer four subscales. In total there were thirty items, ranging from one ('almost never') to four ('almost always'), alternatively referring to positive (for example, 'I can interrupt work when this is necessary for me') or negative working conditions (for example, 'My work consists of physically hard labour'). These statements referred to a subscale of working conditions (six items, for example, noise, ergonomics, breaks), a subscale of job content (ten items, e.g. control, expectations, time constraints), a subscale social relationships at work (nine items, for example, group atmosphere, support of line manager, trust) and a subscale terms of employment (five items, for example, training, overtime, salary, job security). For the subscales 'working conditions' and 'job insecurity' a higher score indicates less favourable conditions. A higher score for 'job content', 'social relationships' and 'terms of employment' means more favourable conditions. The alpha's of the different subscales were 0.66 (working conditions), 0.77 (job content), 0.91 (social relationships) and 0.42 (terms of employment). The latter alpha was low because of a low variation: the majority of the sample described the terms of employment as good.

5   NON-SMOKING PROGRAMME

In this last section, respondents were asked to describe their smoking behaviour, evaluate the quality and their participation in the non-smoking programme at J.P., and to indicate whether they had stopped smoking and why (not). There were twenty-six items, most of them were multiple-choice (three answering alternatives), except for some open questions.

6.4.2   Results

The Department of Psychology of the University of Leuven analysed the surveys. A special task force, consisting of the medical officer, the social worker, the training manager and his assistant, interpreted the data.

1   DESCRIPTION OF SAMPLE

Detailed information on the composition of the work force in J.P. and on the composition of the sample can be seen in Table 6.1 (p. 127).

2   EXPERIENCE OF STRESS

Compared to the norm of the Dutch STAI, the stress-level in J.P. was moderately higher. Both in men and women, the average scores of the Janssen population were higher than the average scores of the population of Leiden. Compared with the norm data (deciles), relatively few of the Janssen employees had a low experience of stress, 25 per cent had a score that corresponded with decile nine or ten- a score that indicates stress with a negative impact- and one in three employees fell within decile 6–7, a risk group that had a tendency to dysfunctioning.

Significant differences in stress-levels were found between different seniority groups, and age groups, with older (> 45 years) and senior (> 15 years) employees experiencing higher stress-levels. No differences were found between different departments, hierarchical levels and sexes (see Appendix Table 1).

3   PSYCHOSOMATIC COMPLAINTS

The most important health complaints were headache (19 per cent), backache (18 per cent), pain in neck and shoulders (18 per cent) and sleeping disturbances (16 per cent) (see Table 6.2).

About 15 per cent of the Janssen sample experienced four or more health complaints. Significant differences in psychosomatic complaints were found, with female and senior (> 5 years) employees experiencing more health complaints than male and junior employees. No significant differences were found between departments, ages and hierarchical levels (see Appendix Table 2).

The Janssen task force considered specific groups as risk groups when 25 per cent or more of the respondents within that group reported four or more psychosomatic health complaints. They identified two risk groups (see Table 6.3):

Table 6.2 Psychosomatic complaints (%)

Complaint	Percentage
Headache	19
Backache	18
Neck and shoulder ache	18
Sleeping disturbances	16
Lack of energy	11
Stomach-ache	10
Oppressed feeling	10
Stool problems	9
Clammy hands	8
Dizziness	7
Shaking hands	6
Heart palpitations	5
Nausea	4
Difficulty in breathing	3
Lack of appetite	2

- Male, senior (> 15 years), no management responsibilities.
- Female, intermediate seniority (5–15 years), no management responsibilities.

4 WORK: WORKING CONDITIONS, TERMS OF EMPLOYMENT, RELATIONSHIPS AND JOB CONTENT

In general the Janssen employees scored positive on (content) satisfaction, working conditions and interpersonal relationships which had a negative correlation with the experience of stress. No relationship was found between the experience of stress and terms of employment, such as training, overtime, salary and job security.

- Production workers and lower level workers experienced less favourable working conditions than workers in the other departments and of a higher level. No significant differences were found between different seniority levels, ages and sexes (see Appendix, Table 3).
- Production workers and lower level workers experienced their job content as less interesting than their colleagues in other departments and at higher levels. No significant differences were found between ages and sexes (see Appendix, Table 4).
- Senior workers judged their social relationships at work less favourably than junior workers. No significant differences were found between different departments, hierarchical levels, ages and sexes (see Appendix, Table 5).

Table 6.3 Absolute number and percentage of employees within that group with four or more psychosomatic complaints

Gender/Hierarchical level	Seniority					
	< 5 years		5–15 years		>15 years	
	Number	%	Number	%	Number	%
Men						
Blue collar	–	–	(1)	(12.5)	(1)	(25.0)
White collar	–	–	9	17.0	10	25.0 *
Management and professionals	–	–	3	10.7	1	7.7
Senior management	–	–	(0)	(0.0)	1	(10.0)
Subtotal	–	–	13	14.3	13	19.4
Women						
Blue collar	–	–	4	33.3*	6	20.0
White collar	1	5.0	14	44.0*	18	15.0
Management and professionals	–	–	(1)	(16.7)	(1)	(0.0)
Senior management	–	–	–	–	–	–
Subtotal	1	3.0	19	38.0 *	25	15.6

Key: * = Risk groups: more than 25 per cent of the respondents within this cell report four or more health complaints.
( ) = Less than 10 observations in total in this cell. No conclusions were drawn from these data.

- Male employees judged their terms of employment as less favourable than their female colleagues. Employees at intermediate and higher levels of seniority and between 31–45 years judged their terms of employment as less favourable than their younger colleagues. No significant differences were found between different departments and hierarchical levels (see Appendix, Table 6).
- Especially older employees, women and lower hierarchical levels experienced more job insecurity than younger employees, men and higher hierarchical levels (see Appendix, Table 7).

6.4.3   Conclusions

Hierarchical level, age and seniority were the major differentiating factors in the experience of stress. Almost all categories of Janssen employees reported they had a job they enjoyed and they could cope with. They did their job under overall good working conditions. The relationships with both colleagues and superiors were good. Terms of employment did not seem to be significant in the experience of stress.

Two risk groups could be identified: (1) male, senior personnel with no

management responsibilities and the (2) female employees with no management responsibilities and intermediate seniority. The task group hypothesis for
explaining the first risk group was that workers with the longest relationship
with the company have more difficulties with the rapidly changing environment. They used to know J.P. 'in the good old days'. The hypothesis for
explaining the second risk group was that this group experience more work–
family conflict because of their double responsibility. This hypothesis was later
rejected by the trade unions although they could not offer an alternative.

The Janssen research report concluded that:

> The experience of stress by Janssen employees cannot be ignored. There
> are quite a few indications that stress can be related to changes that are
> experienced as drastic, especially in senior employees and with the
> combination of professional and family responsibilities, especially in
> female employees with moderate seniority. A lack of work quality plays
> a role, but is not a deciding factor, taking into account the overall positive
> picture.

The first results were made public in a company 'newsflash'. Later on,
more detailed information was given through the company newsletter. The
attitude of the unions and the works council towards the results was positive
but critical.

6.5   Choice of measures

After considering the results, an action plan was developed by the Janssen
task force which consisted of five components:

1   An information session for senior management to involve them in the
    different actions suggested (see section 6.6.1). This was considered as a
    necessary first step in gaining the support of top management.
2   To help individuals at risk, an individual training course to enhance
    coping and stress resistance was proposed (see section 6.6.2.).
3   One of the important risk groups was senior employees who most of all
    experienced the impact of changes in the company. To deal with the
    stress involved in change, the task force proposed a management training
    course to enhance people management in general, and the recognition
    of stress signals in subordinates more specifically (see section 6.6.3).
4   To deal with the psychosomatic complaints and to prevent neck and
    shoulder problems, the task force suggested ergonomic interventions and
    renovation of the office environment (see section 6.6.4).
5   To give special attention to the second risk group, consisting of females
    with intermediate seniority, a special task force on the work–family inter-
    face was recommended (see section 6.6.5).

This action plan was approved by the unions, the works council and senior management.

6.6   Implementation

6.6.1   Sensitising senior management

It is evident that health is of central concern to a company like J.P., operating as it does in the health sector. All the Johnson and Johnson companies have as a common characteristic that in managing their business they are led by the 'Credo', a set of values which indicate the company's attitude towards four groups of stakeholders: clients, employees, the social community and shareholders. Especially with respect to the employees, security and health are regarded as most important values.

Stress management was placed on the agenda of several quarterly information sessions organised for management. The global health policy was presented during a special meeting with the department managers. A special communication session was organised for the senior managers of J.P., to tackle prejudices and taboos, and to explain why stress management was necessary. Special attention was given to:

- the Janssen ethics and corporate values;
- the costs and benefits of these actions;
- the integration in the general health policy, including policies for drug abuse, fitness, healthy eating habits, non-smoking and stress management.

6.6.2   Individual 'coping' training sessions

A series of training sessions in small groups (ten persons, four times half a day) were run by an external trainer, with the title 'Turning stress into vital energy'. The training was announced in the company newsletter and later on in the training catalogue. Employees participated voluntarily during office hours and could subscribe by filling in a form in the newsletter or the catalogue. The fact that 150 employees enrolled, proved the need for this training. One and a half years later a second announcement generated another 100 registrations. The training was experience-oriented, meaning that the focus was on the practice (not theory) and exchange of experiences. Training consisted of improving the body posture, use of humour, improving social support and learning how to put things into perspective. Other topics included work stress, positive stress, insight into individual stressors and stress signals and coping with stress.

The training department is now considering a follow-up training course on 'Recognising stress in others'. Other plans include individual coaching for people with more severe problems and expanding the initiative to the sister companies of J.P., Ortho Diagnostic Systems and Johnson & Johnson.

6.6.3   Management training

This part in the action plan was an obligatory two-day training course called 'Accompanying employees through change' and organised for all managers of J.P. by an external consultancy firm. The goal of the course was to teach management how to lead and support subordinates in periods of change. The first day focused on change and resistance to change, definition and causes of stress, the positive and negative aspects of stress, and different coping reactions in periods of change. The case each participant had prepared became the focus of discussion so as to enhance practical relevance. The second day focused on solutions; how to coach subordinates during important periods of change.

6.6.4   Ergonomic interventions and renovation of the office environment

The ergonomics programme was developed and implemented internally by the medical department, especially to prevent problems in the neck and shoulders. The programme consisted of:

*   adaptation of purchase criteria of office furniture in order to meet higher ergonomic standards;
*   training 'lifting of loads' for logistic and production personnel;
*   medical eye-test for all frequent (daily) computer-users;
*   one thousand workplace analyses were conducted by two company nurses. The desk, the height of the chair and the position of the personal computer was inspected. In case of observation of negative elements, the employee was taught how to adjust his/her posture or the infrastructure was optimalised;
*   information sessions on 'working with a personal computer' were organised in every department;
*   ergonomics training sessions were organised for the chemical plant;
*   all managers received training in ergonomics.

6.6.5   Task force on work–family interface

The special task force, assigned to look at the specific problems of working mothers, was never implemented. This was due to strong resistance from some (female) members of the trade union who suspected that an in-depth study would result in the confirmation of traditional family values. The topic was therefore rescheduled to be included in talks about 'positive actions for female employees' that, at the time of writing, have not yet begun.

6.7   Evaluation

Costs are easier to calculate than benefits. It is difficult to quantify higher moral and better stress resistance. Higher productivity at work was not measured by the Janssen task force. To date there are no 'hard data' available to calculate the benefits. The survey has not yet been repeated, although the Janssen task force is considering further steps, such as identifying organisational stressors. The only information available is to do with costs and the subjective evaluation of the training sessions.

6.7.1   Costs

The costs of the stress management interventions can be seen in Table 6.4. They amount to approximately 476,326 ECU.

6.7.2   Benefits

Absenteeism percentage

Although absenteeism is a result of different influencing factors, it is worth mentioning that the absenteeism percentage went down from 4.3 per cent in 1994 to 3.45 per cent in 1995. This is a significant reduction ($p < 0.1$; NIA, 1996, p. 41). The task force however did not calculate exactly what this means in terms of reduction of costs. We can roughly estimate the benefits of this decrease by multiplying the decrease in absenteeism percentage (0.0085) with the number of full-time employees-equivalents (2,446), times the average salary of a full-time employee (51,840 ECU) (Kompier, 1997). This would

Table 6.4 Costs of the different stress management interventions

Intervention	Cost (ECU)
1 Sensitising senior management	–
2 Individual stress management training, 'Turning stress into vital energy':	
cost of training	35,000
wage costs of participants	124,848
training cost per participant	432 / person
3 Management training 'Change management':	
cost of training	132,500
wage costs of participants	130,628
training cost per participant	452 / person
4 Ergonomic Programme.	
Start-up	25,000
Workplace analysis	27,000
Information sessions	1,350
5 Special task force on work-family interface	——
Total cost	476,326

imply a benefit of 107,780,805 ECU. This benefit clearly exceeds the total costs mentioned in Table 6.4: 1,077,805 − 476,326 brings about a positive difference from *circa* 600,000 ECU. It should be stressed though, that this is a very rough estimate, and that the absenteeism percentage as such is an inaccurate measure of stress. We cannot prove that this decrease is caused by the measures that were taken.

Number of enrolments and evaluation of the training

To evaluate the benefits of the stress management interventions, all interventions were evaluated in terms of number of enrolments as an indication of spontaneous interest in the interventions. These numbers were very satisfactory: 169 employees enrolled after the first announcements. Another 120 enrolments were expected. The training sessions were evaluated by the trainees in terms of the quality of the information, the trainer and his approach, and whether the trainee experienced the training as useful and helpful in recognising and coping with stress or change (see Appendix, Table 8). Again the percentages indicated that the trainees were satisfied with the quality of the stress management sessions.

Qualitative results

Of the reported qualitative results the most important is that stress is no longer considered a taboo subject. Employees can now freely talk about stress and distance themselves from problems. Following the change training programme, managers refer more easily to the health department when confronted with a stress problem in their subordinates. This resulted in an overall increase of number of people referred to the medical officer.

The project not only had a major impact on employees and management–employee relationships, it also generated a lot of positive PR. The systematic approach combining research and training elicited media attention. Janssen set an example for other companies and clearly consolidated its image as an innovative and leading company that cares about its employees. This can have a considerable impact on the labour market where the company image plays a significant role in attracting well-qualified employees and eliciting spontaneous applications for jobs.

6.7.3   Lessons

In the 1994 survey, there was only a very small number of Belgian companies that reported to have examined their employee population with a specific survey, focused on stress, and which had implemented actions to improve working conditions. In that study the authors found that only 12 per cent of the companies occasionally check the stress level, complaints or health risks;

8 per cent reported doing so regularly; and 74 per cent never did. The checking was mainly carried out by medical officers (6 per cent), the personnel department (2 per cent) and others (4 per cent), such as trainees, universities, and the like (Compernolle and Poelmans, 1996). This proves that in Belgium the Janssen case is exceptional and of great importance. It is exceptional because of its systematic approach through research, which is to be expected from a research-driven company. It also is of great importance for the acceptance of stress management in the Belgian business world. Janssen, one of the leading companies in Belgium, both in business and societal terms, set an example for other companies. Extensive media coverage of the stress management approach in Janssen made it a reference in the Belgian business world.

A study revealed that 67 per cent of Belgian companies want to be involved in future initiatives that concern work stress (Compernolle and Poelmans, 1996). These companies mainly wish to be informed on initiatives of other companies (59 per cent), but they are also prepared to co-operate in further research (13 per cent) or to actively participate in a research centre (9 per cent) or a forum (9 per cent). The interest of the companies in receiving more information or participating in research gives an impression of their intention to do something about stress management. Cases such as Janssen and publications such as this book are certainly helpful. Based on the Compernolle & Poelmans study (1996), and the information generated by the Ponos Stress Research Centre, a practical guide was developed to approach stress on an organisational level (Poelmans and Compernolle, 1997).

This chapter indicates the necessity to get the co-operation of senior management to start a systematic approach. To convince senior management, research data can generate persuasive arguments. An interesting fact is that once the Janssen senior management was convinced of the need for a stress management programme, they did not seem to be reluctant to invest a large amount of money (476,000 ECU) in training both employees and managers and implementing large-scale ergonomic workplace improvements. Thus, we can conclude that facts and figures are of prime importance in the political process of approving and supporting a stress management programme. Even though it is much more difficult to generate statistical relevant data on a psycho-social subject such as stress (more difficult than for example generating data on sales), it is important to obtain this data. Moreover, this first survey provides a point of reference for future measurements.

To generate such data, an adequate methodology to measure work stress is very important. Because of the lack of questionnaires tested and standardised on a Belgian representative sample, Janssen used a questionnaire with a cross-section of the population of the Dutch town of Leiden as reference. This is far from ideal for a high-tech pharmaceutical company with highly-skilled engineers and physicians. Obviously, these two populations cannot simply be compared. Moreover, major cultural differences between the two countries certainly distort the comparison.

One of the conclusions of the Compernolle and Poelmans survey (1996) was that research, relevant for the stress management practice in Belgium, is generally lacking. The most urgent needs are standardised instruments and methods and points of reference in different sectors, by means of which a Belgian company can compare itself with other companies. A company that wishes to apply stress management must be able to conclude what actions must be taken, based on measurement and benchmarking of the stress level and the sources of stress (risk inventory).

6.7.4   Conclusion

The case

This case can be considered a successful project. Stress was identified and acknowledged as a topic to be addressed. The task force collected the data in a systematical and methodologically correct way. Risk groups were clearly identified. Measures were taken, at both individual and organisational levels, to help the employees and more specifically the risk groups. With these measures (estimated cost 476,326 ECU), the company management acknowledged that stress is an important topic which can not be ignored. Moreover, the company anticipated government laws, enforcing companies to address stress-related problems. At the time of writing, the company has just finished a second measurement, not as an evaluation of the former actions, but rather as a next step in a continuous process of self-evaluation and improvement. The most important, stimulating factors were the critical openness of senior management and the drive of the task force to assess and confront stress in the company, inviting the employees to improve their coping skills.

The most important weakness of the project is the limited concern to evaluate effects in a systematical way. The attitudes of the participants were evaluated, immediately following and six months after the training, but this doesn't necessarily reflect an actual change in their behaviour or health. The effects of the measures taken were not evaluated. We have no idea of the actual stress-level, and thus no indication of improvement of the situation. Financial benefits were not calculated, apart from the calculations by the authors of the study which point at important benefits due to a reduction of sickness absenteeism. Most of the evaluation was done by the authors while describing the project. The most important hindering factor is probably time or other priorities demanding the attention of the members of the task force.

The Belgian situation

The interest of the Belgian government and companies in stress management at work is very recent. In 1996 the prevention of stress at work became a legal obligation. Several companies, however, did not wait for this law to take initiatives. The actions taken were mostly piecemeal and lacked scientific preparation, analysis and evaluation. In Belgium, Janssen is probably the first company to develop a systematic approach to stress at work. It identified risks and risk groups by studying a representative sample of the organisation and implemented actions addressing the needs: training in stress management for all volunteers, training in change management for all managers and ergonomic interventions.

Only a few companies followed this example. In other countries a well-formulated law stimulated many companies to implement preventive stress management programmes. As this case study shows, even without legislation there are sound business reasons to deal with stress at work. It is clear that a systematic approach towards stress in the workplace is for the benefit of individual workers, the companies and mental health in general.

Appendix

Table 6.A1 Average scores on the STAI questionnaire

Group	Number	Average	Standard deviation	F	Degrees of freedom	Probability
Total	324	40.7	9.9			
Seniority:						
< 5 years	81	37.6	8.4			
5–15 years	143	40.5	9.2			
> 15 years	99	43.4	11.1	7.88	2; 320	**< 0.001**
Department:						
Administration/Finance/ International	96	40.5	9.8			
Production	117	41.4	9.5			
Research	108	39.8	10.0	0.75	2; 318	n.s
Hierarchical level:						
Blue collar	47	42.5	9.7			
White collar	195	41.0	10.3			
Management and professionals	66	39.3	9.0			
Senior management	15	36.7	6.2	1.86	3; 319	n.s.
Gender						
Male	210	40.6	10.1			
Female	113	40.8	9.5	T = –0.22	321	n.s.
Age:						
≤ 30 years	94	38.3	9.3			
31–45 years	168	40.8	9.5			
≥ 46 years	61	44.0	11.0	6.41	2; 320	**0.002**

Table 6.A2 Average scores on scale 'psychosomatic complaints'

Group	Number	Average	Standard deviation	F	Degrees of freedom	Probability
Total	324	1.5	2.3			
Seniority:						
< 5 years	81	0.7	1.0			
5–15 years	143	1.7	2.6			
> 15 years	99	1.8	2.5	6.41	2; 320	**0.002**
Department:						
Administration/Finance/ International	96	1.5	2.5			
Production	117	1.5	2.3			
Research	108	1.4	2.1	0.13	2; 318	n.s
Hierarchical level:						
Blue collar	47	1.4	2.4			
White collar	195	1.7	2.4			
Management and professionals	66	0.8	1.8			
Senior management	15	1.4	1.9	2.54	3; 319	n.s.
Gender						
Male	210	1.2	2.1			
Female	113	1.9	2.6	$T = -2.46$	321	**0.01**
Age:						
≤ 30 years	94	1.5	2.1			
31–45 years	168	1.3	2.1			
≥ 46 years	61	1.9	2.8	1.27	2; 320	n.s.

Table 6.A3 Average scores on sub-scale 'working conditions'

Group	Number	Average	Standard deviation	F	Degrees of freedom	Probability
Total	324	3.37	1.47			
Seniority:						
< 5 years	81	3.2	1.4			
5–15 years	143	3.4	1.4			
> 15 years	99	3.4	1.6	0.51	2; 320	n.s.
Department:						
Administration/Finance/ International	96	3.1	1.6			
Production	117	3.6	1.5			
Research	108	3.3	1.2	4.25	2; 318	**0.01**
Hierarchical level:						
Blue collar	47	4.0	1.4			
White collar	195	3.5	1.5			
Management and professionals	66	2.7	1.1			
Senior management	15	2.5	1.2	11.58	3; 319	**< 0.001**
Gender						
Male	210	3.5	1.5			
Female	113	3.2	1.4	T = 1.58	321	n.s.
Age:						
≤ 30 years	94	3.4	1.5			
31–45 years	168	3.4	1.4			
≥ 46 years	61	3.3	1.7	0.07	2; 320	n.s.

Table 6.A4 Average scores on sub-scale 'job content'

Group	Number	Average	Standard deviation	F	Degrees of freedom	Probability
Total	324	6.75	1.42			
Seniority:						
< 5 years	81	7.0	1.3			
5–15 years	143	6.7	1.4			
> 15 years	99	6.6	1.4	2.52	2; 320	n.s.
Department:						
Administration/Finance/ International	96	6.9	1.4			
Production	117	6.4	1.4			
Research	108	7.0	1.4	4.5	2; 318	**0.01**
Hierarchical level:						
Blue collar	47	6.3	1.3			
White collar	195	6.7	1.4			
Management and professionals	66	6.9	1.5			
Senior management	15	7.5	1.1	3.2	3; 319	**0.02**
Gender						
Male	210	1.2	1.4			
Female	113	1.9	1.5	T = –0.72	321	n.s.
Age:						
≤ 30 years	94	1.5	1.6			
31–45 years	168	1.3	1.3			
≥ 46 years	61	1.9	1.5	0.37	2; 320	n.s.

Table 6.A5 Average scores on sub-scale 'social relationships at work'

Group	Number	Average	Standard deviation	F	Degrees of freedom	Probability
Total	324	6.36	2.24			
Seniority:						
< 5 years	81	6.9	2.2			
5–15 years	143	6.3	2.3			
> 15 years	99	6.0	2.2	4.52	2; 319	**0.01**
Department:						
Administration/Finance/ International	96	6.5	2.3			
Production	117	6.4	2.1			
Research	108	6.2	2.3	0.59	2; 317	n.s.
Hierarchical level:						
Blue collar	47	6.6	2.2			
White collar	195	6.3	2.3			
Management and professionals	66	6.0	2.2			
Senior management	15	7.4	1.9	1.8	3; 318	n.s.
Gender						
Male	210	6.3	2.2			
Female	113	6.5	2.2	T = −1.02	320	n.s.
Age:						
≤ 30 years	94	6.7	2.3			
31–45 years	168	6.2	2.2			
≥ 46 years	61	6.1	2.3	2.01	2; 319	n.s.

Table 6.A6 Average scores on sub-scale 'terms of employment'

Group	Number	Average	Standard deviation	F	Degrees of freedom	Probability
Total	324	6.23	1.42			
Seniority:						
< 5 years	81	6.6	1.5			
5–15 years	143	6.1	1.4			
> 15 years	99	6.2	1.3	3.37	2; 320	**0.04**
Department:						
Administration/Finance/						
International	96	6.3	1.3			
Production	117	6.3	1.4			
Research	108	6.0	1.6	1.29	2; 318	n.s.
Hierarchical level:						
Blue collar	47	6.6	1.3			
White collar	195	6.2	1.4			
Management and professionals	66	6.0	1.4			
Senior management	15	6.5	1.6	2.2	3; 319	n.s.
Gender						
Male	210	6.1	1.4			
Female	113	6.5	1.4	T = –2.32	321	**0.02**
Age:						
≤ 30 years	94	6.6	1.5			
31–45 years	168	6.0	1.4			
≥ 46 years	61	6.4	1.4	5.89	2; 320	**0.003**

Table 6.A7 Average scores on sub-scale 'fear of job loss'

Group	Number	Average	Standard deviation	F	Degrees of freedom	Probability
Total	324	4.7	2.97			
Seniority:						
< 5 years	81	5.3	3.2			
5–15 years	143	4.5	2.8			
> 15 years	99	4.5	2.9	2.24	2; 320	n.s.
Department:						
Administration/Finance/ International	96	4.6	2.8			
Production	117	4.9	3.1			
Research	108	4.4	2.9	0.86	2; 318	n.s.
Hierarchical level:						
Blue collar	47	6.0	3.3			
White collar	195	5.0	3.0			
Management and professionals	66	3.4	2.1			
Senior management	15	3.3	2.2	9.33	3; 319	< **0.001**
Gender						
Male	210	6.1	2.8			
Female	113	6.5	3.1	T = –2.17	321	**0.03**
Age:						
≤ 30 years	94	6.6	3.2			
31–45 years	168	6.0	2.7			
≥ 46 years	61	6.4	3.1	3.4	2; 320	**0.03**

Table 6.A8 Evaluation of the different stress management interventions

1 Individual stress management training	
'Turning stress into vital energy':	
Number of enrolments	169
Number of enrolments expected	120
Evaluation (in per cent):	
Overall evaluation	84
Satisfaction with information transfered through the training	78
Satisfaction with trainer	90
Satisfaction with approach, method	80
Did the training result in more insight in stress	85
Learned how to recognise stressors	82
Learned how to recognise stress-signals	84
Learned how to cope with stress	76
2 Management training	
'Change management':	
Evaluation (in per cent; satisfaction):	
Overall evaluation	75–83
Information transfer	77–82
Trainer	79–89
Approach, method	73–78
Learned how people deal with changes	75–81
Learned how to involve collaborators in change process	76–79
Learned how to help collaborators in stages of change	71–77
Learned how to react when subordinates dysfunction under stress	69–73
3 Ergonomic programme:	
Number of enrolments	250
Evaluation:	Not yet evaluated
4 Non-smoking programme	200
Number of enrolments	
Evaluation:	*circa* 200
Total number of people that stopped smoking (according to indirect evidence [files])	

Bibliography

Belgisch Staatsblad/Moniteur Belge 18/9/1996, Brussels: Belgisch Staatsblad/Moniteur Belge, no. 24309.

Coetsier, P., De Backer, G., De Corte, W., Gheeraert, P., Hellemans, C., Karnas, G., Kornitzer, M., Stam, M. and Vlerick, P. (1996) 'Onderzoeksdesign en instrumentarium van het Belgisch jobstress onderzoek' ('Study design and instruments of the Belgian work stress study'), in *Reeks Theoretische en Toegepaste Psychologie*, Deinze: Infoservice.

Compernolle, T. and Poelmans, S. (1996) *Stress Management in Belgium. Inventory of Initiatives and Experiences of Belgian Organisations*, Sydney: Proceedings Congress International Stress Management Association.

Karasek, R.A. and Theorell, T. (1990) *Healthy Work. Stress, Productivity and the Reconstruction of Working Life*, New York: Basic Books, Inc.

Kompier, M.A.J. (1997) *Personal Correspondence*, Nijmegen: University of Nijmegen, Faculty of Social Sciences, Work and Organisational Psychology, 97.1663/MK/nth, 19 November 1997.

Kompier, M., De Gier, E., Smulders, P. and Draaisma, D. (1994) 'Regulations, policies and practices concerning work stress in five European countries', *Work and Stress*, 8 (4): 296–318.

Kwantes, J.H. and Hoogendijk, L. (eds) (1994) *De Arbouwet compleet. Toelichting/wettekst/register/literatuurlijst* ('The Dutch work environment act complete'), Amsterdam: Nederlands Instituut voor Arbeidsomstandigheden.

NIA: Dutch Institute for Work Environment NIA (1996) *Berekening van ziekteverzuim. Standaard voor verzuimregistratie* ('Calculating Sickness Absenteeism'), Amsterdam: NIA.

Poelmans, S. and Compernolle, T. (1997) 'Stress management', in *Human Resource Management*, Brussels: Ced.Samson.

Spielberger, C.D. (1983) *Manual for the State Trait Anxiety Inventory*, Palo Alto, Calif.: Consulting Psychologists Press, Inc.

Swinnen, L., Moors, S. and Govaert, C. (1994) 'Stress als oorzaak van ziekteverzuim', in S. Moors (ed.) *Stress en werk. Oorsprong en aanpak*, pp. 125–149, Brussels: Nationaal Onderzoeksinstituut voor arbeidsomstandigheden.

Van der Ploeg, H.M. (1979) *Zelfbeoordelingsvragenlijst*, Lisse: Swets and Zeitlinger b.v.

Van Hamme, L. (1997) *Personal correspondence*, Brussels: Ministry for Labour and Employment, LVH/SH/072397.b01, 23 July 1997.

Chapter 7

United Kingdom: Evaluation of a stress management programme in the public sector

Lynne Whatmore, Susan Cartwright and Cary Cooper

7.1 Introduction: Work stress in the United Kingdom

Occupational stress is a significant research area in the United Kingdom. There is a large body of research studies which have sought to identify the stressors associated with a variety of occupations and employee groups and their impact on health and health behaviours (see for example, Cooper and Sutherland, 1991; Rees and Cooper, 1992). As the majority of these studies have been cross-sectional rather than longitudinal in design, there is relatively less research evidence on the effectiveness of any interventions which may have subsequently been introduced in response to the findings.

In the UK, organisational interest in the problems of workplace stress and stress intervention strategies has been motivated by concerns about rising absenteeism due to psychological disorders and stress-related illness. Unlike the United States, the healthcare costs of sick employees are not directly met by UK organisations and so it is the issue of lost productivity that prompts organisational activity in this area. Overall, the annual rate of sickness absence in the UK is 3.5 per cent; which is slightly above the European average of between 1 per cent and 2 per cent (CBI-Percom, 1995). On this basis, it is estimated that the direct cost of sickness absence to British employers is £513 per employee. In UK public sector organisations, the absenteeism rate is notably higher, averaging at around 7 per cent.

According to a survey by the Industrial Society in 1995 (Industrial Society, 1995), UK employers consider the most common causes of stress to be life events such as divorce, moving house and increased workload due to downsizing. Another UK-wide survey by the British Institute of Management in 1997 has also highlighted volume of work to be an increasing problem among managers (Institute of Management, 1997).

In the same way that interest in stress prevention in the US has developed in response to growing and well-founded litigation fears, UK employers are now becoming increasingly aware that their duty of care towards employees can extend to psychosocial risk factors in the work environment.

In this respect, the case of social worker, John Walker, who successfully sued his employers having suffered a second mental breakdown due to work stress (Walker versus Northumberland County Council, 1995) has been particularly influential. Although there have been reports of a number of out of court settlements for stress claims, this was the first case of its kind to come before a UK court.

Types of intervention

In common with the rest of mainland Europe, stress prevention activities in the UK tend to be confined to large organisations employing more than 500 employees (Wynne and Clarkin, 1992). Typically, such activities involve interventions at the secondary and tertiary level (Murphy, 1987) in the form of stress management and health enhancement wellness programmes or Employee Assistance Programmes (EAPs). Evidence based on the experience of Néstlé UK (Cooper and Williams, 1994) suggests that health screening and wellness programmes are well supported by employees although their effectiveness as a means of stress reduction is less rigorously evaluated. Evaluations of stress management programmes have shown that such interventions can make a difference in temporarily reducing experienced stress, although improvements are often modest (Reynolds et al., 1993). The pharmaceutical company, ICI/Zeneca began an extensive in-house stress management programme in the UK in 1988 which has been attended by almost 700 employees. Measures taken two to three months post-workshop attendance have demonstrated a 15 to 20 per cent improvement in self-reported general health and a reduction in the number of referrals to psychiatric help or counselling. Similarly, evidence from the UK Post Office (Cooper and Sadri, 1991) suggests that employee counselling can have a significant impact on improving self-esteem and reducing anxiety and depression. However, as with other individually focused interventions, unless supplemented by other initiatives to directly address the sources of stress inherent in the workplace, counselling does not result in any improvement in job satisfaction or organisational commitment.

Role of stress management programmes

While stress management programmes are criticised because they represent an essentially inoculative approach, the interactive nature of the stress response means that one cannot discount the role played by the individual in the stress appraisal process and the inner resources they possess to cope with experienced stress. In a work context, this is likely to be important in rapidly changing situations such as merger or acquisition which have enormous stress potential (Cartwright and Cooper, 1996), yet generate a variety of possible sources of stress which, because they are often of a temporary rather than enduring nature, cannot be changed by organisational action. Workplace stress management programmes can also be useful in extending the physical and psychological resources of the individual to deal with personal life events and problems outside the work domain.

Because stress management programmes continue to be one of the most popular forms of intervention in the UK, we have chosen to present an evaluative study of the effectiveness of one such programme in a large government department.

7.2 Introduction to the organisation

This case study examines the effectiveness of a stress management intervention aimed at employees in the public sector. The government department concerned employs over 25,000 employees at various locations throughout the UK. In common with other public sector organisations, it had undergone a period of restructuring, when major change initiatives had been introduced, leaving employees with an increased level of uncertainty in respect of continuing career development and in terms of job practices and adherence to organisational systems. As a result, senior management was concerned to address issues of reported strain among employees, along with decreased job satisfaction resulting from a changing organisational climate.

The majority of employees were of professional, managerial and administrative grades; a considerable number interfaced regularly with individual members of the public and with client organisations. The department aimed to provide a high quality service to the public within the regulatory boundaries set by government. Reflecting the period of restructuring and decreased staff levels following voluntary redundancy, a stress audit revealed primary stressors to be volume of work, reductions in staff numbers and coping with change. Cultural changes were moving the department towards a more 'business oriented' approach with an emphasis on implementing strategic plans and performance management systems. For many individuals, particularly those who had worked within the public sector for many years, this cultural change had been difficult and had required a shift in perspective and attitudes.

While employee turnover was minimal, sickness absenteeism was currently around 7 per cent. Although this level was fairly typical of public sector services, an increase in notification of stress-related illness was causing some concern.

7.3 The study: Objectives and administration

7.3.1 Objectives

The study was conducted as an academic research project and the objectives were therefore defined in terms of combining good research methodology with the needs and resource limitations of the participating organisation. The cost of researcher time was not borne by the organisation. Management objectives were to increase understanding of stress and to help employees improve their coping skills. Since management was considering longer term action to reduce stress, systematic analysis of different types of training would provide useful information on which to base decisions for the introduction of stress management training.

The study aimed to improve coping skills among individual employees and thereby reduce reported symptoms of ill health and strain. While it is acknowledged that addressing and changing identified organisational stressors is needed to minimise sources of stress in the workplace (Cooper and Cartwright, 1994), such initiatives generally require longer-term implementation and thorough assessment of stressors and potential alternative working practices. Skills training targeted at the individual level can be introduced within a short time-span and can therefore have more immediate effects on employee strain. Given the potentially high costs to the individual in terms of illness caused by stress (see, for example, Coleman, 1992) and to the organisation in terms of sickness absenteeism (see for example, McHugh and Brennan, 1992), interventions at both an individual level and at an organisational level would constitute an optimal initiative.

Indeed, the department was taking steps to address a number of organisational issues, although no specific initiatives had been introduced at the time this data was collected.

The specific purpose of this study was to examine the effects of individual stress management training on individual outcomes (for example, mental health) and on organisational variables (for example, absenteeism). Given the diversity of programmes offered under the umbrella of stress management and the need for clear comparative evidence regarding the efficacy of programmes with substantive theoretical orientations, the study also set out to examine and compare training based on different theoretical perspectives. These perspectives were:

1   Education and awareness;
2   Exercise;
3   Cognitive restructuring.

Education and awareness

Education and awareness building forms the basis for many stress management programmes. Sutherland (1990) purports that the objectives of this type of programme are to increase awareness of links between stress, illness and personal behaviour. Such programmes usually include identification of personal stressors and symptoms of stress and help individuals recognise the relationship between behaviours, personality, coping skills and outcomes of stress. The premise of an educational approach is that promoting self-awareness helps an individual to take action to reduce their own stress levels. According to Kagan *et al.* (1995), stress reduction is due to 'increased self-understanding and self-awareness of cognitive and affective reactions to interpersonal events'. Educational programmes are not generally used as stand-alone interventions, but commonly provide an introductory element to other stress management techniques (Bunce, 1997). Bunce (1997) suggests that educational programmes per se may be useful as a placebo condition to control for non-specific factors. To increase self-understanding and self-awareness, interventions based on education may require inclusion of an individual diagnostic element to identify personal stressors, ways of behaving and personality factors.

Exercise

Considerable research evidence exists documenting the beneficial effects of physical exercise in reducing reactivity to psychosocial stressors, for example, a review by Crews and Landers (1987). Most exercise studies have used anxiety, depression or mood states as dependent variables and, typically, exercise has been associated with reduced levels of anxiety and depression and positive mood states (Biddle, 1995). Single session exercise has perhaps been researched more thoroughly than longer-term exercise, although in recent years there has been a move towards assessing the effects of a course of exercise on psychological variables. Altchiler and Motta (1994) used both methodologies, finding reduced state anxiety levels following a single session of aerobic exercise and a reduction in post-exercise anxiety over an eight weeks course of exercise. Their study also measured absenteeism, but no changes were found over the course of the study. Reviewing interventions using depression as an outcome variable, Martinsen (1994) concluded that aerobic exercise (longer term) is effective in reducing depression with or without accompanying physiological gains in fitness. Overall, regular exercise appears to have positive effects on psychological health and on an individual's ability to cope with stressful situations, although the mechanisms by which this occurs are not yet clear.

Cognitive restructuring

Interventions directed at improving cognitive skills aim to help an individual use reasoning to assess a situation, rather than reacting emotionally as dictated by past habits (Rosch and Pelletier, 1987). Distortions in cognitive appraisal, such as overgeneralising past experiences, may increase levels of arousal. Cognitive programmes aim to teach people how to recognise these distortions and to help them develop more adaptive methods of thinking (Beck, 1976). Rational emotive behaviour therapy (REBT) is a particular form of cognitive training that has been used traditionally in a clinical setting, but is now also being applied in organisational training (see for example, Neenan, 1993). Originally proposed by Ellis (1962), REBT suggests that individuals hold irrational beliefs which are inflexible and dogmatic and that it is these beliefs that are the major cause of distress, rather than events themselves (Abrams and Ellis, 1994). The technique focuses on helping individuals identify their irrational beliefs and to dispute and change these by examining factual evidence. An ABCDE model is used to analyse and dispute beliefs: 'A' relates to the activating event, 'B' is the belief system that determines the individual's response to the event, 'C' is the disturbed consequence of the event and belief, 'D' refers to disputing and challenging irrational beliefs and 'E' is the effect, i.e. the new philosophy that the individual is encouraged to adopt (Abrams and Ellis, 1994). The degree to which this strategy can be utilised to reduce stress depends on an individual's willingness to accept responsibility for his/her own emotional reactions to difficult situations. In an organisational setting, participants on this type of programme must therefore be prepared to consider workplace stressors in terms of their own reactions and behaviour, and to evaluate alternative interpretations of those stressors.

7.3.2   Responsibilities and administration

In-house responsibility for raising awareness of the study was adopted by senior management, whose role was to facilitate the project by encouraging employee participation. Following introduction of the study, management played no further formal role, since it was considered important that the researcher was viewed as operating independently.

Participating employees were volunteers working within a defined geographical area selected by the organisation. All employees within this area were notified of the project by the researcher; information given related to structure and aims of the project, programme details and role of participants, i.e. questionnaire completion, attendance at training sessions and requirement for practise of skills during the period of the study. Employees at all levels of the organisation were eligible to take part in the study, subject to availability of training places. This approach resulted in a mix of managerial and non-managerial employees in the training sessions. Administration of the project and the actual training was conducted by the researcher. As participants were located on a number of sites, centrally located training facilities were used for session delivery.

7.4   Measures and training sessions

Since the primary objective of the study was to reduce reported symptoms of ill health and strain by improving coping skills, the main considerations in the selection of measures were how specifically the terms ill health and strain should be defined, what effects strain may be expected to have on an individual's interaction with the organisation, the effectiveness of self-report compared to 'hard' data, and practical considerations in terms of time and ease of completion of measuring instruments. It was decided to categorise

outcome variables into 'individual', i.e. reported symptoms, and 'organisational', i.e. reported effects at the individual/organisational interface.

7.4.1   Individual variables

There are several reliable and valid instruments designed to measure symptoms
of ill health and strain. The Occupational Stress Indicator (OSI) (Cooper *et
al.*, 1988) contains two sub-scales, mental health and physical health, which
examine reported symptoms in a way that usefully separates physical manifest-
ations (e.g., headaches) with psychological concepts (e.g., worrying).
However, it is also useful to break down the 'strain' aspect into more specific
elements, for example, anxiety and depression. Exercise research literature in
particular makes considerable use of instruments measuring anxiety and
depression as separate constructs. The Crown-Crisp Experiential Index
(Crown and Crisp, 1979) contains five sub-scales, three of which were
deemed appropriate for this study: free-floating anxiety (anxiety), somatic
anxiety and depression sub-scales. The five scales therefore selected to oper-
ationalise ill health and strain were the following.

MEASURING INSTRUMENTS – INDIVIDUAL VARIABLES:

1   Anxiety, somatic anxiety and depression sub-scales from the Crown-
     Crisp Experiential Index (Crown and Crisp, 1979).
     Each sub-scale comprised eight questions; responses were either in a
     yes/no format or were frequency alternatives, i.e. 'frequently', 'some-
     times', 'never'. Each sub-scale was scored in the direction of high levels
     of the variable being measured. Items typically related to:
     •   Feeling upset, restless, uneasy, worrying (Anxiety scale, reliability
          coefficient: 0.77);
     •   Physical symptoms, for example, indigestion, feeling sick, fatigue
          (Somatic anxiety scale, reliability coefficient: 0.68);
     •   Waking early in the morning, sadness, tearfulness (Depression scale,
          reliability coefficient: 0.72).
2   Mental health and physical health scales from the Occupational Stress
     Indicator (OSI) (Cooper *et al.*, 1988).
     The mental health sub-scale consisted of eighteen items with a six-
     point response choice; a high score indicated less well-being. The physical
     health sub-scale comprised twelve items and was scored in a similar
     manner. Items related to:
     •   Worrying about mistakes, feeling upset, confused thinking (Mental
          health scale, reliability scale: 0.88);
     •   sleeping problems, headaches, fatigue (Physical health scale, reliability
          scale: 0.78).

A biographical questionnaire also collected demographic details relating to age, employment details and health-related behaviours such as smoking, drinking and exercise practices.

7.4.2   Organisational variables

As stated, the term 'organisational' variables in the context of this study refers to the effects of strain on the individual's relationship with the organisation. Two constructs might be expected to suffer as a result of high levels of strain, namely an employee's degree of commitment to the organisation and, potentially, the degree of satisfaction an individual derives from his/her job. These constructs could be measured using the Job Satisfaction sub-scale from the OSI and the Organisational Commitment questionnaire developed by Cook and Wall (1980). A reduction in reported symptoms of ill health should also be observable in terms of sickness absenteeism. Ideally, organisational absence records should be used for this purpose as 'hard data', but there are various difficulties with the collection of this type of information, relating particularly to technical demands of extrapolating data for individuals participating in the study and to issues of confidentiality and the potential implications that collecting this type of data might have on later career decisions involving individual employees. For these reasons, self-report absence data were used. To summarise, the measures for organisational variables utilised were as follows.

MEASURES – ORGANISATIONAL VARIABLES:

1   Organisational commitment (Cook and Wall, 1980).

This questionnaire comprised a set of nine statements; responses were measured on a 7-point rating scale. Reverse scoring was used on three items. A high total score indicated high commitment. Statements related to: being proud of the organisation, feeling a sense of belonging to the organisation, intention to leave. Reliability coefficient alpha was 0.8.

2   Job satisfaction scale from OSI.

Job satisfaction was measured by twenty-two items scored on a 6-point rating scale; a high score indicated high job satisfaction. Statements measured degree of satisfaction with: communication and information, relationships with people at work, volume of work. Reliability coefficient alpha was 0.85 for this scale.

3   Self-reported sickness absenteeism.

This questionnaire asked respondents about the number of occasions and duration of sickness absence over a given period (previous twelve months for pre-intervention questionnaire, previous three months for following questionnaires).

The questionnaire also identified stressors and allowed comparison with normative general population data.

Training sessions

Comparing the effectiveness of different theoretical perspectives in reducing stress requires a baseline level of knowledge among participants across experimental conditions. Since it is obviously impossible to control for prior knowledge, a workable solution was to provide basic information as a starting-point from which to build during the training sessions. The intervention therefore commenced with a one-hour information session, attended by all trainees, covering issues such as causes and symptoms of stress, positive and negative stress, adverse health effects of excessive negative stress and organisational stressors and consequences.

This was followed by two-hour workshops in the separate stress management techniques. The duration of the workshops was deliberately kept to a minimum to facilitate participant attendance. One of the issues in delivering stress management in the workplace is that employees may feel inhibited from attending full-day courses, particularly where individuals are faced with a heavy workload. The workshops therefore concentrated on familiarising participants with the relevant concept and technique; practising the technique outside the workshop aided skill development thereby improving participants' management of stressful situations. The onus was on individuals to maintain skill practice. Workshop details are as follows.

I   PERSONAL STRESS AWARENESS

Participants completed a stress diary to identify personal stressors at work and at home. Having completed the OSI questionnaire pre-intervention, they were also given feedback regarding their personal profile at the workshop. Following group discussions regarding typical behaviour in common stressful situations, participants developed action plans to target their own stressors; participants were asked to follow their action plans for the duration of the study. The programme thus incorporated a behavioural change element.

2   EXERCISE

This intervention was directed at non-exercisers and consisted of a structured exercise programme which participants were asked to complete twice weekly at home for a duration of approximately forty-five minutes. Participants were provided with a detailed schedule that consisted of warm-up, aerobic, muscular strength and endurance, and flexibility components. The workshop concentrated on discussing individual exercises and general guidelines with participants.

3   COGNITIVE RESTRUCTURING

This programme was based on the principles of Rational Emotive Behaviour Therapy (Ellis, 1962). The workshop covered the concept of irrational beliefs and examined how these can affect an individual's perception of a situation and implications for emotional consequences. Group discussions focused on identifying irrational beliefs in common workplace situations. Participants were instructed in the ABCDE framework of challenging irrational beliefs and replacing these with more rational, less destructive ways of thinking. Participants were to follow the ABCDE framework for the duration of the study.

7.5   Implementation of the study

A randomised blocks design with repeated measures was employed for this study. Measures were taken pre-intervention (baseline), three months post-intervention and six months post-intervention using postal questionnaires which were returned direct to the researcher. Type of intervention acted as the independent variable, with three types of stress management training, plus a wait-list control and a full control condition. The wait-list condition acted as a control at the three months stage and was used as a placebo to control for non-specific factors. Volunteers allocated into this condition commenced stress management instruction after three months, and were then able to self select into a particular programme. The full control condition (non–volunteer control) comprised individuals who did not wish to undertake stress management training but were prepared to complete questionnaires pre- and post-intervention. This was to examine the proposition that volunteers for training may be healthier and more 'stress-aware' than non–volunteers (Murphy, 1987).

All employees of the participating organisation were notified in writing of the proposed study and were given details of the programmes to be used. They were informed that volunteers would be allocated randomly into one of the training programmes, or into a wait-list condition. The purpose of control data was explained and employees were asked if they would be willing to complete questionnaires if they did not wish to take part in training.

Following completion of pre-intervention questionnaires, the information session was held for all training volunteers, including wait-list control participants. Workshops were held as detailed earlier, with a maximum number of fifteen participants per workshop. All participants were asked to complete weekly records of their adherence to the programme plan (i.e. action plans, exercise sessions, ABCDE framework). The purpose of this weekly log was to encourage adherence to the programme. However, while some participants were diligent in completing logs, particularly in the early stages of the intervention, compliance with this request diminished over the course of the study. This may reflect decreasing adherence to the programme or it may be that they simply neglected to complete the weekly log. It was not practicable to measure to what extent participants actually followed their programme over the course of the study.

After three months, postal questionnaires were again completed. The control group did not complete questionnaires at this point, this being an interim measure. Wait-list participants then received training in the programme of their choice. After a further three months (six months after commencement of the study), all participants completed a final set of questionnaires. Follow-up sessions were held to discuss participants' experiences and issues arising from the intervention. Group allocation and response is indicated in Table 7.1.

The exercise group has a lower number of participants at the commencement of the study because several participants were either unable to attend the workshop or were advised not to exercise unsupervised because of medical conditions and were therefore transferred to the wait-list group. As can be seen from Table 7.1, attrition mainly occurred between pre-intervention and three months post-intervention.

7.6   Results

7.6.1   Biographical data

Two hundred and seventy individuals participated in the study; of these 113 were male and 157 female. Ages ranged from 23–60 years, with the mean age being 41 years. The age profile of the five groups was very similar, from 39.3 years in the exercise group to 41.9 years in the stress awareness group. Of the sample, 72.3 per cent worked full-time. Most part-time workers were female (31.2 per cent of the female sample compared to 3.5 per cent of the male sample).

In respect of health behaviours, only 23 per cent of the sample smoked, most of whom (85 per cent) smoked between 1 and 20 cigarettes per day. Of the sample, 85 per cent drank alcohol, most of these (92 per cent) limited alcohol to four days per week or less. Only 33 per cent of the sample exercised twice a week or more; the majority of the sample were therefore not exercising sufficiently to have health and fitness benefits (American College of Sports Medicine, 1990).

Table 7.1 Number of participants by group at all periods of the study

Period	Awareness	Exercise	Cognitive	Wait-list	Control (Non-volunteer)	Total
Pre-intervention	48	43	48	52	79	270
Post 3 months	28	25	32	26	—	111
Post 6 months	24	23	26	23	59	155

7.6.2   Pre-intervention data

All outcome variables were examined pre-intervention using analysis of variance technique (ANOVA), to investigate the hypothesis that volunteers for stress management training may, in fact, be healthier than individuals who do not volunteer (Murphy, 1987). No significant differences were found on any measures. This may indicate a similar stress profile in volunteers and non-volunteers. Still conclusions cannot be drawn without examining the attitudes of non-volunteers towards stress management training. Many of the non-volunteers in this study reported that they did not wish to participate in training simply because of time constraints. The implication for organisations wishing to introduce stress management training is that consideration must be given to ease of access to courses, duration and frequency of courses. By facilitating access to training, there will be clearer differentiation between interested employees and those who genuinely do not wish to accept training. The attitudes of this latter group must be investigated for longer-term policies on stress management. There is still, in some organisations, a 'macho' culture in which stress is not an acceptable topic for discussion, leading to a denial of stress symptoms. If 'non-volunteers' are in fact reluctant to admit feeling strained, then it is very important that this is taken into account in the development of stress management policies.

Comparison of the sample with normative data showed that individuals reported significantly more psychological and physical ill-health symptoms than the general population ($p < 0.001$). They also reported themselves as significantly less job satisfied than the general population ($p < 0.001$). Recent normative data for the Crown-Crisp Experiential Index scales (anxiety, somatic anxiety and depression) was not available and it was therefore not considered appropriate to make these comparisons.

7.6.3   Post-intervention data

Individual variables

Using t-tests for paired observations (those who remained in the study), training effects were found after three months on all individual variables, i.e. reductions were found in levels of anxiety, somatic anxiety, depression, mental health and physical health. However, these were specific to the awareness and exercise groups. There were no significant changes in mean scores for the cognitive restructuring group, or for the wait-list group. At the three month time point, the wait-list group acted as a control; training was to commence after questionnaire completion.

In view of the rate of drop-out (42 per cent) at the three month time point, demographics of the remaining participants was examined to determine whether these participants were a representative subgroup of the original sample. Examination of gender, age (mean and range) and full/part-time profiles indicated no strong differences in the two groups. Repeat examination at the six months time point again indicated no strong differences between the original sample and remaining participants. It was therefore concluded that, although a degree of self-selection had taken place during the study, this had not biased the sample in any direction and therefore did not invalidate the results. A further analysis of the baseline measures was conducted to compare 'stayers' with those who subsequently discontinued their participation in the programme. This analysis found that there were no significant differences between 'stayers' and 'drop-outs' on all but three of the individual/organisational variables. Compared to 'stayers' those who discontinued the programme recorded significantly poorer scores in respect of somatic anxiety (p < 0.01), free floating anxiety (p < 0.05) and physical health (p < 0.05). Although this may have contributed to the size of the effect of the programme, we are unable to offer an explanation as to why those who were experiencing poorer health discontinued the programme. Perhaps their poor health affected their ability to apply themselves to the programme or it did not offer them the immediate results they expected and they were discouraged from continuing. Table 7.2 shows mean scores for individual outcome variables. A decrease in mental and physical health mean scores denotes improved health.

Exercise group participants reported improvements on all variables (paired t-test analysis). The improvement in physical health symptoms would be expected within this time frame due to physiological adaptations to exercise. However, the notable improvements in anxiety, depression and general mental health cannot be explained by this mechanism.

The awareness group also improved in depression, physical and mental health states. The mean score for anxiety was considerably lower after training and approached significance.

Table 7.2 Mean scores by group at three-month period on pre-intervention and post-intervention scores on anxiety, somatic anxiety, depression, mental health and physical health scales

	Awareness		Exercise		Cognitive		Wait-list control	
	Pre	Post	Pre	Post	Pre	Post	Pre	Post
Anxiety	6.62	5.19	6.76	4.96**	6.29	6.42	5.12	4.88
Somatic anxiety	5.04	3.77	4.76	2.92***	5.06	4.94	4.31	4.50
Depression	5.77	4.35*	4.92	3.60*	3.05	3.18	4.38	4.50
Mental health	61.21	56.18*	58.84	52.40***	54.53	55.38	52.77	54.43
Physical health	36.82	32.50*	33.44	27.76***	34.28	33.97	31.88	32.35
Number	26	26	25	25	31	31	26	26

Key: *significant p < 0.05; **significant p < 0.01; ***significant p < 0.001

Surprisingly, the cognitive group showed no improvements on any of the variables. There are a number of possible reasons for this finding and these will be discussed later (see section 7.7.2).

At the end of the study, six months following implementation of training, paired t-test analysis revealed significant differences in levels of somatic anxiety and physical health for exercise and wait-list participants. At this time point, the wait-list participants had received stress management training and became an experimental group. The non-volunteer control participants also completed questionnaires and were found to have a significantly reduced mean score on anxiety compared to the experimental groups. Table 7.3 gives mean scores on individual variables for all groups at the six month time-point. A decrease in physical health mean score denotes improved health.

A surprising finding is the reduction in anxiety in control group participants. However, the actual reduction in mean score is less than the corresponding reductions in scores found in the awareness and exercise groups. The number of participants in the control group was considerably greater than in the other groups and thus more likely to be statistically significant, which may explain this anomaly.

Again, the exercise participants showed most benefits from training, with improvements in somatic anxiety and physical health compared to pre-training scores. Improvements in anxiety, depression and mental health were not maintained. This suggests that the physiological mechanisms were perhaps more effective in the longer term than the psychological mechanisms.

The wait-list participants also showed an improvement in somatic anxiety scores. These participants were three months into their training programme at this time point. Since these individuals had elected to follow the cognitive programme, their results would be expected to be in line with those of the cognitive group at the interim stage. This was the case, with the exception of the improvement in somatic anxiety in wait-list participants.

Table 7.3 Mean scores by group at six-month period on pre-intervention and post-intervention scores on anxiety, somatic anxiety, depression, mental health and physical health scales

	Awareness		Exercise		Cognitive		Wait-list		Control	
	Pre	Post	Pre	Post	Pre	Post	Pre	Post	Pre	Post
Anxiety	6.00	4.71	5.87	4.87	7.08	6.62	5.50	4.45	5.30	4.32*
Somatic anxiety	4.88	4.33	4.78	3.48*	5.50	5.15	4.59	3.64*	3.93	4.02
Depression	5.08	4.13	4.43	3.35	5.62	5.73	4.27	4.23	4.11	3.86
Mental health	56.08	53.96	56.43	53.17	58.42	58.15	53.96	55.43	53.61	51.68
Physical health	33.92	32.42	34.13	30.04*	36.77	35.77	32.35	30.96	31.39	30.36
Number	24	24	23	23	26	26	22	22	57	57

Key: * Significant at p < 0.05

Organisational variables

There were no significant effects of training, compared to controls, on either job satisfaction or organisational commitment at three months or six months post-intervention. Self-report sickness absence figures are shown in Table 7.4. Sickness absence rate is calculated as a percentage of workable days based on the formula of 223 workable days/year for each participant.

Compared to the rates for the year preceding the intervention, sickness absence rates increased during the six months following intervention in all groups except the exercise group, which reduced from 3.6 per cent to 0.8 per cent for the period. However, as these figures are self-report there may well be a degree of distortion. The pre-intervention figures are likely to be underestimated, these figures being retrospective. In all except the wait-list group, reported absence rates for the year were lower than the official absence rate for the organisation of 7 per cent. Nevertheless, sickness absence among exercise participants was considerably lower during the study than previously. This finding would be expected under the hypothesis that improved physical fitness boosts immune functioning (Fitzgerald, 1988).

7.7   Discussion

7.7.1   Attrition

Overall, stress management training accrued psychological benefits for individuals engaged in exercise programmes and stress awareness training after three months, with some benefits also reported by exercise participants after six months. The cognitive restructuring programme produced no positive outcomes. The wait-list group was a placebo condition; these participants were accorded training of their choosing after three months. Since no

Table 7.4 Self-reported sickness absence percentages by group for twelve months preceding study

	Awareness	Exercise	Cognitive	Wait-list	Control (Non-volunteer)
% previous year	3.63	3.59	3.34	7.25	2.58
Number	48	42	48	50	79
3-months post intervention	2.69	3.70	4.40	2.48	not calculated
Number	28	25	32	26 (pre-training)	
6-months post intervention	6.46	0.78	7.59	8.03	3.25
Number	24	23	26	23	59

improvements were found in this group in the three months between commencement of the project and implementation of training, it would seem that expectations of training and/or attention are not sufficient in themselves to produce psychological benefits.

Paired t-tests examined pre- and post-intervention data for those participants who remained in the study ('the stayers'). Comparisons of data using only participants who remained in the study raises concerns of self-selection during the intervention. However, since the purpose of the study was to examine effects of and differences between programmes of differing theoretical perspectives, analysing data for the stayers gives a more realistic comparison than would be obtained by using the original sample for pre-intervention data. Also, demographic analysis indicated that the stayers were a representative sub-group of the original sample. It was not possible, given the framework of the study, to determine what percentage of the stayers actually practised the relevant technique and what percentage neglected to follow the programme but still completed questionnaires. Since skill practice was fundamental to this intervention, decreasing adherence to the programmes is likely to confound results. This makes interpretation and generalisation of the results difficult and serves to highlight the need for further research where closer ongoing contact can be maintained with participants.

It would also be productive to examine individuals' reasons for dropping out of the study and whether attrition would have been lower had participants self-selected into the specific training programmes as opposed to random allocation. Attrition may reflect both time pressures on individuals (volume of work was one of the major stressors) and lack of interest in the allocated technique. Again, it was not possible within the framework of the study to investigate reasons for drop-out.

7.7.2   Discussion of specific techniques

Effects and implications of the separate training programmes will be discussed in this section.

I   PERSONAL STRESS AWARENESS TRAINING PROGRAMME

This programme followed an educational perspective. The focus was on recognition of symptoms of stress, personal stressors and coping styles. Workshop instruction culminated in the development of an action plan to address particular stressor situations by adopting more positive coping strategies. This action plan was to be followed for the duration of the study. Analysis of post-training data clearly show that this type of training had a positive effect for individuals in terms of physical and mental health symptoms and on symptoms of depression. However, the crucial issue remains: to what extent does increased awareness of stress facilitate improved coping in stressful situations? Is it realistic to assume that improved understanding will result in behaviour change? As this programme incorporated a behavioural change element, i.e. action planning, it could be argued that it is this, rather than increased awareness, that is responsible for short-term beneficial outcomes. However, the concept of behavioural change and the difficulties attached to changing one's own behaviour was not a feature of the programme. The efficacy of this approach may lie in the degree of perceived control that increased understanding gives an individual. This improved sense of control is likely to be increased if an individual has immediate opportunity to target stressor situations and to set goals, as in this programme.

2 EXERCISE PROGRAMME

This workshop presented participants with a structured exercise programme. Individuals were then asked to exercise twice weekly at home, for the duration of the study. In line with expected findings, exercise participants registered improvements in anxiety, somatic anxiety, depression and mental and physical health after three months. There has been much research into the effects of exercise on anxiety and there is now a considerable body of evidence demonstrating the effectiveness of exercising in reducing anxiety (see for example, Steptoe et al., 1989). The mechanisms by which this occurs are still unclear and there are a number of competing hypotheses, for example, stress inoculation (Keller and Seraganian, 1984), enhanced body image (Tucker, 1990), dissipation of stress hormones (Everly and Rosenfield, 1981). Whatever mechanisms are responsible for producing these effects, exercise is evidently a powerful tool for reducing the negative impact of stress on an individual.

The message for organisations is clear – employee welfare and benefit programmes must disseminate this information and encourage employees to take exercise. Some larger organisations already offer on-site gymnasium facilities for employees. However, employee use of such facilities is not always high. In the UK, the bulk of information aimed at the general public concentrates on the physical health benefits of exercise. While this is important, the psychological benefits are often overlooked and organisations would do well to take on this information role for their own employees.

3 COGNITIVE RESTRUCTURING PROGRAMME

This training programme was based on Rational Emotive Behaviour Therapy (REBT) (Ellis, 1962). During the workshop, participants were instructed in the basis of the theory and had practice in identifying irrational beliefs and completing the ABCDE framework for challenging beliefs and replacing irrational beliefs with more rational and productive ones.

Participants were asked to record stressful situations for the duration of the study and to use the framework to analyse and challenge their beliefs. No significant benefits on any of the measures were found in this group. This was particularly surprising, since it had been anticipated that this technique would have considerable potential to reduce stress, through providing individuals with knowledge of the impact of perceptions on emotion and enabling them to analyse their reactions to stressful situations in terms of a structured framework. There are a number of possible reasons for this lack of effect:

(a)   Is the technique suitable for an organisational setting?
(b)   Did the workshop in this study allow sufficient time for individuals to feel comfortable with the procedure?
(c)   Is the technique appropriate as a 'stand alone' training module?
(d)   To what extent do organisational factors obstruct the technique?

Each of these questions will in turn be addressed.

(a)   Suitability for organisational settings
REBT is most commonly used on a one-to-one basis in a clinical setting. Translating this into an organisational setting and using group training methods, necessitates changing the focus away from a highly personal perspective, involving the psychological history of an individual, and towards a work oriented perspective that examines typical organisational stressors and common reactions to them. In this change of focus, the technique possibly becomes diluted.

(b)   Duration of training workshop
The workshop in this study was only two hours duration, due to organisational time constraints. For a technique as difficult as REBT, this amount of training cannot be sufficient. While trainees certainly appeared to be able to identify certain irrational beliefs in their own behaviours, more practice and discussion was required on the refuting beliefs aspect of the technique. A one-day workshop would be more appropriate for this training module.

(c)   Appropriateness of REBT as a 'stand alone' training module
As a 'stand alone' module, REBT runs into difficulties. The workshop teaches individuals the technique and they are then expected to apply this technique without further support. Should individuals have problems refuting and replacing irrational beliefs, they may become demotivated and withdraw from technique. One solution to this is to hold a 'follow-up' session when common difficulties can be discussed and support given where needed.

(d)   Organisational factors
Organisational factors may also work against the technique. An individual's ability to influence organisational stressors is limited. Although analysis of

irrational beliefs may assist in the promotion of beneficial interpersonal relationships at work, and may modify an individual's behaviour in some situations, there will remain stressors that give little room for manoeuvre. For example, in the case of work overload as an organisational stressor, REBT will help an employee examine their attitudes and behaviours and change any behaviours that may be exacerbating this heavy workload, but it will not reduce the volume of incoming work. Often, there is a sense of frustration and anger among employees about stressors they feel arise unnecessarily from the culture or systems of an organisation. This frustration will not enhance an individual's motivation to use REBT and can result in the feeling that stress is the 'fault' of the organisation and it is therefore the organisation's responsibility to change. REBT as a training programme may therefore be more effective if run in conjunction with interventions aimed at reducing organisational stressors.

The lack of training effects in the cognitive restructuring group does not necessarily indicate that cognitive restructuring as a theoretical perspective cannot be beneficial for reducing stress. Modification of an REBT programme along the lines discussed in this section may bring improved results. There are also other forms of cognitive restructuring that need to be tested empirically in the workplace. REBT is a difficult and possibly ambitious programme and it may best operate as an 'advanced' module, following practice in simpler techniques such as mental diversion, thought stopping and constructive self-talk.

7.7.3 Global issues in stress management training

Sustainability of effects

Most of the benefits apparent after three months post-training were not sustained at six months. This is in line with findings of other studies. In a review of stress management programmes, Everly (1989) reported that positive benefits were generally only demonstrated at immediate post-testings, normally ten to twelve weeks after implementation of training. Reynolds and Shapiro (1991) also conclude that changes have usually dissipated at the follow-up stage. In the present study, the three month time point was an interim measure and skills practice should have continued for the full six months. Since there was no ongoing contact with participants, adherence to the programmes may have diminished over time. This is a particular problem with the exercise programme, since adherence to exercise programmes generally is known to be low (Biddle and Fox, 1989). For any programme to maintain benefits, it is essential that new skills and behaviours are practised until they are assimilated into an individual's normal behaviour pattern. Niven and Johnson (1989) suggest that practice can best be encouraged by holding a series of shorter sessions for discussion of techniques, with time between devoted to skills practice. This methodology is unlikely to be appropriate for workplace stress management training, but it does highlight the importance of practice. A possible solution is to hold short informal support sessions post-training in order to encourage and reinforce skill practice. The period of time over which these sessions took place would need to be determined and would probably vary depending on degree of difficulty of training technique.

Organisational variables

No significant changes were found in levels of job satisfaction or organisational commitment for any group. Empirical research on these variables is more limited and has produced more conflicting findings than research on individual variables. It might be assumed that organisational commitment would increase when stress management training is provided by an organisation. A possible explanation for the lack of such an effect is that employees' awareness of stress is increased, giving rise to concerns that organisational stressors remain unchanged. This hypothesis can only be examined where organisational changes are introduced. One of the issues raised in training sessions targeted at the individual level is 'what is the organisation going to do to reduce stress?' Cooper and Sadri (1991) purport that it may be necessary to effect organisational changes in order to improve employee attitudes towards the organisation. Additionally, Ganster et al. (1982) argue that individually-targeted interventions treat stress as an individual rather than an organisational problem and are applicable only where environmental stressors exist that cannot be changed or modified.

Certainly as far as job satisfaction is concerned, individual stress management training is unlikely to significantly improve an employee's level of satisfaction with their job, unless the major stressors inherent in the job are also addressed. If job stressors remain, an employee's efforts to manage stress more effectively will contrast with lack of initiatives at organisation level, possibly resulting in demotivation on the part of the employee. As with organisational commitment, job satisfaction needs to be examined where organisational changes are being implemented to minimise stressors.

Examination of sickness absenteeism rates indicated increased absence during the period for all groups except the exercise group, whose absence rate decreased from 3.6 per cent pre-intervention to 0.8 per cent at six months post-intervention. This decrease in sickness absence rate among exercisers is in line with findings presented by Cox et al. (1981), who reported lower absenteeism among frequent exercisers than among non-exercisers or infrequent exercisers. As already discussed, this data is self-report and retrospective and therefore susceptible to distortion, thus firm conclusions cannot be drawn. However, there is a clear difference between the post-intervention rate of the exercise group in comparison with its pre-intervention rate and the corresponding rates of the other groups. The evidence regarding sickness absence and general stress management training is still conflicting and will not be resolved without objective data from absence figures collected by the organisation. The problems inherent in this approach, technical issues associated with the collection of data relating to particular individuals, and the reassurance to employees that the data will not be used to their detriment at some point in the future, deter the collection of objective absence data.

7.7.4   Costs and benefits of the project

Financial costs incurred by the organisation were small and related to purchase of questionnaires and photocopying of programme handouts. Indirect financial costs resulted from time lost due to participants attending workshops and completing questionnaires. Limiting training to three hours (a two-hour workshop plus one-hour information session), reduced lost working time.

Benefits of the project were mainly at the individual level and related to fewer experienced symptoms of anxiety, somatic anxiety and depression and more positive perceptions of psychological and physical health. As was discussed in the previous section, data on sickness absenteeism were conflicting, thus it is hard to assess benefits with respect to sickness absenteeism. Indirect benefits may arise from the willingness of the organisation to openly address the issue of stress at work; employees can be reluctant to admit to strain because of fears that career development within the organisation may be impeded (Arroba and James, 1990). Arroba and James also suggest that stress management training makes a statement that the organisation cares about the well-being of its employees.

7.7.5   Stimulating and hindering factors

Promotion of the study was assisted by a concern among many employees about their own levels of stress. While this provided motivation for attending training workshops, it was to some extent offset by time pressures and heavy workloads, leaving many employees feeling that they wanted to take action to reduce their stress levels but did not have the time to learn how to do so. Lack of time was arguably the greatest source of hindrance to the success of the study.

The project was also hindered by a lack of contact with participants during the course of the study. Individual difficulties relating to programme adherence could have been identified and uncertainties clarified. However, owing to the dispersion of participants over a wide geographic area, face-to-face contact during the study was not practicable. Additionally, the support and commitment of senior management to a programme is vital for its success (Seamonds, 1986). Although some members of the senior management team

took part in the project, perhaps more active involvement in project administration would have highlighted management support and encouraged
employee participation.

Follow-up data is not available for this study. Although follow-up data is
important to examine maintenance of effects, it was not feasible to obtain
this data within the current study.

7.7.6 Issues for the future

Aside from technical issues such as duration of training sessions, support
sessions and so forth, one of the more important issues emanating from this
study is the issue of self-selection for training. There are two aspects here –
one relates to who should attend stress management courses and the other
relates to what type of course should be offered by organisations. As demonstrated, there were no differences in this project between volunteers for
training and individuals who did not wish to take part in stress management
training, despite suggestions from the literature that there might be differences in stress profile between these two groups. For example, Sutherland
(1990) describes individuals who attend programmes as the 'worried well',
whereas a review by Conrad (1987) suggests that participants appear to be
healthier and more concerned with fitness and health matters than non-
participants. In practice, organisations wishing to implement an integrated
stress management policy would be advised to develop a culture which recog-
nises stress without viewing it as a 'weakness' and to facilitate and encourage
stress management training for employees. An employee 'assigned' to a stress
management course will not be in a sufficiently positive frame of mind to
benefit from the course and is likely to resent what is seen as an imposition.

Regarding the type of course to be offered by organisations, best practice
may perhaps be served by a stage approach. The first stage would involve
stress awareness coupled with analysis and identification of personal stressor
situations and coping profile, leading to behavioural change and goal setting.
This stage should include the promotion and strong encouragement of exercise as an effective mechanism for reducing stress, with facilitation, as in the
provision of lunchtime exercise classes, where possible. Stage two would
focus on theories underpinning cognitive restructuring techniques and would
include practice in techniques such as constructive self-talk and thought stopping. The final stage would utilise a more advanced technique such as REBT.
Adopting this three-stage approach would address many of the problems from
the present study and would allow time to practice skills learned, with follow-
up support. Although a three-stage (i.e. three-day) approach may seem
onerous to some organisations, since it would be conducted over a period
of months it should not be prohibitive in terms of time or financial costs.
Potential benefits of stress awareness and exercise have been demonstrated in
this study – actual costs have yet to be quantified using organisational absen-

teeism data. Additionally, since stress thresholds and susceptibility to stress vary considerably, not all employees would wish to pursue the full three-stage course. Finally, organisations must not brush aside the need for minimising stressors where possible. The use of a stress audit to identify organisational stressors (Cooper and Cartwright, 1994) is the first step in this process. However, a stress audit can raise hopes among employees that action will be taken by management and it must therefore be used as an indicator for action, not as an end in itself. The stress audit is a very useful tool for identifying problems and is a building block for longer term organisational change. Used in conjunction with interventions aimed at improving individual coping skills, there is high potential for lasting improvements in employee health and well-being. Many organisations in the UK are now beginning to utilize stress audit technique as an initial step towards stress prevention and hopefully this will result in more integrated and better evaluated stress intervention strategies.

7.8 Conclusion

The objectives of the current study were to improve coping skills among employees and reduce reported symptoms of ill health and strain and to examine the effectiveness of different types of stress management programme on individual and organisational variables. Improvements in health were recorded by individuals participating in personal stress awareness and exercise programmes. The cognitive restructuring training programme did not achieve significant health benefits. Organisational variables, i.e. job satisfaction and organisational commitment were not affected by training. Self-reported sickness absenteeism rate was lowered in the exercise group during the period of the study but increased in other groups.

Beneficial effects on anxiety, somatic anxiety, depression and mental and physical health for exercise participants are substantiated by other research findings. Positive influences on depression and mental and physical health in stress awareness participants are also in keeping with other empirical evidence. Less evidence exists regarding the efficacy of cognitive restructuring techniques, but it is suggested here that these techniques also have the potential for positive benefits on employee health. Cognitive restructuring techniques are more difficult to implement and therefore attention must be paid to the format and duration of stress management courses involving this concept, and to skill practice. Certain employee groups may be more receptive to this technique than others.

A three-stage approach is suggested for stress management training at the level of the individual. This should be complemented by the identification, and longer-term minimisation where possible, of common organisational stressors. Improvements in job satisfaction and organisational commitment are unlikely to occur without attempts by the organisation to address major stressors.

With growing awareness in organisations of the deleterious effects of excessive stress, coupled with recent litigation in this country and financial pressures to reduce absenteeism costs, the results of this project give some encouragement for organisations wishing to implement stress management training. Individually-targeted training can produce benefits within a short timespan. However, for these benefits to be maintained, identification and minimisation of organisational stressors is also required. These complementary approaches may, if introduced as part of an integrated policy of stress prevention, also have the additional benefit of increasing employee motivation and commitment to the organisation.

Bibliography

Abrams, M. and Ellis, A. (1994) 'Rational emotive behaviour therapy in the treatment of stress', *British Journal of Guidance and Counselling* 22 (1): 39–50.

Altchiler, L. and Motta, R. (1994) 'Effects of aerobic and non-aerobic exercise on anxiety, absenteeism, and job satisfaction', *Journal of Clinical Psychology* 50 (6): 829–840.

American College of Sports Medicine (1990) 'The recommended quantity and quality of exercise for developing and maintaining cardirespiratory and muscular fitness in healthy adults', *Medicine and Science in Sports and Exercise*, 22: 265–74.

Arroba, T. and James, K. (1990) 'Reducing the Cost of Stress: An Organisational Model,' *Personnel Review*, 19 (1): 21–7.

Beck, A.T. (1976) *Cognitive Therapy and the Emotional Disorders*, New York: International University Press.

Biddle, S.J.H. (1995) 'Exercise and psychosocial health', *Research Quarterly for Exercise and Sport*, 66 (4): 292–97.

Biddle, S.J.H. and Fox, K.R. (1989) 'Exercise and health psychology: Emerging relationships', *British Journal of Medical Psychology*, 62: 205–16.

Bunce, D. (1997) 'What factors are associated with the outcome of individual-focused worksite stress management interventions?' *Journal of Occupational and Organizational Psychology*, 70 (1): 1–17.

Cartwright, S. and Cooper, C.L. (1996) *Managing Mergers, Acquisitions and Strategic Alliances: Integrating People and Cultures*, Oxford: Butterworth Heinemann.

CBI-Percom (1995), *Sickness absence report*, London: CBI.

Coleman, V. (1992) 'Stress Management', *Training and Development*, July: 31–5.

Conrad, P. (1987) 'Who comes to worksite wellness programmes? A preliminary review', *Journal of Occupational Medicine*, 29 (4): 317–20.

Cook, J. and Wall, T. (1980) 'New work attitude, measures of trust, organizational commitment and personal need non-fulfilment', *Journal of Occupational Psychology*, 53: 39–52.

Cooper, C.L. and Cartwright, S. (1994) 'Stress management interventions in the workplace: Stress counselling and stress audits', *British Journal of Guidance & Counselling*, 22 (1): 65–72.

Cooper, C.L. and Sadri, G. (1991) 'The Impact of Stress Counselling at Work', in P.L. Perrewe (ed.) *Handbook on Job stress* (Special Issue), *Journal of Social Behavior and Personality*, 6 (7): 411–23.

Cooper, C.L. and Sutherland, V.J. (1991) 'The Stress of the Executive Life Style: Trends in the 1990s', *Employee Relations,* 13 (4): 3–7.

Cooper, C.L., Sloan, S.J. and Williams, S. (1988) *Occupational Stress Indicator,* London: NFER-Nelson.

Cooper, C.L. and Williams, S. (1994) (eds) *Creating Healthy Work Organizations,* Chichester, England: John Wiley and Sons.

Cox, M., Shephard, R.J. and Corey, P. (1981) 'Influence of an employee fitness programme upon fitness, productivity and absenteeism', *Ergonomics,* 24: 795–806.

Crews, D.J. and Landers, D.M. (1987) 'A meta-analytic review of the aerobic fitness and reactivity to psychosocial stressors', *Medicine and Science in Sports and Exercise,* 19 (supplement): 114–20.

Crown, S. and Crisp, A.H. (1979) *Crown-Crisp Experiential Index,* London: Hodder and Stoughton.

Ellis, A. (1962) *Reason and Emotion in Psychotherapy,* New York: Lyle Stuart.

Everly, B.S. and Rosenfield, R. (1981) *The Nature and Treatment of the Stress Response: A Practical Guide for Clinicians,* New York: Plenum Press.

Everly, S.E. (1989) *A Clinical Guide to the Treatment of the Human Stress Response,* New York: Plenum Press.

Fitzgerald, L. (1988) 'Exercise and the immune system', *Immunology Today,* 9, 338–39.

Ganster, D.C., Mayes, B.T., Sime, W.E. and Tharp, G.D. (1982) 'Managing occupational stress: A field experiment', *Journal of Applied Psychology,* 67, 533–542.

Industrial Society (1995) *Survey of Workplace Stress,* London: Industrial Society.

Institute of Management (1997) *The Quality of Working Life,* London: Institute of Management.

Kagan, N.I., Kagan, H. and Watson, M.G. (1995) 'Stress Reduction in the Workplace: The Effectiveness of Psycho-educational Programs', *Journal of Counseling Psychology,* 42 (1), 71–8.

Keller, S. and Seraganian, P. (1984) 'Physical fitness level and autonomic reactivity in psychosocial stress', *Journal of Psychosomatic Research,* 28, 279–87.

McHugh, M. and Brennan, S. (1992) 'Organisation Development and Total Stress Management', *Leadership and Organisation Development Journal,* 13 (1): 27–32.

Martinsen, E.W. (1994) 'Physical activity and depression: clinical experience', *Acta Psychiatrica Scandinavica,* 89 (377, suppl.): 23–27.

Murphy, L.R. (1987) 'A Review of Organizational Stress Management Research: Methodological Considerations', in J.M. Ivancevich and D.C. Ganster (eds) *Job Stress: From Theory to Suggestion,* USA: Haworth, pp. 215–27.

Neenan, M. (1993) 'Rational-emotive therapy at work', *Stress News,* 1: 7–10.

Niven, N. and Johnson, D. (1989) 'Does Stress Management Work?' *Management Services,* November: 18–21.

Rees, D. and Cooper, C.L. (1992) 'Occupational Stress in Health Service Workers in the UK', *Stress Medicine,* 8, 79–90.

Reynolds, S. and Shapiro, D.A. (1991) 'Stress Reduction in Transition: Conceptual Problems in the Design, Implementation, and Evaluation of Worksite Stress Management Interventions', *Human Relations,* 44 (7): 717–33.

Reynolds, S., Taylor, E. and Shapiro, D.A. (1993) 'Session Impact in Stress Management Training', *Journal of Occupational and Organizational Psychology,* 66, 99–113.

Rosch, P.J. and Pelletier, K.R. (1987) 'Designing worksite stress management programmes', in L.R. Murphy and T.F. Shoenborn (eds) *Stress Management in Work*

Settings, U.S.: Department of Health and Human Services, pp. 69–91.

Seamonds, B.C. (1986) 'The concept and practice of stress management', in S. Wolf and A.J. Finestone (eds) *Occupational Stress: Health and Performance at Work*, Littleton, Massachusetts: PSG Publishing.

Steptoe, A., Edwards, S., Moses, J. and Matthews, A. (1989) 'The effects of exercise training on mood and perceived coping ability in anxious adults from the general population', *Journal of Psychosomatic Research*, 2: 91–106.

Sutherland, V.J. (1990) 'Managing Stress at the Worksite', in P. Bennett, J. Weinman and P. Spurgeon (eds) *Current Developments in Health Psychology*, London: Harwood Academic Publishers, pp. 305–30.

Tucker, L.A. (1990) 'Physical fitness and psychological distress', *International Journal of Sport Psychology*, 21: 185–201.

Wynne, R. and Clarkin, N. (1992) Under Construction: Building for Health in the EC Workplace, Dublin: European Foundation for the Improvement of Living and Working Conditions.

Chapter 8

Denmark: Self-rule on route 166

An intervention study among bus drivers

Bo Netterstrøm

8.1 Introduction: Work stress in Denmark

Denmark has a working population of three million people with a total population of 5.2 million. Only half a million are employed in the manufacturing sector, while almost one million are employed in the service sector. Forty per cent of the working population are women.

In 1990, the unemployment rate was 9.7 per cent, but this rate had decreased to circa 6 per cent in 1998. The unemployment rate among unskilled workers has been relatively high (circa 16 per cent in 1997).

A legal framework for stress policy in Denmark

The Working Environment Act of 23 December 1975 lays down the functions and responsibilities of the institutions, authorities and persons responsible for the working environment in all sectors except domestic work and the armed forces. The Act also defines the structure, responsibilities and powers of the Danish occupational safety and health authorities.

The Act makes it compulsory for work to be conducted in such a way that employees' health and safety are protected. This provision also covers domestic work and the armed forces. The obligation to produce a result implies finding the means and establishing the sort of relationship between the employers' and labour organisations (the social partners) which will ensure that health and safety problems at work are solved and working conditions are improved.

The Act is based on the concept that all sides will co-operate to achieve this objective. Its objective (the preamble to the Act) is to ensure that working conditions are such that workers will not be subject, in the short term, to accident or disease or, in the long term, to physical and psychological problems. The aim is (article 1):

- to create a safe and sound working environment which shall at all times be in accordance with economic and social developments;

- to create the legal basis to enable the undertakings themselves to solve problems relating to health and safety under the guidance of the employers' and workers' organisations, and under the guidance and supervision of the occupational safety and health authorities.

Prevention is based on a number of basic principles:

- the work shall be planned, organised and performed in such a way as to ensure health and safety (article 38);
- the place of work shall be in such a condition that it is safe and healthy (article 42);
- machines, machine parts, containers, prefabricated structures, tools, and other technical equipment shall be designed and used in such a way that they are safe and without risk to health;
- the methods and working processes involved in the production and use of substances and materials shall be such that employees are effectively protected from accidents and diseases.

General goals for the working environment of the future

In spring 1995, the Danish Work Environment Service presented an action programme for a clean working environment by 2005 (Department of Labour, 1995a). This sets out the general goals for preventive health and safety activities up to 2005 and thus provides a general framework for all work in this field in Denmark over a ten-year period. The action programme was preceded by a wide public debate on the issue. The results are reflected in the programme, which was drawn up in co-operation with the social partners, and which received broad support in the Danish *folketing* (parliament).

In conjunction with, the action programme, an agreement has been reached for the first time on an integrated plan for strengthening occupational health and safety at work in Denmark, with a view to achieving safe, healthy and inspiring workplaces for the benefit of the employees and the competitiveness of businesses.

Psychosocial factors

The programme singles out certain sectors for action against psychosocial risk factors. These are:

- transport;
- textile and clothing industry;
- office and administration;
- hotels and restaurants;
- cleaning companies, laundries and dry-cleaners;

- food, beverages and tobacco industries;
- social and health services.

Psychological disorders are also deemed a serious occupational health and safety problem in the 'training and research' sector.

A committee, composed of parties involved with the working environment programme, completed its work in April 1995. The committee's subsequent report agreed there was a need for higher priority in this area and outlined how this should be handled by the Danish occupational safety and health authorities, enterprises and the social partners (Department of Labour, 1995b).

Psychosocial risk factors at work are being reduced in accordance with the recommendations of the committee of the Danish Secretary of State for Employment with respect to the role and methods of the Danish occupational health and safety services.

The prevention and resolution of psychosocial problems require great openness on the part of both the employees and the management at the level of the individual workplace. As in the case of all other working environment problems, psychosocial working environment problems are, according to the policy of the Danish occupational safety and health authorities, best solved by the management and employees of the enterprise, possibly with assistance from their respective organisations, the occupational health service or other external resources.

According to the report, psychosocial risk factors can be divided into two main categories, depending on their cause. The first comprises psychosocial problems arising directly from the management's general decisions concerning the enterprise, the interaction between the management, the employees and their representatives, the interaction between the employees themselves, or factors arising from external circumstances. These factors are not related, either directly or indirectly, to the individual employee's job function. They include:

- pay and pension conditions;
- promotion and training;
- degree of influence on the management's general decisions concerning the enterprise;
- job uncertainty – for example, in connection with personnel redundancies;
- harassment, bullying or conflict between colleagues and role conflict/lack of clarity concerning roles, which may be caused by differences in temperament, natural sympathies/antipathies, and the feeling of being passed over or of being hedged in by job demarcation.

These psychosocial problems must be solved by the management in co-operation with the employees, shop stewards, the liaison committee and the internal safety organisation – if necessary with assistance from the labour market organisations (i.e. employers' and labour organisations). The Danish occupational safety and health authorities do not of their own accord become involved in the resolution of psychosocial problems of this kind.

The second category comprises psychosocial problems which are directly or indirectly related to the individual employee's work situation and which arise from the work process or work methods, the products used or the physical framework for performance of the work. Problems of this kind include:

- organisation of the workplace, noise and temperature;
- monotonous, repetitive work;
- risk of violence;
- solitary work;
- shift work;
- long working hours where this is of more than a temporary nature and is associated with a documented health risk;
- human service work, where the individual's work situation involves a documented health risk, as for example in the case of burn-out.

In these cases, the Danish occupational safety and health authorities can deal with the case after an assessment of the seriousness and extent of the problem and the risk of further harm. The occupational safety and health authorities also seek to establish whether all possibilities of solving the problem without their intervention have been exhausted. Where there is not a serious health risk, the Danish occupational safety and health authorities issue a guidance note. Where there is a proven health risk, an improvement notice is issued. It must be noted that the list of risk factors is not exhaustive, and that a risk factor can be moved from one category to the other in certain instances following a detailed investigation of its cause. To reduce the psychosocial risk factors, the social partners and authorities must either separately or jointly initiate activities within all sectors in which such risk factors are a serious occupational health and safety problem. However, so far only a few cases have been handled according to the guidelines of the report.

The impact of stress on the working population in Denmark is not very well documented. No reliable overall statistics exist on the amount of stress in the workplace. In a survey from 1990–91 made by the National Institute of Occupational Health, one-fifth of the working population reported stress symptoms daily (Nord-Larsen et al., 1992). From specific branches such as slaughter houses (Kristensen, 1994) and bus driving the figures were even higher.

Stress prevention programmes with documented evaluation have not yet been conducted. A few programmes in private enterprises to reduce sickness absenteeism have been made, but they have not been evaluated scientifically.

The primary goal for the project described in this chapter was not stress prevention, but to find ways to reduce costs and improve job satisfaction. Stress was not the specified subject, but reduction of stress was seen as a consequence of improving job satisfaction. However, this project is the first of its kind in Denmark where a radical change in working conditions and a documented evaluation have been made.

8.2 The company

Public transport in Denmark is run by private companies as well as by the state and by semi state-owned companies. There are 25,000 people employed in this sector. The railways are, with few exceptions, run by the Danish National Railway, DSB. This company also runs the bus services in rural areas. In smaller urban areas the buses are in the hands of private enterprises through contracts with the local authorities, while until the early 1990s (see section 8.3) the bus services in the major cities were run by publicly-owned companies.

Since the mid-1970s, Copenhagen's bus company 'Hovedstadens Trafikselskab' (HT), had had a monopoly on the bus service in most of the area around greater Copenhagen, including the counties of Frederiksberg, Roskilde and Copenhagen, as well as the Frederiksberg and Copenhagen councils. Nearly two million people live in this area. The company was owned by these three counties and by the Fredriksberg and Copenhagen councils mentioned above and employed around 4,000 bus drivers. The company had developed a close regional co-operation with the Danish National Railway, especially with regard to co-ordinated planning, and through-ticketing for passengers.

8.3 Motives

At the end of the 1980s, the Danish parliament decided that HT should be divided into a service and a management company. The management company, still state-owned was to put the bus routes out to tender and the service company, also still state-owned, but from then on named 'Bus Denmark', was to submit a tender on equal terms with private bus companies.

At the same time a different financial basis for the bus services in the area was introduced. The bus companies which were awarded the contracts were paid for each hour the buses were in service, in contrast to before when the economy was not dependent on productivity. This led to an increased financial incentive for changes in the organisation of the work.

In 1980, the first Danish study of bus drivers' working conditions and health was published (Laursen and Netterstrøm, 1980). This thorough study of bus drivers predominantly working on routes under the control of Copenhagen and Frederiksberg councils, as well as drivers employed by the bus companies in Århus and Odense (Århus *sporveje* and Odense *bytrafik*), provided the basis for the study outlined in this chapter.

On the basis of the results of the 1980 study, it was recommended that there be changes in the shift system, the organisation of the work into smaller operating units, increased training for the bus drivers and traffic planning initiatives. These recommendations were followed by HT to a minor extent with regard to the traffic planning initiatives in so far as an increased number of bus lanes were introduced in heavy traffic areas in the inner city. Furthermore, several ergonomic improvements were introduced, but hardly any improvements of the work organisation were carried out. For a couple of years there were a few weak attempts at establishing experimental routes with self-rule groups, but these were abandoned due to a lack of support by the bus companies.

However, the Laursen study (Laursen *et al.*, 1980) showed that there was, especially in the large bus companies, a significantly increased absence due to illness and general ill health among the bus drivers. In the late 1970s, absence due to ill health was at 12–13 per cent in Copenhagen. In addition, there was a high turn-over of bus drivers in the companies.

In the early 1990s, the changes in the financial basis of the bus service in the HT area led to discussions between the trade unions and Bus Denmark in order to try to find out how the working conditions of the bus drivers could be improved and thereby, from the bus companies' point of view, the bus service be made more profitable.

8.4   Analysis of the working environment

In 1993, twenty-three bus drivers, independently of the trade unions, participated in development workshops arranged by the company. All the drivers who were invited to participate were actively engaged in improving the working conditions of bus drivers. In these development workshops the existing conditions were appraised, and on the basis of the appraisal and aspirations expressed, concrete suggestions for improvements of the existing conditions were put forward. Six topics were highlighted:

1   *Management and co-operation*:
    The bus drivers had a negative experience of co-operation with the bus company. Particular points of criticism were that they were not involved in the planning to a large enough extent and that they received too little support in connection with illness and complaints from passengers.

2   *The running of the service*:
    The bus drivers pointed out that there was a lack of support from the management's side. Special criticism was directed at the traffic centre which was responsible for the running of the service on a daily basis.

3   *Working conditions*:
    The drivers had experienced a gradual deterioration of their working conditions in recent years, with many drivers quitting the job and

increased driving time. In addition, the uniforms and the staff canteens were criticised.

4   *The buses*:

The drivers criticised the design and maintenance, especially the ergonomic conditions around the driver's seat. The level of cleaning was also criticised, and there was a wish expressed for more bus lanes and for ticket sales to be removed from the buses.

5   *The bus drivers*:

There was internal criticism among the drivers, among other things criticism of those drivers who did not stick to the existing rules, and there was a wish for light duties for drivers with health problems.

6   *The passengers*:

The drivers argued that the passenger service was inadequate and that there should be more time for this.

8.5   Choice of measures

On the basis of the report from the development workshops, Bus Denmark decided to implement an experiment on one bus route, route 166 running from Glostrup to Hellerup in the Copenhagen area. The experiment started on 27 May 1994. Route 166 was an average route with regard to both the number of bus drivers and the level of traffic. From the outset there were in principle only two conditions: (a) the obligations stated in the contract with the management company HT must be fulfilled unless separate agreements and dispensations could be agreed and (2) the drivers had to run the route for the same amount as it would have cost if the route had continued on the standard conditions. This meant that the budget of eleven million kroner (approximately 1.3 million ECU) had to be kept, the timetable could not be changed and the route should remain the same.

Before the project began several working groups were established among the bus drivers, and four seminars for drivers, management and labour organisations were held. These seminars resulted in a final specification agreed by all parties of how the project should be run.

All drivers working on the route at that time were invited to participate in the project. Eighteen drivers chose to participate. One driver declined and the so-called casual drivers without a set rota were not included. However, a number of the drivers who had participated in the development workshops were included, thus twenty-nine drivers were employed at the start of the project. This number was later supplemented with four or five casual drivers. The service was improved concurrently with this increase in the number of drivers.

The introduction to the experiment was a three week full-time course for all twenty-nine drivers. Here the shift and rota planning, finances and maintenance of the buses and so forth, were outlined.

8.6   Implementation

Finance

The budget of eleven million kroner (1.3 million ECU) had to cover wages for the drivers, maintenance of the buses, repairs at a garage which had to be paid for, fuel and other matters of importance for the running of the service. The purchase of new buses was not included in the budget. The drivers were free to organise as they wished within the limits of the budget.

Management

A style of management was chosen whereby the drivers democratically elected four service drivers at general meetings held every three months. At these meetings decisions regarding all aspects of the bus service were also made. The service drivers' task was to manage the daily planning of the bus service, including the calling in of casual drivers, communication with Bus Denmark, book-keeping and so forth.

The service drivers normally worked three hours driving the bus, followed by other duties for the remaining time of their working day. There were no actual superiors among the drivers on route 166 as new service drivers could be elected at the quarterly general meetings.

The tasks of the service drivers were:

- planning of shifts and running of the service;
- appointment of new staff;
- holidays, days off and sabbaticals in agreement with the other drivers;
- sickness;
- administration of ticket sales;
- bonus schemes;
- information to the drivers;
- complaints;
- contact with the management company;
- contact with the service company;
- contact with trade unions;
- contact with the environmental organisation of the management company, HT;
- contact with the safety organisation of Bus Denmark.

In addition, eight working groups were established, and these groups had to work alongside the service drivers, but manage separate issues such as rota planning, advertising and design of the buses, garage and maintenance, passenger service and information, timetables, the bus route, press contacts, personnel management and uniforms.

Planning of the rota

The planning of the rota was based on the wishes of the drivers. All the drivers expressed a preference regarding their working hours, and it turned out that it was possible to cover the whole of the timetable on the basis of the wishes of the drivers. Twelve chose to work the rolling shift counter-clockwise with a late start followed by an earlier and earlier start the subsequent days (see Table 8.1).

The remaining seventeen drivers chose a set rota as shown in Table 8.2. This type of schedule contains nine days off and twenty-one working days.

Working hours for the five casual drivers were not timetabled. All drivers worked Saturday and Sunday every other weekend. During the first year, increased income due to reduced sickness and savings in the running of the service made it possible to employ two more drivers leading to an increase in the length of the breaks. Formerly, breaks were around fifteen to twenty minutes, but now they were frequently around forty minutes, all within the normal working hours. The total working time is different from day to day, but is on average just under thirty-seven hours a week, the typical working day being just over seven hours-long including breaks.

Position with regard to the buses

The drivers now had the opportunity to fit out the driver's seat and the bus cabin in a different way. Coffee vending machines and telephones were installed for the passengers, and the ergonomic conditions for the drivers were improved. New seats were installed in several of the buses.

Social conditions

The running of the service was planned so that breaks could be taken at the bus garage. This means that the driver has the opportunity to talk to colleagues taking their break at the same time. Previously breaks were often taken at the end of the routes when the driver tended to be on his or her own.

Table 8.1 Example of a counter-clockwise rota

Day	Start	End
1	17.26	0.14
2	13.15	20.12
3	12.46	20.2
5	10.58	18.26
6	5.46	14.06
7	Free	

Table 8.2 Example of fixed thirty-day schedule for a driver

Day	Hours worked
Friday–Sunday	6.08–13.22
Monday	off work
Tuesday–Thursday	5.24–11.58
Friday–Sunday	off work
Monday–Wednesday	5.24–11.58
Thursday	off work
Friday–Monday	10.58–18.26
Tuesday	off work
Wednesday–Friday	5.24–11.38
Saturday–Sunday	off work
Monday–Tuesday	5.46–14.06
Wednesday	off work
Thursday–Saturday	5.37–11.58

The general meetings enabled discussions about all sorts of problems in the group. Two and a half years after the start of the project, all drivers are still attending the meetings every three months.

All aspects of personnel management were also the responsibility of the self-governing group. It was agreed that drivers who did not come to work on time and generally failed to fulfil obligations towards his/her colleagues were to receive an oral and a written warning, possibly leading to dismissal. The latter, however, has to date not happened. Only a few discussions about these issues have actually taken place.

The self-governing group also administered sick leave and rules about doctor's certificates for long term illness were introduced as well as discussions with drivers if they were ill for extended periods of time. The doctor's certificate is issued by the drivers' general practitioner, as no occupational health service exists.

A rule that requests to take days off should be granted was also introduced. And the same case was made for requests to take holiday leave.

8.7   Evaluation

An evaluation of objective as well as subjective goals has been made. Among the objective goals have been financial targets, sickness absence and passenger complaints. The subjective evaluation was not planned beforehand, but consisted of questionnaire studies made by a management firm as well as interviews made by the author.

8.7.1   Objective goals

The budgets have kept to their targets. In fact, it was possible to save approximately half a million kroner (approximately 60,000 ECU), and within this budget employ two more drivers. The saving was a result of lower costs for the maintenance and repair of the buses, as well as reduced costs due to fines for disruptions in the service. The service company normally has to pay such fines to HT's management company.

Finally, the change in calculating the funding for the service meant that a decrease in sickness leave resulted in a situation where it was only very rarely necessary to withdraw a bus due to a driver's illness. At the beginning of the project, the absence due to illness was on average fifteen working days per year. One year later it was reduced to 8.9 days and after two years it was just over six days. The increased spirit of solidarity also meant that the drivers were more motivated to help out when a colleague was ill. The number of complaints from passengers had gone down from seventeen (in the year before the start of the project) to three (in the first year of the project).

8.7.2   Questionnaire Study I

During the first year of the project sub-studies were undertaken among the drivers every three months. The overall response rate was 73 per cent (n = 29). The answers to the questions were graded on an eight-point scale in four issues, and it was possible to make comments on advantages and disadvantages. The questionnaire consisted of a few questions encompassing one of each of the following four aspects:

- satisfaction with the project;
- satisfaction with the job;
- influence on the running of the service;
- evaluation of the service drivers.

Satisfaction with the project

Figure 8.1 illustrates a relatively high level of satisfaction with the project, but also that the satisfaction decreased during the first three sub-studies and increased slightly in the last sub-study. Approximately 90 per cent of the drivers questioned were highly satisfied in the first sub-study, approximately half were satisfied in the fourth sub-study. Only 20 per cent of the drivers were generally dissatisfied in the third sub-study. Only one person was highly dissatisfied in the last sub-study. There is no explanation for the relatively high level of dissatisfaction in the third sub-study. The high general level of satisfaction with the project was further illustrated by an additional question

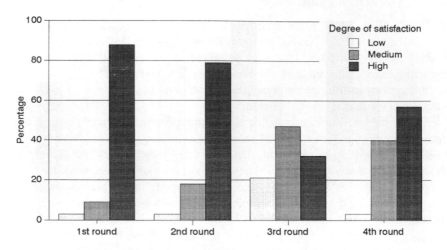

Figure 8.1 Satisfaction with the project, measured every three months

where the drivers had to decide if they would recommend others to participate in similar projects. The majority would.

Those drivers who had participated in the development workshops and
therefore had not previously worked on route 166 were more satisfied than
the original drivers on the route. The original drivers had been more sceptical from the beginning.

Satisfaction with the job

The development of the drivers' level of satisfaction with their job is shown
in Figure 8.2, and also here approximately 60 per cent state relatively high
satisfaction in the first sub-study. The number decreases to around 40 per
cent in the fourth sub-study. Here too, there is a relatively higher level of
dissatisfaction in the third sub-study.

When answering more open questions on the questionnaire, the highest
score as to what was the biggest advantage of the project was the fact that
shifts and breaks had been improved. The new drivers were more positive than the original drivers just as they were in their satisfaction with the
project.

Influence on the running of the service

As illustrated in Figure 8.3, a rather different pattern can be seen. In the first
as well as the fourth sub-study, approximately 40 per cent were highly satisfied with their influence. Generally there were relatively more drivers in the

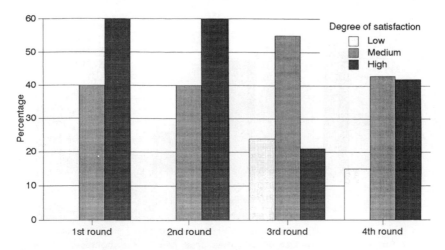

Figure 8.2 Satisfaction with the job, measured every three months

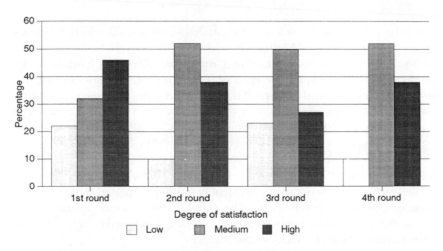

Figure 8.3 Influence on the running of the service, measured every three months

fourth sub-study who were positive with regard to their influence than there were in the previous sub-studies. The drivers who worked on the route before the start of the project assessed their influence on the running of the service more positively than the drivers from other routes who had partici-pated in the development workshops. This can be seen as a sign that improvements actually have taken place, and that the drivers who had been to the development workshops had higher expectations of further improve-ments than those which were actually made.

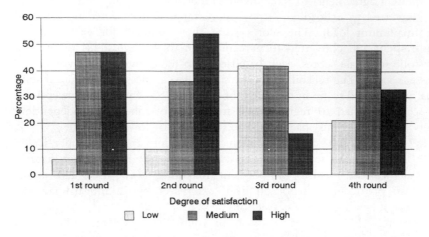

Figure 8.4 Appraisal of the service drivers, measured every three months

Appraisal of the service drivers

Approximately half of the drivers evaluated the work of the service drivers highly positively in the first sub-study, but there was a general development towards a more negative evaluation during the first year (Figure 8.4). However, in the fourth sub-study only approximately 20 per cent of the drivers did express a negative opinion of the work of the service drivers.

Among the negative comments in the questionnaires was the feeling that the service drivers were a clique. The drivers who had participated in the development workshops and consequently had moved to route 166 from other routes were highly critical of the service drivers. They were more critical than those drivers who had worked on route 166 all the time. This was in spite of the fact that drivers from other routes were over-represented among the service drivers.

Those who were service drivers during the study evaluated their colleagues, i.e. the other service drivers, very positively.

8.7.3   Questionnaire Study 2

Nine months after the start of the project, an analysis based on questionnaires was carried out among the drivers on route 166 as well as at a number of other bus stations. In this way it was possible to compare the drivers on route 166 with drivers in other areas. However, the overall response rate among the route 166 drivers was low (41 per cent), and therefore the answers must be taken with a degree of caution.

The questionnaire consisted of 205 items. The items were designed as statements, where the respondent had to indicate agreement on a scale from one (perfect agreement) to five (disagreement). The response for each item was converted to a 'load' or 'stress' score ranging from zero (no load) to four (maximum load). The scores were then summed for each scale of measurement and converted to percentage of total range. This resulted in sixty-four sub-scale scores, each based on two to ten items (on average 3.2 items per scale). The reliabilities of the sub-scales, as measured by Cronbach's alpha, were found to lie in the range of 0.50 to 0.85, with a few exceptions. Sub-scales designed to register total frequency of inherently independent events (e.g., life events) had of course, a somewhat lower alpha.

The sixty-four sub-scales were then averaged into eighteen 'super-scales' for an overview. All sub- and super-scale scores were in the range from 0 per cent (no load/stress) to 100 per cent (maximum load/stress). The super-scales can be further categorised into 'external factors', 'internal factors', 'coping strategies', and 'stress reactions'.

Figure 8.5 shows the comparison of route 166 with the other lines. Compared with the other lines the drivers on route 166 expressed considerably less problems.

The drivers on route 166 scored significantly lower stress levels ($p < 0.01$) regarding work content, work load and control, leadership climate and physical work environment. Generally, the drivers on route 166 felt that they had a better psychosocial working environment, and in particular the relationship with management, with colleagues, and the opportunities for personal development were said to be better among these drivers than the others. Also with respect to the physical working conditions, the drivers on route 166 showed a higher level of satisfaction, whereas other areas such as their self-perception and opinion, the way they handled stress and their behavioural pattern were all similar to the other drivers.

8.7.4 Interview study

The interviews took place at the same time as the questionnaire study. The same volunteer six drivers were interviewed individually each time. The interviews were structured using the same pattern.

In the interview study several types of attitudes to the project among the six drivers and their colleagues were identified: (a) committed, (b) willing, (c) reticent and (d) negative. The initially reticent persons adopted a predominantly positive and accepting attitude. With time this development resulted in approximately one-third of the participants in the project belonging to a core group of very active, committed drivers, whereas the remaining two-thirds constituted a group of more subordinate and passive drivers, 'the ranks'. The active drivers were relatively younger, and the majority of them had worked on other routes before and had participated in the development workshops. The rank and file participants were relatively satisfied with the project because it had brought about some concrete improvements of their

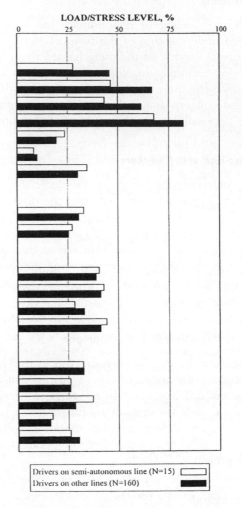

Figure 8.5 Overview of questionnaire results among fifteen drivers from route 166
(light bars), and 160 drivers from surrounding routes (dark bars)

working conditions, but they only participated to a limited extent in discussions at the general meetings, and they were not service drivers at any time.

Evaluation of the advantages of the project

The general evaluation was that it had become easier to be a bus driver because the shifts were shorter and the breaks were extended to forty minutes instead of twenty minutes as before. In addition, the increased influence on the working conditions was considered of utmost importance.

Responsibility

The drivers' feeling of responsibility has increased on several levels. The increased understanding of the finances and the collective responsibility for the financial survival of the route has led to an increased feeling of responsibility, for example in connection with sickness, the maintenance of equipment, the use of fuel, and cancelled departures. However, some drivers expressed concern as to whether the service drivers were qualified to take on the responsibility for the running of the route.

Sickness and relief workers

At the interviews the reason for the decrease in the level of absence due to illness was explained by the fact that the drivers now knew their colleagues better, knew who was working when, and this made the driver more conscious of the consequences of a possible absence due to illness. The absence due to illness had decreased from fifteen days per driver on average before the start of the project. After one year the absence due to illness was 8.9 days, and after two years 6.1 days. A number of drivers had no absence due to illness.

Responsibility towards the equipment

The fact that the drivers on route 166 had their own permanent buses had considerable consequences for the way in which the drivers maintained them. The drivers had also learnt that a different driving technique would reduce the use of fuel. In addition to the decrease in the number of passenger complaints, the drivers felt that the relationship with the passengers had improved, probably, among other things, due to a certain amount of publicity for the project.

Social relations

The contact among the colleagues was improved considerably as the project made it possible to take breaks at the bus garage which meant that the drivers met each other daily. The meeting place was usually the operations office, where it was possible to confer with the service driver on duty. The extension of the breaks enabled a further increase in the social contact. However, the increased leisure time did not lead to more contact among the drivers outside of working hours.

From the interviews it was clear that the team spirit had increased, as had the level of flexibility and attentiveness towards colleagues. In addition, several of the drivers were willing to spend some of their spare time on the project, something which would have been unthinkable before.

Finally, the increased experience and understanding of the financial and co-operative rules of the game on a bus route developed a higher level of loyalty towards the employer and better understanding of the measures taken by top management.

Participation

The bus drivers previously had not had any influence on their working conditions. The introduction of general meetings as the highest authority on the route is perhaps the most significant change in this situation. At these meetings a number of working groups were established, these groups made decisions on uniforms, rota, matters concerning the bus stops, personnel management and so forth.

Several drivers expressed their satisfaction with the fact that the channels of command between the drivers and the final decision-makers within the company had become clearer and shorter. The present and former service drivers had the strongest feeling of influence.

8.7.5   Conclusion of evaluation

The conclusion of the evaluation is that there has been a relatively high level of satisfaction with the project, the organisation of the work, and the service drivers' influence, although the satisfaction declined during the first year. Also sickness absenteeism and passenger complaints have decreased. The project is an experiment in introducing new organisational structures from the bottom up with extensive transfer of power to the drivers themselves. It could be said that the project is democracy at work carried through to its logical conclusion. The core of the project has been that the drivers have gained control over their working conditions through increased influence on the planning of the work, and through the power they have been delegated they have gained certain skills.

The longer breaks enabled social contact and this social dimension and support from work colleagues have been significant. These factors appear to act as an alleviating measure from the demands associated with bus driving. The project has not been able to greatly alter the actual demands of driving a bus, the contact with the passengers, the timetables, the level of traffic and so forth.

One criticism is the level of education of the drivers in how to handle situations of conflict, for example with the passengers, while on the route, which is somewhat lacking. The education of the service drivers may not have been sufficient either, and as they to some degree act as team leaders, a better education with regard to personnel management would be advantageous.

It has been positive for the running of the project that the service drivers could be replaced using normal ballots and that they worked as regular drivers at the same time as being service drivers.

8.8 Implementation of similar projects within Bus Denmark

The success on route 166 has resulted in experiments with the implementation of the project in three other towns. However, there have been considerable differences between the various projects, and in none of the other projects were the drivers delegated the same degree of power given to the drivers on route 166.

In one of the projects, in Gilleleje, the obvious mistake of not enabling replacement of the service drivers by balloting of the other drivers was made. This resulted in a situation whereby the service drivers in time acted as a sort of middle management without the necessary contact and co-operation with the drivers which the service drivers had on route 166. In another project, in Roskilde, the drivers were not given the same degree of financial responsibility and opportunity to handle the budget as the drivers on route 166 had. Therefore a possible saving on the budget did not enable the employment of more drivers, and there were limited opportunities for changing the rota planning. Here the social dimension must be seen as the principal factor.

Tendering

It is one of the rules that the bus routes in question, including route 166, are offered for tender every four years. The increased financial profitability which the project on route 166 brought about, will to some extent be part of the tender which will mean that a project such as this one can appear to be a money-saving exercise. We feel that this development is unfortunate and will certainly have an effect on the route 166 drivers, who, at the time of writing, have been disposed of by tender to another bus company. Negotiations concerning the continuation of the project under another management company are taking place. It could have been expected that the invitation to tender would include the condition that the aims of the project were to be maintained in the future, but apparently this has not been the case.

8.9 Conclusion

The introduction of wide-ranging democracy at work and the associated responsibility, including financial matters, was shown to be successful on a bus route.

So far the project has run for three and a half years, and despite some reduction in the satisfaction with the project and its effects during the first year, it still stands as a textbook example of how improvements in the psychological working environment can be initiated, an example worthy of imitation. The fact that absence due to illness, which was reduced to about one-third of its previous level, has stayed low, that the drivers are generally satisfied, and that the budgets have been kept, speak for themselves.

The job of a bus driver is demanding: the driver has to keep to the timetable, as well as attending to the passengers, coping with the traffic and working odd hours. These demands are inherent to the job and are difficult to reduce. However, traffic initiatives and increased education of the drivers in handling difficult situations are areas which could be given more attention.

The introduction of a democratic system at work, as happened on route 166, can help to reduce the health related and social consequences of these work-related demands. The drivers feel that they have considerably more control over their own working conditions due to their having an influence on the planning of the rota, the equipment, the choice of the immediate team leader as well as the increased level of competence brought about by more responsibility. In addition to this, there is the social dimension which enables support between the colleagues in the extended breaks as well as discussions with colleagues at the general meetings about the running of the route as a whole. This has altered the situation of the drivers from being one which is characterised by high demands and low control to one which is characterised by high demands and a higher degree of control. This is equivalent to a move which, in the terminology of Karasek's job strain model (Karasek and Theorell, 1990), takes the group of drivers from high job strain towards the activity group.

The most serious criticism of the project is the uncertainty caused by the fact that the bus route is offered for tender every four years, without the drivers having any guarantee that they can continue the work in the way they have chosen to organise it.

Bibliography

Department of Labour (1995a) *Clean Working Environment Year 2005*, Copenhagen: Department of Labour.

Department of Labour (1995b) *Psykosociale risikofaktorer i arbejdslivet* ('Psychological risk factors in working life'), Copenhagen: Department of Labour.

Laursen, P. and Netterstrøm, B. (1980) *Buschaufførers arbejdsmiljø* ('Work environment of bus drivers'), Institut for Social Medicin, Copenhagen: Copenhagen University.

Nord-Larsen, M., Ørhede, E., Nielsen, J. and Burr, H. (1992) *Lønmodtagernes arbejdsmiljø 1990* ('Work environment of employees 1990'), Copenhagen: Arbejdsmiljøfondet.

Karasek, R.A. and Theorell, T. (1990) *Healthy Work*, New York: Basic Books.

Kristensen, T.S. (1994) *Arbejdsmiljø, stress og helbred i den danske slagteribranche* ('Work environment, stress and health in Danish slaughter houses'), Thesis, Copenhagen: FADLs forlag.

Chapter 9

Sweden: Mail processing

Töres Theorell and Kurt Wahlstedt

9.1 Introduction: Work stress in Sweden

9.1.1 Emphasis on work organisation and work redesign

For a long period of time, Sweden was considered a role model with regard to its attitude towards the work environment. There were several reasons for this. In 1945 Sweden was one of the few countries in Europe which had not been exposed to two world wars, and this was one of the factors behind its material affluence. The affluence of the country created a good climate for social research and reforms. Historically, Sweden had had a relatively strong tradition in these fields. Slavery had been abandoned much earlier in Sweden than in most other European countries. One of the basic fundamentals of social research – population statistics – also had early beginnings in Sweden, in the eighteenth century. Four decades of uninterrupted social democratic rule contributed to the climate of social reform, which resulted in the creation of a special agency for the protection of workers, the National Board of Occupational Safety and Health, a large institute for Research on Occupational Health and Safety, and a national research council, the Work Environment Fund, for research grants. The latter has contributed financially to a large number of research projects.

In comparison to many other European countries, Swedish research had been more oriented towards public perspectives – which resulted in an emphasis on epidemiological research dependant on person identification numbers and large population registers. Regularly recurring national surveys of living conditions including the working life in representative population samples, was a practice also started early on in Sweden (LNU, Level of Living Examination, Institute for Social Research, University of Stockholm, in 1968) and expanded both qualitatively and quantitatively in the national bureau of statistics in the 1970s (ULF, Examination of Living Conditions, Statistics Sweden). Links were created between basic psychological and physiological research on the one hand and work organisation research on the other hand. The most well-known examples of these links were:

1   The long-lasting collaboration (Frankenhaeuser and Gardell, 1976) at the University of Stockholm between Bertil Gardell – who formulated the Swedish version of alienation theory applied to work organisation (Gardell, 1971) – and Marianne Frankenhaeuser (see Frankenhaeuser and Johansson, 1975), who had been studying basic mechanisms of psychophysiological arousal for many years.

2   Lennart Levi's stress research laboratory which was expanded to become a national institute for psychosocial factors and health in 1980. Levi, a physician, had collaborated with Ulf von Euler and Hans Selye, both pioneers in physiological stress research, and he decided to start an extensive cross-disciplinary scientific group which included physicians, psychologists and sociologists.

Work environment regulation also included psychosocial factors and work organisation. This was enshrined in the Swedish law of 1976 (Arbetsmiljölag, 1976) which stated that psychosocial factors were of the same importance as the physical working environment. In terms of government policy, democratization of the working life was seen as an important agenda. The arena of paid work is one that traditionally has been regarded as the most amenable to social interventions. Workers tend to be gathered in a defined geographical location and meet regularly. Legal constraints are fewer in collective job interventions than in interventions to do with residential areas or the family. Historically this has been reflected in the establishment of structures for negotiations – workers' unions and employers' federations. This was particularly evident in the Swedish case, which resulted in a treaty (Saltsjöbadsavtalet, 1938) that included the creation of central structures for negotiations, as well as laws protecting against the dangers of certain kinds of strikes. This resulted in a relatively peaceful and successful Swedish system for the negotiation of wages.

Stress at work has been an important issue in Sweden since the 1970s. The Work Environment Act (section 1, see Arbetsmiljölag, 1976) states among many things that working conditions should adapt to people's differing physical and mental aptitudes, that the employee should be given the opportunity to participate in designing his/her own working situation, and in processes of change and development affecting his/her work and technology, work organisation and job content should be designed in such a way that the employee is not subjected to physical or mental strains which could lead to illness.

A long tradition of work redesign efforts have helped Swedish practitioners identify a list of common workplace stressors, such as the following introduced by Levi (Levi and Lunde-Jensen, 1996):

•   Inadequate time to complete our job to our satisfaction or that of others;
•   Lack of a clear job description or chain of command;

- No recognition or reward for good job performance;
- No opportunity to voice complaints;
- Lots of responsibilities but little authority or decision-making possibility;
- Unco-operative or unsupportive superiors, co-workers or subordinates;
- No control, or pride, over the finished product of our work;
- Job insecurity of no permanence of position;
- Exposure to prejudice regarding age, gender, ethnicity, race or religion;
- Unpleasant or hazardous physical work conditions;
- No opportunity to use our personal talents or abilities effectively.

The interest in stress at work has been especially pronounced among white-collar worker organisations. Among blue-collar workers, physically adverse conditions were considered more important than psychosocial factors, but explorations of stressful conditions were already made during the 1970s by the central labour union (LO) in questionnaire surveys. Because of the long historical tradition with regard to democratization of work in Sweden, stress has been associated with the workers' possibility to influence working conditions. For instance, the central organisations arranged courses for local unions in the introduction of computers and word processing software in offices in the early 1980s, with the specific aim of increasing the influence of employees.

Another feature of Sweden's attitude to stress at work is that the emphasis has been on primary prevention of stress through changing or redesigning work organisation (Kompier et al., 1994). Various large funds have been formed to promote a healthy work environment and work organisation, under the guidelines of the Work Environment Act. Another characteristic in the Swedish system is that the Labour Inspectorate has the power to stipulate improvements in an inspection report addressed to the employer. Notice of measures taken and planned is requested within a certain period of time, for instance within two or three months. If no acceptable measures have been presented by then, the Labour Inspectorate can order the employer, under threat of a fine, to make the improvements and can even prohibit certain kinds of activity, conditionally or otherwise. These penalties are, however, seldom imposed.

As a general preventive strategy, the Labour Inspectorate gives priority to supervising and inspecting the systems of internal control – the so-called systems supervision. Each employer has to present a system for internal control of the work environment including the psychosocial aspects.

Several occupational groups in Sweden have been the focus of stress research and interventions, for instance professional drivers – especially bus drivers (Belkic et al., 1994) – air traffic controllers (Theorell et al., 1990), nurses and nurses' aides (Petterson et al., 1995) and industry workers (Arbetsmiljökommissionen, 1989). In the late 1980s, the Swedish government began a special investigation into the most dangerous occupations (Arbetsmiljökommissionen 1989), which stimulated an integration of research in the areas of accident risks, cardiovascular and suicidal epidemiology and working hours. Stressors considered to be of particular importance include a lack of democracy, poorly organized shift work systems, lack of possibility for development of competence and, especially during the later decade, severe systematic maltreatment of employees ('mobbing').

9.1.2 Recent developments

The development of some of the relevant work environment variables can be seen in Table 9.1. Data are presented for men and women separately and for all of Sweden. The source is the ULF, the Examination of Living Conditions, Statistics Sweden, for the years 1975 to 1995. With regard to physically demanding conditions, i.e. heavy lifting and noise, the conditions in general seemed to improve between this period, at least for men. For one physical aspect, inconvenient postures, the conditions deteriorated, particularly for women. For psychosocial conditions, emotional demands increased during the 1990s particularly for women. This has been compensated for partly by improved possibility to learn new things. To some extent this may reflect the rising level of education of the Swedish working population and also the work environment orientation of the society. Longitudinal data published from representative groups of the working population (Fritzell and Lundberg, 1994)

Table 9.1 Developments with respect to the quality of working life of Swedish working men and women (percentages), 16–64 years of age

		% change 1975–1995	prevalence % 1992–1995
Lifting of heavy objects	men	−0.6 o	23.5
	women	+ 4.4 *	24.9
Inconvenient postures	men	+ 5.9 *	41.6
	women	+ 15.7 *	42.1
Deafening noise all the time	men	−5.9 *	11.8
	women	−1.1 o	5.0
Psychological effort	men	+ 4.9 *	38.9
	women	+ 15.6 *	46.4
Hectic and monotonous work	men	+ 1.9 o	10.8
	women	−2.3 *	10.6
Possibilities to learn new things	men	+ 8.5 *	67.7
	women	+16.2 *	60.6

Key: o = not significant   * = significant (p < 0.05)

Note: Trends have been calculated on the basis of all successive surveys, the Examination of Living Conditions (ULF)

Source: Välfärd och ojämlikhet i 20-årsperspektiv 1975–1995 (Welfare and inequality in a 20-year perspective 1975–1995), Statistics Sweden no. 91, 1997

showed that among women increasing demands – and in this particular case also lowered decision latitude – were reported first in transportation and health care. Among men the most striking observation was increasing demands in the hotel/restaurant, transportation and bank/insurance sectors. These latter observations may show the effect of global trends on Swedish working life in the late 1980s.

The situation has changed drastically during the 1990s. Pressure from the financial markets and Sweden's preparation for the entrance into the European Union (which took place after a referendum in 1994) influenced the government to change the tax system as well as the system for international financial exchange. A financial crisis in the Swedish state reached its peak in the early 1990s. This resulted in a dramatic increase in the unemployment rate, to a continuous level of around 10 per cent from the previously low level – by European standards – of 3 per cent. This has of course had an influence on the activities regarding work redesign – when employees fear losing their jobs they may be less willing to discuss work environment problems. Another significant change is that governmental support of the occupational health care system (which accounted for one-third of the budget) was withdrawn, resulting in a decrease in staff. Thus, the occupational health care teams have less resources to make explorations of psychosocial work environments and to participate in workplace redesign. There is also more emphasis on financial effectiveness and profit. This means that clients (employers) must buy the services that the occupational health care team provides. Since work environment explorations, not least in the psychosocial area, may be perceived as a threat to the acting parties in the work site, this could mean that there will be less emphasis on preventive work in the future.

The increasing emphasis on effectiveness and profit can be seen throughout the public services in Sweden. Economists for some time have been making a plea for privatization and competition to achieve these goals. However, to implement privatization and competition within the public service has been problematic, for instance in the health care sector where some reforms have been poorly prepared and have resulted in serious psychosocial work problems (see, for instance, Gustafsson, 1994).

The recent trends are reflected in the prevalence of 'casual employment': that is temporary employment in the form of project employment, practice periods, employment during periods of excessive work load and so forth. This prevalence towards casual labour has been rapidly rising in Sweden during the 1990s (Aronsson and Sjögren, 1994), despite an emphasis on employment security as set out under the law. During the period August 1993 to August 1994, 85,000 employees lost their permanent position while during the same period 100,000 men and women became temporarily employed (Aronsson and Sjögren, 1994). In the present labour market situation, a division is developing between on the one hand a 'favoured' group who have stimulating jobs and life-time job security and on the other a growing 'disfavoured' group with psychosocially bad jobs and periods of unemployment interrupted by periods of temporary employment. All of these developments are threatening the basic sense of job security and may result in increasing psychosocial tensions.

As Sweden abandons some of its previous welfare principles, there is at the same time an accumulated experience in job redesign aimed at improving productivity and the psychosocial climate. In order to explore these experiences, an interview study with the management in 2,000 worksites was performed (Le Grand et al., 1993). The participation rate was 93 per cent. The management interviews were correlated with results from employees in the same worksites participating in the survey of working Swedes performed by Statistics Sweden the same year (AKU, labour market study). The results (see Table 9.2) showed that Swedish management has been greatly influenced by work organisation research and laws. Quality circles and development groups were reported in more than half of the worksites. Industry took the lead in 'decentralized responsibility for results' and 'wages in relation to flexibility of employees' – changes which are influenced by current economy discussions. Industry, however, also had a good position with regard to possibilities for employees to develop skills and to create equal opportunities for blue- and white-collar workers. One of the surprising findings was that 'good work' (no excessive demands, an influence over decisions and opportunities to develop and use skills) was not determined statistically by a flattened hierarchy per se. The interpretation of this finding could be that the simplistic application of a flattened hierarchy may not lead to 'good work' if it is not coupled with other reorganisation efforts as well. In this study conditions were operationally defined for the labelling of a worksite with 'new' management and work organisation. There were nine conditions: (1) quality circles, (2) thorough introductory courses, (3) planned systematic within-company formal education for at least some of the employees, (4) individual development planning talks with employees, (5) responsibility for results below management level, (6) some degree of flexible salaries, (7) decisions about which work tasks to be performed, (8) decisions about how to perform work tasks at least to some extent made below the management level and (9) decreasing differences between white- and blue-collar workers. By adding the number of positive conditions a measure was created which reflects the degree to which 'new' ideas had been instituted. Table 9.2 shows the results of this analysis for different branches. The branches of health care (18 per cent at least 7 'good' conditions) and trade (17 per cent at least 7 'good' conditions) had instituted the least 'new' ideas and the manufacturing industry (42 per cent at least 7 'good' conditions) had been the most attentive to them. Another clear result was that small companies had instituted few and large companies many 'new' ideas.

The relationship between the psychosocial environment at work and health has attracted considerable attention during recent years. Surveys during the two latest decades have shown that the physical environment at work has

Table 9.2 Number of fulfilled conditions (adoption of new management principles) in different sections of the Swedish labour market

Conditions	Private	Public	Production industry	Other industry	Trading	Care	All	50–99 employees	100–499 employees	500– employees
0–3	17.6	14.2	13.8	12.2	26.4	14.0	15.9	27.0	16.4	5.0
4–6	52.2	64.1	43.7	60.9	56.8	68.2	58.0	54.9	60.9	55.9
7	19.0	12.6	21.4	18.9	12.6	13.4	15.9	12.7	15.2	20.1
8	7.6	8.3	13.9	5.0	4.1	4.4	7.9	5.4	5.1	15.1
9	3.6	0.8	7.1	3.0	0.0	0.0	2.2	0.0	2.4	3.9
Total(%)	100	100	100	100	100	100	100	100	100	100

improved whereas several aspects of the psychosocial environment have deteriorated (see for instance the Stockholm county statistics in Arbetsmil-jörapport, 1995). The increasing complexity of modern western society increases the demands on psychosocial interaction. In several countries an increasing number of employers' unions and trade unions have realized that a functioning psychosocial work environment is heavily dependent on good work organisation.

9.1.3 Demand-control-support model

An integrated theory which has been greatly influential on work redesign efforts in many countries, and particularly in Sweden, was formulated by Karasek (1979), an American sociologist who has been working for several years in Scandinavia and who created a two-dimensional model amalgamating stress research traditions with alienation theory. According to Karasek's theory, alienation – in his own terminology, a lack of decision latitude – interacts with psychological demands in generating long-term effects on health. Excessively high psychological demands are adverse to health only when decision latitude is low. When the decision latitude is high (and the worker can influence decisions regarding how and when to perform work tasks and also develop and use his/her own skills) excessive psychological demands may not be so harmful. This theory from an early stage incorporated social support at work (Karasek and Theorell, 1990), the importance of which has been discussed by other authors (see House, 1981). The role of the social support in the demand-control-support model was theoretically developed by Johnson (Johnson and Hall, 1988). Social support from superiors and work colleagues could serve as a buffer against the combination of high demands and low decision latitude. The worst combination, iso-strain – high demands, low decision latitude and low support – would have the most adverse health consequences (Johnson et al., 1989).

The importance of various combinations of psychological demands, decision latitude and social support has been discussed in relation to different kinds of illnesses. Empirical findings from sixteen out of twenty different epidemiological studies have indicated that there is a clear relationship between low decision latitude and elevated coronary heart disease risk and that excessive psychological demands and low support may add to this risk (Theorell and Karasek, 1996). Of particular importance to job intervention research is that decreased decision latitude may be associated with increased risk within a five year period of development of myocardial infarction in middle-aged men (Theorell et al., 1996). If this result can be verified in other research, it indicates a potential for disease prevention in this group of men by means of job redesign aimed at the prevention of decreased decision latitude. With regard to functional gastrointestinal disorders, there is also empirical evidence of a relationship between job strain and lack of social support on the one hand and risk of illness on the other hand (Westerberg and Theorell, 1997). In the case of musculoskeletal disorders, some studies indicate relationships between illness and excessive psychological demands while others show relationships between illness and low decision latitude or low social support. Findings depend to a great extent on the samples studied, with different findings in office workers versus manual workers, in older versus younger, in men versus women and so on (Bongers et al., 1993).

The empirical findings on the relationship between the demand–control–support model and illness risks indicate that there is a health promotion potential in job redesign aiming at improved decision latitude and social support in work places.

The demand–control–support model does not incorporate individual reactions and characteristics. The interaction between the individual and his/her environment has been explored more systematically in other theoretical systems (Cooper and Marshall, 1976; French, 1963; Katz and Kahn, 1966; Siegrist, 1996). Most importantly, there is no empirical evidence, however, that the observed relationships between decision latitude and coronary heart disease risk can be 'explained away' by self-selection processes based upon individual personality (which would mean that workers with risk behaviour work in the risk occupations). According to this argument, there is reason to believe that collective reorganisation may be of importance. On the other hand, it is also clear that some individuals will benefit more and others less from social interventions. It is important to take into account published knowledge regarding the interaction between individuals and environment in the planning of job redesign processes.

Techniques for the achievement of improved decision latitude and social support

Quality of working life experiments have been going on for at least two decades. They have been evaluated in terms of productivity – but not frequently in health terms – and it has been shown that they have often been associated with a lasting increase in productivity (see for instance Kopelman, 1985). These experiments have built on principles outlined in this chapter so far. Increase in intellectual discretion has been achieved by means of job enrichment or increased worker responsibility for the complete product. Increase in decision authority has been achieved by means of job enlargement or a flattened organisation hierarchy. Increase in social support, has been achieved finally by means of improved feedback and formation of more cohesive work groups. During later years, both in the United States and in Scandinavia, the implementation of regular staff meetings for the systematic discussion of important decisions regarding work routines and goals has been used as a tool for increased decision latitude and social support.

The occupational health care team has often been an important vehicle in Scandinavian job redesign (see for instance Wallin and Wright, 1986). The occupational health care team has the possibility to work both with the structure of the company and with the individual workers. It has the possibility to carry out individual measurements of psychological and somatic health indicators and to monitor these through the change process. It has been the experience of health-oriented job redesigners that the concomitant emphasis on structure and individuals is helpful both for individual motivation to follow health promotion advice (which is strengthened when workers discover that there is willingness in management to improve the structure) and for success in instituting structural change (which will be of benefit if individuals are strengthened).

The redesign process will now be illustrated by two related case studies. The experiences of these cases will be discussed and put into a larger framework. The focus will be on the second study since this represents a more 'controlled' evaluation study. The first study is related, however, to the second one.

9.2 Organisational interventions in mail processing: Introduction

The interventions described in this section deal with mail processing in two Swedish urban regions (Uppsala and Spånga/Kista in the northern Stockholm region). The job redesign processes were prompted by current demands for effectiveness and speed in public service, but also by concerns caused by a high sick leave prevalence among the employees. Mail processing has been a state-run public service in Sweden. No competition has existed so far, but recently small-scale efforts to create competing mail service organisations have started and due to national financial problems, discussions regarding the effectiveness in the governmental mail system have taken place. These discussions have dealt both with the postal sorting systems – which are now concentrated at postal sorting terminals – and with the delivery, i.e. the work of the mailmen. Accordingly, a number of job redesigns have been tested in both these areas which the examples here illustrate.

9.3 Motives, signals and project organisation

The postal sorting terminal

Due to problems with the high level of sick leave and decreased productivity, a number of organisational changes were introduced by management at a postal terminal on 1 October 1987. The principles underlying the changes were founded on a pilot study and on exploratory interviews including all employees. The pilot study had been instituted by the occupational health care team and the interview study by the regional postal head office.

In the Swedish postal system, occupational health care teams have been quite active in the psychosocial field (from Previa, previously Statshälsan). It has developed both a system for exploring the psychosocial work environment and for instituting beneficial organisational changes within it. These programmes designed for state employees in general, have been extensively used throughout Sweden and by other organisations. In this particular postal worksite, the occupational health care team was responsible for the follow-up of the consequences of the organisational changes. Academic support was given by the department of occupational and environmental medicine at the Uppsala university.

Mail delivery

This organisational change was initiated by the regional head office in Spånga/Kista. The intention was to decrease the prevalence of musculo-skeletal disorder which was common among employees.

9.4 Analysis

Mail sorting is a monotonous kind of work. Before his untimely death, Gardell (1971; and Gardell and Svensson, 1981) and his co-workers had started redesign experiments in a large postal sorting terminal in Stockholm. The experiences from these experiments, which were aimed at decreasing sick leave rates (which had been high in this group), indicated that it was important to clarify goals and to change work organisation as well as to try to increase cohesiveness in the worksite in order to achieve improvement in health.

Mail delivery is a physically demanding job. The physical demands increase as one becomes older. Accordingly, it is uncommon to work as a mailman or mail woman after the age of fifty. The traditional way of reducing physical demand has been to reduce ergonomical loads. There is also a possibility to change the work organisation, however, since increased variation may reduce tissue strain and an improved psychosocial climate may decrease vulnerability (see for instance, Theorell, 1996). The health consequences of such changes in work organisation, however, have not been studied extensively. Increasing observation of dynamic and less stable organisations in which several changes take place concomitantly has been recommended from this point of view (see Silverstein, 1992). If many such evaluations are published, a total scientific evaluation will be facilitated. In line with this recommendation, the evaluation of this experiment in mail delivery was performed (Wahlstedt et al., 1996).

9.5 Choice of measures

The theoretical background of the instituted changes was the demand-control-support model (Johnson and Hall, 1988; Karasek and Theorell, 1990). In both experiments, there was an emphasis on improvement of authority over decisions.

9.5.1 Postal sorting terminal

In the postal sorting terminal, which was located in Uppsala, an urban region approximately forty miles north of Stockholm, the practical aims were to increase decision latitude, social support and contacts between management and staff and to create an improved shift working schedule as well as the possibility of obtaining meals on site. More specifically:

1   Two separate production areas were formed, each with its own management and budget. The role of management was clarified and production goals, for instance quantitative goals – such as how much mail would be handled during a shift – were stated more precisely than before. The total number of supervisors was decreased and those who remained were carefully selected. This increased the possibility of the staff to influence the work situation. The ex-supervisors either obtained other positions in the post office or continued at the terminal as senior postmen.

2   The number of senior postmen, i. e. employees intermediate in position between supervisors and other postal workers, was reduced from twelve to seven. At the same time they were given the authority to act as assistant supervisors in the new teams during the day and as full supervisors during night shifts. This group had previously been very dissatisfied with their work.

3   To handle periods of excessive work load more effectively, the number of staff was increased by five letter sorters which corresponded to an increase in number of 2.5 per cent.

4   Working groups of four to five individuals were created, with the groups working together. The work tasks, however, were not changed.

5   The information system was improved, through regular weekly staff meetings and by keeping noticeboards up to date. Previously, information had been relayed to the employees sporadically and feedback was almost completely lacking. Employees had not known the supervisor previously.

6   The shift work schedule was changed and meal breaks became more regular, whereas previously they had been very irregular. The original aim was to introduce a clockwise rotation system, which has been shown in two previous controlled studies to be associated with lowered prevalence of psychosomatic complaints (Fredén et al., 1985). This was not

Table 9.3 Changes in Spånga ('traditional') and Kista ('modern') postal stations

Changes	Spånga	Kista
New localities	0	++
Restoration of localities	+	++
New sorter tables	+	++
Separate rooms for the teams	0	++
Organisationally cohesive teams	+	++
Increased foreman responsibility	+	++
Budget responsibility	++	++
Recruitment of temporarily employed to foreman	++	++
Planning of vacations to foreman	0	++
Bonus system	0	++

Key: 0 = unchanged
      + = little change
     ++ = big change

possible, however, due to different opinions among older and younger employees, with older workers being more interested in the 'healthy' clockwise schedule starting with the morning shift and ending with the night shift and younger workers more interested in shifts resulting in periods of several consecutive days off work, beginning with the night shift and ending with the morning shift

7 The introduction of an automatic food vending machine and microwave ovens. Previously there had been little possibility of obtaining hot meals at the plant or in the immediate vicinity.

9.5.2 Mail delivery

In the mail delivery study the intervention was based on the following practical premises. The postal station in Spång/Kista, close to Stockholm, had started in 1975. Since this time the region had increased its number of inhabitants, companies and mail districts.

In 1988, a plan to divide the station into two work sites was started. In summer 1990 the plans became more concrete when convenient sites became available. The two new stations opened in April 1991. Employees were given the option of choosing one of the two stations. The more traditional organisation was planned in Spånga and the more modern one in Kista. There were changes in both places, however. Table 9.3 summarizes these changes. Improved authority over decisions and social support were effected by means of changes in clarification of the role of the management. Furthermore, the number of foremen was reduced and the information system improved by means of regular staff meetings and noticeboards. In order to avoid uncontrolled periods of excessive workload, the number of staff was increased by 2.5 per cent. The foremen were given increased authority in both stations but particularly so in the Kista station. Since the foremen were closer to the individual delivery workers, it was hoped that this would result in improved authority over decisions.

An important difference between the two work sites was that the employees in the Kista station had joint responsibility for all the districts of the team, whereas in the Spånga station they had responsibility only for their own district. In the Kista station the teams also had joint responsibility for partially new work tasks such as delivery of large collections of letters, sorting of boxes as well as handling of precious mail and parcels. Two new persons were recruited to act as back-up staff at Kista when short leaves occurred. They were stationed in one of the teams but were available for the other teams in cases of emergency. Time was allocated for planning and foreman activities in the Kista station, and cohesiveness was strengthened in this station by means of a team-based bonus system. Each team in the modern station had a room with windows for mail sorting.

All delivery men and women in the Kista station rode bicycles when delivering mail, whereas some of the employees in the traditional station used cars and some used bicycles – as previously – even after the changes had been instituted.

In both intervention studies, the organisational changes could also have resulted in improved intellectual discretion.

9.6 Implementation

9.6.1 Postal sorting terminal

In the postal sorting terminal, the staff were invited to co-operate in the planning of the organisational changes. It was considered that a positive change in the psychosocial work climate would lead to improved working conditions which would result in a lower prevalence of, in particular, functional gastrointestinal symptoms and sleep disturbance. And as a consequence this would also lower sick leave rates (Wahlstedt and Edling, 1994; 1997).

9.6.2 Mail delivery

In the mail delivery study the employees had a certain amount of influence over the process. Since the regional office reasoned that the changes instituted in one of the sites were profound (and according to the hypothesis more effective and therefore important to test) and could be perceived as threatening, the employees were given the opportunity to choose which site they wanted to work at.

In both interventions the occupational health care team played an important role in the co-ordination of the activities.

9.7 Evaluation

9.7.1 Introduction: Design and measurements

Postal sorting terminal

In the postal sorting terminal the only possibility was to perform a before and after comparison. The pre-intervention measurements were performed in September 1987. Two follow-up measurements were performed, one in May 1988 and the other in October 1988. The follow-up measurements represent first the final stage of the intervention and second a one-year follow-up after the initiation of the whole process

Mail delivery

In the mail delivery service it was possible to perform a before and after comparison both in the intervention group and in a group with less extensive intervention. The participants in the intervention group moved to a new station and went through a change in work organisation. Employees were allowed to select which station they would belong to. Measurements were performed before intervention and twelve months later (1991 and 1992 respectively).

Postal sorting terminal

In the postal sorting terminal analysis the evaluation question was: 'Can improved work organisation decrease sick leave and improve psychosomatic condition?' The final study group comprised the 136 subjects (105 men and 31 women) who had answered the baseline questionnaire and whom it was possible to identify – eight answered anonymously. The 144 subjects who responded to the baseline questionnaire constituted 75 per cent of potential participants. Of the 136 identifiable subjects, 100 completed all three questionnaires. Before all subjects in the study population were asked to participate (n = 191) 59 subjects had been excluded who were on long-term sick-leave or who were absent for other reasons during the initial study period.

Mail delivery

The main question in the evaluation of the mail delivery intervention was: 'Can improved work organisation result in a decrease in the prevalence of locomotor disorder?' The study group consisted of 106 persons after exclusion of those who had served as assistants working only every second Saturday, those who were on long-term sick-leave and those who had stopped working during the study period. Eighteen persons did not answer the first questionnaire in 1991 and six did not answer the twelve-month follow-up questionnaire in 1992. Accordingly the final study group consisted of 82 persons. The persons who chose to move to the modern station (n = 27) were comparable with regard to gender and age to those who stayed in the traditional station (n = 55). Those who moved had in general been working in mail delivery for a significantly shorter period than those who stayed (median 2 and 4 years respectively).

Measures

In both comparisons psychosocial work conditions were measured by means of a Swedish-established self-administered questionnaire for the recording of psychological demands (five questions), intellectual discretion (four questions) and authority over decisions (two questions) (Theorell et al., 1988). Cronbach's alpha coefficient for the three indices was 0.78, 0.68 and 0.71 respectively in the postal sorting terminal study. In the mail delivery study intellectual discretion and authority over decisions were added into one composite measure, decision latitude. In that study Cronbach's alpha coefficient for psychological demands and decision latitude was 0.84 and 0.83 respectively. In addition, on the basis of factor analysis, two indices were constructed for the measurement of contact with superiors (five questions) and contact with team mates (four questions). Cronbach's alpha coefficient for these two measures in the postal sorting terminal study was 0.77 and 0.69. The corresponding coefficients in the mail delivery study were 0.78 and 0.67. In the mail delivery study nine different questionnaire-based indices of physically adverse conditions were computed – such as awkard working positions sitting, twisted working postures, heavy lifting and repetitive work with the arms (Wahlstedt and Björkstén, 1993). The number of questions included in these indices ranged from two to five, and the alpha coefficients from 0.58 to 0.84.

In the postal sorting terminal study sick leave was recorded from registered data. Psychosomatic symptom scores were computed from a self-administered questionnaire. On the basis of factor analysis a gastrointestinal symptom score was computed, as in previous studies. An index of sleep disturbance was also constructed according to previous psychometric analysis (for a description of gastrointestinal symptom index and sleep disturbance index, see Theorell et al., 1991). Symptoms from the locomotor system were recorded by means of a self-administered questionnaire (the Nordic Council questionnaire, see Andersson et al., 1984) which has been well established in previous research.

9.7.2 Results

Postal sorting terminal

At the occasion of first follow-up study when the changes had recently been introduced, the contact with superiors had changed in a positive direction, but skill discretion, authority over decisions, contacts with team mates and psychosocial work demands remained unchanged. At the second follow-up when the changes had been in place for a time, contact with superiors had returned to the level that it had before the changes were instituted. Contact with team mates and psychological work demands remained unchanged whereas skill discretion and authority over decisions had improved significantly.

Sleep difficulties had increased significantly on the first follow-up occasion but were unchanged compared to the second follow-up occasion. Gastrointestinal complaints did not change during the study period. Both short-term and long-term sick leave decreased significantly. The reduction was most evident during the first follow-up period but remained significant on the second follow-up occasion. Among full-time employees a lasting decrease in total sick leave of 15 per cent was observed ($p = 0.02$), whereas for the part-time employees it was reduced by 30 per cent ($p = 0.02$).

Subjects who reported improved contact with team mates and superiors improved significantly more with regard to sleep difficulties and gastrointestinal symptoms than other subjects on the second follow-up occasion. The same was true of improved skill discretion and authority over decisions. Thus, lasting improvements in psychosomatic conditions were observed among those subjects who had improved social support and decision latitude at work.

Mail delivery

Ergonomic conditions (repetitive arm movements, uncomfortable standing and uncomfortable sitting positions, leaning and twisted postures, heavy lifting, repetitive leg work, uncomfortable arm work) did not change significantly according to the questionnaires. Social support increased significantly in the modern station only and psychological demands decreased significantly in both stations. Authority over decisions increased in the traditional but not in the modern station – somewhat contrary to expectations. A combined index of neck, shoulder and chest back pain as well as shoulder and chest back pain (see Table 9.4) decreased significantly in the modern but not in the traditional station (see Table 9.5). The favourable musculoskeletal changes were more pronounced in participants below 35 years than among those above this age (see Table 9.6). A logistic stepwise regression analysis of individually perceived changes in working conditions in relation to perceived

Table 9.4 Mail delivery: Self-reported psychosocial/organisational conditions at the old (A) and the new (B) stations, 1991 and 1992 (n = 82)

Index (possible variation)	Stayed in A (n = 55) 1991	1992	Moved to B (n = 27) 1991	1992	Total group (n = 82) 1991	1992
Social support* (16–64)	29.1	27.3	28.2	**25.8**[1]	28.8	**26.8**[2]
Contact with supervisors* (5–20)	7.7	7.7	6.8	7.4	7.4	7.6
Contact with work mates* (4–16)	6.2	6.5	6.2	5.7	6.2	6.2
Psychological demands** (5–20)	12.9	**11.6**[3]	13.2	**11.6**[4]	13.0	**11.6**[5]
Intellectual discretion** (4–16)	10.0	9.8	9.2	9.9	9.8	9.9
Authority over decisions** (2–8)	5.3	**5.8**[6]	5.8	5.7	5.5	5.8

Key: *The higher score the lower degree of support.
**The higher score indicates more demands, more intellectual discretion and more authority over decisions.
[1]$p = 0.04$ [2]$p = 0.02$ [3]$p = 0.001$ [4]$p = 0.006$ [5]$p = 0.000$ [6]$p = 0.03$

Table 9.5 Mail delivery: Prevalence (%) of symptoms from the locomotor system at the old (A) and the new (B) stations, 1991 and 1992 (n = 82)

Anatomical region	Stayed in A (n = 55) 1991	(n = 27) 1992	Moved to B (n = 82) 1991	1992	Total group 1991	1992
Neck	40	26	46	44	42	32
Shoulders	51	37	52	**28**[1]	51	**34**[2]
Thoracic spine	29	21	33	**8**[3]	30	**17**[4]
Lumbar spine	43	30	42	36	43	32
Arm*	31	24	27	24	30	24
Leg**	48	54	41	29	46	46
Neck/shoulders/ thoracic spine***	56	44	69	**44**[5]	61	**44**[6]

Key: *Symptoms from elbows and/or symptoms from wrists/hands.
**Symptoms from hips and/or symptoms from knees and/or symptoms from ankles/feet.
***Symptoms from neck and/or symptoms from shoulders and/or symptoms from thoracic spine.
[1]$p = 0.02$ [2]$p = 0.009$ [3]$p = 0.02$ [4]$p = 0.02$ [5]$p = 0.04$ [6]$p = 0.006$

Table 9.6 Mail delivery: Prevalence (%) of symptoms from the locomotor system in younger and older subjects

Anatomical region	< 35 years (n = 51)		≥ 35 years (n = 31)	
	1991	*1992*	*1991*	*1992*
Neck	39	23	48	45
Shoulders	54	29[1]	46	43
Thoracic spine	35	17[2]	21	17
Lumbar spine	46	27[3]	38	40
Arm*	29	27	31	18
Leg**	53	55	32	31[5]
Neck/shoulders/ thoracic spine***	62	36[4]	59	58

Key: *Symptoms from elbows and/or symptoms from wrists/hands.
**Symptoms from hips and/or symptoms from knees and/or symptoms from ankles/feet.
***Symptoms from neck and/or symptoms from shoulders and/or symptoms from thoracic spine
[1]p = 0.003 [2]p = 0.01 [3]p = 0.04 [4]p = 0.006 [5]p = 0.04

changes in health showed that subjects who had shoulder pain in 1991 and who reported improved contact with their superiors between 1991 and 1992, had an increased likelihood of becoming free of symptoms in 1992 compared to other subjects with these symptoms (odds ratio = 4.0; 95 per cent confidence interval: 2.4–6.4). Other changes in ergonomic and psychosocial factors had no statistical independent relationship with changes in symptoms from the locomotor system.

Discriminant analysis showed that those who were older than 35 years and reported little authority over decisions in 1991 were the least likely to become free of symptoms from neck, shoulder, chest and back pain. The effect of age was not explained by the number of years in service – this factor was included in the discriminant analysis and was shown to be not significant.

9.8 Discussion

Neither of the two evaluations was a classical evaluation in the sense that two randomly selected samples were followed and compared with regard to the outcome after the intervention. In both experiments, the main follow-up was made twelve months after the start. This precludes effects of seasonal variations. In the postal service there was no comparison group at all, but there is reason to believe that the work site was in a steady state with regard to work organisation and health when the experiment started. In the postal station, two groups were compared. These two groups were self-selected and there is a possibility that more healthy and satisfied workers could have selected one of the two alternative stations. The available information would contradict this interpretation, however. The experiments have the advantage from a practical standpoint that they represent changes that arose within the system as a response to external demands for improvement and adjustment. Management instituted the changes after having contacted the occupational health care team in the first experiment. In the second study, management also initiated the changes. External consultation was used only for the evaluation. Accordingly they reflect real-life phenomena which could be translated into viable follow-up experiments in other sites. In the postal service experiment as well as in the delivery station change the selection procedure and the participation rate were acceptable.

The other main emphasis was on improved social support/climate. Improved social support is often difficult to disentangle from increased authority over decisions. Frequently, an improved sense of individual control is obtained by means of collective actions of the total working group. In the postal sorting terminal the tool for improved social support/climate was the formation of work-groups of 4–5 individuals. In the modern postal station the corresponding tool was the formation of working groups with joint responsibility for several districts, allocation of these groups to separate rooms and financial group bonus.

The two studied settings are of course different in nature. While the postal sorting functions very much like an industrial setting, mail delivery is more variable, more physically demanding and there is more direct interaction with customers. This may to some extent explain why the organisational changes and its results in the former case were clearer with regard to lasting effects on authority over decisions and intellectual discretion and, in the latter case, were clearer with regard to social support and interaction. In several previous experiments, effects have been documented after group feedback and group intervention either on different aspects of authority over decisions/intellectual discretion (Gardell and Svensson, 1981; Karasek and Theorell, 1990, p. 211) or on social support (Orth-Gomér et al., 1994; Theorell et al., 1995). In previously published experiments, a decrease (Karasek and Theorell, 1990, p. 211; Orth-Gomér, 1994) as well as an increase in psychological demands (Gardell and Svensson, 1981) have been reported following the changes. In the present case studies no consistent finding was made in this respect – there were no changes in the postal sorting terminal and demands decreased in both the traditional and the modern stations in the delivery experiment. The organisational outcome depends on initial problems, work content and strategy for change.

Few studies have been published regarding mail processing and its psychosocial work environment. But one of the largest studies published in this area was by Amick (1991). On the basis of his study of nearly 5,000 postal sorters, Amick suggested that influencing supervisor support is the most effective way to affect a person's job satisfaction and level of psychosomatic symptomatology.

The organisational intervention in the postal sorting terminal took place before the dramatic changes in the Swedish economy, described earlier, had become manifest. Thus, a dramatic decrease in the sick leave rate could not be expected during this period. Accordingly the observed decrease in sick leave in the terminal could be a consequence of improved working conditions. In the postal delivery change, the study of sick leave as an outcome measure would have been meaningless since the changes in sick leave rates in Sweden had already started during this period, with dramatically decreased rates as a consequence of changes in law practice and the labour market. Decreased sick leave has indeed been observed previously in similar experiments on health care facilities in which changes have aimed at improved authority over decisions, intellectual discretion and social support (Arnetz, p. 194–197, in: Karasek and Theorell, 1990; Jackson, 1983; Lazes, 1978; Lazes et al., 1977). The main health outcome result in the delivery stations was that neck, shoulder, chest and back pain decreased. This is consistent with observations which indicate that good social support at work may have a statistically significant protective effect in relation to locomotor disorder (Ahlberg-Hultén et al., 1995; Bongers et al., 1993).

Although no significant decrease in psychosomatic complaints was observed in the postal service intervention, it was still shown that those individuals who reported improvement in social support and decision latitude had decreased sleep disturbance and gastrointestinal complaints. This is consistent with longitudinal observations which indicate that variations in job strain (high demands and low decision latitude) are associated with intensity of functional gastrointestinal complaints and sleep difficulties (Theorell, 1989). It is also supported by findings of an increased prevalence of low self-reported authority over decisions at work among men and women who consult primary care centres in Sweden because of such symptoms (Westerberg and Theorell, 1997). In that study it was also shown that men with low social support at work had less likelihood of becoming free of symptoms after one month than other men.

Even in Sweden with its long tradition of work redesign, very few studies have actually documented health consequences of this type of job interventions. Most of the published work has been based on self-administered questionnaires. One study of cardiovascular risk factors (Orth-Gomér et al., 1994; Theorell et al., 1995) showed that a similar programme (which was evaluated in a controlled study) was followed by a reduced ratio of LDL/HDL cholesterol in the experimental group but not in the comparison group. As in all experiments of this kind, the design was not 'clean' in the sense that all other changes had been ruled out, but the findings could be interpreted to mean that job redesign aiming at improved social relationships and decision latitude could lead to decreased cardiovascular risk. In the same study, it was also shown that the psychosocial job changes were more beneficial in worksites which had an active attitude to change. In those with a more passive attitude, feedback from superiors deteriorated and the psycho-endocrinological arousal – as reflected in serum cortisol levels during the intervention – was more pronounced.

Self reported psychosomatic symptoms, such as gastrointestinal symptoms, tiredness and depression, decreased among a section of employees working for the car company Volvo after a number of psychosocially-oriented job changes had been instituted, such as role change in supervisors in the direction of more facilitation, less authoritarian leadership style, promotion of personal contact between customers and employees and increased teamwork (Plate *et al.*, 1985; Wallin and Wright, 1986).

Costs and benefits

In these two studies no financial cost benefit analysis was performed. It is clear, however, that the decrease in sick leave (the mail sorting terminal) and musculoskeletal morbidity (the mail delivery) are obvious financial gains. No external extra resources were used for the intervention since those instituting the changes were the management, representatives of the workers and the occupational health care team. The only extra resources that were needed were for the five extra letter sorterers in the mail delivery intervention, but this addition represented a much smaller amount of money than the gains in morbidity. Accordingly, although no detailed financial analysis was performed the evidence points to a financial gain in both studies.

9.9 Lessons

In the Scandinavian context, considerable experience has built up regarding the know-how of instituting job organisation improvements. The large occupational health care organisations, such as the organisation for state employees, have formulated strategies for this in manuals. The most important general principles:

1   Job changes require considerable time. When an exploration (which is always regarded by the employees as a start of the change process) is planned, the team must have the resources and allocate the time to follow-up the consequences. Social changes always take more time than expected – months and years rather than days and weeks are required. In the case descriptions presented in this chapter, the role changes that were asked of the foremen groups demanded extensive time.

2.   The different groups involved should be informed before and continuously during the process. Processes that arise as needs formulated by the workers are more likely to be successful than top-down processes (see for instance, Gustavsen and Hunnius, 1981). The managers and superiors should be informed regarding important findings and developments

during the process, for instance when group feedback is planned. In the experiments described in this chapter, management in general collaborated well with the representatives of the employees, although in both cases the initiative came mainly from the management. The occupational health care team members played an important role, since they provided pilot studies and experience.

3   Group feedback and discussion are important components in the change process. The importance of group feedback is illustrated by the findings in a study of six occupational groups, with each participant being monitored on four occasions during a year. On the one hand, very small changes in the perceived work environment were reported in relation to individual feedback occasions. On the other hand, after group feedback had taken place, measurements indicated that psychological demands had decreased and intellectual discretion had increased significantly. More conflicts and greater awareness of work environment problems were also reported after the group feedback occasion (Karasek and Theorell, 1990). In the mail sorting terminal the group of foremen was resisting the changes and considerable efforts were made to give feedback and hold discussions with this group.

    Group feedback and discussion has to be organized in a systematic way. What is found in the exploration is compared with other groups which are used as a reference. Both strengths and weaknesses are identified. The positive aspects are important since the workers need to feel a sense of pride and self-esteem. But the worksite has to identify problems that are important to ameliorate. In the ideal situation, special employees are elected who have the task (within a specified time frame) of formulating practical solutions. These solutions are discussed on the next occasion. Several such groups may work concomitantly on different specified problems. The employees were quite active in the change process itself in the interventions described in this chapter.

4   The potential for conflict with regard to opinions about solutions needs to be addressed. After the initial phases of 'engagement' and 'search', the 'change' phase occurs. During this phase there are always differing opinions regarding the best solutions. If the initiators of the process are unprepared for this diversity of opinions (and the potential for serious conflicts) they may not facilitate the redesign in a helpful way.

9.10 Conclusion

This review and the case descriptions illustrate that work redesign for the improvement of the psychosocial environment has held a strong position in Sweden's working life for a long time. Due to the economic downturn, however, health promotion work in relation to work organisation has weakened. The case description illustrates that it is possible to improve the work organisation of a public service body and that such changes may benefit employee health.

Acknowledgement

The second intervention case ('mail carriers') presented in this chapter was performed and analysed by Kurt Wahlstedt (National Institute for Working Life, Stockholm), Clas Håkan Nygård, Kristina Kemmlert and Margareta Torgén (Department of occupational and environmental medicine, University Hospital, Uppsala) and Marianne Gerner Björkstén (National Institute for Working Life, Stockholm), whose help is gratefully acknowledged.

Bibliography

Ahlberg-Hultén, G., Theorell, T. and Sigala, F. (1995) 'Social support, job strain and musculoskeletal pain among female health care personnel', *Scandinavian Journal of Work, Environment and Health*, 21: 435–39.

Amick, B. (1991) 'Structural determinants of the psychosocial environment: introducing technology in the work stress framework', *Ergonomics*, 34: 625–46.

Andersson, G., Biering-Sorensen, F., Hermansen, L., Jonsson, B., Jorgensen, K., Kilbom, Å., Kuorinka, I. and Vinterberg, H. (1984) 'Nordiska frågeformuläret för kartläggning av yrkesrelaterade muskuloskeletala besvär' ('The Nordic questionnaire for the assessment of work related musculoskeletal symptoms'), *Nordisk Medicin*, 99: 54–5.

Arbetsmiljökommissionen (1989) *Arbeten utsatta för särskilda hälsorisker* ('Occupations exposed to pronounced health risks'), Gotab, Stockholm: Allmänna förlaget.

Arbetsmiljölag ('Swedish Law on Work Environment') (1976) Stockholm: Sweden SOU 1976, 1.

Aronsson, G. and Sjögren, A. (1994) *Samhällsomvandling och arbetsliv. Omvärldsanalys inför 2000-talet* ('Societal change and working life. Analysis of the international perspective facing year 2000'), Solna, Sweden: Arbetsmiljöinstitutet

Belkic, K., Savic, C., Theorell, T., Rakic, L., Ercegovac, D., and Djordjevic, M. (1994) 'Mechanisms of cardiac risk among professional drivers', *Scandinavian Journal of Work, Environment and Health,* 20:73–86.

Bongers, P.M., De Winter, C.R., Kompier, M.A.J. and Hildebrandt, V.H. (1993) 'Psychosocial factors at work and musculoskeletal disease', *Scandinavian Journal of Work, Environment and Health*, 19: 297–312.

Cooper, C.L. and Marshall, J. (1976) 'Occupational sources of stress: A review of the literature relating to coronary heart disease and mental ill health', *Journal of Occupational Health*, 49: 11–28.

Department of Occupational Health (1995) *Arbetsmiljörapport för Stockholms län*, Stockholm: Karolinska Hospital, Department of Occupational Health.

Frankenhaeuser, M. and Gardell, B. (1976) 'Underload and overload in working life: Outline of a multidisciplinary work', *Journal of Human Stress*, 2: 34–46.

Frankenhaeuser, M. and Johansson, G. (1975) 'Behaviour and catecholamines in children', in: L. Levi (ed.) *Society, Stress and Disease, Childhood and adolescence*, 2, Oxford: Oxford University Press, pp. 118–26.

Fredén, K., Ohlsson, I.L., Orth-Gomér, K. and Åkerstedt, T. (1985) 'Positive effects of displacing night work to the end of the shift cycle', in M. Haider, M. Koller and R. Cervinka (eds) *Night- and shiftwork: Long-term effects and their prevention*, Proceedings of the VII international symposium on night- and shift-work, Igls, Austria, Frankfurt: Peter Lang Verlag.

French, J.R.P. (1963) 'The social environment and mental health', *Journal of Social Issues*, 19: 39–56.

Fritzell, J. and Lundberg, O. (1994) *Vardagens villkor* ('Conditions of everyday life'), Stockholm: Brombergs.

Gardell, B. (1971) *Technology, alienation and mental health*, Stockholm: Personaladministrativa rådet.

Gardell, B. and Svensson, L. (1981) *Medbestämmande och självstyre: En lokal facklig strategi för demokratisering av arbetsplatsen* ('Worker participation and autonomy: A local union strategy for democratization of the workplace'), Stockholm: Prisma.

Gustafsso, R.Å. (1994) *Köp och sälj, var god svälj? Vårdens nya ekonomistyrningssystem i ett arbetsmiljöperspektiv* ('Buy and sell, please swallow? The new financial controlling systems in health care in a work environment perspective'), Stockholm: Arbetsmiljöfonden.

Gustavsen, B. and Hunnius, G. (1981) *New patterns of work reform: The case of Norway*, Oslo: Oslo University Press.

House, J. (1981) *Work, Stress and Social Support*, Reading, MA, USA: Addison-Wesley.

Jackson, S. (1983) 'Participation in decision making as a strategy for reducing job related strain', *Journal of Applied Psychology*, 68: 3–19.

Johnson, J.V. and Hall, E.M. (1988) 'Job strain, work place social support and cardiovascular disease: A cross-sectional study of a random sample of the Swedish working population', *American Journal of Public Health*, 78, 1336–342.

Johnson, J., Hall, E., and Theorell, T. (1989) 'The combined effects of job strain and social isolation on the prevalence and mortality incidence of cardiovascular disease in a random sample of the Swedish male working population', *Scandinavian Journal of Work, Environment and Health*, 15: 271–79.

Karasek, R.A. (1979) 'Job demands, job decision latitude and mental strain: Implications for job redesign', *Administrative Science Quarterly*, 24: 285–307.

Karasek, R.A. and Theorell, T. (1990) *Healthy Work*, New York: Basic Books.

Katz, D. and Kahn, R. (1966) *Social Psychology of Organisations*, New York: Wiley.

Kompier, M., De Gier, E., Smulders, P. and Draaisma, D. (1994) 'Regulations, policies and practices concerning work stress in five European countries', *Work and Stress*, 4: 296–318.

Kopelman, R.E. (1985) 'Job redesign and productivity: A review of the evidence', *National Productivity Review*, Summer: 237–55.

Lazes, P. (1978) 'Health workers and decision making', *Urban Health*, April: 34–55.

Lazes, P., Wasilewski, Y. and Redd, J.D. (1977) 'Improving outpatient care through participation; The Newark experiment in staff and patient involvement', *International Journal of Health Education*, 20: 61–8.

Le Grand, C., Szulkin, R. and Tåhlin, M. (eds) (1993) *Sveriges arbetsplatser – organisation, personalutveckling, styrning* ('Sweden's work places – organisation, personnel development and management'), Stockholm: SNS.

Levi, L. and Lunde-Jensen, P. (1996) *A Model for Assessing the Costs of Stressors at National Level*, Dublin: European Foundation for the Improvement of Living and Working Conditions.

Orth-Gomér, K., Eriksson, I., Moser, V., Theorell, T. and Fredlund, P. (1994) 'Lipid lowering through stress management', *International Journal of Behavioral Medicine*, 1: 204–14.

Petterson, I.L., Arnetz, B.B. and Arnetz, J.E. (1995) 'Predictors of job satisfaction and job influence – results from a national sample of Swedish nurses', *Psychotherapy and Psychosomatics*, 64: 9–19.

Plate, R., Gal, I. and Schütz, F. (1985) 'Ny syn på produktionen' ('New view of production'), in *En bok om Volvo* ('A book about Volvo'), Göteborg: AB Volvo.

Siegrist, J. (1996) 'Adverse health effects of high effort/low reward conditions', *Journal of Occupational Health Psychology*, 1: 27–41.

Silverstein, B. (1992) 'Design and evaluation of interventions to reduce work-related musculoskeletal disorders', *Arbete och Hälsa*, 17: 1–7, Stockholm: Lecture at PREMUS.

Statistics Sweden (1997) *Välfärd och ojämlikhet i 20-årsperspectiv 1975–1995* ('Welfare and inequality in a 20-year perspective 1975–1995'), Sockholm: Statistics Sweden, no. 91.

Theorell, T. (1989) 'Personal control at work: A review of epidemiological studies in Sweden', in A. Steptoe and A. Appels (eds) *Stress, Personal Control and Health*, New York: Wiley, PP. 49–64.

—— (1996) 'Possible mechanisms behind the relationship between the demand-control-support model and disorders of the locomotor system', in S.D. Moon and S.L. Sauter, (eds) *Beyond Biomechanics: Psychosocial Aspects of Musculoskeletal Disorders in Office Work*, London: Taylor and Francis.

Theorell, T., Perski, A., Åkerstedt, T., Sigala, F., Ahlberg-Hultén, G., Svensson, J. and Eneroth, P. (1988) 'Changes in job strain in relation to changes in physiological state', *Scandinavian Journal of Work, Environment and Health*, 14: 189–96.

Theorell, T., Ahlberg-Hultén, G., Sigala, F., Perski, A., Söderholm, M., Kallner, A., and Eneroth, P. (1990) 'A psychosocial and biomedical comparison between men in six contrasting service occupations', *Work and Stress,* 4 1: 51–63.

Theorell, T., Konarski-Svensson, J.K., Almén, J., and Perski, A. (1991) 'The role of paid work in Swedish chronic dialysis patients – a nation-wide survey', *Journal of International Medicine*, 230: 501–9.

Theorell, T., Orth-Gomér, K., Moser, V., Undén, A.L. and Eriksson, I. (1995) 'Endocrine markers during a job intervention', *Work and Stress*, 9: 67–76.

Theorell, T. and Karasek, R.A. (1996) 'Current issues relating to psychosocial job strain and cardiovascular disease research', *Journal of Occupational Health Psychology*, 1: 9–26.

Theorell, T., Tsutsumi, A., Hallquist, J., Reutervall, C., Fredlund, P., Emlund, N., Alfredsson, L., Hammar, N., Ahlbom, A., Johnson, J. and the Stockholm Heat Epidemiology Programme (SHEEP) (1996) *On the Relationship Between Decision Latitude and Myocardial Infarction – Methodological of Men in Stockholm*, Stockholm: National Institute for Psychosocial Factors and Health, (submitted).

Wahlstedt, K. and Björkstén, M.G. (1993) *Arbetskrav och belastningsbesvär i sex postala yrken − enkätundersökningen* ('Work demands and symptoms from the locomotor system − the questionnaire study'), Stockholm: Arbetsmiljöfonden.

Wahlstedt, K.G.I. and Edling, C. (1994) 'Psychosocial factors and their relations to psychosomatic complaints among postal workers', *European Journal of Public Health*, 4: 60–4.

Wahlstedt, K.G.I, Nygård, C.H., Kemmlert, K., Torgén, M. and Gerner Björkstén, M. (1996) 'Påverkan av en organisationsförändring på arbetsmiljöfaktorer och upplevd hälsa inom brevbäring' ('The impact of organisational changes on work, environmental factors and on perceived health of mail men'), Stockholm: *Arbete och hälsa*, 15: 1–29.

Wahlstedt, K.G.I. and Edling, C. (1997) 'Organisational changes at a postal sorting terminal − their effects upon work satisfaction, psychosomatic complaints and sick leave', *Work and Stress*, 3 (11): 279–91.

Wallin, L. and Wright, I. (1986) 'Psychosocial aspects of the work environment: A group approach', *Journal of Occupational Medicine*, 28: 384–93.

Westerberg, L. and Theorell, T. (1997) 'Working conditions and family situation in relation to functional gastrointestinal disorders', The Swedish Dyspepsia Project, *Scandinavian Journal of Primary Health Care*, 15 (2): 76–81.

Chapter 10

Germany: Reduction of stress by health circles

Beate Beermann, Karl Kuhn and
Michiel Kompier

10.1 Introduction: Work stress in Germany

10.1.1 The German legal system

The German industrial relations system is characterised by 'co-operative conflict solution' mechanisms based on a broad societal and industrial consensus which, even in periods of recession, has not (yet) been substantially damaged.

In the area of work safety and health there are two types of public law, and they reflect the so-called 'dual legal system' in Germany. One set is based on the national labour law and the other is based on the social security law that was developed by the Accident Insurance Funds ('Berufsgenossenschaften'). The first group comprises state regulations, i.e. laws and ordinances. The second group relates to accident prevention regulations of employers. These accident prevention regulations are prescripts which are comparable with legal ordinances and are aimed at preventing industrial accidents and industrial diseases. Both ordinances and accident prevention are not as comprehensive as the law, and each of them regulates a certain section. The number of cases that they cover is more limited than for the law, although still fairly large. The orders and prohibitions stipulated in the ordinances and accident prevention regulations are more concrete than in the law. Other levels are required to cover the application of orders and prohibitions to individual cases.

All those who can contribute to reducing the risks of accidents and hazards to health in the company have an obligation to co-operate. The following parties are involved in the organisation of health and safety in companies:

* employers;
* works councils as representatives of the employees;
* work safety experts and company doctors;
* health and safety committees.

The Employer

The employer is responsible for implementing health and safety measures. He/she must ensure the protection of employees by early prevention, and one of the most important duties of the employer is to inform and instruct employees. Depending on the size of the company, the employer must either implement an internal health and safety organisation or use external prevention services. The employer also must inform the employee of the scope and responsibility of his/her work and its significance within the production process of the company. Before an employee begins a new job, the employer must inform him/her of the risks of accidents and any health dangers he/she may be exposed to, and of the measures to be taken and facilities available to reduce the risks.

Works councils

The establishment of a works council is obligatory in companies with more than ten employees. The works councils have a special responsibility since they represent the interests of those who voted for them in the company. The council is particularly committed to ascertaining the health and safety of the workforce they represent. The collaboration of the works councils in implementing health and safety measures is, therefore, one of their most important tasks. Their legal status in matters of industrial health and safety takes account of this special role. According to the co-determination act, the works council is responsible for the following aspects of industrial health and safety:

DUTY TO MONITOR

Within their duty to monitor, the works council has the right and the obligation to point out to the employer or the responsible works manager any inadequacies in preventive measures, and to insist that faults be remedied with all means available to him/her.

DUTY TO ORGANISE

The council may deal with any health and safety problem and insist that the employer carries out proper measures. This also applies to measures which are not specified in the relevant regulations.

The duty to organise not only applies to existing companies and technical equipment, but the works council should also be allowed to participate in the planning of new construction, conversion and expansion of production, administrative and other factory premises; of technical systems, work procedures and work processes; and of jobs.

RIGHT OF CO-DETERMINATION

If health and safety measures are to be carried out in the company, the works council usually has a right of co-determination.

DUTY TO PROVIDE ASSISTANCE

The works council is obliged to assist the authorities with their activities in the company by making suggestions, giving advice and information. On the other hand authorities are obliged to permit the works council to participate in all plant inspections, investigations into accidents and discussions on questions of health and safety and to offer advice if required. The works council may consult work safety experts and company doctors as well as the supervisory authority.

RIGHT TO INFORMATION AND PARTICIPATION

The right to information is based on the principle that in order to fulfil their duties the employer and the works council should have equal access to the same information in the field of health and safety and accident prevention.

Work safety experts and company doctors

According to law, work safety experts and company doctors have the following duties:

1   To advise the employer and any other persons responsible for work safety and accident prevention, in particular with respect to:

    • planning, execution and maintenance of company plants and welfare and sanitary facilities;
    • the provision of technical work devices and the introduction of work procedures and use of dangerous substances;
    • the selection and testing of personal protection equipment;
    • questions of work physiology, psychology and other ergonomic or welfare problems, in particular work rhythm, the organisation of work time and breaks, the design of workplaces, work flow and the working environment; the organisation of first aid in the company;
    • questions of workplace changes and the integration or reintegration of handicapped people in the work process.

2   To check the safety aspects of machines, equipment and technical systems before they are put in to operation as well as work procedures and dangerous substances, before they are introduced.

3   To see that industrial health and safety and accident prevention measures are carried out.

Company doctors have the additional duty of examining employees, assessing and advising them on their fitness for work and compiling and evaluating test results. They also assist in planning the operation and training of first aid and auxiliary medical personnel.

An important aspect of the Work Safety Law is the co-ordination between company doctors and work safety experts. By linking the insights of industrial medicine and safety technology, solutions can be found to the problems of industrial health and safety. Company doctors and work safety experts must therefore work together closely, particularly by carrying out joint company inspections.

Health and safety committees

The various actions in the field of company health and safety are co-ordinated or represented by the health and safety committee. Health and safety committees need to be installed in all companies in which company doctors and work safety experts have been appointed. It is evident that bargaining by intensive co-operation between various parties is a characteristic of problem solving in German companies.

10.1.2 Stress as an issue

With the transposition in 1996 of the Framework Directive 89/391/EEC in the German Health and Safety Law, stress at work has become an issue for all employers. There now is a general obligation for employers to reduce stress at work. Still, the German health and safety system is relatively technically oriented. Official German government documents do not pay much attention to stress at work or to psychosocial work demands (Kompier *et al.*, 1994). There are no special legal regulations related to stress at the workplace. However, the Ministry of Labour is certainly interested in the matter. A problem for the German government is the question of how stress and well-being can be measured more or less objectively. The Bundesanstalt fur Arbeitsschutz und Arbeitsmedicin (the Federal Institute for Occupational Safety and Health) holds a special place within the work and health debate. This institute supports the federal government in Bonn with its research and advice. It also supports German industry on questions relating to safety and health.

As in many other countries, improving the health of the workforce does not seem to be a particularly high priority for employers in Germany. Their principal concern relating to personnel is more to do with such factors as salaries, new technologies, lean production methods and sickness absence rates. Many German employers like to think of stress and well-being as a personal matter rather than a work-related issue. Trade unions rarely participate in discussions on stress and workplace health promotion, as they often see this as having little to do with the reality of the workplace. In addition, occupational health services in Germany devote more attention to chemical, physical and biological hazards than to psychosocial problems such as monotonous work, social climate and working hours.

From time to time stress-monitoring surveys are carried out on representative samples of employees in Germany to ascertain the level of their work and job satisfaction. For example, in 1991, an important monitoring study was carried out by the Federal Institute for Working Education and the Institute for the Labour Market and Work Research. Their BIBB/IAB survey, a representative survey of the German working population on specific aspects of work, demonstrated that 55 per cent of all employees experienced time pressures, 48 per cent performed repetitive and monotonous tasks, and 62 per cent performed high concentration tasks. Although such studies give important indications, nationwide work and health monitoring systems are perceived as lacking in Germany. Still it seems that in the 1990s stressful working conditions are a common phenomenon in Germany.

10.1.3 Problem solving groups in German companies

In the areas of human resources management, work productivity and working conditions policies, various types of problem-solving groups have been introduced and developed in recent years in German companies. These include 'health circles' 'health and safety circles', 'quality circles', and 'learning workshops'. Although there are differences between and also within each type of group, the fundamental philosophy which links them is that it makes sense to recognise and eliminate problems at their source. This seems appropriate for several reasons (Johannes, 1995):

- since employees are the ones who are confronted with everyday work problems, many of them are in fact expert on work issues;
- many employees have the potential for creativity and problem-solving which up to now has hardly been used;
- a company's 'professional problem solvers' are usually so overloaded with other work tasks that they often lack the time for recognising and dealing with (minor) work problems;
- when combined, a large number of minor weak spots ('daily work hassles') may result in major errors, costs and a potential for dissatisfaction. Therefore these factors should be dealt with.

In their ideal form, these various groups are only seldom put into practice in German companies. Moreover, in recent years there has been a trend towards a convergence between the various groups. For example, the idea that quality circles should concentrate exclusively on improving production is slowly dissolving. In recent years quality circles have become increasingly concerned with improving working conditions, interpersonal relationships, safety at work, and the health of the workforce.

Changes in objectives over the course of time can also be observed with respect to learning workshops. Originally, learning workshops dealt with functional language teaching. These workshops place an emphasis on the general personal development of the workforce (Breisig, 1990). They aim to promote joint learning and co-operation in small groups, while trying to create a balance between the development of the participants' professional and social competences. Now, however, learning workshops also deal with specific problems of work organisation and or quality management (Kunzmann, 1991). Accordingly, the aims of the learning workshop approach those of the quality circle.

In the last few years in German companies different types of problem-solving groups have dealt with occupational health and safety problems, including the assessment and prevention of stress at work. This trend is influenced by indications that working conditions may cause or contribute to cardiovascular, gastrointestinal and musculoskeletal diseases (Slesina, 1990). In a similar vein, working conditions may cause or contribute to psychosomatic symptoms. Health circles may therefore be utilized to counter signs of ill health among employees.

Two health circle concepts: The Berlin and the Düsseldorf model

A comparable development in objectives has taken place in the case of health circles. Their original, almost exclusive emphasis on the prevention of chronic-degenerative diseases at the workplace was replaced by a broader conceptualization of work-related problems and hassles that employees may face. In addition, the reduction of working difficulties has increasingly been connected to the company's operational objectives. It is argued that the elimination of various interference factors, for example, accidents or health impairments, via the improvement of working conditions, may cause an improvement in product quality. Improving working conditions therefore bears a direct relationship to economic production (Schröer, 1992).

At the end of the 1980s, two different health circle concepts – the Berlin model and the Düsseldorf model – were developed and tested at about the same time. According to Brandenburg (1991), 'These concepts display some basic similarities, but diverge from one another to some extent quite significantly in basic aims, theoretical references and in practical methods'. The basic scheme of the 'Berlin model' is as follows: (1) a small group consisting of fifteen members, (2) from a single hierarchical level, (3) meets twelve times over a limited period of time, (4) under the leadership of an external moderator, (5) stress situations are revealed, (6) experiences exchanged, and (7) a new method of coping with stress and preserving health is developed and tested.

The Berlin model's aim is to change the way people deal with the phenomenon of stress, to learn new patterns for coping with stress, and to create a new working climate which supports a healthy stress management.

The 'Düsseldorf model' can be defined as follows: (1) a small mixed group of employees, foremen, a safety officer, a works council member, a plant medical officer and a plant manager, (2) meets at regular intervals, (3) approximately eight to ten times over a limited period of time, (4) the employees are voted into the group by their colleagues, and (5) under the leadership of a trained external moderator, (6) are to deal with all the demands of work in their own field which are felt by the workforce to be damaging to health.

Both types of circles try to promote broad, open communication concerning illness symptoms resulting from work and their causes, in order to guarantee the health of the workforce and the company's efficiency and performance. Under the 'Berlin model' there is a strong emphasis on stress and stress management ('stress awareness', and 'coping'), whereas in the Düsseldorf model the scope is broader. It attempts to make a connection between the expert knowledge of the employee and the medical and ergonomic knowledge of the work and safety experts. In this way, expertise is developed of psychosocial stressors at work that significantly affect health. According to Schröer et al. (1991) there are two main steps that health circles should follow:

1   The circle should clarify those work requirements that are particularly demanding and challenging, their rate of occurrence, and the possibilities which exist to deal with them. In addition, the circle should try to answer the question whether these work situations may lead to medical complaints and infirmities.
2   The circle should determine whether and how tasks and work situations which are particularly demanding can be improved. The focus should be on technical, organisational and person-related measures.

The 'Düsseldorf model' provides the framework for the health circles which are now offered as a service by the Federal Association of Company Health Insurance Funds (BKK BV). This service covers the analysis of the health situation in the company (health situation reporting), moderation of the health circle meetings, preparatory work and an evaluation of the circle findings. 'Düsseldorf model' health circles have been and are being used in a large range of sectors, for example, in the steel and automotive industries, in public transport companies, in commerce and in the food industry. With a health situation report as its starting point, in the near future more health circles will also be employed in the service sector (e.g., hospitals).

10.2 Introduction to the case study

This case study concerns the introduction of a health circle in a German hospital. There are over one million people in Germany employed in hospitals and nursing homes. A typical problem in this type of working organisation is the coordination of the different professions. Furthermore, German hospitals are characterized by their strict hierarchical form. Traditionally, the medical department is dominant and authorised to instruct the nursing staff. Hospitals in Germany are still anchored in tradition.

Work in hospitals in both the medical and nursing areas is marked by a high level of physical and psychological stress. This often leads to 'burn-out' which is prevalent in the area of nursing (e.g., Gerhards, 1988; Kleiber and Enzman, 1990; Hoffmann, 1997). Symptoms of burn-out include a gradual loss of interest in work; employees are unable to cope with high, often conflicting job demands and with the high emotional workload and irregular work and rest schedules. Hospital employees need to provide constant care. At the same time, limited numbers of staff means a considerable amount of overtime is necessary. The resulting stress symptoms often result in illness and absence due to sickness (Dietrich, 1994). This creates a cycle whereby, colleagues must work overtime and thus stress levels are increased (Schmeikal and Nowak, 1994; Fick, 1993; Landau, 1991).

In nursing the proportion of female workers is very high, about 85 per cent (Dietrich, 1994), and sickness absence figures are above average. The average number of years of service in the profession is no more than five years (Dietrich, 1994). Thus, in hospitals and nursing homes a considerable proportion of qualified and experienced staff is lost after a relatively short time.

In general, the situation in hospitals and nursing homes is marked by strong economic pressures. Due to budgetary constraints, high potential in the work force and in work quality is lost through dissatisfaction with working conditions and with work itself. Without doubt, and especially in hospitals, there is the potential for improvement in the work organisation structures.

Work place health promotion is one way of using the employees' potential in optimising the working conditions. In such a programme employees may play an active role in (re)organising job content and work processes. Accordingly, employees may acquire a stronger feeling of responsibility and influence in the organisation. As on-site experts, they have considerable competence concerning possibilities for improvement. Health circles and staff interviews are important tools in this programme.

Because of the number of problems experienced by the employees and the expense caused by ill health and sickness leave, a project was sponsored to be carried out by the BAuA (Bundesanstalt fur Arbeitsschutz und Arbeitsmedizin). Through the implementation of health circles, its aim was to identify work-related stress factors and to define possibilities for improvement.

10.3 The hospital and the two wards

10.3.1 The hospital

The health circle in question is one of the few health circles to be found outside industry. A total of three health circles were implemented within the framework of the research project. One of these health circles was concluded during the period of this report and is outlined in this chapter.

The hospital under study is a general hospital with a surgery, an internal medicine ward and a geriatrics department. Its focus is on 'medical rehabilitation'. It has a total of 144 beds and 69 rooms. About 230 staff members are employed in the hospital. About 110 of these work in the area of nursing. Sickness rate statistics were not available.

10.3.2 The health work group

First a health work group was appointed by the management of the hospital. It consisted of the following members: the general manager of the company health insurance (the BKK), as representative of the hospital authorities; senior hospital physicians; nursing service management; and representatives of the works council.

The company health insurance of the hospital kept in contact with the Federal Association of Company Health insurance funds. This association offers a consultancy service to its members.

The hospital management revised the basic questionnaire that BKK uses for interviewing employees. It was adapted according to specific conditions of the hospital. In part, these adjustments were in line with adjustments that had previously been made in the context of an interview in another hospital. In part this previous interview served as a basis for comparing the case hospital scores with another comparable hospital. For more details about the questionnaire, see section 10.4.2.

Furthermore it was agreed that the questionnaires would be distributed to all wards and that the employees would be extensively informed about the health circle programme in both verbal and written form. It was also decided that the intervention would take place in a geriatric ward and in an internal ward. The geriatric ward had thirty-three beds. The internal medicine ward counted thirty-four beds. Each ward was managed by the respective ward sister in charge. In the two wards under study, the employees worked in shifts. In addition to the early, late and night shift a so-called supplementary service existed. The employees were responsible for general nursing services as well as the co-ordination of the 'function services' in the hospital. There were also extensive administration tasks. On these wards many patients required a very high amount of care due to their advanced age and often serious illnesses. The employees' peak work load was in the mornings since this was the time when the patients required a lot of help in getting up, dressed and washed and having breakfast. Whereas the rooms in the geriatric ward had already been partly reconstructed and renovated, so far nothing had been done to renew the internal medicine ward.

It was decided that the health circle would consist of: a ward sister for ward 2b, a ward sister for ward 3a, a nurse for ward 2b, a nurse for ward 3a, a student nurse, a member of the nursing service management, a safety expert, a representative of the works council, and, finally, a representative of the medical profession. Furthermore it was agreed that the health circle should meet every two weeks for a total of five meetings each lasting one and a half hours. Variations in the intervals between and the length of the meetings would be possible. Usually in health circles there is a series of about eight meetings lasting approximately fifty to sixty minutes. In the 'hospital version' the same period of time was divided over fewer meetings. The amount of time that the employees 'used' in order to participate in the health circle would be credited to their working time.

It was also agreed that the small-scale improvements would be implemented immediately. Throughout the study, the hospital management had overall responsibility. Suggestions for medium or large-scale improvements would be presented to the hospital management for decision. The decision for the implementation of the suggestions would be made in a special meeting after the health circle had finished. It was decided that the local branch of the BKK or the hospital would make available company data and documents to the BKK BV (Federal Association of Company Health Insurance) for the purpose of evaluation of this type of programme.

10.4 Introduction of the health circle, workplace observations and questionnaire study

10.4.1 Introduction of the health circle and workplace observations

Before the start of the health circle, hospital employees were informed about the project, both verbally and in writing. There were several informational meetings with the relevant departments. In addition, the moderator and a BKK secretary carried out workplace observations. These observations served two purposes: on the one hand more insight could be obtained towards the actual work organisation and work processes. On the other hand employees could become more familiar with the concept of the health circle. The aim was to enable fluent and smooth processing in the circle meetings. Observations also intended to overcome remaining irritations and opposition among health circle participants, and to increase the employees' acceptance by means of more personal contact.

10.4.2 Questionnaire

In addition to the written information, all employees of the hospital received a questionnaire (see section 10.3.2). This questionnaire included questions about: personal data, work schedules, work organisation, social relations at work and working climate, work-related risk factors, health complaints and the extent to which these were work related, work changes, work satisfaction, and suggestions for improvement.

This questionnaire was administered to get an initial idea of the relationship connection between work demands and complaints of employees. From the 228 distributed questionnaires, 135 could be included in the evaluation (response percentage of 60 per cent). The respondents may be regarded as representative for the whole staff. The proportion of administrative staff in comparison to the care personnel was minimal (n = 10). Data were compared with those of another hospital (external comparison), and within the hospital itself (internal comparison, i.e. between the nursing service and other services in the hospital). Compared to the other hospital, employees in the study hospital had more complaints regarding health, physical and psychological strains. The results with respect to the nurses and from the internal comparison (nursing, i.e. the internal medicine ward and geriatric department versus the other area, i.e. administration) are reported in the following sections.

Work-related health complaints

From Figure 10.1 it can be seen that in this hospital employees report very high levels of work-related health complaints. Scores with respect to the musculoskeletal system (backaches, arms and legs) are especially impressive. Ninety-five per cent of the nursing staff report work-related backaches and 87 per cent mention work-related pains in arms or legs. Moreover, the nursing staff report substantial fatigue and sleep problems, gastric disorders, and so on. It seems as if the nurses report more health complaints than other employees in the hospital. This seems to be a relative difference, however, since the other employees also report high levels of work-related health complaints.

Physical strains

Figure 10.2 demonstrates important risk factors with respect to the musculoskeletal system. Almost all (98 per cent) of the responding nurses report that lifting and carrying constitutes a load to them. Also a compulsive work position is a common risk factor among nurses (65 per cent), and also for the other employees in the hospital.

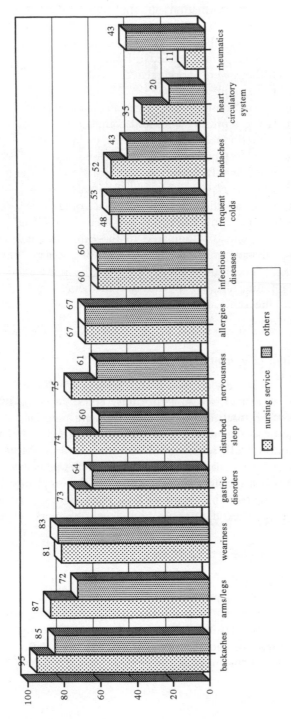

Figure 10.1 Work-related health complaints among nurses and other employees (percentages)

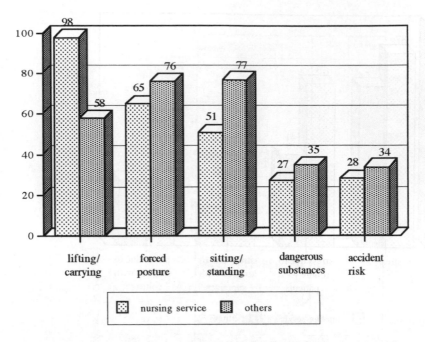

Figure 10.2 Physical strains among nurses and other employees (percentages)

Psychological stress

From Figure 10.3 it is clear that stress is a very common complaint among nurses (87 per cent). Patients seem to cause stress, since 73 per cent of the nursing staff report this complaint. Superiors as well seem to cause stress among nurses (32 per cent). Colleagues hardly constitute a source of stress among the nurses (12 per cent). Stress is also a common phenomenon among non-nursing staff (72 per cent).

10.5 Implementation of the health circle

10.5.1 Timetable and participation

The constituting meeting of the health circle took place on 1 July 1993. The full timetable for the total project is shown in Table 10.1.

In addition to the arrangements in the health workgroup (see section 10.3.2), it was decided that the nursing service management should only participate in the first, the fifth and the last meeting as their presence might exert a hierarchical influence. The participation in the health circle is shown in Table 10.2.

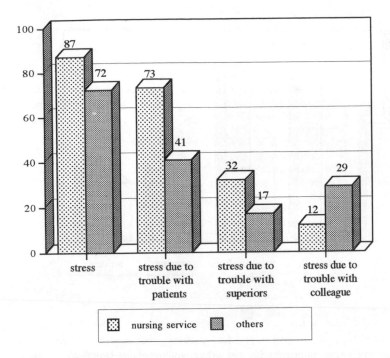

Figure 10.3 Stress among nurses and other employees (percentages)

The presence of the several circle members indicates the general interest in the circle work. Table 10.2 shows that, in contrast to the five circle meetings, only two employees took part in the evaluation meeting. This was attributed to holidays and illness at that time, but also to the fact that the doctor, the student nurse and a person serving alternative national service left the hospital.

10.5.2 Health circle meetings

First, an introduction circle took place in the first meeting of the health circle. All participants were asked to state their expectations, aims and hopes about the project. Major points that were mentioned were: identification of work strains, improvement of work satisfaction, improvement in communication and improvement of the spatial conditions.

After this introduction and an evaluation of the rules of collaboration, the definition of work strains formed the main issue of the first meeting. Participants were asked to note the strains that were relevant to them on cards. On a meta-plan board these cards were then assigned to three different categories, i.e. physical, psychological and environmental strains. This gave

Table 10.1 Timetable of the 'health circle project'

Period	Measures
May 1993	Health work group/meeting of the hospital management • presentation of the concept 'health circle' • presentation of the research project 'evaluation' • decision to include a geriatric and an internal ward in the research project for the health circle
June 1993	Meetings of the wards • information in verbal and written form • interview of all employees
June 1993	Workplace observations
July to August 1993	Five health circle meetings of one-and-a-half hours in fortnightly periods
September 1993	Health work group • presentation of the circle results • initiation of the proceedings of translation
April 1994	Final meeting of the health circle
1995	Evaluation of the health circle results

an extensive overview of the stressful working situations which were to be analysed step by step. At the end of the first meeting the moderator requested to carry out a priority meeting. The employees expressed the wish to first discuss the strains that resulted from adverse environmental influences, as these were very important to them.

The process of the following meetings was structured by different focal points. Two meetings were used for in-depth discussion of environmental strains, as well as suggestions for improvement. One meeting was devoted to the discussion of physical problems and 'their' possible improvements, and to the discussion of psychological strains. Each meeting was minuted and these were later distributed to all circle participants to inform them of the

Table 10.2 Participation in the meetings

Circle meeting	Participants total	Employees	Nursing service management	Doctor	Works council	Safety expert
1	9	5	1	1	1	1
2	8	5	1	1	1	0
3	9	6	*	1	1	1
4	7	4	*	1	1	1
5	9	5	1	1	1	1
Evaluation meeting	5	2	1	0	1	1

Key: * = participation was not planned

Table 10.3 Stressful working situations and suggestions for improvement

	Physical strains	Environmental strains	Psycho-social strains	Other strains (organisational)
Strains	6	30	13	3
Suggestions for improvement	9	29	10	5

current state of discussion. A copy of the minutes was sent to each department for their information. At the beginning of each meeting a discussion on the minutes from the previous meeting took place.

10.5.3 Identified stressful work situations and suggestions for improvement

A total of fifty-two different stressful work situations was voiced in the five meetings, and fifty-three suggestions for improvement were developed.

In Table 10.3 we can see that the meetings focused on environmental influences and on psychosocial strains. Among the most important strains and suggestions for improvements were strains caused by lack of space and missing or insufficient installations in bathrooms and showers. These could only be reduced by suitable measures or reconstruction. Better ventilation was suggested in order to improve the air-conditioning of several rooms including the examination rooms. There were considerable problems with regard to the collaboration of the different occupational groups (lack of co-ordination, bad information). It was therefore considered necessary 'to approach each other' and to achieve a closer and regular co-ordination with the help of programmed circle discussions. With regard to physical strains, major causal factors related to the long passages in the wards, bent postures while washing the patients and heavy lifting and carrying while repositioning them. It was therefore suggested to offer courses in lifting and carrying techniques.

10.5.4 Implementation of the recommendations

After the five regular health circle meetings had been concluded, the hospital management initiated the implementation of the suggested improvements. Table 10.4 reflects the improvement suggestions which were or were not implemented in the several strain categories. Suggestions were categorised according to their feasibility and based on the evaluation of the health work-group meeting after the circle meetings. In this evaluation the hospital management made a corresponding rating. There were four categories:

A   'Simple suggestions'
These were suggestions that could be implemented easily within a relatively short period of time. They cover suggestions that relate to smaller
structural measures, to the improvement of information flow as well as
to class and training arrangements. Examples from this category are the
fixing of handles, a non-slip paint in the showers, cleaning of toilets, the
restructuring of the billeting of rooms, and certain types of training.
B   Suggestions that needed more preparation
These suggestions would be implemented but only after certain preparations. These suggestions were for instance new low-cost purchases and
smaller technical modifications, such as the sealing of windows and the
reconstruction of toilet doors.
C   Suggestions included in investment plans
These were suggestions that were not yet implemented but were included
in investment plans and/or in reconstruction plans. Examples from this
category are the installation of additional baths for the patients, the reconstruction of toilets and other specific items.
D   Suggestions that would not be implemented
These were suggestions that were labelled as not suitable for implementation. These suggestions were larger reconstruction measures which were
considered not realistic because of their costs or because it was assumed
that they would cause a lot of other problems in the hospital. Examples
were the installation of a new water pump or the modification of
washrooms.

Table 10.4 shows that by April 1994, eight months after the conclusion of
the circle, thirty-four suggestions for improvement had been implemented

Table 10.4 Four strain categories and four types of suggestions for improvement

	Total	A Suggestions that were implemented	B Suggestions ready for implementation after preparation	C Suggestions included in reconstruction/ investment plans	D Not possible to implement
Physical strains	9	4	1	3	1
Environmental strains	29	18	1	4	6
Psycho-social strains	10	9	1	–	–
Other	5	3	2	–	–
Total	53	34	5	7	7

Table 10.5 Amount of improvement in percentages with respect to work stress through implemented suggestions

	Physical	Environmental	Psychological	Other	Total
Intensity					
Very high	16	6	3	2	6
High	61	61	58	30	54
Somewhat	21	23	36	55	33
Very little	2	8	3	10	5
None	–	2	–	2	1

from a total of fifty-three (category A). The implementation of five additional suggestions is possible after certain preparations (category B), and the implementation of seven additional suggestions had been included in the budgeting (category C). Category D counted seven measures.

10.6 Evaluation

Approximately six months after the conclusion of the health circle (in February 1994), employees in the intervention areas were questioned about the changes with respect to stress at work. Questions were asked about improvements with respect to stress at work, information and communication within the company; and improvement of social support and acknowledgement of achievement (working atmosphere). For this evaluation again a questionnaire was sent to the two wards.

Improvement with respect to work stress

From Table 10.5 it appears that most of the employees place high value on the measures that have been implemented. According to approximately 60 per cent of the employees these improvements have had a high or very high impact on stress at work. Positive results were mentioned with respect to all three major categories: physical, environmental and psychosocial constraints. Only a small minority (approximately 6 per cent) mentioned very little or no effect at all.

Communication and social support

Since another aim of the health circle concept was to improve communication patterns and abilities on all hierarchical and professional levels, in the evaluation the question was asked whether communication had improved. All supervisors, the health and safety experts and 87 per cent of the employees mentioned an improvement in communication. Furthermore, with respect to social support, 80 per cent of the supervisors and 56 per cent of the employees mentioned that 'inter-group' relationships and behaviours had been improved. Also all supervisors, and 60 per cent of the employees were of the opinion that the working atmosphere had improved.

10.7 Conclusion

A series of stressful situations was subject for discussion in this health circle project. Many organisational problems were discussed during the health circle work and greater transparency was achieved for the employees. In addition to the identification of stressful situations, stress reduction suggestions were developed that from the employee's point of view could improve their working situation. In this respect the fact that the original questionnaire did not provide the possibility of examining strains caused by the working environment, proved to be a deficiency in the circle work right from the beginning. The questionnaire was therefore adapted for the purpose of this study.

As was expected, the main suggestions that were put into practice soon after the study were the 'small-' to 'medium-sized' suggestions. Six months after the circle work had ended at least 50 per cent of the suggestions had been implemented or at least initiated. In this health circle project employees were committed and participated in an active way.

With respect to the results of the interventions no objective measures (sickness absenteeism, productivity indicators, and so forth) were available. However, the results from the evaluation survey clearly point to a decrease of stress at work, and an improvement in information and communication patterns and in social support (a 'positive' working atmosphere). These positive effects are not limited to only those employees who directly participated in the health circle meetings, but relate to all employees in the intervention wards.

Currently, an ongoing project of the BauA's is the evaluation of approximately one hundred company health circles. The interim results from this large study seem to confirm the value of the 'health circle' as a tool in reducing stress at work.

Bibliography

Brandenburg, U. (1991) 'Gesundheitszirkel in der Volkswagen AG – Konzept und Erfahrungen' ('Health circles in Volkswagen AG – concept and experiences'), in A. Schöer, R. Sochert and R. Stuppardt (eds) Gesundheitsberichterstattung und Gesundheitszirkel ('Health report and health circles'), Essen: BKK.

Breisig, Th. (1990) Betriebliche Sozialtechniken ('Company's social techniques'), Band 3, Neuwied/Frankfurt am Main: Luchterhand.

Dietrich, H. (1994) Wege zur Verbesserung des Ansehens von Pflegeberufen ('Ways of improving the professional image of caring occupations'), Nurnberg: Institut für Arbeitsmarkt und Berufsforschung für Arbeit.

Fick, D. (1993) *Der Krankenstand im Betrieb. Eine Analyse von Entwicklungen, Ursachen und Massnahmen* ('Sickness absenteeism in the company. Analysis of developments, causes, and measures'), Konstanz: Hartung-Gorre.

Gerhards, J. (1988) *Soziologie der Emotionene. Fragestellungen, Systematik und Perspektiven* ('The sociology of emotions. Questions, systematics, and perspectives'), München: Weinheim.

Hoffmann, P. (1997) 'Das Burnout-Syndrom und seine Folgeerscheinungen beim diplomierten Pflegepersonal' ('Burn-out syndrome and its consequences in care personnel'), in A. Grundböck, P. Nowak and J.M. Pelikan (eds) *Gesundheitsförderung – eine Strategie für Krankenhäuser im Umbruch. Projekte aus Österreich und Deutschland* ('Health promotion – strategy for hospitals in development. Projects from Austria and Germany'), Wien: Facultas Universitätsverlag, pp. 176–92.

Jansen, R. and Stooss, F. (eds) (1993) *Qualifikation und Erwerbssituation in geeinten Deutschland,* ('Qualification and work in united Germany'), Berlin: BIBB/IAB–Erhebung 1991/1992.

Johannes, D. (1995) *Quality Circles, Health Circles and Other Problem-solving Groups,* Dortmund: Federal Institute for Occupational Safety and Health.

Kleiber, D. and Enzmann, D. (1990) *Burnout. Eine internationale Bibliographie* ('Burn-out, an international bibliography'), Göttingen/Toronto/Zürich: Verlag für Psychologie Hogrefe.

Kompier, M., De Gier, E., Smulders, P and Draaisma, D. (1994) 'Regulations, policies and practices concerning work stress in five European countries', *Work and Stress,* 8, (4): 296–318.

Kunzmann, E.-M. (1991) *Zirkelarbeit* ('Working in health circles'), München und Mering: Rainer Hampp Verlag.

Landau, K. (ed.) (1991) *Arbeitsbedingungen im Krankenhaus und Heim. Bericht über ein Symposium* ('Working conditions in hospial and at home'), München: Bayensches Staatsministerium für Arbeit, Familie und Sociales.

Schmeikal, B. and Nowak, P. (1994) *Time Strucures at the Ward. An Analysis of Sick-leave Rates Within Nursing Personnel,* Vortragsmanuskript.

Schröer, A. (1992) *Gesundheitszirkel* ('Health circle'), Essen: BKK.

Schröer, A., Sochert, R. and Stuppardt, R. (eds) (1991) '*Gesundheitsberichterstattung und Gesundheitszirkel*' ('Health report and health circle'), Essen: BKK.

Slesina, W. (1990) 'Gesundheitszirkel: Ein neues Verfahren zur Verhütung arbeitsbedingter Erkrankungen' ('Health circle: A new method for preventing work-related sickness'), in U. Brandenburg et al. (ed.) *Prävention und Gesundheitsförderung im Betreib* ('Prevention and health promotion at the workplace'), Dortmund: Schriftenreihe der Bündesanstalt für Arbeitsschütz.

Chapter 11

Ireland: Stress prevention in an airport management company

Richard Wynne and Rose Rafferty

11.1 Introduction: Work stress in Ireland

The legislative situation in Ireland had for most of the twentieth century been influenced by the United Kingdom approach. After the formation of the State in 1922, Ireland inherited the UK body of legislation on health and safety and many of the administrative structures which implemented this legislation. Over the next sixty years various updates were made to legislation on a piecemeal basis. However, as late as the early 1980s, no more than 30 per cent of the workforce were covered by health and safety legislation of any kind and no mention was made of the issue of occupational stress in any part of the legislation.

In 1984, a government commission (the Barrington commission) was set up to investigate the issue of health and safety legislation, as it was recognised that the then current body of legislation was inadequate for a range of reasons. First, there was the need to comply with the regulations which were being issued by the European commission. Second, it was recognised that the then current legislation was inadequate and in some cases anomalous. Finally, it was also appreciated it was no longer sufficient for legislation to cover less than a third of the workforce. When the Barrington Commission reported in 1986, it recommended a major overhaul of legislation in the area. Specifically, it recommended the drafting and implementation of framework-type legislation to cover all workers and the establishment of a new agency (the Health and Safety Authority – HSA) to, *inter alia*, police the legislation. These recommendations were acted on by the Government in the 1989 Safety, Health and Welfare at Work Act (SHAW), which replaced much of the existing legislation.

This legislation does not specifically require employers to act on occupational stress by name, but its provisions concerning the work environment and working methods in effect cover many of the workplace elements which give rise to occupational stress. Stress prevention, therefore, in the context of health and safety has only become an issue since 1989 with the passing of SHAW. This legislation states general duties on employers to manage systems of working so that they are not injurious to health. This has been interpreted to cover occupational stress.

The social partners have gradually become more aware of the issue. For example, the VDU usage guidelines issued by the Health and Safety Authority in 1990 specifically mentioned stress as an issue for the first time. The HSA has also issued more general guidance on the issue. Trade unions have generally been in favour of dealing with stress at work, while employers have been more reticent. Priorities in the past have focused on traditional health and safety issues, and still do to a great extent.

No national statistics on stress are available from official sources. However, there have been a number of nationwide studies commissioned by specific occupational groups, for example, first- and second-level teachers (WRC, 1992), medical nurses (WRC, 1993), and a number of other major initiatives have been undertaken at company level, for example, Aer Rianta (Wynne and Conroy, 1991) and Dublin Bus. Therefore there is no reliable picture of at risk groups or situations. These and other smaller initiatives provide examples of good practice.

There has also been a tradition among some companies (especially United States multinationals with operations in Ireland) to treat stress at work as an individual problem to be managed by enhancing the personal coping skills of the individual worker. This has emanated mainly from two sources – the US health promotion tradition and a desire to improve employee performance. These individually-oriented interventions (which may be termed stress management) constitute the vast bulk of activities in the occupational stress area in Ireland.

However, there have been a number of developments in recent years which have begun to lead to a change in approach to dealing with workplace stress. First, stress in general and occupational stress in particular has begun to lose its taboo status and its previous association with mental illness in the public mind. There have been many conferences, newspaper articles and television programmes which have dealt with stress in a more open manner, and recently we have begun to see the emergence of litigation against employers citing occupational stress as the ground for their case. Second, anecdotal evidence would indicate that medical practitioners are beginning to use the term stress as a reason for absence from work. Third, the growing exposure of all sections of society to the issue has led to a more sophisticated approach being at least talked about in the workplace, and this would appear to be followed up by at least some companies. These changes, though difficult to quantify, offer the hope that occupational stress will be dealt with more coherently in the future.

11.2 Introduction to Aer Rianta

Aer Rianta is a state company with responsibility for the management and development of the three state airports Dublin, Cork and Shannon.

In addition, the company operates an international commercial division with airport management interests in Britain and Germany and duty-free interests in east Europe and Asia. It also owns a major hotel chain in Ireland. They are a semi-state company, i.e. all shares in the company are held by the Irish Government, but they have considerable freedom to operate in a commercial manner. Their ownership structure is roughly equivalent to that of public utilities such as electricity and telecommunications in other European countries.

Aer Rianta's core mission is to be the best organisation in the world in the field of managing airports and associated commercial activities. It aims to achieve this through the fundamental values of excellence, customer service, humanisation and open management systems. Equal opportunity is an internal aspect of management procedure in Aer Rianta.

The organisational structure is based on a hierarchical form with the Aer Rianta group employing the equivalent of 2,742 full-time employees during 1996. Total group revenue for 1996 reached an all-time high at IR £231 million, with profits of IR £39.4 million. Passenger numbers have increased from 7.5 million in 1993 to 11.96 million in 1996. Quality is one of the key factors in the success of the organisation with the acquisitions of various international standards, ISO 9002 and E3 10.

The company is responsible for all aspects of airport management, including maintenance, policing, fire and safety services (this latter function in conjunction with the airlines), duty-free sales, car parking and cleaning. They work closely with the airlines which use the airports and with air traffic control. Working conditions vary considerably, with some staff being office based, duty-free shop based, others being mobile within the airport terminal and some staff working outdoors.

11.3 Evolution of the project

The initial stimulus for the project arose when a member of staff wrote to the chief executive of the company in September 1988 expressing the view that occupational stress was a significant issue in the organisation. This issue was further discussed with a member of the Staff Development Department and a group known as the 'Stress Working Group' was established in December 1988. The aim of this group was to investigate stress within Aer Rianta at Dublin airport and to identify, as far as possible, where such stresses originate. Ultimately the aim was to formulate a plan for the prevention and management of stress within Aer Rianta. An additional aim was to disseminate relevant information which would be helpful to staff in coping with stress, and this was achieved in the summer of 1989 with the publication of a booklet listing external help agencies. This booklet was distributed to all staff at Dublin airport and was also made available to the other airports.

To achieve the aim of investigating stress and identifying its origins within Aer Rianta, it was decided to undertake a survey. Contracts were made with a number of outside bodies including academics and external consultants. While there was a lot of interest in the concept of a survey, many of the contacts were only interested in becoming involved at the results stage. Finally a three-dimensional approach was used and a working partnership evolved between Psychological Consultancy Services (PCS), the Work Research Centre (WRC) and the Aer Rianta Stress Working Group.

The survey was supported financially by Aer Rianta Dublin Management team who were also very encouraging. Full support to the initiative was also given by the Aer Rianta staff representation and several union groups.

Following initial discussions, it was decided that the survey should run in two phases. The first phase consisted of extensive piloting activities, and the second would consist of the survey itself. Piloting activities involved pilot questionnaire development, the pilot survey, analysis of the results from the pilot survey and alterations to the survey questionnaire on foot of the pilot results. The surveying activities project was conducted between January and July 1990, with the analysis of results taking place over the remainder of 1990. The setting up of project actions teams (see section 11.6) took place early in 1991 and the stress prevention activities have taken place from late 1991 up until the present day (1998).

11.3.1 Piloting activities

Developing the pilot questionnaire involved two processes. In the first process, the WRC/PCS proposed a questionnaire which examined generic sources of stress, coping health-related behaviours and the outcomes of stress. The second process involved an intensive series of discussions with the Aer Rianta Stress Working Group in which the questionnaire was contextualised and made appropriate to the specific situation of Aer Rianta. During these discussions additional questions were suggested and incorporated into the questionnaire.

The pilot questionnaire was issued to fifty people selected by the Stress Group covering all areas of Aer Rianta. The aim of this pilot study was to assess the acceptability of the questionnaire to potential survey participants, to assess procedures for maintaining confidentiality and to provide input to modification of the survey questionnaire. Approximately 60 per cent of the pilot sample replied to the questionnaire, and the principal modifications to the questionnaire concerned reducing its length, modifications to layout and the alteration of specific questions concerning life events and social support.

11.3.2 Main survey

Some modifications to the procedures for maintaining confidentiality were made as a result of the pilot study. In essence this involved the use of detachable identification numbers, which gave respondents the option of remaining completely anonymous, or of receiving personalised feedback from the survey. The pilot questionnaire proved completely acceptable to the sample.

The survey instrument was issued to all 953 workers at Dublin airport. The instrument was extensive and comprehensive and covered the following areas:

- Respondent personal and work-related demography (11 items)
- Sources of stress at work (55 closed items, 4 open-ended questions)
- Personal life events (43 items)
- Coping styles (34 items, 2 open-ended questions)
- Social support at and outside of work (19 items)
- Physical health status (39 items)
- Psychological well-being status (28 items)
- Health-related behaviours (18 items)
- Job satisfaction (17 items)

The questionnaire was constructed from a variety of sources and consisted of a number of standard instruments used in occupational stress research, (for example, Cooper's Occupational Stress Indicator (Cooper *et al.*, 1988), the General Health Questionnaire (12 items; Goldberg, 1978), the Crown–Crisp Experiential Index (Crown and Crisp, 1979), the Ways of Coping Checklist (Lazarus and Folkman, 1984), a health symptomatology scale published by NIOSH (Tasto *et al.*, 1978), the Holmes and Rahe Life Events Scale (Holmes and Rahe, 1967), and the Job Satisfaction scale (extrinsic and intrinsic) published by the Social and Applied Psychology Unit in the United Kingdom (Warr *et al.*, 1979). In almost all cases these standard scales were augmented by additional items which the WRC had been using in their own research work and which were of specific interest within the context of Aer Rianta. The demography section of the questionnaire was based on items commonly used by the WRC.

In all cases the reliability coefficients (Cronbach alpha) of the scales used in the questionnaire fell within acceptable ranges. The survey itself proceeded by setting up a project committee with representatives from the ad hoc committee and the consultants. The concepts measured in the questionnaire are outlined in Table 11.1

11.3.3 Response rates

In all, 489 people responded to the survey which represented a response rate of 51 per cent. The response rate varied somewhat between company departments, ranging from 34 per cent (cleaning section) to 92 per cent (clerical section). These variations were confounded by gender and by whether the employee was full-time or part-time, as the cleaning section had predominantly female workers, while the gender balance in other sections was more even. The cleaning section were also predominantly part-time workers.

Table 11.1 Concepts measured by the survey

Background information: Respondent demography	Sources of stress at work: Nature of the job	Outside of work stress: Number of life events Impact of life events
	Role stress	
Outcomes of stress	Relationships at work	Social support:
Shiftwork effects	Career development	Sources of support
Digestive symptoms	issues	Adequacy of support
Musculoskeletal	Organisational structure	
symptoms	and climate	Health/coping
Psychosomatic symptoms	Home–work interface	behaviour:
Total symptomatology	Conditions of work	Smoking
Serious illness	The physical environment	Alcohol consumption
Cognitive anxiety		Caffeine consumption
Physical anxiety		Exercise
Mental well-being		Sleep
Job satisfaction		Type 'A' behaviour
		Coping style

There was also a tendency for response rates to be associated with grade levels, with the highest responses coming from the higher grade levels.

11.4 Analysis: Risk factors and risk groups

The analysis strategy employed in the study focused on identifying the principal psychosocial features of the work environment which were associated with reduced health and well-being (the identification of at risk situations). In addition, the analysis focused on characterising the experience of stress for specific groups within the workforce.

11.4.1 Sample demography

The study population were relatively old by Irish standards (Ireland has the youngest age profile in the European Union) with 33 per cent aged under 30 years, 31 per cent aged between 30 and 39 years and 35 per cent aged over 40. However, 49 per cent of the sample were working for the company for less than ten years. Sixty-five per cent of the sample were male, and 65 per cent were married. Fifteen per cent of the sample worked as operatives, 24 per cent worked at lower grade administrative and clerical work, 9 per cent were graded as technicians (largely trades and crafts), 20 per cent worked in the airport police and fire service, 20 per cent were graded as supervisors and 3 per cent were graded as management. Eighty-five per cent were employed on a permanent basis. Overtime working was common, with 17 per cent of the sample working an average of 41–50 hours per week and 3 per cent working an average of more than 50 hours per week.

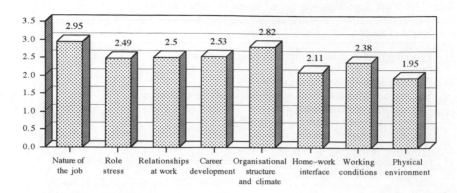

Figure 11.1 Main sources of work stress (0 = never; 1 = rarely; 2 = sometimes; 3 = frequently)

Note: Physical environment refers to physical sources of stress such as noise, heat and dust. Working conditions refers to contractual issues such as tenure and hours of work.

11.4.2 Sources of stress

Sources of stress were measured in a number of ways, principal among them was the use of the Occupational Stress Indicator (Cooper *et al.*, 1988). This instrument yields eight factors, and the prevalence of stress among the entire population is illustrated in Figure 11.1. In all subsequent Figures relating to sources of stress 0 = never, 1 = rarely, 2 = sometimes, and 3 = frequently.

Respondents were also asked to name the three most important sources of occupational stress in their own words. The main findings from these questions are outlined in Table 11.2.

The ten highest ranking sources of stress confirm the findings from the structured part of the questionnaire, where items relating to workload, the climate of the organisation and communications were rated as being among the most stressful features of working in Dublin airport.

Respondents were also asked about the most important sources of stress they experienced outside of work and also about the major life events of their recent past. These questions were asked in order to be able to control for these factors when assessing the nature of the impact of occupational stress on health and well-being.

The principal findings from these questions revealed that more than 75 per cent of outside work stressors was due to a combination of family problems relating to children, in-laws and bereavement, money problems, interpersonal relationships and recreational arrangements. In addition, six life events were reported as having occurred in the past year by more than 25 per cent of the sample (nine with a frequency of more than 20 per cent). These six life events were: a changed work situation, a big change in financial state,

Table 11.2 Most important sources of stress (in order of rank)

Source of stress
1   Working time pressures/responsibilities/overwork
2   Pay
3   Promotion/permanency/job security
4   Supervision difficulties (staff supervisors/outside contractors)
5   Lack of resources/staff/equipment
6   Poor management support and planning
7   Lack of information and communication
8   Work environment/working conditions
9   Feeling undervalued/receiving no feedback/no recognition for work done
10 Overtime/shiftworking/working hours

Note: Overwork refers to perception of qualitative and quantitative overload, while overtime refers to the practice of working hours in excess of contracted hours

borrowing less than IR£10,000, a major change in social activities, a new job, and an outstanding achievement. Interestingly, all of the top nine life events were rated as having a positive impact on respondents' lives. The major burden of negative stress therefore did not come from major life events, but from a combination of occupational stress and ongoing problems outside of work.

11.4.3 Health and well-being

The health and well-being of the sample was assessed in multiple ways. In addition to assessing physical and psychological health, respondents were asked questions about a range of what were classified as health-related behaviours, including social support, coping style, eating, drinking, exercise and sleeping behaviours.

Social support

The social support available to the sample was assessed in two ways: (1) the availability of support from a range of work-related and non-work-related sources, and (2) the adequacy of support from these sources. Particular attention was paid to the levels of support available from work sources, as previous studies have shown that this source of support is more effective in combating occupational stress than outside of work support. The findings from the questions on work-related support are presented in Figure 11.2.

The findings in relation to work-related sources of support were of interest for two reasons. First, they are of theoretical interest because of their capacity to buffer the effects of stressors on health and well-being. Second, and more importantly from the point of view of stress prevention, they provide an indication of how a range of organisational functions are perceived in relation to the support they provide.

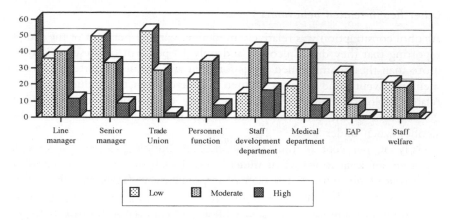

Figure 11.2 Work-related support (percentages)

Note: Numbers do not add up to 100 per cent as some of these sources of support were not available to all of the sample. EAP refers to Employee Assistance Programme.

The highest levels of support from non-specialist functions came from line managers and senior management. However, the findings indicated that there could be considerable room for improvement here, as only about one in eight people rated line management as providing high levels of support, while only one in eleven rated senior management as providing high levels of support. Even allowing for the fact that not all employees might perceive a need for support from these sources, the potential for improvement here was obvious.

Of the other potential sources of support, the staff development department (training) and the medical department were rated most positively, while employee assistance programme function and the trade unions were rated least positively.

The findings with regard to adequacy of support indicated that 30 per cent of the sample rated work-related sources of support as being inadequate for their needs, while 31 per cent rated it as being adequate. This finding supports the interpretation that there is room for improvement with regard to the provision of support by the various support related agencies present in the company.

Sources of support outside of work was assessed by combining levels of support available from four potential sources – spouse or partner, other relatives, friends and neighbours. This composite index revealed that 32 per cent of the sample had low levels of support available, 47 per cent had moderate levels of support while 21 per cent had high levels of support available to them. The findings with regard to adequacy of support indicated that 22 per cent of the sample rated outside of work-related sources of support as being inadequate for their needs, while 46 per cent rated it as being adequate.

Other health-related behaviours

Alcohol consumption was relatively moderate, with 87 per cent of the sample reporting that they drank alcohol, and only 18 per cent of these consuming more than the recommended limits for men and women (fourteen units for men and twenty-one units for women – these differences are due to gender-related biological differences in the capacity to metabolise alcohol). Only 26 per cent of the drinkers in the sample indicated that they used more alcohol when under stress.

Only 30 per cent of the sample smoked, but 86 per cent of smokers reported smoking more when under stress. Levels of caffeine consumption were quite high, with 55 per cent of respondents reporting that they drank a pharmacologically active dose (more than six cups) each day. Exercise levels were quite low among the sample, with 28 per cent reporting that they took no exercise at all, and only 17 per cent reporting that they took daily exercise (this could consist of relatively gentle exercise such as walking or gardening or more strenuous forms). On the other hand, sleep quality was surprisingly good for a workforce containing so many shiftworkers – only one in eight employees reported sleeping badly or very badly.

Coping behaviour

Coping behaviour was assessed in two ways – first, using an open-ended question ('What are the three most important ways in which you cope with stress') and second, using a standard questionnaire (the Ways of Coping Checklist; Lazarus and Folkman, 1984). The results from the open-ended

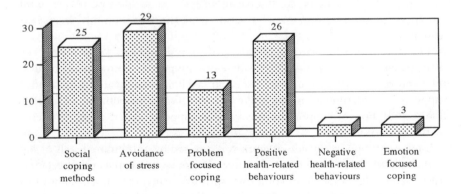

Figure 11.3 Summary of coping styles in the sample

Note: The figures illustrated above refer to the numbers of coping responses reported by the overall sample, not to the percentage of respondents reporting a specific method of coping.

question are more revealing, and are presented in Figure 11.3. These represent a summary of 1,224 responses to the open-ended question from 489 respondents. The data were analysed using content analysis.

Perhaps the most interesting feature of these findings is that coping with stress (from any source) is largely undertaken through indirect methods, only some of which could be viewed as being positive. Specifically, problem focused coping (trying to solve the problem, figuring out the best way of coping) accounted for only 13 per cent of all coping responses, while more palliative strategies accounted for the remainder. Of these palliative strategies, avoidance of stress (e.g., being alone, use of hobbies, turning off, thinking of something else) was the most prevalent, closely followed by social coping methods (engaging in social support), and by positive health-related behaviours (e.g., exercise, rest). There were relatively few negative or actively damaging coping strategies reported by respondents.

The health and well-being of the sample

The health and well-being of the Aer Rianta workforce was measured using the following indices:

- Cognitive and physical anxiety
- Psychological well-being
- Musculoskeletal, psychosomatic, digestive and general physical symptoms
- Intrinsic, extrinsic and overall job satisfaction

Over the past decade, the WRC have collected psychological well-being data from more than 5,000 Irish workers and members of the labour force. In addition, a nationally representative survey of the labour force was carried out by the Economic and Social Research Institute (ESRI) which enables national-level comparisons to be made using the GHQ-12 measure (Goldberg, 1978). While most of the samples examined by the WRC were samples of convenience, there were also two nationally representative surveys of teachers and nurses conducted. The rates of 'caseness' on the GHQ from the Aer Rianta study can then be compared with confidence to national-level data. This is illustrated in Figure 11.4.

The employed sample from the ESRI were reported as having a 7.5 per cent rate of psychological disturbance, which can be taken as a national average for the entire workforce. The Aer Rianta sample had a rate of psychological disturbance of 25 per cent which is more than three times the national average. However, the other nationally representative samples of teachers and nurses showed rates of psychological disturbance in excess of this, ranging up to 37 per cent, while some of the samples of convenience reported rates of almost 50 per cent. As might be expected, unemployed samples showed, broadly, the highest rates of all. These findings indicate that the psychological

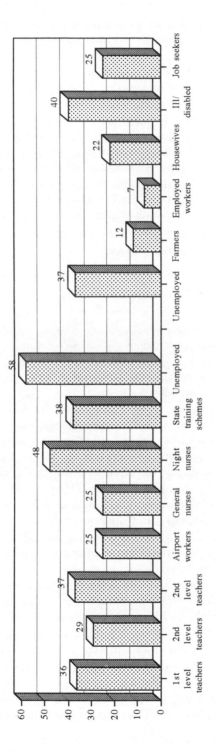

Figure 11.4 Rates (percentages) of disturbed psychological well-being in the Aer Rianta workforce compared to other Irish samples

Note: The right section of Figure 11.4 has been extracted from the ESRI nationally representative study, while the left section is taken from various WRC studies. The three teachers' samples and the nurses' samples represent more than 2,000 workers and are nationally representative.

well-being of the Aer Rianta sample were a cause for concern, though how much of this problem was due to working conditions had yet to be established.

The physical well-being of the workforce was measured in a number of ways. As indicated earlier (see section 11.3.2), four dimensions of physical symptomatology were measured using a scale developed in the 1970s by NIOSH, while a number of other questions relating to chronic illness were also asked. In general, the findings indicated that physical health was not a serious problem within Aer Rianta at that time. Comparisons with other Irish working groups indicated that there were no anomalous findings in the Aer Rianta sample. Musculoskeletal symptoms and psychosomatic symptoms were the most prevalent physical complaints among the sample.

The levels of job satisfaction (as measured by a standard seven-point bipolar scale; Warr et al., 1979) were generally low in comparison to other Irish samples, with employees reporting themselves to be 'neither satisfied nor dissatisfied' with their work.

Potential prevention strategies

As a contribution to the process of developing a stress prevention strategy for Aer Rianta, respondents were asked (in an open-ended question) what would be the most effective response which the company could make in this regard. Figure 11.5 summarises the responses to this question.

The most interesting feature of these findings is that there was overwhelming support given to taking preventive action to deal with occupational stress, rather than to taking palliative, individually-focused actions. In all, more than 90 per cent of suggestion to deal with stress referred to changing some aspect of the structure of work, the working environment and the management of work. This finding was perhaps surprising, as the then prevalent approaches to dealing with occupational stress in Ireland largely consisted of coping skills training and the provision of staff welfare activities. This study was one of the first studies in Ireland to indicate that the demand for change lay elsewhere, and that stress was seen by the workforce as a problem of work and working conditions rather than one of a failure to cope by individual workers.

At risk groups in the workforce

The identification of at risk groups constituted a major part of the analysis of the survey data. This was done by undertaking a set of inferential statistical tests (analyses of variance and multiple regressions) to identify whether personal demographic or work demographic characteristics were associated with higher levels of psychological and physical well-being and job satisfaction. A similar set of analyses was conducted to identify at risk situations

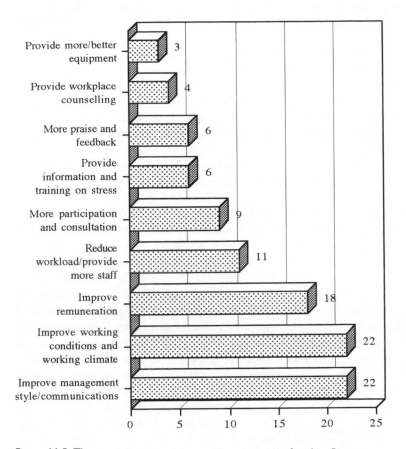

Figure 11.5 The most important prevention strategies for Aer Rianta

within the workplace. These extensive analyses are too complex to report on fully in this chapter, so a summary of the main results is presented in the following sections. All of the results presented here relate to statistical differences at $p < .05$ or better (for details of these analyses, see Wynne and Conroy, 1991).

Gender

Male workers tended to be more at risk from stress when compared to their female colleagues. They reported more problems in relation to five of the seven sources of stress dimensions (intrinsic factors, role stress, relationships at work, career development and working conditions). These findings were not surprising, as more men tended to work full time, and to work at higher grade levels. In addition, women reported higher levels of social support both inside and outside of the workplace. Men also reported higher levels of cigarette and alcohol consumption. Men also reported themselves to be more affected by shiftwork than women. However, a different picture emerged in relation to the outcome variables. Women tended to report higher levels of anxiety and impaired psychological well-being. Similarly, women reported higher levels of all types of physical symptomatology when compared to men. These paradoxical findings were interpreted as being largely cultural in origin, where men tend to be more involved in their jobs, while at the same time being less supportive and less likely to report health impairment of any kind.

Age

The age of the sample was also significantly associated with many indices of stress. However, the effects of age were not linear – the under 29 years age group were least affected by the sources of stress or the outcomes of stress, the 30–39 year age group were most affected, while the older age groups were affected in an intermediate way. Interestingly, the oldest age groups reported the highest levels of social support. These findings were interpreted as indicating that the youngest age groups were not yet fully committed to their jobs, the middle age groups were most ambitious and were under most pressure for promotion at work (and also undergoing a major stress load outside of work), while the oldest age groups had become relatively settled both in their jobs and in their outside of work life. In addition, a 'healthy workers' effect might also have been operating.

Company department

The range of jobs involved in running an airport is very large compared to most companies. It can involve indoor and outdoor work; professional, skilled and non-skilled work; and manual and clerical work. It was therefore expected the department which an employee worked in (which reflects the different kinds of jobs the sample worked at) would have a role to play in differentiating the experience of stress and its outcomes in Aer Rianta. These expectations were realised. When the sample was divided into seven departments a clear pattern emerged in relation to the sources of stress examined in the survey. This pattern was consistent across all of the sources of stress and it showed that the airport police/fire service (APFS) and the trading department reported most stress. Further investigations and analyses revealed the reasons for this pattern. First, both groups worked shiftwork (in the case of the APFS this was a current industrial relations issue). Second, the APFS essentially fulfil a conflicting role, that of being a policeman (with powers of arrest) and that of being an unofficial source of information to airport users. Workers in the trading department were also subject to major levels of demand from working constantly with the public and having the responsibility of being one of the major revenue earning groups within the company (duty-free sales currently account for approximately one-third of company income).

These groups also were at higher risk in terms of low social support at work and health related outcomes. In all cases the APFS tended to have the highest risk profile and these generally were followed by the trading section.

Shiftwork

There is a large and venerable literature on the direct effects of shiftwork on health (Thierry and Meijman, 1994). However, there has been relatively little work on how shiftwork might interact with sources of stress in the workplace. The findings from the Aer Rianta project are of significance in this regard. There were 200 shiftworkers in the sample of over 400 respondents. Shiftworkers reported significantly higher levels of sources of stress in relation to all eight of the indices measured in the study. Aspects of stress such as working long hours, management style, differences between policies and practice, lack of consultation and the demands that work makes on private life were all more frequent for shiftworkers. In addition, shiftworkers reported that they received less support from work-related sources. Shiftworkers also tended to report more physical symptomatology than non-shiftworkers, especially in relation to musculoskeletal symptoms, but not in relation to digestive symptoms, which are often associated with shiftworking. There were no shift-work-related differences in psychological well-being, but shiftworkers did report lower job satisfaction than non-shiftworkers.

Grade levels

There are strong reasons for expecting that grade would be associated with the experience of stress in any organisation. Accordingly, an analysis of the relationship between grade and the various indicators of stress was conducted. It should be noted however, that a company such as Aer Rianta which employs workers of widely different skills tends to have a very complicated grade structure, and it was sometimes difficult to assign grades across disparate occupations. However, the grades which were assigned to the sample do represent equivalence as far as it was possible to do so. Numbers in each grade varied between 44 and 102. Grade levels were significantly associated with a wide range of stress indices in Aer Rianta. Specifically, it was associated with sources of stress, sources of work-related support, psychological well-being, psychosomatic symptoms and job satisfaction. All of these associations were very strong, and pointed in the expected direction, i.e. the lowest grades reported the highest levels of stress.

11.5 Choice of measures

The findings from the survey were comprehensive and complex and developing a coherent set of intervention actions took some time. The approach taken was a participative one, whereby the project team were consulted about potential measures and where subsequent actions teams set up by the company consulted widely on what interventions to make. The stages which followed are outlined below.

1   The results from the survey were presented and explained to the Aer Rianta survey team. This involved a series of presentations by the consultants where the findings, and particularly their significance for action were explained.
2   Drafting of recommendations from the survey. This was undertaken by the consultants and presented to the survey team. It seemed clear that a dual approach to intervention was called for. First, there should be a preventive approach, whereby actions would be taken to change aspects of working practices and company policies which were giving rise to stress (this was called the organisational development (–'OD approach'). This approach was influenced by the data collected from the survey and reported on in Figure 11.5 (p. 255). The second approach was to examine and improve the health and welfare services of the company to take greater account of the outcomes of stress (this was labelled 'the health promotion approach' – HP). The finalisation of recommendations was also undertaken in a participative manner in order to ensure that the survey team and Aer Rianta would have a sense of ownership of the recommendations and that they were culturally appropriate for the company. The recommendations from the survey are outlined in Table 11.3.
3   The survey results were presented to Aer Rianta staff at a series of meetings, in addition to receiving a summary of the report. All staff were also invited to view the report and about seven did so.

An important part of the recommendations concerned the setting up of two action teams to examine, amend and implement the recommendations. This effectively involved the breaking up of the survey team and their replacement by teams which would have more influence within the company and would therefore be better positioned to implement the recommendations.

11.6 Implementation

At the time of delivering the agreed recommendations to the survey team, the involvement of the external consultants to the project effectively ended.

Table 11.3 Recommendations from the survey

Organisational development	Health promotion
Establish an OD programme	Establish a HP programme
Alter shift schedules	Address high levels of anxiety
Improve communications and	Improve work-related coping skills
consultation	Provide gender-based programmes
Improve career development	Address alcohol problems
practice	Implement smoking reduction
Improve organisational climate	programme
Address job satisfaction	Address sleep problems
Provide support services	
Address pay and salary	
Examine grade issues	
Improve home–work interface	
Improve performance appraisal	
procedures	

This much reduced involvement had been planned as part of the project, mainly to ensure that implementation activities would attract the ownership of the Aer Rianta staff who would be affected by any changes made. As a result, the conduct of the project differed in its implementation phase, where the emphasis shifted from analysis and recording towards pragmatic action.

Implementation was organised around the setting up of two high-level action teams, one for each of the HP and OD programmes. Their function was to examine and prioritise the recommendations, and to develop an action programme in each of these areas. Training and consultancy input was provided to the teams by the external consultants, who had no direct involvement after this point, except where specific skills which were not available in-house were called for.

Both teams were active for more than a year after their establishment. For the OD team, their main task was to adapt the recommendations into ongoing programmes which were taking place within the company, and where appropriate and possible, to establish new ones. In general terms it was recognised that not all of the recommendations could be acted upon at once, and in the case of some recommendations, that they may be very difficult to implement for a variety of internal organisational reasons. However, there were a number of notable interventions implemented.

One of the main tasks of the HP team was to repackage existing services, rather than developing new ones. These services included the medical department, the employee assistance programme service, the staff welfare department and the staff development (training) department. Part of the problem with regard to these services was their lack of visibility to staff, and their relative lack of integration. In addition, these services lacked a coherent philosophy. They had developed over a relatively long period of time for a range of

Table 11.4 Short- and medium-term stress prevention and management actions under-taken by Aer Rianta (key to notes 1–5 on p. 261)

Recommendation	Actions	Current status
Shiftwork[1]	Education programme for shift–staff; line managers and supervisors to be trained	Action completed
	Training session on shiftwork and its effects to be carried out on all introduction courses	Ongoing
	Information booklet to be issued to all shift staff	Work in progress
	Redesign of shift roster	APFS completed, work in progress in other sections
	Job sharing introduced to APFS-section	Action completed
Improve communications[2]	Increase access to information–staff representatives to attend management meetings	Ongoing
	All noticeboards to be covered by glass to prevent information notices from being removed	Action completed
	Continue yearly staff Communication Event	Ongoing/action completed
	Update management development programme	Action completed
Career development	Conduct career development training for staff	Action completed
	Encourage internal work experience	Ongoing
Home-work interface[3]	Encourage more family participation in social activities at Dublin airport	Ongoing
	Introduce smoke alarm system for all staff	Ongoing
Performance appraisal	Develop performance appraisal system for all staff	Work in progress
Staff health and well-being[4]	Develop awareness of stress through training courses	Ongoing
	Increase awareness of negative effects of smoking	Ongoing
Health awareness	Conduct health screening	Action completed
	Promote health as an issue[5]	Ongoing
	Introduce healthy eating policy	Ongoing
	Develop nature walks around the airport	Work in progress

reasons, and had not been viewed as an integrated service dealing with all aspects of staff health and well-being.

The OD and HP teams each produced a report which transformed the recommendations of the consultants report into an action plan, taking into account criteria such as feasibility, importance and available resources. These reports outlined a set of short-term and longer-term actions which the company wished to undertake, and the principal actions and their current status are outlined in Table 11.4. In addition, the role and functioning of the employee assistance programme was reviewed.

In all, Aer Rianta undertook twenty distinct actions to help prevent and manage stress and improve staff health and well-being. These actions were sometimes directed at the sources of stress, for example, the redesign of shift schedules, the actions taken to develop and improve communications and a performance appraisal system, while others were protective in nature and were directed at improving the ability of staff to cope with specific work stressors, for example, the training and information booklets provided to staff on dealing with shiftwork. In addition, more general health promotion activities were undertaken in the areas of tobacco consumption, fitness and diet.

A significant feature of the Aer Rianta response to occupational stress has been its commitment: of the twenty actions developed by the OD and HP teams, no less than fourteen are either still ongoing or in progress some six years after the consultants report was issued. Moreover, the actions which were indicated by the project teams were not necessarily without cost, for they often involved the ongoing provision of training and information materials.

11.7 Evaluation

No formal evaluation

The stress prevention initiative in Aer Rianta was undertaken as a pragmatic exercise with the aim of reducing the levels of occupational stress for the workforce as a whole as far as this was practically feasible. An extended effort was placed on the identification and description of the problems associated

---

Notes to Table 11.4

1 Other actions in this area included the airport duty manager working night shifts.

2 There were many interactions between these actions and the other areas of intervention. For example, covering the company notice boards had the effect of internal job advertisements being seen by all interested staff, thereby improving career development opportunities.

3 Many staff, especially female staff within specific departments already worked part-time or job-shared. In practice the new initiatives here were an extension of existing programmes to new categories of staff.

4 There were a wide range of activities undertaken within this area, only some of which are listed in Table 11.4. Others included healthy eating cookery courses, weight reduction programmes, a nutrition survey, lifestyle programmes, cancer screening, and glaucoma testing.

5 This activity involved running a Health Exhibition, i.e. a concentrated set of health-related activities with a high public profile within the company.

with stress, and the results of this phase were taken as a springboard for the development of a dual approach to the prevention of stress. As a result, the formal evaluation of the stress prevention initiative by Aer Rianta was not a high priority.

The role of the two contractors in the stress prevention initiative was as consultants rather than as academic investigators. This role meant that the consultants were engaged as experts in relation to the assessment of occupational stress and as providing input to the design of appropriate interventions. In addition, support was provided on an 'as needs basis' to the activities of the two intervention teams. A major limitation of this role, but a strength of the intervention, was that the two intervention teams took effective ownership of implementation and to the extent that it was relevant to company needs, evaluation of the initiative. It was therefore not possible for the external consultants to the initiative to undertake a formal evaluation either.

Major outcomes

However, despite this lack of formal evaluation of the initiative, it is possible to describe in anecdotal terms some of the major outcomes of the interventions which were undertaken. These included:

- Redesign of shift schedules for the airport police/fire service;
- Design and implementation of a support manual for new and existing shiftworkers;
- Implementation of training for new shiftworkers and for supervisors;
- Improvements in communications practices. As a result of the activities of the OD team, a number of practical steps were taken to improve communications. These included placing glass doors on noticeboards where jobs were internally advertised, thereby preventing their removal. Prior to the intervention it was common for interested employees to remove these notices, thereby leading to allegations that there was a 'golden circle' in relation to who got to hear about new posts. Since this intervention, the numbers applying for these posts has increased markedly.

While these observations do not amount to an evaluation of the intervention, they none the less indicate that the programme had positive effects. The members of the two intervention teams report that while the problems of occupational stress have not been eradicated in Aer Rianta, they have been addressed in a serious manner. Perhaps more importantly, the experience of undertaking the project has created an awareness of occupational stress and its implications which did not exist prior to the project, and it has helped develop a set of skills within the company which is in a position to deal more effectively with the problems of occupational stress which can affect even the most successful of companies.

Bibliography

Cooper, C., Sloan, S. and Williams, S. (1988) *The Occupational Stress Indicator*, Windsor: NFER–Nelson.

Crown, S. and Crisp, A.H. (1979) *Manual of the Crown-Crisp Experiential Index*, London: Hodder and Stoughton.

Goldberg, P. (1978) *Manual of the General Health Questionnaire*, Windsor: NFER–Nelson.

Holmes, T.H. and Rahe, R. (1967) 'The Social Readjustment Rating Scale', *Journal of Psychosomatic Research*, 11: 213–18.

Lazarus, R. and Folkman, S. (1984) *Stress, Appraisal and Coping*, New York: Springer.

Tasto, D., Colligan, M., Skjei, E. and Polly, S. (1978) *Health Consequences of Shiftwork*, NIOSH publication, no. 078–154, Washington DC: DHEW, US Government Printing Office.

Thierry, Hk, and Meijman, T.F. (1994) 'Time and behaviour at work', in H.C. Triandis, M.D. Dunnette and L.M. Hough (eds) *Handbook of Industrial and Organisational Psychology*, 4, Palo Alto: Consulting Psychologists Press, pp. 314–413.

Warr, P.B., Cook, J. and Wall, T.D. (1979) 'Scales for the measurement of some work attitudes and aspects of psychological well-being', *Journal of Occupational Psychology*, 52: 129–48.

Work Research Centre (WRC) (1992) *The Experience of Stress Among Irish First and Second Level Teachers*, Dublin: Work Research Centre.

—— (1993) *The Experience of Stress among Irish Nurses*, Dublin: Work Research Centre.

Wynne, R. and Conroy, H. (1991) *Stress Amongst Dublin Airport Aer Rianta Employees*, Dublin: Work Research Centre.

Chapter 12

Portugal: Preventing occupational stress in a bank organisation

Luís Graça and Michiel Kompier

12.1 Introduction

12.1.1 Important transformations

Since the end of the 1950s drastic transformations have occurred in the Portuguese economy and society. There have been large political, social, technological and economic changes: the establishment of a democratic political system, a redefined relationship between the State and the Catholic Church, the end of the colonial empire, the growth of the middle class, better school education, and 'open frontiers' to people and goods. In addition to these changes, in 1986 Portugal joined the European Union. These developments also influenced, and were influenced by public health, for example, a decrease in the fertility rate and in child mortality, changes in consumption patterns, improved health care and social security services (e.g., Barreto, 1996).

During the last three decades Portugal has transformed itself from an economy based on agriculture, forestry and fisheries to a 'service economy'. In 1960, 44 per cent of the population was employed in agriculture, forestry and fisheries, 29 per cent was employed in manufacturing industry, building, energy and water, whereas 27 per cent was employed in the service sector (including distribution). Table 12.1 presents data on the Portuguese workforce in 1995. 'Services' are now by far the largest sector (56 per cent) and women comprise 45 per cent of the total employed population. The rate of unemployment (7.1 per cent) is higher than in 1993 (5.5 per cent), but lower than in 1986 (8.0 per cent).

It is clear that both modern life in general and modern working life in particular are totally different compared to the situation thirty years ago. The question is whether the Portuguese working population has paid a price, in terms of health and well-being, as a consequence of all these changes. There is no sound social epidemiological research on this issue, but it seems that in the last ten years the experience of work-related stress is more common in various occupational groups. According to an ongoing survey study among

Table 12.1 Portugal: population, employment and unemployment, by gender (1995)

	Female (%)	Male (%)	Total (×1000)
Total population	52.0	48.0	9846.8
Working population (48%)	45.0	55.0	4754.3
Employed population (45%)	45.0	55.0	4415.9
Broken down by activity sector:			
• Agriculture, forestry and fishing (12%)	48.0	52.0	508.9
• Industry, Building, Energy and Water (32%)	32.0	68.0	1415.3
• Services (56%)	51.0	49.0	2491.7
Unemployment rate (%)	8.1	6.3	7.1

Source: Portugal, INE (1995 Statistical Yearbook of Portugal) 1996

a sample of approximately 1,500 companies equal to or over seventy-five employees, in all business sectors, an increasing number of companies is concerned with stress at work (22 per cent), with work-related mental health problems (16 per cent) or at least, with their employees' difficulty of coping with stress (32 per cent) (Graça, 1997).

Although it may be hypothesised that work-related stress is responsible for an important part of employee absenteeism, and negatively affects company performance, clear Portuguese data are lacking with respect to (a) stressful working conditions, (b) stress reactions, and (c) the relationship between stress at the workplace and absenteeism. There are, however, four sources that at least shed some light on these questions:

1   Studies with respect to sickness absenteeism;
2   Eurobarometer survey (1991);
3   Monitor on working conditions (Paoli, 1992);
4   Research into mental disorders at work (Graça, 1995).

12.1.2 Occupational stress and sickness absenteeism

Studies with respect to sickness absenteeism

Detailed statistics on sickness absenteeism of the working population are not available. There are, however, data published on absenteeism for the 2,000 largest companies in Portugal. These data are taken from the Corporate Social Audit by the Ministry of Employment and Social Security. They relate to 1989–1993. The companies involved, each with one hundred employees or more, currently employ about 25 per cent of the total working population (Graça, 1996a).

In 1993, the absenteeism percentage is highest in transport and communication (9.7 per cent), and lowest in banking and finances (4.8 per cent).

Table 12.2 Percentage absenteeism days per person, due to sick leave, injuries and other reasons, by economic sector. Portuguese companies equal to or over 100 employees (1989–1993)

Economic sector	1989	1990	1991	1992	1993
1 Agriculture, forestry and fisheries (n = 5.0)	5.7	4.1	6.6	8.4	9.2
2 Mining (n = 4.9)	10.1	9.8	11.0	9.2	7.7
3 Manufacturing industry (n = 394.1)	9.4	10.1	6.9	7.1	6.5
4 Energy and water (n = 22.8)	10.9	11.5	12.4	9.8	7.9
5 Building and civil engineering (n = 57.2)	6.9	6.9	7.5	8.3	7.2
6 Distributive trades, hotels and catering (n = 86.8)	6.1	7.1	7.2	7.7	7.6
7 Transport and communication (n = 105.2)	7.8	7.6	11.2	11.0	9.7
8 Banking and finance (n = 91.9)	4.5	4.1	4.5	5.0	4.8
9 Other services (n = 35.6)	6.5	7.3	6.0	7.7	7.4
Total (n = 803.6) (n)	8.1	8.5	9.2	9.5	8.7

Source: Portugal, Ministry of Employment and Social Security (1989–1993 Corporate social audit), quoted by Graça 1996a
Key: (n) Average yearly number of employees, during this period (in thousands)

The interpretation of these data is not without problems: in Portugal, by definition, absenteeism not only relates to absences due to unfitness for work, caused by illness, occupational diseases or injuries. It also includes work absences due to other reasons such as maternity/paternity leave, compassionate leave, disciplinary suspension, and so-called voluntary, very short-term absenteeism. Sick leave (56 per cent) and accidents (7 per cent) account for less than two-thirds of the absence volume in paid employment. Their direct, indirect and hidden costs have recently been estimated at approximately 3,000 million ECU, i.e. equivalent to the 1995 National Health Service budget (Graça, 1995 and 1996a; Gründemann and Van Vuuren, 1997).

In the same period, Social Insurance Funds paid a yearly average of approximately 63 million days of sickness benefits to 800,000 employed and self-employed workers (not including civil servants). The average duration in calendar days of sick-leave benefits calculated per person, increased from 67 days in 1989 to 92 days in 1993. This increase relates to men and women, but among the latter absenteeism is higher (see Figure 12.1).

The advantage of the information in Figure 12.1 in comparison to Table 12.2, is that data in Figure 12.1 only relate to absenteeism related to sickness and not to other causes. However, Figure 12.1 does not include absences from civil servants. Still, data from Figure 12.1 seem to be better suited for assessing possible trends in sickness absenteeism over years. They strongly suggest an increase in sickness absenteeism among Portuguese workers.

Interpretations of these data are far from unambiguous. By governmental and employers' representatives these figures are often interpreted as indications of a clear misuse of sickness benefits and as a serious threat to the future

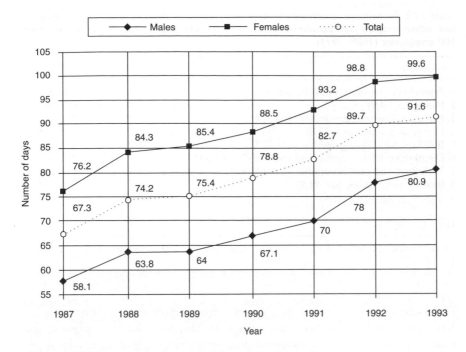

Figure 12.1 Average duration, in calendar days, of temporary sick-leave benefit, by person, paid by Social Security (1989–1993)*

Source: Portugal, Ministry of Employment and Social Security (1987–1993 Social Statistics), quoted by Graça (1995)

*Note: Sick-leave spells having finished during the year and not including tuberculosis and occupational diseases; spells may last longer than 365 days (in paid employment); Social Security does not pay the first three days (for employees) or the first thirty days (for the self-employed)

social insurance system. On the other hand, organisations of employees point at the underlying role of possible causal agents such as stress at work, and the high demands placed on today's employees.

Academic researchers also point to the fact that one should not underestimate the inequalities in health and health care, due to lay-off, unemployment, precarious employment, pre-retirement, ageing, lack of resources and skills, lack of social support, lack of preventive health services at the workplace, waiting lists on the National Health Service, poverty, gender, region, social class, and so on (Graça, 1996a; Pereira, 1995).

Eurobarometer survey (1991)

In order to prepare for the European Year of Safety, Hygiene and Health at Work (1992), a 'Eurobarometer survey' was carried out in spring 1991, on behalf of the Commission of the European Union (1992). The study sample comprised approximately 12,500 employed and self-employed persons in all sectors of economical activity, representing the national working population in the twelve EU member states. One of the main conclusions from this study is that Portuguese workers (n = 952) 'agree with the average European about the level of risk perceived, but are markedly less satisfied with prevention'. This Eurobarometer also presents data on the work-related health risks as perceived by Portuguese workers in comparison to the total EU sample (see Table 12.3).

Compared to the 'European worker in general' the Portuguese working population reports more musculoskeletal problems: more than half of the Portuguese workers report backache and muscular pains. About 50 per cent of the Portuguese workers complain of 'overall fatigue', this is twice as much as is reported in Europe. Twenty-eight per cent of the Portuguese workers mention 'stress', whereas that percentage 'in general Europe' is higher: 48 per cent. With respect to the other items, there are no important differences between the Portuguese workers and the average European worker. The differences in 'overall fatigue' and in 'stress' are remarkable. Overall fatigue seems to have both a physical and a psychological or mental component. This might indicate that at least a part of the high Portuguese score merely reflects work-related mental problems, such as depression, exhaustion or burn-out. It might even be that the word 'stress', although nowadays part

Table 12.3 Work-related health risks as reported by Portuguese workers and 'the average European worker*

Self-reported work-related health risk	Portugal (%) (n = 952)	EU (%) (n = 12,819)
• Backache	58	47
• Muscular pains in the limbs	55	33
• Overall tiredness, work that is too tiring	51	26
• Stress	28	48
• Eyestrain	27	27
• Breathing difficulties	22	21
• Ear problems	20	17
• Skin problems	11	11
• Personal problems at the workplace	3	5
• Other	6	8
Don't know	1	1

Source: Commission of European Communities (1992), p. 125
Note: Question: 'In which way(s) does your work affect your health ?' (Multiple answers possible)

of ordinary vocabulary in Portugal, is not recognised as the more common concept of 'fatigue', so that the same psychological problems that, for example in western Europe, may get labelled as 'stress', are conceptualised as 'overall tiredness' in Portugal. In sum, Table 12.3 suggests that in Portugal musculoskeletal problems are the most prominent, directly followed by more psychological problems such as stress and fatigue.

The Eurobarometer also suggests that 38 per cent of Portuguese respondents (against 23 per cent of the EU sample) felt that they would benefit from an improvement of health and safety standards at the workplace, 'definitely' to perform their work in a more efficient way. Also it appeared that only 13 per cent of the Portuguese sample (against 27 per cent of the EU sample) had followed a training course on Occupational Health and Safety (OHS).

Monitor on working conditions

Another cross-national survey was carried out in 1991, on behalf of the European Foundation for the Improvement of Living and Working Conditions (Paoli, 1992). This study was based on direct interviews with a sample of 12,500 employed and self-employed workers, throughout the twelve member states of the European Union; circa 1,000 per country. The total sample, and the sample for each member state, may be regarded as representative for the European (and national) labour force, with respect to sector, gender, age group and professional status (for details see Paoli, 1992).

According to this survey, the physical work environment of Portuguese employees (n = 952) was worse than on average in the EU. Portuguese employed and self-employed workers were more exposed to weather constraints, heat and cold than the average European. Also 'having painful positions' (42 per cent) and 'carrying heavy loads' (21 per cent), at least 50 per cent of the time, are more often mentioned by Portuguese workers. Concerning the psychosocial working environment (e.g., time pressure, time constraints, repetitive tasks), percentages were very close to the EU average. However, 'working to tight deadlines' was significantly lower (Portugal: 23 per cent; EU: 40 per cent). Also 'using computer equipment', at least 50 per cent of the time (Portugal: 12 per cent; EU: 22 per cent), was lower in Portugal, whereas the dependence of income on work rate was higher (36 per cent) than the EU level (26 per cent). With respect to working time arrangements, the average working week in Portugal (45.6 hours) was longer than in Europe (40.8 hours). Finally, 32 per cent of Portuguese workers considered their health and safety at risk because of their work. This percentage is comparable to the general EU percentage (30 per cent).

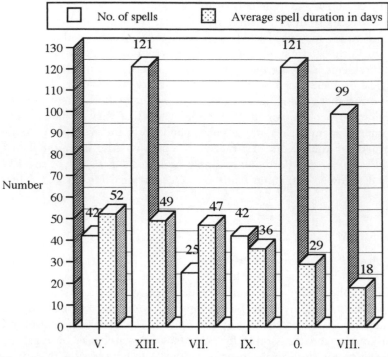

Figure 12.2 Multinational electrical engineering plant: distribution of main causes of diseases, according to ICD-International Classification of Diseases, by number of spells and average spell duration in days (1992–1994)
Source: Graça 1995

Research into mental disorders at work

Graça (1995) and Graça *et al.* (1997) analysed absenteeism data of three Portuguese companies that had taken initiatives in order to reduce and prevent work disability (a copper mine, a municipality and a manufacturing industry). In this study it is suggested that mental problems are among the most important causes of long-term sick leave. Figure 12.2 presents data from one of these companies, a local business unit of a German multinational electrical engineering plant employing *circa* 350 persons (69 per cent being staff production and 23 per cent women) (see also Graça, 1996b). Sickness data were combined over 1992–1994. Figure 12.2 demonstrates that, at least in this organisation, mental disorders were the leading cause of sick leave, not in terms of absence frequency but in terms of average duration in days.

12.1.3 Legal regulations

In July 1991, a so-called 'historic social agreement' was signed by the government and the social partners. This agreement included new OHS legislation and regulations, that were based on European Framework Directive 89/391/EEC and ILO Convention no. 155 (Graça and Faria, 1993). It was expected that this agreement meant more than merely updating 'old' legislation and regulations on occupational health and safety, issued during the last period of Salazar's dictatorship, but meant the development and implementation of new forms of workplace action for health (innovative strategies, structures, policies, programmes and activities). Notwithstanding this agreement, serious criticisms on working conditions policies and practices in Portugal still seem prevalent. Graça and Faria (1992, 1993) have argued that in Portugal:

- the concept of safety at work is neither practically nor conceptually related to the worker's health and his/her psychosocial working environment;
- there is no tradition of paying attention to job satisfaction, occupational stress and job-related mental health problems;
- the OHS approach is usually top-down, the leading role is played by experts and professionals, without effective involvement of employees;
- the biomedical approach of health at work and work-related diseases is prominent;
- OHS services at company level only focus on the prevention of occupational diseases and accidents, they are person-oriented and not environment-oriented;
- trade unions have called for updating the compensation system, and accidents and occupational diseases are under-reported;
- policies and programmes on workplace health promotion are generally lacking;
- policies and programmes on rehabilitation and reintegration after a long-term sickness spell are lacking;
- there are hardly any programmes directed towards addressing the unhealthy lifestyles of employees;
- finally, that workplace health action is not related to individual and organisational development.

This rather pessimistic view is being underlined by a current social agreement (between the period of 1996–1999) between the government and the social partners. The main goals of this agreement, signed by government, employers' representatives and one trade union confederation (UGT), are 'to support employment, improve competitiveness and promote development without social exclusion'. In this document no reference is made to concepts such as workplace health promotion or stress at work. This is remarkable since this social agreement addresses national strategies with respect to economic globalisation and technical and organisational innovation, including 'the improvement of the working environment'.

12.1.4 Conclusions

In summary, we would conclude that during the last fifty years (working) life in Portugal has gone through remarkable changes. It is not yet entirely clear what consequences these changes will have on Portuguese companies and employees, for example in terms of workers' well-being and health. There is not enough empirical data on this issue, but it seems that sickness absenteeism is increasing in the Portuguese working population. Furthermore, musculoskeletal problems seem to be the most prominent, directly followed by more psychological problems such as stress and fatigue. The physical work environment in Portugal seems to be worse than on average in the European Union. There are indications that in the last ten years the experience of work-related stress is becoming more common in various occupational groups. Although the word 'stress' is part of 'everyday vocabulary' in Portugal, there is no tradition of monitoring causes and consequences of stress or of stress prevention. Also with respect to other constraints in the work situation (e.g., biological, chemical, physical), such a tradition of risk-assessment and risk-control is scarce in Portugal.

With respect to legal regulations concerning working conditions, some important steps forward have been taken. Portugal now follows the European Framework Directive 89/391/EEC and ILO Convention no. 155. There are no specific legal regulations concerning stress at work or work-related mental health problems. Although some advances have been made, there are still serious criticisms regarding working conditions policies and practices. These criticisms, among others, point at a lack of attention for the psychosocial work environment ('occupational stress', 'job satisfaction'), and at a conceptualisation of risks and prevention that is only individually-oriented, and is 'reactive' as opposed to being proactive.

12.2 Banking and financing: Goodbye to the old times

12.2.1 Impressive changes

In the second section of this chapter we will provide a characterisation of a major branch in the service sector: banking and financing (including insurance). In the third and last section, an ongoing stress prevention project in a large bank organisation will be discussed.

Table 12.4 Milestones in the recent history of Portuguese banking

Year	Events
1975	• Nationalisation of most commercial banks and insurance companies, owned by the leading economic groups, closely connected with manufacturing industry
1984	• Banking sector opens its doors to the private-owned banks (including the foreign companies)
1985	• Three new private-owned banks (BCP, BC, BPI) are established: a 'revolution' with respect to the banking corporate culture, work methods, services, products and market
1986	• Portugal and Spain join European Community
1988	• Favourable legislation on holding companies, given opportunities to corporate mergers and concentrations in the banking and financial sectors
1989	• Beginning of the privatisation process of the state-owned banks and insurance companies
	• Banking employees and their representatives are more and more afraid of future implications of privatisation (e.g., unemployment, early retirement, labour market deregulation, flexibility, new forms of employment and work organisation, according to the neo-liberal management ideology)
1993	• Increasing deregulation of the banking activity, in order to meet the criteria required by third phase of European Monetary Union
	• Increasing technical innovation and re-engineering in order to improve productivity and competitiveness
	• Downsizing of the banking and other financial companies,including the State Central Bank of Portugal
1995	• The private-owned BCP/BPA group is now the leading group in the financial sector, after CGD, the only existing public-owned financial group.

Traditionally, the bank employees' job is a prestigious one: among white-collar workers the bank employee ranks in the highest position on the 1988 scale of occupational prestige. He or she has a better ranking than, for example, a scientist or a nurse. Employee absenteeism and turnover are low in this branch (see Table 12.2). Union membership is high and trade unions play a strong role, even before the 25 April 1974 Revolution. The most important and influential trade union in this branch of industry is the Sindicato dos Bancários do Sul e Ilhas (South and Islands Bank Employees' Trade Union). Many of the developments discussed in section 12.1 of this chapter have been influential in this branch of industry, especially since the 1980s. The most important milestones in the recent history of Portuguese banking are listed in Table 12.4.

These developments were accompanied by a new language and a new way of working: the supply of new financial products and services, small teams running corner-street bank branches, client needs and expectations oriented marketing, output oriented management, new corporate culture, downsizing, re-engineering, flexibility, quality, productivity, competitiveness, and so forth.

According to economic analysts, there are too many banks in Portugal for such a small market. Moreover, compared to other European countries operative banking costs are much higher in Portugal. One of the management strategies that companies have chosen to diminish these operating costs, is an increased rationalisation of work, i.e. 'working harder and working smarter'. Today in banking, according to union representatives (interviewed by the authors for the purpose of this case study), four to seven employees carry out tasks that used to be performed by a large work team of fifteen to twenty people. According to these union representatives, the bank clerk must sell more products and process more information than ever before. He/she is permanently placed under time pressure by clients, co-workers, supervisors, managing directors, computer system failure, paperwork, training, etc. As a consequence, he/she is compelled to work overtime: often three or more hours a day, without extra pay.

The management of banking companies question whether a further work rationalisation will be enough to improve productivity and competitiveness. Therefore a related management strategy is to diminish the number of employees, mainly by means of early retirement and a more flexible workforce. According to union representatives, some thousand bank clerks have been invited or compelled to retire or take early retirement, many of them in the age group of 40 to 50 years. Meanwhile, the work pace has accelerated for those who had the luck of keeping their jobs. Unions can be critical towards the labour inspectorate and towards labour legislation, which they characterise as too permissive. Trade unions are also opposed to the new type of corporate culture, work organisation, work ethics and productivity-related pay system. According to workers' representatives, BCP have introduced new work ethics in banking, which they call 'workaholism', and even a new bank employee, who is expected to identify with the corporate image, and is fully committed to perform his/her job. This new-style employee is highly motivated by the expectancy of receiving extrinsic rewards (e.g., extra pay, share profits, production bonus, merit advancement and other fringe benefits). 'It is a new individualistic and materialistic culture', one trade union leader has commented, 'where one sacrifices not only the family and one's social life, but also one's health and well-being. The price to be paid is high, since there remains no time for family or leisure'.

Given this type of criticism, it is not surprising that the banking trade union press – the fortnightly journal, 'O Bancário', published by Sindicato DOS Bancários do Sul e Ilhas (and circa 55,000 copies) – is paying more attention to issues of work (over)time and stress. Recently, Sindicato dos Bancários do Sul e Ilhas launched a campaign against non-paid overtime. A booklet, which contains three vignettes, illustrates 'the assault [by employers] to the bank employees' pocket and life':

- First scene: 21.00 p.m. Three people are still working in a corner-street bank branch: 'What are these guys doing in the bank office?';
- Second scene: 21.45 p.m. A young woman is waiting in front of a cinema: 'My husband is late again. He is a bank employee';
- Third scene: In a surgery, a young man is late for his appointment with the medical doctor, after failing it three previous times: He says: 'I'm sorry, doctor, I'm a bank employee'.

12.2.2 Research on stress

Unfortunately, as in other sectors of industry, there is a lack of epidemiological research on the causes and consequences of stress in banking. There is also little data on work satisfaction and sickness absenteeism. Recently, though, on behalf of the largest banking trade union, the Portuguese epidemiologist, S.M. Cardoso (1994), carried out questionnaire studies among bank employees. Respondents in the first study totalled 1,750 bank employees, both unionised and non-unionised workers. In the second study there were 210 respondents, all union members, working in thirty-two different banks.

Cardoso computed an index of job satisfaction, based on attitudes towards supervisors and co-workers, the job, the tasks performed and the workplace. Approximately 23 per cent disliked their work and 37 per cent would like to change their job. Furthermore, about 30 per cent of the bank employees were smokers and 63 per cent drank alcohol. About 17 per cent of the respondents reported the occurrence of infectious diseases as a cause of sick leave during the previous year.

Despite some methodological constraints (with respect to the design of the questionnaire and the construction of the job satisfaction index), results of this cross-sectional study are of interest. At the very least, it opens up an unexplored research field in Portugal: the link between negative psychosocial factors at work and immunological diseases.

12.2.3 Conclusions

Banking and finance are important branches in the service sector. Especially since the mid-1980s, dramatic changes have taken place. An increased rationalisation of work and an increased flexibilisation of the workforce are two examples of recent and influential management strategies. These changes and new production concepts face resistance from the trade unions, strongly opposed to what they conceive as a new type of organisational culture and work ethic: 'workaholism'. Trade unions emphasise that these new concepts lead to an increase of stress and time constraints, and working overtime, and to a decrease of (the quality of) leisure time. At the moment there is not much empirical data on the amount of stress-related problems in this sector.

12.3 Current project in a bank organisation

12.3.1 MA/CB: The bank and its health policy

In Portugal in the 1990s, in-depth case studies in stress prevention have not as yet been performed. No examples of good preventive practice have been published, nor are they known to us by other means. Therefore, in this section we will introduce a stress prevention project that is currently being carried out in a large banking organisation. The project we have selected concerns a mutual insurance and pension association, established in 1840. In 1844 it created its own savings bank (or credit union). Today in 1998 there are about 61,000 associates and approximately 6,000 'old pensioners'. It is the leading Portuguese organisation operating in this field. Its headquarters is located in Lisbon.

The selected case study fits into an important tradition in Portuguese banking and insurance, the mutual aid movement. This movement, based on benevolent or friendly societies, flourished in Portugal during the second half of the nineteenth century (Goodolphim, 1974), after the liberal revolution of 1820. At that time, as in other European countries, medieval craft guilds had disappeared. Their insurance function was gradually taken care of by groups of employed and self-employed workers who contributed to a common fund. This fund was intended to provide 'protection for all' in the case of illness, work accidents, unemployment, poverty, retirement, death or other hazardous events. In 1934, there were more than 500 mutual insurance, pension and credit associations. Salazar's fascist regime (1932–1974) put an end to the majority of these associations of this kind. As a consequence, ten years after the 1974 Revolution, there were only 117 associations left. In Portugal today, there is an increasing interest in the role these mutual insurance associations might play in the field of social protection, health care and quality of life, due to what is considered to be the crisis of the welfare state.

The mutual insurance association in this study is best known for its commercial activity as a popular deposit and investment bank. We do not have the authorisation to identify it by name thus, the organisation will be referred to as a 'mutual association and commercial bank' (MA/CB). It employs over 2,000 people and has 115 bank branches throughout the country. At the time of writing, its aim was to open sixty-five new branches before the end of 1997. Two-thirds of the employees are male. In 1995, the average age was about 38 years and seniority was 12 years. The largest group of employees was production staff (58 per cent), followed by the top, middle and bottom line managers (17 per cent). The level of temporary or precarious employment was fifteen per cent, which today in Portugal is very low. CB is by far the largest part of the company (1,863 employees); MA has only fifty-three employees.

Technically, MA/CB only became a fully recognised bank in 1995. Since then, it has operated overseas and carried out the same type of financial activities as other joint-stock banking companies. In fact, the most important difference, in comparison to the private-owned companies, concerns its ownership and organisational culture. There are no stockholders, only policyholders. Every year these policyholders elect a board of directors. This board appoints the chief executive officers who are responsible for operating the commercial (CB) and non-commercial (MA) activities, including a foundation. The social and cultural activities of MA are, to a large extent, supported by the financial profits of CB.

In the banking and finance business, MA/CB is an example of corporate success. Ten years ago, it employed 1,200 people and had only thirty-two bank branches. The profits per employee have increased significantly in the last three years. Productivity is also improving. The average number of employees per bank branch decreased: from 17.2 in 1993 to 13 in 1996. The present, MA/CB organisational strategy is 'to modernise, grow up, and consolidate'.

Health policy

Since 1981 MA/CB, has had its own occupational doctor, and since 1989 an occupational health nurse. At the time of the study, the health team included two occupational nurses, two occupational physicians and one administrative staff member. The occupational health service is oriented towards disease prevention and health promotion. Its four main goals are:

* Protecting and promoting worker's health;
* Monitoring and improving the working environment;
* Preventing occupational hazards (including work-related health problems);
* Assuring quality and efficiency of services provided by the health team.

Up until now, the preventive activities of MA/CB's Occupational Health Service has mainly been person-oriented. These activities include a periodical health screening and risk assessment, health education and health promotion. Those preventive measures that are primarily work oriented are limited to the monitoring of major risk factors – both physical and psychosocial (e.g., temperature, VDU work, eye fatigue, back complaints, job satisfaction, stress due to workload). The health team also takes part in ergonomic analyses of appropriate premises, furniture and computer equipment. Occupational health professionals have not been in a position to influence the design of the work organisation. The design of work processes is primarily the task of the re-engineering department.

In addition to the services delivered by the occupational health team, MA/CB's employees are also covered by SAMS, a health care service, financed by both banking employers and employees but owned and operated by Sindicato dos Bancários do Sul e Ilhas. SAMS also runs a modern hospital (130 beds), including a psychiatric service. Furthermore, the MA/CB employees are covered by a complementary health insurance scheme, as part of their fringe benefits. They also have access to the National Health Service (e.g., family doctor, hospital care).

12.3.2 Risk factors and risk groups

The periodical health screening and risk assessment include:

- An interview carried out by the occupational health nurse;
- A medical examination by the occupational physician;
- Additional medical and nursing examinations (e.g., electrocardiograms, clinical tests, ophthalmological and radiological exams).

The occupational health nurse is responsible for identifying and assessing the main health risks. This 'health interview' is a comprehensive risk inventory, concerning both individual factors (e.g., family and social background, health-risk behaviours such as smoking, drinking, eating, exercise, sexual behaviour) and the physical and psychosocial working environment (including occupational stress and job satisfaction).

The main perceived risk factors are broken down by employee health status and the International Statistical Classification of Diseases and Related Health Problems (ICD-10).

Table 12.5 Main reported risk factors, in percentages (n = 80)

Risk factor	%
Health-risk behaviour:	
Lack of regular exercise	45%
Inappropriate nutrition	45%
Lack of use of preventive health care services outside	
company	35%
Smoking	30%
Drinking	20%
Organisational pressures:	
Poor working conditions, job overload, professional role,	
career development and other organisational stressors	80%

Source: MA/CB's Occupational Health Service

Risk assessment

In order to prepare the future workplace health action, an employee's random sample was drawn (n = 80), broken down by gender, age group and department. The sample was drawn from the total population (n = 1,263), that is excluding the northern commercial department (n = 443). About 54 per cent of the sample was production staff. The others consisted of managerial and technical staff based at the company's headquarters. The sample was surveyed by means of a confidential health needs questionnaire (including questions on behavioural and organisational risk factors). The main reported risk factors are listed in Table 12.5.

In addition to the results of the periodical health screening and risk assessments mentioned in Table 12.5, this small sample points to the prevalence of various unhealthy behaviours: lack of physical activity, smoking, drinking and unhealthy eating habits. Other data from this sample seem to point to the fact that male and female employees are not overly concerned with primary prevention of gender diseases and/or health promoting activities.

With respect to organisational factors, the main stressors, as in other banking companies, appear to be:

- Poor or unpleasant working conditions (e.g., lighting, temperature, lack of physical space). The physical working environment is perceived to be a risk factor mainly by the employees at headquarters.
- Work organisation, new technologies, new products and services, quantitative and qualitative overload – but also repetitive, routine, boring work – the role performed within the work team, relationships at work, career development, organisational structure and climate. These factors were especially mentioned by local bank clerks.
- Working overtime. This is perceived as a major source of stress, as is the case in many other banks. Often working overtime is partially compensated by extra pay.

Table 12.6 MA/CB: Percentage absenteeism days per person, in non-commercial (MA) and commercial (CB) activities (1993–1996)

	1993	*1994*		*1995*		*1996*	
	MA/CB	*MA*	*CB*	*MA*	*CB*	*MA*	*CB*
Sickness, accidents and other causes	4.5	6.2	3.5	6.7	4.2	5.2	3.5
Only sick leave	2.7	4.2	2.0	3.3	2.4	2.9	2.2

Source: MA/CB 1996 Social Audit

Table 12.7 MA/CB: Proportion of short- and long-term sick leave in the total volume of working days lost due to illness, accidents and other reasons (1993–1996)

Sick-leave duration	1993 MA/CB	1994 MA	1994 CB	1995 MA	1995 CB	1996 MA	1996 CB
Long-term (≥ 31 days)	28.3	29.1	27.5	49.6	34.9	38.3	47.0
Short-term (≤ 30 days)	31.6	37.1	30.2	0.0	21.5	17.6	14.6
Total	59.9	66.2	57.7	49.6	56.4	55.9	61.6

Source: MA/CB 1996 Social Audit

Sick leave, turnover and work disability

Sick leave and turnover are very low. Work accidents are relatively rare. Nevertheless, employee absenteeism is higher in MA than in CB (see Table 12.6).

Sick leave represents approximately 60 per cent of the total working days lost due to illness, accidents and other absence reasons (e.g., maternity/paternity leave). In 1996, both in CB and MA, the proportion of long-term sick leave (31 days or more) is higher than the proportion of short-term sick leave (Table 12.7).

In 1996, the main causes of ill health were cardiovascular diseases. Among the work-related diseases, eye fatigue and other clinical eye problems, typical of VDU workers, were the most prevalent. Mental problems ranked second. These work-related diseases seem to be related to the high degree of computerisation (and the frequent utilisation of VDU screens) in banking and finance activities. From the First European Survey on the Work Environment, as mentioned in section 12.1.2, it appears that 40 per cent of the respondents in this sector indicated permanent use of computers, a very high proportion when compared with the EU average (14 per cent) (Paoli, 1992). In the same survey it is shown that, of all sectors studied, banking and finance has the lowest level of complaints with regard to the physical environment and to physical constraints. 'Working times are also among the lowest (39.7 hours per week on average) but are compensated by higher than average time pressure, in particular due to tight deadlines' (Paoli, 1992, p. 156).

12.3.3 Choice of measures

MA/CB's Occupational Health Service is preparing an action plan that is to be implemented in 1998. Given the analysis of risk factors, priority has been given to the reduction of causes and symptoms of job-related stress. The principal objective is to reduce the stress level, as experienced by MA/CB employees. More specifically, the objectives are:

- To decrease by 10 per cent the level of stress reported by the Lisbon bank branches' employees;
- To increase by 10 per cent the number of actions by occupational health nurses, in co-operation with the heads of regional commercial departments, in order to reduce and to prevent stressful situations at the workplace;
- To increase by 50 per cent information to and training of employees, in order to improve their knowledge about stress and their coping skills and in order to prevent the negative effects of stress on health and performance.

12.3.4 Action strategies and implementation

These objectives are provisional and a basis for discussion-negotiation and decision-making among management, the works council and the occupational health team. MA/CB's Occupational Health Service's strategy is to build up, step by step, an organisational climate that is supportive to dealing with stress at work. It goes without saying that the involvement of bank directors and managing directors is essential in creating such a climate. Therefore a first report was sent to all commercial and non-commercial departments. As a next step, discussion meetings took place with heads of these departments and top executive management.

It seems the most difficult task up to this point has been to gain and keep the interest and goodwill of bottom and middle managers. The main barriers being lack of time and the ongoing process of commercial expansion.

Generally, most employees and their representatives (mainly the works council) are open-minded with respect to the needs of a comprehensive and participatory programme for job-related stress. This attitude was probably influenced by regular contributions of the occupational health team in *Entre Nós*, the newsletter edited by the works council.

With respect to their own roles, the health professionals feel that they have not enough knowledge and skills to perform all the roles that might be necessary in such a workplace health promotion process (see Wynne, 1994). Various skills are needed, since the prevention of stress at work is complex, and it presupposes measures targeted at the individual, the group and the organisation as a whole. The occupational health team is also very sensitive to the risk of a top-down approach, and has rejected the typical US stress management programmes. These programmes are viewed as only directed at improving individual coping skills.

Although in this company stress is now perceived as a major health issue that calls for action, several questions still have to be answered. The most difficult question is how to combine preventive actions on the individual level and on the organisational level. Another question is whether the organisational climate is ready yet for, and supportive to, organisational change. Are the board of directors, the heads of departments and the supervisors really willing to eliminate or minimise the main organisational pressures? And what will be the cost and benefits of the intended measures?

12.3.5 Evaluation and follow-up

Since at the time of writing this project is still in progress and the actual implementation of preventive measures has not yet taken place, it is not yet possible to evaluate this project in a systematic way. It is also too early for a cost benefit analysis. One of the positive outcomes of the project, is that top and middle managers have become more sensitive to the social and economic costs of stress and ill health, including their negative effects on job performance and corporate image. But still many managers feel that job-related stress is a price worth paying, as a consequence of the expansion of commercial activities. However, they conceive stress at work is a serious issue, and are relatively open-minded towards a comprehensive health promotion programme at the workplace. Moreover, many managers support the idea of designing, planning, implementing and evaluating such a programme, in co-operation between management' representatives, the occupational health team and workers' representatives.

Another way of evaluating the project is by comparing the amount of occupational health and safety attention that MA/CB provides to each employee, to the service level provided in other companies. In 1995, MA/CB has spent about 190 ECU per employee for 'services and activities' with respect to occupational health and safety. In addition, social welfare programmes, run by MA/CB, cost 320 ECU per employee (not including free meals, health insurance premium and other fringe benefits). In paying attention to the health and safety of its employees MA/CB can be considered a pioneering organisation in Portugal: in 1993, only 14 per cent of the 2,000 largest Portuguese companies spent more than 100 ECU per employee, for OHS services and activities (Graça, 1995 and 1996a). There are clear indications that the lower management levels have also become more sensitive to work-related stress. Directors of local bank branches are expected to give more social support to their work teams and to provide support to those employees who might be at risk (e.g., those suffering from emotional disturbance and personal problems). Without a doubt, the communication with the occupational health team has improved. Its role is now better understood by both management and employees.

Presently, the occupational health team spends one day per week discussing and planning the stress prevention project. Occupational health nurses are playing a leading role in this project. Since a tradition of occupational health nursing is lacking in Portugal, this new development is a rather unusual one in Portuguese OHS company services.

Conclusion

It is hard to predict how this project will develop over the next few years. Still, we would argue that MA/CB, in starting an ambitious stress prevention project, has taken an important initiative which is very welcome in an economic sector where the traditional OHS services and programmes need to urgently be re-oriented towards health promotion.

Bibliography

Barreto, A. (ed.) (1996) *A Situação Social em Portugal, 1960–1995* ('Social Trends in Portugal: 1960–1995'), Lisboa: Instituto de Ciências Sociais da Universidade de Lisboa.

Cardoso, S. M. (1994) 'Dissatisfaction in the Workplace and Prevalence of Infectious Diseases. New Epidemics in Occupational Health', proceedings of the International Symposium on New Epidemics in Occupational Health, May 16–19, 1994, Helsinki, in J. Rantaten *et al.* (eds), *People and Work*, Research Reports, 1. Helsinki: Finnish Institute of Occupational Health, pp. 76–8.

Commission of European Communities (1992) *Europeans and Health and Safety at Work. A Survey*, Luxemburg: Directorate-General for Employment, Social Affairs and Education, Health and Safety Directorate, Unit V/E/5.

Goodolphim C. (1974) *A Associação. História e Desenvolvimento das Associações Portuguesas* ('A history of the Portuguese mutual insurance and pension associations'), Lisboa: Seara Nova (1st edition, Lisboa: Imprensa Nacional, 1876).

Graça, L. (1995) *Ill-health and Workplace Absenteeism in Portugal: Initiatives For Prevention*, Dublin: European Foundation for the Improvement of Living and Working Conditions (working paper).

——(1996a) 'Um problema de saúde pública: O absentismo por incapacidade' ('Unfitness for work: A public health problem'), *Revista Portuguesa de Saúde Pública* (Portuguese Journal of Public Health), 14 (3): 5–19.

——(1996b) 'The example of the electronic industry', in O. Brown Jr. and H.W. Hendrick (eds), *Human Factors in Organisational Design and Management-V*, Amsterdam: North-Holland., pp. 345–50.

——(1997) *Corporate Modernising and Workplace Health Promotion. Mail Questionnaire Survey and Case Studies: Preliminary Conclusions*, Lisbon: New University of Lisbon, National School of Public Health working paper; in Portuguese.

Graça, L. and Faria, M. (1992) *Innovative Workplace Action for Health: Mechanisms for Establishing Initiatives, Portugal*, Dublin: European Foundation for the Improvement of Living and Working Conditions (working paper, no. WP/92/organisat/EN).

——(1993) 'Ano Europeu da Segurança., Higiene e Saúde no Local de Trabalho', ('European Year of Safety, Hygiene and Health at Work in 1992'), *Revista Portuguesa de Saúde Pública,* 11 (1): 15–20.

Graça, L., Gonçalves, A.I., Semedo, and Silva, R. (1997) 'Iniciativas para prevenir e reduzir o absentismo por incapacidade: três estudos de caso' ('Preventing ill health and absenteeism at the workplace: Three Portuguese case studies'), *Revista Portuguesa de Saúde Pública*, 15 (2): 21–44 (in Portuguese).

Gründemann, R. and Van Vuuren, C. (1997) *Preventing Absenteeism at the Workplace: European Research Project*, Dublin: European Foundation for the Improvement of Living and Working Conditions.

Paoli, P. (1992) *First European Survey on the Work Environment (1991–1992)*, Dublin: European Foundation for the Improvement of Living and Working Conditions (EF/9211 I/EN).

Pereira, J.A.C.G. (1995) *Equity, Health and Health Care: An Economic Study with Reference to Portugal*, Ph.D. thesis. York: University of York, Department of Economics and Related Studies.

Portugal, INE (National Institute of Statistics) (1996) *1995 Statistical Yearbook of Portugal*, Lisbon: INE.

Wynne, R. (1994) *Workplace Health Promotion: A Specification for Training*, Dublin: European Foundation for the Improvement of Living and Working Conditions, (Working paper no. WP/94/22/EN).

Chapter 13

Greece: Stress management in the health care sector

Elisabeth Petsetaki

13.1 Introduction

The relationship between stress and the workplace has long been recognised (Yates, 1979). Stress occurs in a relationship between the worker and the work environment (Blau, 1981). The extent of stress in the workplace is difficult to define though some stress is seen to be helpful, as it increases concentration, effectiveness and performance. In the view of many practitioners, the management of stress in the workplace is usually associated with human resource management (Quick and Quick, 1979).

This chapter will focus on human resource management in the public sector and specifically in the area of health care in Greece. Emphasis will be placed on the reasons for the lack of stress management programmes. The regulations on health and safety in the workplace will be reviewed along with policies regarding human resource management. Finally, a review of cases of stress management programmes in the workplace in the greater Athens area (Attica) will be discussed.

13.1.1 Stress and human resource management

In Greece, stress in the workplace is not considered an important aspect of human resource management (Papadatou and Anagnostakis, 1995). Furthermore, the area of human resource management is underdeveloped. This is demonstrated by the absence in both the public and private sector of the basic functions of human resource management (Andrioti and Kyriopoulos, 1989). Experts in the area are absent from leadership positions. Personnel departments function with minimal duties and responsibilities and are plagued by a bureaucratic management style, with human resource management limited to routine procedures (Merianou, 1994). These include the payment of salaries, transfers, promotions and the monitoring of insurance benefits. Functions such as job development, training, employee evaluation, health and safety, counselling and labour relations are almost absent. The important areas in human resource development, such as training programmes, counselling in career paths and sound promotion procedures, are hardly to be found in Greek organisations. Furthermore, there is a lack of a culture in effective management specifically in human resources, often exemplified by the confusion of expectations between employers and workers. In such a working environment, interest in stress management in the workplace is certainly not a priority in work policy in Greece.

The public sector is the largest employer in Greece. The largest percentage of public employees work in the area of health care. Even though it offers low salaries, the public sector still attracts workers for the reason that a salary and benefits (health and retirement) are assured for life (Abel-Smith *et al.*, 1994). Given these low salaries, many public servants have a second job. In many cases these second jobs pay more than the public salary and are more satisfying (Xenos, 1996).

Within the existing work policy and management style, it is indicative that the Greek public sector chooses to ignore worker problems concerning their job, working conditions, management and co-workers, instead generating a 'public employee' profile characterised by boredom, alienation, burn-out, and apathy towards work and the workplace. Work results and effectiveness is very difficult to measure since there is no planning, feedback or any type of evaluation of work performed.

Supervisors lack skills in all areas of management. Very few supervisors have received any further job-related training or opportunities to develop new skills after their formal education. In addition the position they hold may be totally unrelated to their formal training or work experience. Though the public sector has a formal body responsible for the continuous training of civil servants, this has not been an effective resource in promoting the development of training programmes within institutions. Furthermore, straightforward yet essential orientation programmes for new employees on the policies and procedures of the organisation have been lacking.

Low salaries have been an issue for workers and unions for decades, with the result that other important areas have been left behind (Agavanaki, 1997). Low salaries are only part of the problem for workers in the public sector. Unions rarely address other issues of core importance to the worker. Work policies and procedures do exist, but they seem to exist only on paper with there being very little interest in applying them to real work situations. Job descriptions, job enrichment, and job development are critical aspects of clarifying roles and responsibilities, but these topics are absent from union and management debate. The civil servant after a few years of work assumes the 'public employee' profile in order to function and survive in such an ambiguous and unsupportive environment.

Ignoring worker problems runs counter to contemporary human resources management philosophy (Handy, 1985). Organisations, public or private, should respond at least partially to worker problems, but it is crucial that they also have the capacity to offer solutions. Unfortunately, the role that giving attention to worker problems can play in improving motivation and enhancing the productivity of the workforce is still very much underestimated in the Greek public sector (Gana, 1989).

Major shortcomings in human resource management in Greece include the following (Velonakis, 1989):

- Role ambiguity: the individual does not have a clear understanding of the behaviours expected in the job. This is mostly due to lack of appropriate experience, training and consistency in work behaviours.
- Responsibility and authority ambiguity: the worker is not clear about the various components of the job, the expected outcome, the responsibility of the outcome and the connected authority. Internal politics are dominant and the worker is very much aware of the dynamics involved. Taking initiative, being innovative and other such 'progressive' work behaviours are met with suspicion and only in rare situations is such behaviour encouraged.
- Outcome ambiguity: the worker does not receive feedback on performance or a sense of how each part contributes to the whole. There is a feeling of endlessness, a beginning without an end. The work is just measured on time sheets, hours, days, months, years with little connection to performance.

The lack of effective management of human resources in combination with a working environment not responsive to worker needs is a big contributor to work stress (Xidia-Kikemeni, 1997).

13.1.2 Legal framework

The legal framework regarding working conditions in Greece follows the regulations of the European Union. The area of health and safety of workers in Greece is regulated by law 2224/94. The regulations outline the guidelines and standards regarding the protection of workers from occupational hazards. The guidelines specifically cover such areas as the prevention of work accidents and occupational diseases. Another section in the regulations covers the area of training, counselling workers and abiding by the guidelines. These regulations apply to all places of work, including the private and public sectors. To emphasise the importance of these guidelines for occupational health and safety, the law makes specific mention of high-risk work including: mining, heavy-duty transport, the handling of explosive/hazardous materials, work involving radioactivity and so forth.

Specific articles in the law cover the organisational structure in the workplace for the improvement of working conditions (Articles 3–6). Workers have the right to choose their representatives on health and safety. Specific areas of concern include:

- provision of services in the area of protection and safety and the prevention of work accidents;
- the employment of an occupational health doctor and a technical specialist in work safety;
- training for the technical specialist in safety, occupational health doctors, representatives of workers (this is carried out usually through the Greek Institute of Hygiene and Work Safety).

Other responsibilities for employers are outlined in these articles:

- provision of health benefits and the protection of health;
- procedures for first aid, fire safety, other internal and external dangers;
- training of workers in health and safety and the safe operation of equipment and hazardous materials;
- procedures for implementation and assurance/control methods for following standards and guidelines;
- procedures for penalties.

In general, it is mandatory that the employer assures the health and safety of workers in the workplace. The employer has to have set policies and procedures in the compliance with the regulations including a warning and penalty system. Training of workers on health and safety is specifically mentioned in the regulations.

In practice, what occurs in the workplace is a very different story. What prevails is a lack of consciousness by both employer and worker on the importance of health and safety in the workplace. Health and safety is not a priority even in high-risk jobs. The adherence to safety guidelines is not enforced on the part of management (Politis, 1991), which is evident on examination of the following:

- unsafe handling of equipment and hazardous materials (storage, safe operation according to guidelines, safety gloves, masks, helmets, etc.);
- unsafe working environment (floor and wall safety, electrical outlets, etc.);
- absence of comprehensive training programmes in all areas of health and safety and especially orientation procedures for new employees;
- absence of up-to-date fire safety procedures and regular training of workers;
- unsafe working practices (lifting, transporting, general movement in the workplace).

To summarise, health and safety in the workplace in Greece is still not considered a priority. This is reflected in the inability to enforce health and safety regulations and to increase public awareness on health and safety. The development of specific issues regarding health and safety in the workplace such as stress management programmes and the prevention of stress is even less of a priority. There is a lack of awareness of stress in the workplace and its effects on health, safety, morale and the productivity of workers. Programmes on stress management are few, are not well developed, and, in general, are not reflective of a general policy on stress in the workplace (Papadatou and Anagnostopoulos, 1995).

13.2 Management of stress in the health care sector: Introduction

A national health system was established in Greece in 1983 (Law 1937/83). Core principles of this major reform, such as equity in care provision, decentralisation of decision-making on health and primary health care provision, are still blocked in the implementation process due to poor planning, know-how and funds (Dervenis and Polyzos, 1995). The organisation and management of the health service is still highly centralised and regulated (Abel-Smith et al., 1994). Furthermore, there is a lack of experienced manpower in the planning and management of health services which could support and implement necessary changes in health care regulations (Yfantopoulos, 1993). Well-trained and experienced health service managers, as well as comprehensive structures of control and regulation are lacking in the health sector.

Human resource management in this sector, and specifically the health and safety of workers, reflects a similar situation found in other work sectors in Greece. Even in the work environment of health care, when health care and safety practices are examined it is apparent that there is room for improvement. In hospitals basic procedures are not well developed, are out of date or are totally absent. These include procedures for fire safety, natural physical disasters, accidents and hazardous incidents. The control of hospital infections is one area which has received some attention, even though hygiene protection throughout hospitals is generally lacking.

The overall hospital working environment appears unsafe. This is reflected in the design of the buildings, and the organisation of the various hospital functions. Natural physical barriers, passageways, stairs, elevators, the blockage of hallways, all hinder the safe movement of workers, patients and visitors, especially during emergency (Niakas, 1997). Furthermore, the protection of workers and patients cannot be assured with the current 'open-door' policy that operates at all hours, and which is the practice in most public hospitals. Multiple entrances, the lack of observation of visiting hours, smoking regulations and the overall relaxed behaviour patterns regarding health and safety is very characteristic of Greek public hospitals.

Greece's population according to the 1991 census was 10,259,000, with over one-third residing in its capital, Athens. The Athens area, with its hospitals, private clinics and diagnostic centres is the centre for health care provision, closely followed by Thessaloniki. These two cities and their surrounding environs are the providers of most health care services, also attracting patients from other regions who prefer to seek care in Greece's two largest cities (Niakas and Petsetaki, 1995).

13.2.1 Methods used for the survey

A review or any type of description of stress management programmes cannot be found in the Greek literature. In March 1997, an initiative was taken by the Department of Health Services, National School of Public Health to locate and describe the ongoing programmes in both public and private hospitals in the general Athens area (Attica). Contacts made with practitioners in the health care area resulted in references to other possible ongoing programmes in companies. Information provided by the contact person in the companies, though often very limited, is also described in this section.

A survey was developed with open-ended questions to gain information on stress management programmes. The main questions of the survey were:

*   does the organisation have a stress management programme?
*   how was the programme started; motives, responsible person, support from management?
*   description of the programme; methods used;
*   evaluation, effects of the programme.

There are twenty public hospitals and six main private hospitals in the Athens area. Telephone contacts were made with the personnel manager of these hospitals and information on stress management programmes was requested. From the twenty hospitals, seventeen agreed to give information on stress management. After a further contact with these seventeen, only five hospitals gave any meaningful information on stress management. With these five hospitals a contact person and an interview time were established. The contact person in most cases was a psychologist who was responsible for the stress management programme. Two private hospitals also provided minimal information on their stress management programmes (see Table 13.1).

13.3 Motives for the programmes

We found that the development of the programmes came from individuals who are aware and knowledgeable in the area of stress in the workplace and who have taken the initiative. These programmes were not part of a comprehensive and progressive human resources management initiative. The information available on the programmes was limited. It is the opinion of

Table 13.1 Survey of stress management programmes (SMP) in hospitals and companies in the Athens area

Public hospitals	(SMP)	
	YES	NO
Saint-Anargiry	X	
Dafni	X	
Metaxa	X	
Saint–Sofia	X	
Agl. Kyriakou	X	
Agios Savas		X
Alexandra		X
Laiko		X
Euagelismos		X
Elpis		X
Sotiria		X
Ipokratio		X
Patision		X
Spiliopoulio		X
Laiko		X
Sygros		X
Benakio		X

Private hospitals	(SMP)	
	YES	NO
Ygia		X
Iaso		X
Mitera		X

List of companies	(SMP)	
	YES	NO
Sida		X
Bayer		X
Bioser		X
Bristol		X
Erfar		X
Glaxon		X
Fage (Milk Products)		X
Federation of Greek Industrialists		X
Olympic Airways		X

the researcher that a more comprehensive approach to stress did not exist in the workplaces surveyed. For this reason the information available was limited to the specific programmes described.

In our survey we found several support groups, mostly for nurses, on stress management. Similar to support groups in other work areas, their aim is the reduction of stress and the increase of self-esteem of workers. Support groups provide opportunities for the strengthening of communication between members of the health team and helps to decrease the feelings of isolation, depression and burn-out. In this way support groups can help health teams work more effectively with patients and their families.

Specific objectives of support groups include:

- to provide to the health care team the opportunity to share their feelings and perceptions about incapacity, life and death;
- to understand their reactions and to work through painful experiences;
- to seek alternative ways of dealing with difficult situations;
- to discuss and share successful interventions which strengthens their confidence.

13.4 Support groups in public hospitals

13.4.1 Oncology hospital of Saint-Anargiri

The support group in this hospital developed due to a need for staff support in response to interest expressed by the nursing staff at large. Trained specialists developed a support group for the nursing staff. The group meets for three months once a week for one to two hours. At the end of the three months a new group is formed. The group consists of around ten members and is led by a psychologist trained in support groups. A group usually consists of nursing staff from the same unit who attend on a volunteer basis and usually after referral from the head nurse.

Time constitutes a strong obstacle for group meetings. Holding the groups during working hours presents a problem on the ward since there is no possibility for replacements. Holding the groups after work hours is difficult for those nurses who have young children. The interest is there, the need has been identified, but the time constraint hurdle has not been worked out.

The psychologist leading the groups gave us a brief description of the methods and techniques used in the sessions. The drawing of pictures is used to open discussion with the members. The members express their feelings through focusing on areas seen in the picture which are common to the group. Members then relate their reactions to the group as a whole and to their work experience.

Knowledge of self is a predominant focus for group discussions. Members learn techniques to 'explore themselves' and to express their experiences and their development of the group. Through this exploration of self their work experience is examined and shared with the group. Group dynamics, conflicts with co-workers and patients, job satisfaction and many other concerns are discussed.

The psychologist reported that many members of the various groups felt that being together and sharing thoughts and feelings about self and work is rewarding enough to ease some of the isolation and feelings of stress felt at work. The group offers an opportunity to be together, to talk, to discuss problems and to generate a feeling of group identity. This is something which is very much lacking in the organisational culture of Greek hospitals. Formal means of communication through regular staff meetings in an effective and consistent manner is absent.

The psychologist described four other possible structures of support groups which can be developed to provide support to the health care professional.

GROUP A:

This type of group focuses on offering support to its members through training them in specific skills in how to relate to patients, families and co-workers. The emphasis is on effective communication. The objective is to increase knowledge and develop capabilities towards a better understanding of the behaviour of patients, families and co-workers. Short presentations are made on specific topics followed by discussion, role play and practical exercises.

GROUP B:

This group focuses more on discussions of cases which concern the health team. The emphasis is on learning skills to deal with aggressive behaviour and conflict. The members learn effective ways of resolving conflict through various methods, similar to the ones mentioned in group A.

GROUP C:

Working with terminally-ill patients over a long duration can cause tremendous stress. Stress felt at work especially when experienced over an extended period of time can lead to depression, detachment and burn-out. In this group members learn to deal with stress through using various relaxation techniques. The objective is to learn to deal with stress more effectively at work and to learn not to transfer destructive behaviours to the home.

13.4.2 Psychiatric hospital Daphni

This is the largest psychiatric hospital in Greece and is based in Athens. The hospital staff had expressed a great need for support groups in this workplace.

Our contact person in the hospital provided us with minimal information on the existing support groups. The purpose of the support groups is to help the members express their feelings of stress, fear, isolation and depression and, from the discussions within the group, find ways to resolve them. The groups consist of nurses and doctors and are usually limited to twelve to fifteen members. The group is led by a trained psychologist and does not have a specific format or structure. The discussion may start spontaneously by any of the members who has a concern, and then the rest of the members contribute to the discussion. Hospital staff here have an increasing interest in support groups and feel that they are very beneficial. It is hoped that the hospital will have the capacity and interest to develop more of them.

13.4.3 Other hospitals

Three other public hospitals in the Athens area were visited to learn about their stress management programmes. The Children's hospital responded very positively with respect to the need for such programmes, especially for nurses working with terminally-ill children. Once a month a group meets with participants from the intensive care unit and the cancer ward. An external consulting psychologist holds the sessions. Unfortunately, we were not able to get any further details. In another cancer hospital the individual responsible felt that programmes in stress management would be very beneficial to the staff. Unfortunately the hospital does not have specialised staff to develop such programmes. In addition it was mentioned that the general attitude of the staff is not very supportive of such programmes. They feel they would not offer much in dealing with the stress they experience in working with terminally-ill patients. In a large general hospital management does not support such programmes, since it is of the opinion that work stress is secondary to other problems of the hospital such as poor planning and overall management.

Three of the largest private hospitals in Greece were visited to learn about the existence of any stress programmes. One of the hospitals did not give us any information on stress management while the other two felt that they have not observed any need for such special programmes for their staff. It is interesting that they also added that the benefit of such programmes is not very well known in Greece nor are there any findings in support of investment in such programmes.

13.4.4 Other companies

Six of the largest pharmaceutical companies in the Athens area were visited as well as the Federation of Greek Industrialists (SE). Personnel directors were approached and were asked if any stress management programmes existed in their companies.

Though they reported that such programmes are beneficial, they felt that they are not necessary and are considered as a luxury in their organisation. They felt that any problems workers may have can be resolved through one-to-one counselling with the supervisor or with the personnel director.

One of the largest milk product producing companies was also approached. The personnel director reported that the prevention and management of stress is best dealt with through sound human resources management procedures. They have a keen interest in the health and safety of their employees. Any problems encountered by employees are resolved with the supervisor or the personnel manager. In special cases the worker may be referred to the staff psychologist or may take some days off work. Additional information on stress reduction through the company's human resource procedures was not provided by the contact person.

Olympic Airways is the Greek flag carrier and is state owned. We were not able to meet with the personnel director but were referred to a responsible employee and to the legal department. The general attitude here was similar to that experienced in other places we studied. Problems are dealt with through the hierarchy on an individual basis. What is interesting in the case of the Civil Aviation Authority is the lack of specific programmes for air traffic controllers. Though the contact person recognised that the profession is a high-risk one, problems of stress, depression, isolation and burn-out are only resolved with special sessions with a staff physician and days off work. There is no in-house psychologist, so in special cases the employee will be referred to a consulting psychologist.

13.5 Conclusion

Stress in the workplace in Greece is much talked about by workers but little attention is given to examining the causes or to developing programmes to reduce stress. The lack of interest mostly stems from the general management style and more specifically the management of human resources. Departments of human resource management are not well developed, with wider functions and policies being minimal. The workplace in Greece seems to forget its most essential asset, the worker. If workers are not well matched to the organisational needs and are not managed effectively, then work quality and output are negatively affected.

Attention to more specialised worker needs and how this can affect performance is not given priority by those in leadership positions. Embryonic programmes described in this chapter are initiatives of individuals in response to worker needs. Well developed comprehensive programmes on stress management will only happen as the result of improved and strengthened policies on human resources management.

Acknowledgement

This chapter would not have been possible without the valuable assistance of Spiridoula Spiliopoulou, research assistant, National School of Public Health, Athens, Greece.

Bibliography

Abel-Smith, B., Calltorp, J. and Dixon, M. (1994) *Report on the Greek Health Services*, Athens: Ministry of Health and Social Welfare of Greece.

Agavanaki, D. (1997) 'Old and New Public Salary Scale', *Public Sector*, 128: 28.

Andrioti, D. and Kyriopoulos J. (1989) 'Health Manpower in Greece', *Health Review*, 3, (34), no. 6: 47–54.

Blau, G. (1981) 'An Empirical Investigation of Job Stress, Social Support Service Length, and Job Strain', *Organisational Behaviour and Human Performance*, 27: 280.

Dervenis, C. and Polyzos, N. (1995) *Study and Proposal on the Organisation and Management of the NHS and the Development of Health Care Personnel*, Athens: Ministry of Health and Welfare.

Gana, A. (1989) 'Medical Training Results in Greece', *Proceedings, First Conference in Health Care Finance*, Athens.

Handy, C. (1985) *Understanding Organisations*, Harmondsworth: Penguin.

Merianou, M. (1994) 'Development and Management of Human Resources' in *Health Care Medical Review*, 6: 33–6.

Niakas, D. (1997) 'The Cot Syndrome and the reasons behind it', *Health Review*, 8: 48.

Niakas, D. and Petsetaki, E. (1995) 'Problems and Perspectives in Health Care Policy in Greece', *Public Budgeting and Financing Management*, 7, (2): 250–79.

Papadatou, D. and Anagnostopoulos, F. (1995) 'Psychology in the Health Sector', *Greek Letters*, Athens, pp. 242–58.

Politis, D. (1991) 'Health and Safety of Workers', *Public Sector*, 70–71: 73.

Quick, J.C. and Quick, J.D. (1979) 'Reducing Stress through Preventive Management', *Human Resource Management*, 18: 17.

Velonakis, M. (1989) 'Work Health, the Economy and Development', *Proceedings, First Conference in Health Care Finance*, Athens, pp. 84–9.

Xidia-Kikemeni, N. (1997) *Work Organisation, Work Environment and Stress*, Departmental Document, Athens: National School of Public Health.

Xenos, A. (1996) 'Tenure of Public Employees', *Public Sector*, 123: 43–44.

Yates, J.E. (1979) *Managing Stress*, New York: American Management Association.

Yfantopoulos, J. (1993) 'Health Manpower Needs in Greece 1980–2000', *Report to DGV of European Union*, Athens.

Chapter 14

Italy: A school of nursing

Sebastiano Bagnara, Alberto Baldasseroni,
Oronzo Parlangeli, Stefano Taddei and
Riccardo Tartaglia

14.1 Introduction

It is difficult to identify specific political interventions to do with stress in
the workplace in Italy that are both global and effective, though there are
local services, co-ordinated by the national health system, particularly
concerned with working conditions and risk factors. In the past, the national
unions have collaborated in some pilot studies aimed at a deeper comprehension of stress factors with relation to the working conditions of specific
professionals, such as bus-drivers, pilots and workers under thermal stress risk
(for example, in glass works) (Bagnara and Rizzo, 1990; Strambi, 1991;
Strambi *et al.*, 1991).

However, these studies have been somewhat sporadic and lacking in overall
co-ordination. One notable example is the homogeneous factory group
evaluation programme in operation from the end of the 1960s to the 1980s.
Within this program representatives of the unions and workers met to discuss
issues such as 'group IV risk factors', a label identifying such risk factors
related to work organisation, as mental fatigue, monotony and erratic rest
breaks. In these discussions it was concluded that working conditions and
different methods of organisations may produce stress, and the unions
made a commitment to combat work-related stress. Interventions that
followed these discussions were not structured as systematic studies, however
they could be considered practices aimed at improving workers' mental well-
being.

The focus at the moment on safe working conditions by the national
unions in Italy is once again creating an interest in stress prevention. Precise
indications as to how work stress can be monitored and prevented are,
however, still missing. The frame of reference usually adopted is the law
which governs the healthy working conditions at national level. This Act
(the Ministerial Decree 626/94) was presented and passed to conform with
European Union directives concerning work safety and is based on the
assumption that the assessment of risk factors is a basic measure for the safeguard of workers' well-being. The innovations of this Act are related to a

broader concept of health, which also implies 'psycho-physical integrity'. In addition, the decree involves the consideration of such factors as work organisation, ergonomics and the level of usability of information systems, assuming that such factors, when they are not adequate to support work activities, can have negative consequences on workers.

As a result of the enforcement of this Act, all firms in Italy are obliged to train workers in issues related to health and safety. Companies must organise annual meetings in which these issues are discussed. When problematic conditions arise, they must adopt the necessary measures to improve the situation.

The legislation makes a distinction between different risk factors. However, although for many problems, in particular those related to physical well-being, a direct causal relation with the workplace is acknowledged, this is not so with respect to stress. It is clearly established, for instance, that there is a link between noise and deafness, benzene and leukaemia, whereas factors that can cause stress are not univocally determined. Stress is not seen as being related to specific risk agents. Instead it is considered to be the result of more general conditions involving exposure to different and interacting factors that can be present both in the work setting and in private life. Thus, occupational health practitioners, responsible for the evaluation of safety conditions in companies, even when they might assess stress risk factors, tend to avoid doing so due to the difficulty in proving whether such factors are ascribable to work or not.

The Ministerial Decree 626/94 does not differentiate between public and private enterprises, thus the activities that it prescribes to guarantee workers' well-being must be performed by public institutions as well. Some public professions have been recognised as being particularly vulnerable to stress risk factors. Among these, the nursing profession has received considerable attention due to the fact that different studies (Del Rio, 1993; Di Martino, 1994; Sirigatti *et al.*, 1988a; 1988b; Sirigatti and Menoni, 1993; Sirigatti and Stefanile, 1993) have shown that nurses are particularly exposed to risk factors for occupational stress.

In relation to the nursing profession, it should be pointed out that over the last few years there have been rapid changes in Italy. The nursing profession has developed from one based on low qualified tasks to one that involves the assumption of responsibility. In short, the profession has become more comparable to those in other European countries. These transformations were accompanied by legislative directives which were aimed at updating training programmes. As a consequence, new regional schools have been established and a university course in nursing has been opened. New educational programmes provide considerable training practice in real contexts, such as hospitals and clinics. Both Italian (Sirigatti *et al.*, 1988a; 1988b; Sirigatti and Menoni, 1993) and non-Italian (Haack, 1988; Haack *et al.*, 1988; Lees and Ellis, 1990) researchers have focused their studies on the psychological factors involved in stress perception by young nurses. These studies have shown the relevance of such factors as motivation and expectations, collaboration among peers during the early periods of training, and perceptions of the results of one's activity. However, although the nursing profession is one of the most thoroughly studied, there is no national programme for stress prevention and data on how work activities affect the mental well-being of student nurses are still missing.

This chapter is a report of a study that shows an example of 'current Italian practice' in work stress. Student nurses participated in a study that was aimed at determining the effectiveness of supervision and group problem management for stress reduction. Results should be considered as a preliminary indication as to how to reorganise student nurses' working practice in order to minimise stress effects.

14.2 Introduction to the school of nursing

The company under study is the Unità Sanitaria Locale (USL) 10D in Florence. This Local Health Unit, offers different health services, and is located throughout different centres in the region. The most important section, with the largest number of clinics, is the Careggi's hospital, in north Florence and is well connected by a freeway. This public body has recently become a health company. It adds to the financial support it receives from the regional government, by offering additional medical services that are not included in the set of services which receive regional grants. In the past these kind of services were essentially provided by private companies. These companies, in turn, can now offer services that were formerly only provided by public health institutions. Competition with private health companies is now occurring, and new managerial staff, responsible for the final balancing of accounts, has been appointed to ensure a more profitable presence on the market.

The USL 10D is connected to a three-year regional school of nursing. This school is open to 200 students per year who are admitted after the consideration of their qualifications and an entrance exam. In the past, there were less people applying for this school than the number of available places. However, the number of applicants has increased to the extent that applicants are now subjected to a strict selection process. Students must have at least a high school diploma. Nursing students undergo 200 hours of theoretical training in the first year. The number of hours decreases in the second and third year (to 150 hours and 100 hours respectively). More importantly, the school provides for the completion of a large number of remunerated hours of nursing practice in a hospital or clinic. In the first year they must work in a clinic for a total of 400 hours. In the second year this increases to 500 hours and in the third year 600 hours. In the first year they work in non-specialised clinic wards such as general medicine or general surgery. Subsequently students have to work also in such specialised wards as ophthalmology, gynaecology, neurology and heart surgery.

When professions in which helping activities play a major part are considered (Dick and Anderson, 1993; Rosa *et al.*, 1994), research into stress prevention and burn-out has generally focused on educational and support programmes. There are a number of studies indicating a trend toward the reduction and the removal of the causes which give rise to stress instead of – as frequently happened in the past – trying to treat the effects of stress (Del Rio, 1993; Karasek and Theorell, 1990). In this respect, both the consideration of motivational aspects and the enactment of support activities proved to be effective strategies in the reduction of the effects of stress, and have been adopted in some stress prevention programmes (Di Martino, 1994; Lees and Ellis, 1990). At least three different models of burn-out have been put forward in relation to strategies for prevention and management of work distress: the Cherniss (1983), the Golembiewsky (1982), and the Leiter (Leiter, 1992; Leiter and Meechand, 1986) models, each one of them deriving from specific hypotheses on stress prevention.

The Cherniss process model of burn-out is based on the consideration of two factors. The first is related to job characteristics such as orientation, workload, stimulation, scope of client contact, autonomy, institutional goals, supervision and social isolation. The second concerns the expectations (careers orientation and extra-work supports or demands) that an individual has when he/she enters the job. Sources of stress, that result from the combination of these two factors, may be negatively dealt with by the individual. Thus, negative attitudes or changes that Cherniss identifies as burn-out, may develop. In Golembiewsky's model, burn-out is examined as a process involving the notion of phases. Using the three sub-scales of the Maslach Burn-out Inventory (MBI; Maslach and Jackson, 1981), i.e. Depersonalisation, Personal Accomplishment and Emotional Exhaustion, eight phases of burn-out were generated, ranging from low to high levels of stress. Also in Leiter's model the three components of burn-out defined by the MBI are considered. They are supposed to have distinct relationships with environmental conditions and individual differences, though they can influence one another over time. The Emotional Exhaustion dimension is the most prominent dimension in this model.

From interventions aimed at reducing burn-out (Burke and Richardsen, 1996) it is known that those models that focus on organisational interventions have highlighted the support of superiors and colleagues (Leiter, 1986), participation in discussion groups (Golembiewsky, 1982), professional training and the possibility of having formal and informal contacts with other members of the team (Cherniss, 1983). These factors, together with other educational and social factors, seem to have a worthwhile effect in the reduction and prevention of stress.

Using this as a background, a study was carried out with first-year students of the USL 10D nursing school. In particular, the study aimed to analyse changes between two groups of student nurses in psychological conditions (psychological disorders and anxiety), in expectations and in work involvement at the beginning and at the end of the first half year.

14.3 Motives, signals and project organisation

During training and in their early work experience young nurses are 'ideal' subjects since they are obliged to complete one full working semester per year and to participate in discussion groups under the supervision of an older colleague.

Some authors have found that nurses, in their working conditions, are prone to an erosion of their helping disposition ('burn-out') and are subject to notable stress agents such as, for instance, shift work. In particular, the nursing profession has manifested a substantial turnover and a considerable drop-out rate has been associated with trainee nurses (Sirigatti et al., 1988a). Other authors have underlined the relevance of educational interventions to prevent the risk of stress and burn-out (Maslach, 1984; McCarty, 1994). Great attention is thus paid to the period in which trainees undergo the first working experiences. This is a period in which work styles, attitudes towards work and strategies to cope with stress develop.

With this in mind, the study reported here was carried out over the first year of training for the nurses, since during this year, in addition to the theoretical work, they must attend nursing practice in a clinic. The first nursing experience means acquiring new knowledge in relation to working conditions and stress management strategies. This experience is managed, supervised and supported to such an extent that it can not be compared to 'real' work. By and large, new organisational models and strategies for coping with stress can be profitably verified. Many models of stress and burn-out have emphasised the effectiveness of supervision and group problem management for stress reduction. The Italian school of nursing is thus one such a situation in which these activities may be assessed.

14.4 Analysis: Risk factors and risk groups

The identified risks are related to the enactment of operative styles which give rise to burn-out. The study focuses on the improvement of supervision and social support and may thus be considered as an example of primary prevention. The objective of the intervention is to foster the personal development of effective coping strategies in relation to those stressing events which characterise nursing activities.

The study started with the administration of a questionnaire to the first year trainees involved in this study. This questionnaire was set up to obtain information on the students background, for example, parents' age and work, the number of members in the family, relatives' education and so forth. Another set of questionnaires for the analysis of some psychological scales, the reaction to the new situation and the level of psychological well-being was also administered. The following self report measures were taken into account:

- General Health Questionnaire (GHQ, Goldberg, 1972) using the twelve items version, translated and validated for the Italian linguistic context by Bellantuono *et al.* (1987) and elaborated adopting the standard method. This test assesses psychological well-being (for example, 'I have lost confidence in myself') by a four-point Likert scale: subjects were asked to rate how frequently they felt each items sentences (1 = not at all; 4 = frequently).
- State Trait Anxiety Inventory (STAI, Kellner and Uhlenhult, 1993; Spielberger, 1983) using the Y1 version (state anxiety) and Y2 (trait anxiety). Both versions are twenty items questionnaires (for example, 'I feel calm' for Y1 and 'I feel well' for Y2) assessed by a four-point Likert scale (1 = not at all; 4 = very much).
- Self-esteem Scale (SELFES, Rosenberg, 1965), a ten items scale (e.g., 'usually, I'm satisfied with myself') that measures self-esteem by a four-point Likert scale rating the level of agreement with the items. In this scale high scores reflect a bad self perception while low scores reflect a good self perception (minimum 10, maximum 40).
- Working Expectation Measuring Scale (EXPECT, Hackman and Oldham, 1975), this six item questionnaire (for example, 'a job to put into practice my aspirations of independence') assesses the attitude and the expectations about the job with a three point Likert scale (1 = just a little; 3 = very much). High scores in this scale reflect high work expectations (minimum 6, maximum 18).
- Work Involvement Measuring Scale (WINVO, Warr *et al.*, 1979), this six items questionnaire (e.g., 'the job is very important for me') assesses work involvement by a seven point Likert scale (1= I do not agree at all, 7 = I strongly agree) in a continuum from 6 to 42.

The GHQ and the STAI in the Y1 version are situational psychometric scales. The STAI in the Y2 version and the self-esteem scale represent measures of more stable traits of personality. The final two scales, EXPECT and WINVO, provide some indications as to motivation in relation to work. These instruments were used in order to collect information on psychological well-being, some personality traits and the attitude towards work.

The subjects originally involved in the study (n = 131) are nursing students attending the first course in the main centre of the school (Careggi's hospital). Another group of students (n = 69) had not been involved in this study since they were attending classes in different health centres far from the main hospital. During the six months that the intervention lasted three students gave up school. Data analysis is thus related to a group of 128 subjects.

Subjects (n = 128) had been randomly allocated to two groups: an experimental group (n = 66) and a control group (n = 62). Subjects in the experimental group participated in discussion groups and were supervised by a team of experts while the control group had to follow the traditional working experience with no specific 'extra' psychological support.

14.5 Choice of measures

Work socialisation offers important opportunities for developing strategies for stress prevention, especially in those professional training programmes which are combined with work experience. In the past (Sutherland and Cooper, 1990) three fundamental issues have been studied by student nurse researchers:

1 the psychological characteristics of the young nurse, her/his motivations and expectations as well as her/his difficulties to cope with professional demands;
2 first working and training days, with a focus on changes related to cognitive processing, habits and lifestyle;
3 their environmental and organisational surroundings, in order to collect information for the development of strategies to reduce stress.

A more global approach aimed at determining effective strategies for work stress management would thus have to rely on the knowledge of the psychological characteristics, and role modifications that occur during the early period of training and practice. Psychological monitoring of trainee nurses, the consideration of indicators for psychological well-being, the determination of the perceptions related to one's working condition, are all activities which may be used for an improvement in the organisation of healthy working conditions.

Taking these considerations into account, the treatment for the subjects in the experimental group was based on the participation of each student in the same discussion group. The treatment lasted six months during which every two weeks, the student had an individual meeting with one of the supervisors who co-ordinated his/her discussion group.

Table 14.1 shows that each group had twelve to fifteen students, that there were two supervisors, and an expert in group discussion management. During twelve meetings, the discussion of the group dealt essentially with practical issues, the most relevant working experiences of the students. The co-ordinator of the group, the expert in group discussion management, had to facilitate the individual expression of difficult experiences and to foster a generally sympathetic attitude. During the individual meetings the supervisor,

Table 14.1 Experimental design and educational characteristics of the prevention project

Class	Activity	Time (6 months)	Aims	Expert/ student ratio	Professionality
Experimental (n = 66)	Individual supervision	12 meetings	Tutoring and counselling	2 : 12–15	Tutors
	Discussion group	12 meetings	Experience of group	1 : 12–15	Psychologist
	Ward activity	40-hours weekly	Training	—	—
	Refer to older nurse	Daily contact	Model of an expert	1 : 4–5	Expert nurse
Control (n = 62)	Refer to older nurse	Daily contact	Model of an expert	1 : 4–5	Expert nurse
	Ward activity	40-hours weekly	Training	—	—

without adopting directive interview techniques had to elicit the expression of doubts, and uncertainties, and the account of particular difficult experiences at work.

The programme adopted was worked out with the co-operation of the nursing school supervisors, the professionals of the Service of Occupational Health and researchers from the University of Siena. The assumption behind this programme was that more functional and effective coping strategies may be elaborated through the sharing of experiences with colleagues. This was supposed to bring about a clearer comprehension of a problem, the knowledge about the way in which others have dealt with similar situations, and an awareness of the availability of social support.

Whereas the experimental group received individual supervision, participated in regular group discussions, performed normal nursing tasks ('ward activity') and referred to older nurses, the control group 'only' followed the two latter activities, that is ward activity and reference to an older nurse. The two latter activities constitute the 'traditional' form of training.

As can be seen from Table 14.2, the sample consisted of 128 subjects: 66 in the experimental group (9 males and 57 females) and 62 in the control group (15 males and 47 females).

14.6 Implementation

Supervisors were the key figures in the treatment. First, in a three-day course, they were trained by interview experts in techniques for leading the discus-

Table 14.2 Experimental and control group

	Males		Females		Total	
	no.	%	no.	%	no.	%
Experimental group	9	13.6	57	86.4	66	51.6
Control group	15	24.2	47	75.8	62	48.4
Total	24	18.8	104	81.2	128	100

sion groups. Later supervisors were involved in the introduction of the programme to the trainee nurses. During a meeting with all students of the experimental group, supervisors explained the aim of the study and how the discussion groups were to be organised. A schedule of meetings was then prepared. All students in the experimental group were also invited to keep a written diary of their work experience and to produce a written report at the end of the first six months. These reports have not been analysed in the study reported here.

14.7 Evaluation

14.7.1 Time 1 comparisons

Table 14.3 presents average scores and standard deviations for each sub-scale of the questionnaire. Differences between both groups were tested (unpaired T-test) at both Time 1 and Time 2. Differences between Time 1 and Time 2 were also tested (paired T-test).

At Time 1 there are no significant differences between the experimental and control group with respect to STAI (Y1 and Y2 forms), the Self-esteem Scale, the Expectations Scale and the Work involvement scale. With respect to General Health Questionnaire scores, there is a significant difference, the experimental group reporting more health complaints. Their average score (2.4) is a relatively high score, over two points indicating psychological stress (Bellantuono et al., 1987). At Time 2 there are no significant differences between the experimental group and control group.

14.7.2 Time 1 versus Time 2

Table 14.3 shows a clear improvement from Time 1 to Time 2 for all student nurses. Work experience was accompanied by a decrease of anxiety and a better psychological condition for both groups. Since there are no differences between the two groups, it seems that the experimental condition has little 'extra' influence on anxiety assessed with the STAI (Y1 and Y2 scales).

Table 14.3 Average scores and standard deviations in the scales STAI Y1 and STAI Y2, GHQ, Self-esteem, Work Expectation and Work Involvement for the experimental and control group. Comparisons between experimental group and control group (unpaired T-test) and between Time 1 and Time 2 for both groups (paired T-test)

| Scales | Group | Time 1 | | Time 2 | | Time 1 vs Time 2 | |
		M	s.d.	M	s.d.	diff.	sig.
STAIY1	Experimental	38.5	8.15	34.7	7.8	3.8	0.001
	Control	37.8	7.6	33.9	6.3	3.9	0.0002
Significant		n.s.		n.s.			
STAIY2	Experimental	39.5	7.7	36.3	6.9	3.2	0.0005
	Control	39.0	7.2	35.4	7.1	3	<0.0001
Significant		n.s.		n.s.			
GHQ	Experimental	2.4	2.3	1.0	1.6	1.4	<0.0001
	Control	1.4	1.7	1.1	1.7	0.3	n.s.
Significant		0.004		n.s.			
SELFES	Experimental	18.8	3.7	16.9	3.8	1.9	<0.0001
	Control	18.6	3.9	17.2	3.7	1.4	0.0004
Significant		n.s.		n.s.			
EXPECT	Experimental	15.5	2.3	15.5	2.6	0	n.s.
	Control	15.3	1.2	15.5	2.6	−0.2	n.s.
Significant		n.s.		n.s.			
WINVO	Experimental	35.1	4.8	36.7	4.1	−1.6	0.003
	Control	35.7	4	35.1	5.4	0.6	n.s.
Significant		n.s.		n.s.			

Key: STAI Y1   State Anxiety Inventory
     STAI Y2   Trait Anxiety Inventory
     GHQ   General Health Questionnaire
     SELFES   Self-esteem scale
     EXPECT   Working Expectations scale
     WINVO   Working Involvement scale

As to the GHQ the improvement of the experimental group (from 2.4 to 1.0) is statistically significant. The decrease in the control group (from 1.4 to 1.1) was not significant. It is worth bearing in mind that the experimental group had at Time 1 a considerably higher average score and a consistently higher standard deviation. At Time 2, both score and standard deviation are reduced to levels similar to those of the control group. In Table 14.5 the Time 1 versus Time 2 decrease in general health complaints will be studied in more detail.

Self–esteem (SELFES) also tended to improve in both groups (18.8 versus 16.9 and 18.6 versus 17.2) while expectations (EXPECT) did not change. Work involvement (WINVO) seemed to improve in the experimental group.

In Table 14.4, for both the experimental and control group, the numbers of students who were admitted to the upper grade and who were not, are

Table 14.4 Cross table of admission to upper grade by experimental and control group

	Not admitted		Admitted	
	no.	%	no.	%
Experimental	8	12.1	58	87.9
Control	18	29.0	44	71.0
Total	26	20.3	102	79.7

Note: $\chi^2 = 5.7$; d.f = 1; p < .01

Table 14.5 Mean questionnaire scores before and after 'experimental' and 'traditional' training by low or high GHQ score

	Experimental group (n = 66)				Control group (n = 62)			
	Low GHQ (n = 40)		High GHQ (n = 26)		Low GHQ (n = 52)		High GHQ (n = 10)	
	Time 1	Time 2	Time 1	Time 2	Time 1	Time 2	Time 1	Time 2
STAI Y1	35.8	32.9*	42.5	37.6*	36.9	33.5**	44.9	37.1
STAI Y2	37.2	35.2	43.1	38.1**	38.6	34.2***	41.8	43
GHQ	0.9	0.7	4.9	1.5***	0.8	0.6	5	3.9
SELF-ES	18.3	16.6***	19.5	17.3*	18.4	16.9***	20	19.1
EXPECT	15.6	15.4	15.4	15.8	15.4	15.6	14.9	15.0
WINVO	35.5	37.1	34.4	36.1	35.9	35.6	34.3	32

Note: Paired *T*-test
   *   p ≤ .05
  **   p ≤ .001
 *** p ≤ .0001
Key: STAI Y1   State Anxiety Inventory
     STAI Y2   Trait Anxiety Inventory
     GHQ   General Health Questionnaire
     SELF-ES   Self-esteem Scale
     EXPECT   Working Expectations scale
     WINVO   Working Involvement scale

presented. Examiners were not aware of the membership of a student nurse to either the experimental or the control group. Differences in success, i.e. admission to the upper grade were tested (Chi-square) and were significant. More students from the experimental group passed the exams.

As a whole, the monitoring activities before and after the training support process gave encouraging even if not final results. It could be hypothesised that an improvement in well-being may be due more to the effects of the first work experience (Hagström and Gamberale, 1994) than to the training itself. However, we might also conclude that, within the general Time 1 –

Time 2 improvement, especially those subjects showing signs of distress when first monitored benefited from the treatment.

The prevention programme seems therefore to act directly on those subjects who need it: it supported those nurses who showed initial distress and uncertainty. To test this assumption we analysed data by dividing the subjects into two groups: those who at Time 1 showed signs of psychological distress measured by GHQ (score > 2 'psychologically unstable') and those who had an adequate index of psycho-physical well-being (< 2, 'psychologically stable'). This selection was done in accordance with a standard evaluation method and considering the score of 2 to be a cut-off between well-being and psychological distress (Bellantuono et al., 1987). We then crossed the various scales score with the two groups (low GHQ and high GHQ; see Table 14.5).

From Table 14.5 it follows that state anxiety (STAI Y1) improves in a statistically significant way for both experimental and control students who had been measured as being stable (low GHQ), and considerably in distressed (high GHQ) students belonging to the experimental group. Trait anxiety (STAI Y2) improves in unstable students (high GHQ) of the experimental group, and improves in steady students (low GHQ) of the control group. General well-being (GHQ) improves in unstable students (high GHQ) of the experimental group while it does not change in any other case. Self-esteem (SELFES) showed a trend similar to that of STAI Y1, while expectation (EXPECT) and work involvement (WINVO) did not change in any subgroup. The data lends preliminary support to the hypothesis that the training was particularly effective for at risk subjects who needed help. It is important however to underline that, in relation to the control group, the absence of any statistical significance for what concerns the comparisons between Time 1 and Time 2 (Table 14.5) could be ascribed to the small number of subjects (n = 10) considered in this analysis.

14.8 Conclusion

Until now a tradition of stress monitoring and stress prevention has been lacking in Italy. However, various studies have been made that look at stressful occupations, for example, nursing and other health professions, whose aim is to understand the causes and identify strategies for prevention. Trade unions are becoming increasingly interested in stress and well-being at work. The project discussed in this chapter complements this recent interest from unions and health institutions (USLs).

The experimental programme design is comprised of a prevention project integrated with the monitoring of the intervention itself. In particular, two groups of student nurses were studied during their first work experiences. A control group carried out activities as normal while the experimental group took part in a controlled programme of support and supervision. Well-being of members of both groups was monitored via self-report instruments.

Our study design makes it possible not only to verify the effectiveness of the intervention but also to understand some of its dynamics. With some caution, we hypothesise that the intervention supports those subjects who are more psychologically stable.

Moreover our data suggest that both types of experiences, normal ward activity and the 'social support treatment', were successful in improving the well-being of student nurses. The study provides evidence for the success of the interventions for both groups: 'for all nurses' the well-being indexes (STAI Y1 and Y2, GHQ, SELFES, EXPECT and WINVO) were improved. However, it is also suggested that in the experimental programme more student nurses pass the exam. In addition, there is also evidence that the more intensive intervention programme (experimental group) lowers the GHQ scores. Thus, the more intensive programme seems to have an additional value compared to the traditional mode of intervention, that given its Time 1 to Time 2 improvements, already has a value *per se*.

However, we should be careful in drawing firm conclusions since:

1   the number of subjects is sometimes small (for example, for one of the subgroups in Table 14.5);
2   we cannot completely exclude the possibility that the positive effects might be primarily due to the first work experience as a nurse and not to the interventions;
3   the decrease in GHQ scores for those students with high scores at Time 1 might be related to the statistical phenomenon 'regression to the mean';
4   at this present time the study has not yet been repeated.

From this study, some preliminary indications for the re-organisation of student activity in hospital wards can be identified. It confirms the necessity of social support practices like group discussions and the importance of individual supervision.

This process turned out to be also particularly efficient in the relation between possible economic investments and the results achieved. We made use of already available resources, such as those of the unit of industrial medicine, and we simply worked at reorganising supervision activity in the school of nursing. The only actual expenses were those for administration, questionnaire collection and processing, while knowledge, the assuming of responsibility and the effects on the psychological condition of at-risk students were considerably benefited, thus supporting the early hypothesis of the study.

Bibliography

Bagnara, S. and Rizzo, A. (1990) 'Indagine sullo stato di fatica e stress del personale viaggiante TRA-IN' ('Fatigue and stress in coach drivers'), proceedings of *L'autobus come ambiente di lavoro*, Siena: 16 March 1990, pp. 69–76.

Bellantuono, C., Fiorio R., Zanotelli, R. and Tansella, M. (1987) 'Psychiatric screening in general practice in Italy', *Social Psychiatric*, 22: 113–17.

Burke, R.J. and Richardsen, A.M. (1996) 'Stress, burn-out and health', in C.L. Cooper (ed.) *Handbook of Stress Medicine and Health*, Florida: CRC Press, pp. 101–17.

Cherniss, P. (1983) 'The ideological community as an antidote to burn-out in the human services', in B.A. Farber (ed.) *Stress and burn-out in the human services profession*, New York: Pergamon Press, pp. 198–212.

Del Rio, G. (1993) *Stress e Lavoro nei Servizi* ('Stress and Work in the Services'), Roma: La Nuova Italia Scientifica.

Dick, M. and Anderson, S.E. (1993) 'Job burn-out in RN-to-BSN students: Relationships to life stress, time commitments, and support for returning to school', *Journal of Continuing Education in Nursing*, 24 (3): 105–9.

Di Martino, V. (1994) 'Stress lavorativo, un approccio per la prevenzione', ('Stress at work, prevention strategies'), in M. La Rosa, M. Bonzagni and P. Grazioli (eds) *Stress at Work. La ricerca comparativa internazionale* ('Stress at Work. Comparative International Research'), Milano: Franco Angeli, pp. 17–46.

Goldberg, D.P. (1972) *The Detection of Psychiatric Illness by Questionnaire*, London: Oxford University Press.

Golembiewsky, R.T. (1982) 'Organizational Development Intervention, Changing Interaction, Structures and Policies', in S.S. Paine (ed.) *Job Stress and Burn-out: Research, Theory and Intervention Perspectives*, Beverly Hills: Sage Publications, pp. 232–51.

Haack, M. R. (1988) 'Stress and impairment among nursing students', *Research in Nursing and Health*, 11 (2): 125–34.

Haack, M. R., Harford, T.C. and Parker D.A. (1988) 'Alcohol use and depression symptoms among female nursing students', *Alcoholism, Clinical and Experimental Research*, 12 (3): 365–7.

Hackman, J.R. and Oldham, G.R. (1975) 'Development of the job diagnostic survey', *Journal of Applied Psychology*, 60, 159–70.

Hagström, T. and Gamberale, F. (1994) 'What is a good job? Young people's values and attitudes toward work', *The 4th Biennial Conference of the European Association for Research on Adolescence*, Stockholm, Sweden.

Karasek, R.A. and Theorell, T. (1990) *Healthy Work. Stress, Productivity and the Reconstruction of Working Life*, New York: Basic Books.

Kellner, R. and Uhlenhult, E.H. (1993) 'La valutazione psicometrica dell'ansia' ('Anxiety assessment'), *Bollettino di Psicologia Applicata*, 205: 43–54.

Lees, S. and Ellis, N. (1990) 'The design of stress-management programme for nursing personnel', *Journal of Advanced Nursing*, 15 (8): 946–61.

Leiter, M.P. and Meechand, K.A. (1986) 'Role structure and burn-out in the field of human services', *Journal of Applied Behavioural Science*, 22: 47–52.

Leiter, P.P. (1992) 'Burn-out as a crisis in professional role structures: measurement and conceptual issues', *Anxiety, Stress and Coping*, 5: 79–93.

McCarty, M.M. (1994) 'Stressors and coping in the school setting', *Journal of School of Nursing*, 10 (1): 20–25.

Maslach, C. (1984) 'Patterns of burn-out among a national sample of public contract workers', *Journal of Health and Human Resources Administration*, 7: 189–212.

Maslach, C. and Jackson, S.E. (1981) 'The measurement of experienced burn-out', *Journal of Occupational Behaviour*, 2: 99–113.

Rosa, M., Bonzagni, M. and Grazioli, P. (eds) (1994) *Stress at Work. La ricerca comparativa internazionale* ('Stress at Work. Comparative International Research'), Milano: Franco Angeli.

Rosenberg, M. (1965) *Society and the Adoloscent Self-image*, Princeton, NY: Princeton University Press.

Sirigatti, S. and Menoni, E. (1993) 'Una ricerca sulla formazione nelle scuole infermieri in Toscana' ('Research on the Nursing School Education'), *Salute e Territorio*, 86: 59–61.

Sirigatti, S. and Stefanile, C. (1993) 'Correlati individuali e ambientali del burn-out in infermieri professionali' ('Individuals and environmental aspects in nursing burn-out'), *Bollettino di Psicologia Applicata*, 207: 15–24.

Sirigatti, S., Stefanile, C. and Menoni, E. (1988a) *Aspetti Psicologici della Formazione Infermieristica* ('Psychological Aspects of Nurse Education'), Roma: La Nuova Italia Scientifica.

——(1988b) 'Sindrome del burn-out e caratteristiche di personalità' ('Burn-out Syndrome and Personality'), *Bollettino di Psicologia Applicata* 187–188: 55–64.

Spielberger, C.D. (1983) *Manual for State Trait Anxiety Inventory*, (revised edition), Palo Alto (CA): Consulting Psychologist Press.

Strambi, F. (1991) 'Problemi inerenti il lavoro al caldo in Italia' ('Thermal stress work in Italy'), proceedings of *Valutazione dello stress termico: gruppo di lavoro e seminario*, Siena: 5–9 September 1991.

Strambi, F., Valentini, F., Bartalini, M. and Brighi, C. (1991) 'Stress termico e lavoro in cristalleria' ('Thermal stress in glass work'), *Health Safety Seminar*, Lisbon: 15–16 July 1991.

Sutherland, V.J. and Cooper, C.L. (1990) *Understanding Stress, a Psychological Perspective for Health Professionals*, London: Chapman and Hall.

Warr, P.B., Cook, J.D. and Wall, T.D. (1979) 'Scales for the measurement of some work attitudes and aspects of psychological well-being', *Journal of Occupational Psychology*, 52, 129–48.

Chapter 15

Stress prevention: European countries and European cases compared

Michiel Kompier and Cary Cooper

15.1 Introduction

In this summary chapter, we will consider the current status with respect to occupational stress and its prevention in the various countries that are discussed in this book (section 15.2). Next, we will compare and evaluate the eleven cases that are presented in Chapters 3 to 14 (section 15.3). First, we will summarise each of these projects by presenting a brief description of the five consecutive steps for each project (section 15.3.1). Second, we will discuss the methodological quality of the eleven cases (section 15.3.2). Third, we will compare our cases in more detail, in a step by step comparison in terms of: preparation, problem analysis, choice of measures, implementation and evaluation (section 15.4). Finally, we will draw several conclusions and formulate some recommendations (section 15.5).

15.2 European countries compared

15.2.1 General characteristics of stress compared

For the purposes of this book we asked the contributors – all specialists in the field of psychosocial factors at work and health – to characterise the current state of occupational stress and its prevention in their country. We have summarised this information in eleven country profiles, presented in Table 15.1. Each profile is based on short answers to six questions (see also section 1.3):

1   Is stress an important policy issue? ('policy issue'.)
2   Is there a legal framework for stress prevention? ('legal framework'.)
3   Is there a national monitoring system (identification of risk factors and risk groups)? ('monitoring'.)
4   Are there examples of good preventive practice available? ('examples'.)
5   Are stress interventions mainly orientated towards the (work) organisation or the individual employee, or both? ('work/employee'.)
6   Are there reliable data on the costs of stress at work and the benefits of stress prevention? ('costs and benefits'.)

Table 15.1 Comparison of general characteristics of stress at work for the eleven countries

	1 Policy issue	2 Legal framework	3 Monitoring	4 Examples	5 Work/ individual	6 Costs/ benefits
Sweden	+	+	+	+/–	work	?
Finland	+	+	+	?	work	?
The Netherlands	+	+	+	+	ind./work	+/–
Belgium	+	+	–	–/+	?	–/+
Denmark	+	+	–	–	?	–
United Kingdom	+	+	–	–/+	individ.	–
Germany	–/+	+	–	–	?	–
Ireland	–/+	+	–	–	individ.	–
Portugal	–	+/–	–	–	–	–
Greece	–	+/–	–	–	–	–
Italy	–	+/–	–	–	–	–

Key: + Indicates whether country is with listed aspect
    – Indicates whether country is without listed aspect
    ? Not specified

Before commenting on the country profiles as outlined in Table 15.1, we should make some caveats. It should be borne in mind that the characterisations of the various countries were not fully standardised. Some authors were able to provide detailed answers to all six questions (for example, Sweden, the Netherlands). Other authors could not. The country characterisations were also made by various authors. Although in all cases these authors are specialists in this area, it is hard to assess whether (and to what extent) inter rater differences played a role in analysing and characterising their country situation.

Nevertheless, since consistent and comparative studies on the quality of the psychosocial work environment of employees in different countries are not available (Smulders et al., 1996), and since there is a need for more information on national and international policies on stress prevention and healthy working conditions (Kompier et al., 1994), these country profiles are at least important indicators of the current status with respect to occupational stress and its prevention in Europe.

15.2.2 Three separate clusters of countries

When comparing the eleven countries in Table 15.1 one may distinguish three separate clusters.

1   There is a first group of countries that already pay a lot of attention to (preventing) work stress and that consider work stress as a relevant health

and safety issue. This first cluster consists of Sweden, Finland and the Netherlands. These three countries have a legal framework on working conditions that also explicitly addresses psychosocial factors at work. There is national data on the working population and specific risk factors and risk groups, and increasingly there is an increasing orientation on costs and benefits of improving working conditions, and on examples of good preventive practice. Still, there are some differences within this group. For example, with respect to stress interventions, in Sweden and Finland the emphasis is more on organisational than on individual factors, whereas in the Netherlands there also exists a tradition of merely individual directed measures.

2   The second cluster takes in an 'in-between position': Belgium, Denmark, United Kingdom, Germany and Ireland. In these countries stress is more or less (Germany) considered as a policy issue, i.e. it has earned its place on the agenda of government and social partners. These countries also have implemented the European framework directive on health and safety, but there are no specific regulations regarding stress at work. With respect to these first two items these countries hold a position that seems comparable to that of countries in the first group. However, with respect to the general stress characteristics three to six in Table 15.1 (monitoring, examples of good preventive practice, stress interventions, data on costs and benefits), the developments in group two countries are still less pronounced.

3   The third cluster consists of the three southern European countries: Italy, Greece and Portugal. In these countries work stress is not yet recognised as an important policy issue. Although these countries have implemented the European framework directive on health and safety, occupational stress is not considered a real issue; there is not much empirical data on risk groups and risk factors, and there are hardly any preventive actions undertaken. More than the other two groups these countries face typical blue-collar occupational hazards, such as noise, safety risks and so forth.

In Europe, although work stress is an important subject in some of the countries under study, most of the attention in the field of occupational health and safety is still being devoted to 'traditional topics' such as ergonomics, somatic health, (technical) safety and toxic agents. Significantly more attention is being paid to chemical, physical and biological hazards than to psychosocial risks such as poor job content, monotonous work, lack of control and poor social support. This conclusion supports the results of the survey by Wynne and Clarkin (1992) reported in Chapter 2 of this book. This study showed that actions which are often related to problems in connection with stress at work, do not have high priority when compared to chemical and physical hazards. However, increasingly, and especially in the first group of countries, a balance is being reached with respect to attention for 'more classical' and 'more modern' psychosocial occupational hazards.

15.2.3 Spain, France and Austria

Although we discussed this book with several experts in the field of occupational health and safety, of work and organisational psychology, and of public health we did not succeed in identifying cases in Spain, France or Austria. It proved difficult to examine the situation with respect to work, stress and health in Austria. In other words, we do not know whether 'much is going on in this field'. We hypothesise that the absence of cases from the two other countries, France and Spain, may be explained by the north–south division in Europe as discussed in Section 15.2.2. It seems probable that Spain and France would be located in the third country group (see also Kompier et al., 1994; Smulders et al., 1996).

15.2.4 The three clusters and other studies

Comparative studies on the quality of the work environment in different countries are scarce (Smulders et al., 1996). More recently however, important contributions in this field have been made by the European Foundation for the Improvement of Living and Working Conditions (Paoli, 1992; 1997). Our cluster classification fits in reasonably well with the 1992 survey (Paoli, 1992). In their secondary analysis of this 1992 study (a large sample, n = 12,500, representative for the workforce distribution in the European Union according to occupation, gender, age, sectors and company size), Smulders and colleagues (1996) identified four clusters of countries that best describe the situation in Europe (at that time twelve countries) with respect to the working environment. The four clusters were: the 'northern' cluster (Denmark, Germany, the Netherlands, Great Britain), the 'middle' cluster (Belgium and Luxemburg), the 'southern' cluster (Spain, Portugal, France, Italy and Ireland), and the 'isolated southern' cluster (Greece). The overall quality of working life in Greece, the other southern countries and Ireland – in comparison to the other European countries – was below average. In the northern and middle European countries the quality of working life was above average. Physical working conditions, psychosocial job demands (for example, speed, deadlines, repetitive tasks) and the length of the working week played a significant role in these differences between country clusters. In general, physical working conditions were less favourable in the southern countries, whereas psychosocial job demands were highest in the northern European countries and in Greece. Also in other studies a clear north–south differentiation is seen in Europe with respect to work characteristics (for example, Near and Rechner, 1993; see for a discussion Smulders et al., 1996). It seems probable that economic as well as cultural factors play a role in these differences in the quality of the work environment in European countries.

15.3 Comparison of the cases

15.3.1 Summary of the eleven cases

In order to compare the eleven cases in more detail, a brief description of the five consecutive steps for each project is presented in Table 15.2.

15.3.2 Research design rating and methodological critique

Selection

A first comment concerns the selection of these eleven projects. They do not constitute a random sample of prevention projects. A quantitative comparison between cases (in terms of absolute figures) does not make much sense. Thus, conclusions drawn from analysing and comparing these cases do not relate to 'average', but rather to 'current' or 'good' practice. To give an example, the fact that eight out of eleven cases involved external consultation, does not imply that (successful) stress prevention projects often use consultants. The relatively frequent use of external consultants is probably due to the fact that the authors selected projects in which they themselves were involved as researcher and consultant.

Research rating

A second methodological issue relates to the research rating of these projects. In order to examine the methodological quality of the projects, each case received a research rating, according to Murphy (1996). The rating could vary from one (★) to five stars (★★★★★):

★   evidence that is descriptive, anecdotal or authoritative;
★★   evidence obtained without intervention, but that might include long-term or dramatic results from general dissemination of information or medical agent into population;
★★★   evidence obtained without a control group or randomisation but with an evaluation;
★★★★   evidence obtained from properly conducted study with control group but without randomisation;
★★★★★   evidence obtained from properly conducted study with a randomised control group.

One case from these eleven studies (Greece) received a one star rating. Also one country (Portugal) was given a two star rating. Six countries received a three star rating (Finland, Belgium, Denmark, Germany, Ireland and Italy). A four star rating was given to two cases (the Netherlands, Sweden 'B';

Sweden 'A' received three stars). Finally, one case received five stars (United Kingdom).

It is not surprising that it is the two countries from the southern European cluster that receive the lowest methodological marks and that the other countries receive higher ratings. The high rating from the United Kingdom case may be related to the content of the intervention which, in a United Kingdom tradition of emphasising interventions at the individual level, was primarily a training programme directed at the employee. For such a programme, it is easier (although not easy!) to develop a randomised control condition than for a programme which places the emphasis on changing stressful working conditions (for example Finland, Sweden). Overall, in three cases (United Kingdom, the Netherlands, Sweden 'B') a genuine control condition existed (rating four and five stars) Apart from Greece and Portugal the other projects receive a three star rating.

Although from a methodological point of view these three star designs may seem somewhat 'meagre', we considered them acceptable for the type of study we performed. First, as discussed previously, the hectic organisational arena, rapid changes in companies, and the fact that management and not scientists run companies, means that it is almost impossible to 'play fully by the methodological rules'. Second, we think there is some 'methodological compensation' in many of these cases. Many of these cases receive good marks on other methodological criteria: reliable and valid assessment of stressors and outcomes, appropriate statistical analyses of the data, and 'good' sample or population size, ranging from 29 (Denmark) to 19,000 employees (Finland).

15.4 The cases compared: a step-by-step comparison

15.4.1 Step 1: Preparation

In two cases (the Netherlands and Sweden) high absence figures formed the starting point of the project. In these cases sickness absenteeism was presumed to be a result of a high psychosocial and musculoskeletal workload. Among the consequences of high absence rates were high costs, inefficiency in the organisation of work, disturbances in work processes and a decreasing social climate. In addition to these so-called 'internal' motives, 'external' motives also played a role, such as shortages in the labour market (for example, the Netherlands). For example, the Dutch hospital explicitly chose to transform into 'a better than average hospital' in order to attract new personnel. Other main motives for starting these projects were: paying attention to 'human capital', prevention of work-related health problems, prevention of stress symptoms, promotion of workers' health, jointly improving working conditions and productivity, finding out whether there was a stress problem, and providing more social support to the staff (see Table 15.2, p. 318).

Table 15.2 Characterisation of the eleven cases

Case (n)	Step 1: Preparation	Step 2: Problem analysis	Step 3: Choice of measures
1 Finland (n = c. 19,000) Chapter 4	Motives: paying attention to 'human capital', prevention of work-related health problems, stress, and promotion of workers' health. Organisation: complex action-research programme; Programme Advisory Committee, Programme Management Committee; Outside consultancy. Research design rating: ***	Instruments: questionnaires, job analysis, psycho-physiological stress study. Risk factors: for example, little possibilities for advancement and for participation, lack of feedback, time pressure. Risk groups: some factors the total personnel, other factors specific groups, for example, office personnel (mostly women) and foremen.	Two basic approaches chosen: reorganisation of work and training of management; implementation of specific development projects. Work directed: reorganisation of work (for example, reorganisation of monotonous tasks, integration of maintenance and support functions with production) and training of management (for example, leadership style); development of work and training of foremen; development of co-operation of office personnel and management; development of psychosocial services in occupational health, and of personnel development. Person directed: training (workshops, seminars).
2 The Netherlands (n = 850) Chapter 5	Motives: high sickness absenteeism, difficult to hire new personnel. Organisation: initiative by management, steering committee, external consultant, participative approach, comparison with 'control-hospital'. Research design rating: ****	Instruments: interviews, checklists, questionnaire, analysis of sickness absenteeism and turnover. Risk factors: high psychosocial workload, interior climate, leadership style, physical workload, shift system, insufficient training and career opportunities. Risk groups: some factors: total organisation; others: certain departments. Control condition: other hospital.	Work directed: changes in interior climate, work and resting times schedule, technical devices, reduction in physical workload, work organisation, job enrichment. Person directed: managerial information with regard to sickness absenteeism figures and procedures with regard to sickness absenteeism, training for supervisors, better guidance in case of sickness, health promotional initiatives, various trainings (for example, coping with agression, individual stress management, alcohol, smoking).

Step 4: Implementation	Step 5: Evaluation
Well-planned seminars (after piloting); principles of participatory action research.	Comprehensive survey studies. (Scientific) analyses are still being carried out. Mainly process evaluation, more than outcome evaluation. Absence %: not clear.
Action plans carried out on nine important topics, for example: reorganisation of monotonous work; personnel development; encouragement of shop floor participation; increasing psychological resources and preventing stress. Responsibility: management.	Subjective evaluation of work changes: overall positive, but time pressure had increased for both office personnel and foremen, and also (ten-year follow-up study) for total company. Health complaints: no differences. Costs and benefits: hard to assess in such an extensive project, for example, due to changes over time in workforce, unit-differences in recording absenteeism. The fact that the process still goes on after 10 years is seen as an indicator of its value. Obstructing factors: sometimes differences in interests between company and consultants/researchers (more practical versus more scientific aims). Stimulating factors: using direct assessments of employees and management. Follow-up: yes, actions taken with respect to management procedures, personnel development, performance of the personnel, and work and workplace changes.
Organisation: various sub-projects with a participative approach. Responsibility: final responsibility by top management; co-ordination by steering committee; practical implementation of sub-projects by (line) management in departments. Duration: c. four years	Comparing pre-test and post-test: improvement in working conditions, intensified attention for sick employees and for working conditions, better psychosocial work climate. Comparison with 'control-hospital': control-hospital scores better at some variables in questionnaire (post-test). Absence %: 8.9% (1991) —> 5.8% (1994) (significant, $p < 0.05$) now below average hospital level and below control hospital. Costs and benefits: positive, benefits exceed costs. Obstructing factors: difficult to keep middle management committed, differences in steering committee, unclear what are the responsibilities of the steering committee, 'everything takes a lot of time', difficult to keep employees involved in a four-year project, difficult to assess objectively 'which is a serious constraint and which is not'. Stimulating factors: stepwise approach, adequate instruments, course in guidance in case of absenteeism, employees very committed in sub-projects, information and discussion day for all employees. Follow-up: yes, increasing responsibility for supervisors.

Table 15.2 cont.

Case (n)	Step 1: Preparation	Step 2: Problem analysis	Step 3: Choice of measures
3 Belgium (n = 3,261) Chapter 6	Motives: unions and works council considered stress as a topic; employees asked for measures to be taken against stress; signals to medical officers; need to know whether there was a stress problem. Organisation: taskforce with important role for health department and training manager; questionnaire study evaluated by university. Research design rating: ***	Instruments: questionnaire study (personal data, experience of stress, psychosomatic complaints, work factors) on representative sample of 324 employees. Risk factors: for example, poor job content, social relationships at work, terms of employment. Risk groups: (a) men, senior (> 15 years), no management responsibilities; (b) women, medium seniority (5-15 years), no management responsibilities.	Work-directed: ergonomic interventions. Person-directed: information session for senior management; training course 'coping with stress'; obligatory training for managers in 'people management' and recognition of stress signals; managers trained in ergonomics.
4 United Kingdom (n = 270) Chapter 7	Motives: senior management wanted to decrease reported strain among employees and to improve their coping skills. Organisation: Initiative: senior management; important, independent, role for external researcher (university) being the 'motor' of the study; attempt to combine 'good research methodology' with company wishes. Research design rating: *****	Instruments: pre-test and post-test with reliable questionnaires. Individual variables: for example, anxiety, depression; mental and physical health. Organisational variables: organisational commitment, job satisfaction. Also biographical data. Self-reported sickness absenteeism (frequency, days). Risk factors: (from previous stress audit) volume of work, reduction in staff numbers, coping with change. Risk groups: all employees.	Work-directed: no specific initiatives. Person-directed: three training programmes: • Personal stress awareness • Exercise • Cognitive restructuring Participants (managerial and non-managerial employees) were volunteers, and were randomly allocated into one of these three training programmes. There was also a wait-list control group and a full control group (non-volunteers) (groups 4 and 5). Training programmes consisted of one-hour general session and one two-hour workshop.

Step 4: Implementation	Step 5: Evaluation
Action plan approved by senior management, unions, works council.	Absence %: significant reduction of sickness absenteeism (from 4.3% to 3.45%; p < 0.1).
Many information and discussion sessions in company.	Other effects: stress is no longer a taboo subject and is now on the company agenda. A lot of positive attention in media.
Circa 1,000 workplace analyses (ergonomics) by two company nurses.	Costs and benefits: no detailed calculations but benefits from decrease in absenteeism clearly exceed the extra costs. Obstructing factors: time constraints. Stimulating factors: critical openness of senior management; using clear facts and figures to convince top management; drive of taskforce to assess and reduce stress.
Special task force on 'work–family interface' planned but never started.	Follow-up: yes, in company.
Responsibility: senior management, but central role for researcher. Duration: after baseline recording, first measurement after 3 and second measurement after 6 months.	Questionaires: no pre-test differences between conditions. Post-intervention: after 3 months exercise group improved on all 'individual health variables'. Some improvements in 'awareness group', no changes in the 'cognitive group'. After 6 months some positive effects left in exercise group, but not in awareness group or cognitive group. No changes after 3 or 6 months in organisational commitment or job satisfaction. Absence %: self reported absence decreased in exercise group, but increased in other two groups. Doubts about quality of sickness data (self-report, retrospective). Costs and benefits: no detailed analysis. Costs are reported to be small. Obstructing factors: lack of time (time pressures and heavy work loads); lack of contact with participants during the study. Stimulating factors: some concern among employees about their own levels of stress. Follow-up: no follow-up data.

Table 15.2 cont.

Case (n)	Step 1: Preparation	Step 2: Problem analysis	Step 3: Choice of measures
5 Denmark (n = 29) Chapter 8	Motives: jointly improving working conditions and increasing productivity. Organisation: development workshops, seminars for drivers, management and labour organisations. Research design rating: ***	Instruments: previous studies on bus drivers, discussions among bus drivers. Risk factors: for example, management style, running of the service, ergonomics. Risk groups: all bus drivers.	Work-directed: introduction of self-regulating (autonomous) team; drivers were free to organise as they wished within the limits of the budget. Person-directed: three week full-time introductory course.
6 Sweden (n = A: 136; B: 82) Chapter 9 The 'mail processing' case exists of two sub-cases: mail sorting (A), and mail delivery (B)	Motives: (A and B): high sickness absenteeism, decreased productivity, demands for effectiveness and speed; (B) decrease musculoskeletal disorders. Organisation: management initiated changes; active occupational health care team; academic support for evaluation. Research design rating: A: *** B: ****	Instruments: valid questionnaires. Risk factors: (A): monotony; (B): high physical demands. Risks groups: A and B. (A): mailsorters (B): mail (wo)men	Work-directed: (A): Smaller more autonomous production units; small increase in staff (+2.5%); introduction of small working groups; improved information systems; change in shift systems; new food vending machine/microwave ovens. (B): Two stations, a more traditional and a more modern station, changes in both but more changes in the latter: for example, improved control and social support, roles of management more clear; less foremen; better information systems; increase of staff (+2.5%); increased authority for foremen. Person-directed: not specified.

Step 4: Implementation	Step 5: Evaluation
Eight working groups were established (for example, rota planning, advertising and design of the buses, personnel management and uniforms); quarterly general meetings, where decisions were made; service drivers elected.	Absence %: decrease from 15 working days on average to 6 days (after 2 years). Passengers complaints decreased. Relative high levels of satisfaction among drivers (with respect to project, job, running of the service, elected service drivers). Costs and benefits: budget had been kept, and even two extra drivers could be employed. Obstructing factors: tendering-system. Stimulating factors: participative approach. Follow-up: yes, in some other companies, but 'less far reaching'.
(A): Employees participated in planning of organisational changes. (B): Employees could choose between two stations. Important role for occupational health care team.	(A): Two follow-up measurements, valid questionnaires on work and health (for example, job demands, control, social support); sickness absence data; first follow-up represents final stage of intervention; second follow-up one year after start. (B): Follow-up measurement (after 12 months) and comparison between more traditional and more modern stations. Questionnaires: (A): After one year skill discretion and authority over decisions had improved significantly. (B): Psychological demands decreased in both stations; social support increased in the modern site only; ergonomic conditions did not change; authority of decisions increased in the more traditional station only; less musculoskeletal symptoms in modern station only and more pronounced in younger employees. Absence %: (A) Significant reduction of sickness absenteeism (full-time and part-time employees). (B): Study and interpretation 'meaningless' due to drastic social political changes and changes in social insurance system. Costs and benefits: no detailed analysis made, but it is clear that decrease in sick leave (in A) and decrease in musculoskeletal morbidity (in B) are financial gains. Evidence points at a financial gain in both sub-studies. Obstructing factors: not specified. Stimulating factors: co-operation between management and representatives of employees Follow-up: not known.

Table 15.2 cont.

Case (n)	Step 1: Preparation	Step 2: Problem analysis	Step 3: Choice of measures
7 Germany (n = 230) Chapter 10	Motives: workplace health promotion. Organisation: central role for health work group. External consultancy. Installation of health circle. Research design rating: ***	Instruments: questionnaire on work and health; workplace observations; discussions and interviews. Risk factors: high musculoskeletal work load (for example, lifting and carrying) and high psychosocial work load (stress, for example, through patients, supervisors). Risk groups: all nurses, and on certain factors also other employees.	Work-directed: a.o., changes in information flow and communication, better co-ordination, ergonomic and technical improvements. Person-directed: a.o., training of personnel.
8 Ireland (n = 953) Chapter 11	Motives: to investigate stress and identify stressors, ambition to formulate a prevention plan; wish to disseminate relevant information on stress management among staff. Organisation: 'stress working group' installed. External consultancy. Support by management, representatives of employees, and unions. Research design rating: ***	Instruments: extensive survey, after piloting, among all employees: demography, sources of stress at work and outside of work, social support, outcomes of stress, health/coping behaviour. Risk factors: a.o., working time pressures, responsibilities, overwork; pay; promotion, permanency, job security; supervision difficulties; lack of resources; poor management support; lack of information; work environment. Risk groups: some factors: total organisation; specific groups at risk were a.o.: 30-39 years of age; certain departments (airport police/fire services trading department); shiftworkers; lower grades (these factors are not independent of each other).	Before starting, two approaches were chosen: (1) organisational development, and (2) health promotion approach (examining and improving the health and welfare services of the company to address stress). From a long list of recommendations with respect to both areas several measures were selected. Work-directed: improving shift work regulations (a.o. redesign of shift rosters); improve communications (a.o. increase access to information, update management development programme); performance appraisal for all staff. Person-directed: career development (training for staff, encourage internal work experience); health awareness and health promotion programme (a.o., development of awareness of stress through training courses; increase awareness of negative effects of smoking; health screening; healthy eating policy).

Step 4: Implementation	Step 5: Evaluation
The health circle identified stressful work situations and suggestions for improvement. The hospital management approved of these measures and the planning with respect to implementation of these measures.	Subjective effects: after six months the project was evaluated by means of a questionnaire study. Improvements were said to have a high impact on stress reduction; communication and social support had improved. Absence %: no data available. Costs and benefits: unknown. Obstructing factors: the 'original' questionnaire needed to be adapted since it did not include questions about work. Stimulating factors: participative approach. Follow-up: not known.
After the analysis and after the list of recommendations was made, the involvement of the external consultants ended. The approach taken was a participative one (employee involvement). Two new 'high level action teams' were set up: one for the organisational development programme (track 1) and one for the health promotion programme (track 2). It was recognised that not all recommendations could be acted on at once. Both teams developed an action plan (with criteria such as feasibility, importance and resources). In all, Aer Rianta undertook twenty distinct actions.	Of those twenty actions, six years after the analysis, fourteen are still ongoing or in progress. The project was undertaken as a pragmatic exercise. The tasks of the external consultants ended after the analysis. Formal evaluation was not a high priority. Still there are some clear positive outcomes, such as better shift regulations, a support manual for shiftworkers, training for new shiftworkers and supervisors, and improvements in communication practices. Absence %: not known. Costs and benefits: not known. Obstructing factors: not specified. Stimulating factors: the two intervention teams (and not the external consultants) took effective ownership of the implementation. Other effects: the project has created an awareness of occupational stress and a set of skills within the company which did not exist before. Follow-up: yes, ongoing project (14 from 20 'original' actions are still ongoing or in progress).

Table 15.2 cont.

Case (n)	Step 1: Preparation	Step 2: Problem analysis	Step 3: Choice of measures
9 Portugal (n = 1,263) Chapter 12	Motives: promoting workers' health, monitoring and improving work environment, preventing occupational hazards. Organisation: central role for occupational health service. Research design rating: ** (no evaluation yet).	Instruments: interviews, medical examination, questionnaire for small random sample of employees, analysis of sickness absence, turnover and disability. Risk factors: poor working conditions, poor work organisation, working overtime; lack of exercise, inappropriate nutrition, smoking, drinking. Risk groups: all employees.	The action plan is currently being prepared by occupational health service. Objectives: decrease stress level (10%); increase (10%) number of preventive workplace-directed actions by occupational health nurses; increase (50%) information and training (for example, coping skills). Work-directed: not specified. Person-directed: not specified.
10 Greece (n = unknown) Chapter 13 The case presented is Oncology Hospital Saint-Anargiri	Motives: need for more support for staff. Organisation: not specified. Research design rating: *	Instruments: no specific instruments used. Risk factors: not specified. Risk groups: volunteering nurses, usually after referral by head nurse.	Work-directed: support groups. Person-directed: support groups.
11 Italy (n = 128) Chapter 14	Motives: preventing risks of stress and burn-out by developing effective coping styles. Organisation: co-operation of nurse school supervisors, occupational health professionals and university. Research design rating: ***	Instruments: validated questionnaires on work and (psychological) health. Risk factors: based on 'nurses burn-out' literature. Risk groups: all student nurses.	Difference work-directed versus person-directed hard to assess: controlled programme of support and supervision. 'Work directed': experimental group: regular group discussions, control group: none. 'Person-directed': experimental group: individual supervision, support from older nurse Control group: support from older nurse only.

Step 4: Implementation	Step 5: Evaluation
Action plan to be implemented in 1998. Strategy is to gradually build up organisational climate that is supportive to dealing with stress at work. Central role for occupational health nurses.	Action plan to be implemented in 1998. Therefore an evaluation study has not yet been performed. Stress has now become a serious issue, and has been 'put on the company agenda'. Absence%: not known yet. Costs and benefits: not known yet. Obstructing factors: not specified. Stimulating factors: not specified. Follow-up: yes, this is an ongoing project.
Not part of human resource management strategy. Guided by psychologist.	Absence %: not known. Costs and benefits: not known. Obstructing factors: time constraints: support groups during work interferes with 'production', after work interferes with home care. Stimulating factors: not specified. Follow-up: not specified.
For both the experimental and the traditional groups measures were implemented and combined with 'ward activity'.	Absence %: not measured. Questionnaires: in general various positive effects from Time 1 to Time 2 in both the experimental and the traditional groups (for example, decrease of anxiety, better psychological condition, higher self-esteem). Other benefits: significantly more students from the experimental group passed the exams. Costs and benefits: not known, presumably positive. Obstructing factors: not specified. Stimulating factors: combining monitoring and intervention; making use of already available resources. Follow-up: unknown.

Various organisations, especially the large-scale projects in Finland, the Netherlands, Belgium and Ireland installed a project-structure (project group or steering committee) on a temporary basis. Such project groups formed a representation of the most important organisational 'parties'. In all cases, however, management remained responsible for the chain of events and often chaired the meetings. In several projects (Finland, the Netherlands, Denmark, Sweden, Germany and Ireland), a basic assumption was that employees whose 'work was in discussion' needed to have an important role in the execution of the project. In eight projects (Finland, the Netherlands, Belgium, United Kingdom, Sweden, Germany, Ireland and Italy) external consultants or researchers, mostly from a university, were involved. Especially in Sweden and Portugal, an active role was (is) played by the occupational health service.

15.4.2 Step 2: Problem analysis

A wide range of instruments was used in order to assess risk factors and risk groups. Most projects combined several instruments, ranging from simple instruments used for 'first line monitoring' (for example, checklists and interviews) to more sophisticated 'professional' ones (instruments for task analysis, a psycho-physiological study, for example, Finland; for analysing work organisational processes, for example, the Netherlands). Also questionnaires and analyses of administrative data (such as sickness absenteeism, turnover, work disability) were used. In identifying risk factors, several companies (for example, Finland, the Netherlands, Germany and Ireland) differentiated between factors that affect the organisation as a whole, and factors that affect one or more specific departments or groups of employees. Accordingly, risk groups were mostly defined in terms of specific departments or positions or involved all employees in the organisation (for example, United Kingdom, Denmark, Portugal and Italy). Ideally, such an approach may enable a company to make an assessment of its relative position (compared to 'the average employee' and to specific norm-scores of the branch), and to make internal comparisons between departments or groups in the organisation (on the basis of age, gender, blue versus white collar, and so on), otherwise known as 'benchmarking'.

15.4.3 Step 3: Choice of measures

Table 15.3 provides an overview of work-directed and person-directed measures from the eleven projects.

Among the work-directed interventions are work redesign, changes with respect to work and resting time regulations, social support and ergonomic and technological actions. The most important person-directed interventions relate to training of employees and of management (seven companies).

Table 15.3 The most important interventions in the eleven projects

Work-directed
- Work redesign (Finland, the Netherlands, Denmark, Sweden)
- Work time schedules (the Netherlands, Denmark, Sweden, Ireland)
- Improved social support (Sweden, Germany, Italy, Greece, Ireland)
- Ergonomics and technology (the Netherlands, Belgium, Germany)
- Small increase in staff (Sweden)
- Changes in interior climate (the Netherlands)

Person-directed: human resources management and training
- Training (Finland, the Netherlands, Belgium, Denmark, United Kingdom, Germany, Ireland)
- Training of management (Finland, the Netherlands, Belgium, Ireland)
- Promoting healthy lifestyle (the Netherlands, United Kingdom, Ireland)
- Training modules personal stress awareness, cognitive restructuring (United Kingdom, Ireland)
- Career development training (Ireland)
- Coping with aggression (the Netherlands)
- Performance appraisal system (Ireland)

Other measures
- Development of occupational health service (Finland)
- Improved registration of sickness absence and managing the sickness report (the Netherlands)

As demonstrated in Tables 15.2 and 15.3, eight cases (Finland, the Netherlands, Belgium, Denmark, Germany, Greece, Ireland and Italy) explicitly decided on the combination of work-directed and person-directed measures. One case (United Kingdom) 'only' opted for employee-directed measures, whereas another case (Sweden) 'only' addressed work-directed measures. The project in the Portuguese bank organisation is still underway and therefore can't be classified.

15.4.4 Step 4: Implementation

Most organisations have chosen to integrate the interventions into the regular company and management structure. This implies that (line) management is responsible and that stress prevention (for example, introducing the interventions) belongs to the 'normal daily duties' of supervisors. Sometimes (for example, Finland) measures were pre-tested, before implementing measures on a larger scale.

In various cases principles of worker participation were explicitly chosen, for example, in the Finnish case, in the Danish bus company (where in fact worker participation was the heart of the intervention), in the Sweden case, in the German health circle and in the Irish airport management company.

Implementing improvements was not always easy and did not always proceed according to plan. In the final step, we will discuss both obstructing and stimulating factors.

15.4.5 Step 5: Evaluation

Our overview of these eleven cases demonstrates that stress monitoring and stress reduction is not merely a technical process (based on a technical analysis and on the simple, straightforward realisation of recommendations and receipts), but relates to changing and improving organisations and organisational processes. This may be a time consuming process (as in the Finnish case), and often this does not seem to be a 'one off event'. Several organisations continued their efforts to reduce occupational stress after the evaluation step. In some cases stress prevention now seems to be 'business as usual', that is part of the normal company processes and related to the company's aims (for example, Finland, the Netherlands, Belgium, Ireland). In other projects it is not clear to what extent there existed a follow-up.

Objective effects

With respect to the effects of these intervention programmes we can differentiate between more objective and more subjective effects. As to the more objective data, changes in company registered sickness absenteeism were measured in four cases (the Netherlands, Belgium, Denmark, Sweden 'A'; not in Sweden 'B'). In three cases (the Netherlands, Belgium, Sweden A) sickness absence percentage was significantly ($p < 0.05$) decreased post intervention. In the Danish bus company, the change in absence percentage was in the expected direction, but this effect was not significant, probably since the number of employees was rather small. In the other projects, more objective data on absenteeism could not be provided. Since the absence data in the United Kingdom were 'only' self reported, they have not been taken into account here. In addition to the absence data, other objective outcome measures have hardly been studied. An exception is in the Italian case, where more student nurses from the experimental group passed the exam.

Subjective effects

Regarding subjective, i.e. self-reported effects, more data are available. Mostly these data relate to (changes in) evaluations of work factors, to evaluations of changes that were implemented and to (changes in) health complaints. Subjective evaluations were recorded in all cases, with the exception of Belgium, Ireland and Portugal (preventive measures not yet implemented, two star research rating) and Greece (one star rating). Sometimes pre- and post-intervention comparable questionnaires were administered (for example, the Netherlands, Sweden, United Kingdom and Italy). In general, positive self-reported results stem from these evaluations (Finland, though time pressure had increased; the Netherlands; United Kingdom, especially in the exercise group; Denmark; Sweden; Germany; Italy, both in the experimental and in the traditional group).

Costs and benefits

None of the projects (or project teams) involved in the current study was equipped with a specialised economist. Furthermore in only one project were the financial costs and benefits assessed in detail (the Netherlands). In the Dutch hospital, the benefits clearly exceed the costs (see Table 5.9). Some organisations (for example, the Finnish corporation) found it too difficult to estimate these figures. Indeed, as discussed in Chapter 3, assessing and comparing costs and benefits is difficult. A theoretical and empirical tradition in this field is absent, although recently some progress has been made (see also Cooper et al., 1996). Still there are clear indications from several cases that these projects may be regarded as successful from a financial perspective. In the pharmaceutical company in Belgium there is no doubt that the benefits related to the decrease in absenteeism exceed the costs of the intervention programme. In the Danish bus company the budget had been kept by the drivers, but they were able to hire two new drivers from this same budget. Furthermore, it seems at least probable that the decrease in sickness absence and in musculoskeletal morbidity in the Swedish case brought about financial gains. In the other cases there is no or hardly no data in this respect.

Obstructing and stimulating factors

Of course, en route there have been various obstructing factors (see Table 15.4).

The first factor seen in Table 15.4, 'time constraints', is paradoxical as it is directly coupled to the stress issue itself. Especially in those companies where psychosocial demands (for example, work pace, deadlines) are very high, and therefore stress may constitute a major problem, there is not much

Table 15.4 Main obstructing factors in the eleven cases

- Time constraints (Belgium, United Kingdom, Greece)
- 'Everything takes a lot of time' (the Netherlands)
- Differences in expertise in steering committee (the Netherlands)
- Difficulty in keeping middle–level and employees involved (the Netherlands)
- What is a constraint and what is not? (20% complaints?, 30%?) (the Netherlands)
- Differences between practical and scientific aims (Finland)

Table 15.5 Stimulating factors in the projects

1   Project organisation and process–variables: • Stepwise and systematic approach (the Netherlands) • Clear structure (tasks, responsibilities) (Belgium) • Participative approach (Denmark, Germany, Ireland) • Cooperation between management and representatives of employees (Sweden) • Recognition of employees as 'experts' (the Netherlands) • Emphasising the responsibility of management/critical openness of senior   management (Belgium) • Combining monitoring and intervention (Italy)
2   Analysis and instruments: • Proper risk assessment/adequate instruments (the Netherlands) • Assessment of risks for whole company and certain departments/positions • (the Netherlands, Germany) • Using direct assessments of employees and management (Finland) • Using clear facts and figures to convince top management (Belgium) • Combining monitoring and intervention (Italy)

time for 'extra' effort in a new stress prevention approach. For example, key figures who might be the right people to participate in a steering committee, are often overloaded with other tasks and simply lack the time to chair and prepare meetings. Another example is in the case of high work-related sickness absenteeism where it becomes difficult to organise training sessions during work time, since so many employees are sick and management's attitude is that 'production must go on'.

The second factor, 'everything takes a lot of time', follows on from the fact that serious stress prevention relates to changing and improving organisations, which indeed often is a time consuming process. It is foolish to consider successful stress prevention as a marginal activity. Furthermore, especially 'when things take time', it may be difficult to keep middle level supervisors and employees involved.

To conclude, on the one hand we would argue that obstructing factors are natural, and on the other hand, as follows from these cases, that they can be overcome.

Apart from these obstructing factors, several factors were mentioned as being stimulating (see Table 15.5). More attention will be paid to these factors in section 15.5.

15.5 Discussion and recommendations

15.5.1 Were these cases successful?

Are these indeed examples of good preventive practice? Generally, in most cases the answer is 'yes'. No evaluation data were available in two companies, those cases with the lowest research rating (Greece and Portugal). Therefore it is not (yet) possible to decide on the level of success in these two cases. In the remaining nine cases, there are four that do offer more objective data on sickness absenteeism. In three of these four cases (the projects from the Netherlands, Belgium and Sweden) a significant reduction of sickness absence is demonstrated. In the fourth case (the Danish bus company) the reduction is not significant, probably due to the small sample size.

Self-reported effects were available in seven cases (not in cases from Belgium, Ireland, and again from Greece and Portugal). In general there are positive outcomes, for example, less constraints in the work situation, decreased health complaints and positive evaluations of implemented measures. Furthermore there are clear indications from several cases (the Netherlands, Belgium, Denmark, Sweden) that they may be regarded as successful from a financial perspective.

Are improvements due to the interventions?

A key question is whether these positive outcomes may be interpreted as a direct consequence of the projects' interventions. Although it is difficult to provide strong evidence for such a direct relationship, it does at least appear plausible. In most cases, a systematic assessment was made of constraints in the working situation that might contribute to health complaints or high absence figures. Next, tailormade interventions were introduced, sometimes after pre-testing. Thus, we can assume that the measures taken have – at least in part – contributed to the positive self-reports in the evaluation step and to the reduction of sickness absence (in four cases).

A difficult question is what exactly were the effective 'medications' implemented in the various projects. One of the problems of a post hoc analysis, as performed in this book, is that it is almost impossible to find out what specific measure had what effect. Not only did the starting situation differ between cases, but also the interventions and outcomes differed accordingly. Most companies preferred a range of interventions, often combining work-directed and worker-directed measures. From these cases we cannot tell whether comparable results would have been obtained had other interventions been implemented.

15.5.2 Key factors to success: recommendations

Since it may well be that successful stress prevention depends not so much on a specific measure taken, but rather on the general approach that was followed, we will now discuss some key factors from these eleven cases that, in our opinion, seem to be at the heart of a successful approach in stress prevention (see also Table 15.5 p. 332). At the same time, these factors may be regarded as recommendations for both companies and researchers with respect to the identification and reduction of occupational stress (see also Kompier et al., 1998). These key factors are:

1 A stepwise and systematic approach. In addition to the proper sequence in problem solving, this involves a clear determination of aims, tasks, responsibilities, planning and financial means. The stepwise approach can be compared to the 'control cycle' introduced by Cox (1993).

2 An adequate diagnosis or risk analysis. 'An organisation needs to know its starting point in order to assess the benefits derived' (Cooper et al., 1996). Although this statement may seem obvious, the practice of stress prevention is different, as we have emphasised in the first chapter of this book. In a similar vein, Kopelman (1985) concluded: 'All too often, though, job redesign interventions are undertaken without adequate diagnosis' (p. 245).

3 A combination of work-directed and worker-directed measures. Many organisations on the one hand focused on primary prevention, that is, prevention at the source and simultaneously combined this approach with measures which aimed at improving the coping capacity of the employees.

4 A participative approach: involvement and commitment of both employees and middle management is crucial, since they may be considered experts with respect to their own working situation. This principle is linked to that of 'participatory action research' (Israel et al., 1989; Landsbergis et al., 1993). This kind of approach in the work setting involves both outside experts (i.e. researchers or consultants) and organisation members in a joint process aimed at meeting both research and intervention objectives. This participatory approach has shown progress in the area of ergonomics. Studies on 'participatory ergonomics', that is, a practice of field-oriented ergonomics using reciprocal communication flows among managers and employees, show that ergonomic improvements are best implemented when employees themselves as well as other 'company parties' are actively involved (Noro and Imada, 1992). Good results are obtained in a stepwise participative process (Noro and Imada, 1992; Vink and Kompier, 1997).

5 Top management support. The initial success and subsequent survival of the stepwise and participative approach we suggest, depends largely on the sustained commitment of top management (see also Kopelman, 1985). It is important that top management incorporates preventive activities in regular company management. Paying attention to (psychosocial) working conditions should become 'business as usual', that is, a regular task of supervisors. Only with such an approach can work stress management be regarded as a 'normal' company phenomenon, i.e. a phenomenon that can be understood and therefore dealt with.

To sum up, it may be hypothesised that the success of stress prevention depends on a subtle combination of two approaches, that is, 'bottom-up' (participation) and 'top-down' (top management support). This combination strongly resembles a route to job redesign that was first advocated by Kopelman (1985): on the one hand assigning responsibility and accountability, and on the other, ensuring, through external monitoring, that the work is performed satisfactorily.

Conclusion

In this book, by analysing and comparing various stress prevention projects, we have tried to contribute to both stress research and practice by reducing the gap between both fields, strongly suggesting that stress prevention may be beneficial to both the employee and the organisation.

Bibliography

Cooper, C.L., Liukkonen, P. and Cartwright, S. (1996) *Stress Prevention in the Workplace: Assessing the Costs and Benefits to Organizations,* Dublin: European Foundation for the Improvement of Living and Working Conditions.

Cox, T. (1993) *Stress Research and Stress Management: Putting Theory to Work,* HSE contract research report, no. 61/1993.

Israel, B.A., Schurman, S.J. and House, J.A. (1989) 'Action research on occupational stress: Involving workers as researchers', *International Journal of Health Services,* 19: (1): 135–55.

Kompier, M.A.J., De Gier, E., Smulders, P. and Draaisma, D. (1994) 'Regulations, policies and practices concerning work stress in five European countries', *Work and Stress,* 8 (4): 296–318.

Kompier, M.A.J., Geurts, S.A.E., Gründemann, R.W.M, Vink, P. and Smulders, P.G.W. (1998) 'Cases in stress prevention: the success of a participative and stepwise approach', *Stress Medicine,* 14, 155–68.

Kopelman, R. (1985) 'Job redesign and productivity: a review of the evidence', *National Productivity Review,* summer 237–55.

Landsbergis, P.A., Schurman, S.J., Israel, B.A., Schnall, P.L., Hugentobler, M.K., Cahill, J. and Baker, D. (1993) 'Job stress and heart disease: Evidence and strategies for prevention', *New Solutions,* Summer: 42–58.

Murphy, L.R. (1996) 'Stress management in work settings: A critical review of the health effects', *American Journal of Health Promotion,* 11 (2): 112–35.

Near, J.P. and Rechner, P.L. (1993) 'Cross-cultural variations in predictors of life satisfaction: A historical view of differences among West European countries', *Social Indicators Research,* 29: 109–21.

Noro, K. and Imada, A. (1992) *Participatory ergonomics,* London: Taylor and Francis.

Paoli, P. (1992) *First European Survey on the Work Environment 1991–1992,* Dublin: European Foundation for the Improvement of Living and Working Conditions.

Paoli, P. (1997) *Second European Survey on Working Conditions 1996,* Dublin: European Foundation for the Improvement of Living and Working Conditions.

Smulders, P.G.W., Kompier, M.A.J. and Paoli, P. (1996) 'The work environment in the twelve EU-countries: Differences and similarities', *Human Relations*, 49: 10, 1291–313.

Vink, P. and Kompier, M.A.J. (1997) 'Improving office work: a participatory ergonomic experiment in a naturalistic setting', *Ergonomics*, 40 (4): 435–49.

Wynne, R. and Clarkin, N. (1992) *Under Construction: Building for Health in the EC Workpace*, Dublin: European Foundation for the Improvement of Living and Working Conditions.

Index